The Fundamentals of Digital Currency

Yun Wu · Wei Zhu

The Fundamentals of Digital Currency

Demystifying the Social Experiment of New Money

ZHEJIANG UNIVERSITY PRESS
浙江大学出版社

Springer

Yun Wu
The People's Bank of China
Beijing, China

Wei Zhu
Aldelo LP
Beijing, China

ISBN 978-981-97-8260-4 ISBN 978-981-97-8261-1 (eBook)
https://doi.org/10.1007/978-981-97-8261-1

Jointly Published with Zhejiang University Press
The print edition is not for sale in China (Mainland). Customers from China (Mainland) please order the print book from: Zhejiang University Press

Translation from the Chinese language edition: "数字货币" by Yun Wu and Wei Zhu, © Zhejiang University Press 2022. Published by Zhejiang University Press. All Rights Reserved.

This Springer imprint is published by the registered company Springer Nature Singapore Pte Ltd.
The registered company address is: 152 Beach Road, #21-01/04 Gateway East, Singapore 189721, Singapore

Preface

Amidst a rapidly transforming global financial landscape, *The Fundamentals of Digital Currency: Demystifying the Social Experiment of New Money* emerges as a timely work that offers comprehensive insights into the conceptual and practical underpinnings of modern digital currencies. This book is intended to serve as a navigating tool through the complex terrain of cryptocurrencies, blockchain technologies, as well as the broader implications of this new and intriguing form of money for society and governance.

As a foreword to this foundational work, we invite readers to embark on a journey deep into the underpinning of digital currencies, beginning with the enigmatic inception of Bitcoin and delving into the profound questions and historical significance rooted in the birth of this groundbreaking currency. This narrative not only covers technological innovation but also involves philosophical and sociopolitical exploration that can challenge our very notions of money, authority, and associated social contract.

Through a meticulously structured narrative, the book expounds on the topic in three parts, each dissecting the critical aspects of digital currency revolution. Part I, "Understanding Digital Currency", first provides a historical perspective, contextualizing Bitcoin within the grand tapestry of monetary evolution. It then raises compelling questions about the intentions and philosophical stance of the anonymous creator, Satoshi Nakamoto, and how the architecture of Bitcoin may signify more than just a currency: possibly a blueprint for a new form of societal governance.

As we peer into Part II, "Social Experiment of Digital Currencies", we dissect the milestones of private digital currencies and the audacious question of whether they represent failed experiments or comprise the harbinger of a financial paradigm shift. We are then driven to consider the emergence of Central Bank Digital Currencies (CBDCs) as a counterpoint to decentralized cryptocurrencies, examining the two development paths these state-sponsored digital currencies could take and their potential impacts on the global financial landscape.

In Part III, "When it Comes to Regulation", our focus shifts to the implications of digital currencies within the context of financial regulation. We dissect the formation of a global anti-money laundering regulatory network and anticipate the inevitable fate of cryptocurrencies towards transparency and ordinance.

This book culminates in Part IV, "The Future of Digital Currency", in which we are prompted to envision the possibility that blockchain technology will give rise to a new super-regulator, a digital 'pontiff' that could redefine national sovereignty and global hegemony. We then explore the concept of "machine power" and the emerging digital order that blockchain and digital currencies could establish.

"The Fundamentals of Digital Currency" is not only an academic treatise but also a clarion call to readers to reflect upon the changing essence of money and its role in modern social contract. As digital currencies continue to evolve and challenge the status quo, we aim to enlighten the path ahead and ensure that readers turn from passive observers into informed participants in this unfolding captivating digital currency narrative.

Beijing, China

Yun Wu
Wei Zhu

Contents

About the Authors

Dr. Yun Wu, with a role at the People's Bank of China, holds advanced degrees in law and economics. His expertise in financial regulations is reflected in his meaningful contributions to anti-money laundering standards, including the pioneering AML framework for e-CNY. He has co-authored several publications on financial oversight and digital currencies, establishing him as a respected figure in the field.

Mr. Wei Zhu, a seasoned computer science expert, is pursuing a doctorate in engineering at Renmin University of China. With a solid foundation in blockchain and AI, he leads various software development initiatives and actively contributes to scientific discussions through his writings. Two decades of industry experience make him a key player in technological innovation.

Part I
Understanding Digital Currency

Chapter 1
The Context and Technology of Bitcoin

What did Satoshi Nakamoto intend to convey by entering his birthdate as April 5, 1975?

What are the historical and philosophical underpinnings of Bitcoin as an attempt to create a private currency?

To what extent is the design of Bitcoin consistent with and beyond Hayek's economic theory of private currencies?

What novel concepts has Bitcoin introduced beyond a new form of currency, such as possibly reflecting a new mode of social governance?

To find answers to the above captivating questions, in this chapter, we explore the enigmatic identity of Satoshi Nakamoto, particularly the symbolic meaning behind his chosen birthdate, linking it to pivotal moments in monetary history. We contemplate the historical events and philosophical motivations for Bitcoin's inception as a private currency that challenges traditional paradigms. We further suggest that the architecture of Bitcoin introduces groundbreaking concepts that extend beyond its function as money, suggesting transformative implications for social governance.

1.1 The DNA of Bitcoin

In the forest, the same soil and sunlight nourish all plants, while some grow as twining vines, others as small patches of grass, and still others develop into tall trees that outgrow all plants in the competition for light. The fundamental differences between them lies in their unique DNA. Similar to exploring the genetic makeup of flora and fauna, to truly understand the essence of a social phenomenon, one must examine its deepest philosophical roots.

Y. Wu and W. Zhu, *The Fundamentals of Digital Currency*,
https://doi.org/10.1007/978-981-97-8261-1_1

1.1.1 Satoshi Nakamoto's Birthday: Why April 5, 1975?

April 5th: The day when the U.S. government openly robbed its people of their gold.

On April 5, 1933, facing the Great Depression, President Roosevelt issued Executive Order No. 6102 under the Trading with the Enemy Act of 1917, declaring a state of emergency and prohibiting the hoarding of gold by Americans. It required all American citizens to surrender all stored gold (coins, bullion, and certificates) to the Federal Reserve by May 1, 1933 in exchange for $20.67 per ounce; failure to comply with this order would result in fines of up to $10,000 and imprisonment to five to ten years (Fig. 1.1).

The Trading with the Enemy Act authorized the U.S. president to impose restrictive measures on trade with "enemy" nations, but the presidents abused this authority by exercising emergency powers during non-wartime and within the United

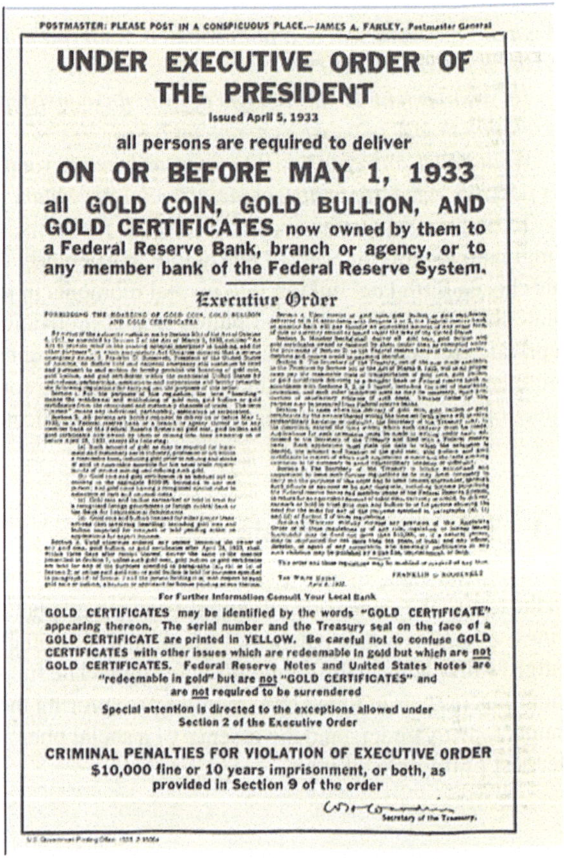
POSTMASTER: PLEASE POST IN A CONSPICUOUS PLACE.—JAMES A. FARLEY, Postmaster General

UNDER EXECUTIVE ORDER OF THE PRESIDENT

Issued April 5, 1933

all persons are required to deliver

ON OR BEFORE MAY 1, 1933

all GOLD COIN, GOLD BULLION, AND GOLD CERTIFICATES now owned by them to a Federal Reserve Bank, branch or agency, or to any member bank of the Federal Reserve System.

Executive Order

For Further Information Consult Your Local Bank

GOLD CERTIFICATES may be identified by the words "GOLD CERTIFICATE" appearing thereon. The serial number and the Treasury seal on the face of a GOLD CERTIFICATE are printed in YELLOW. Be careful not to confuse GOLD CERTIFICATES with other issues which are redeemable in gold but which are not GOLD CERTIFICATES. Federal Reserve Notes and United States Notes are "redeemable in gold" but are not "GOLD CERTIFICATES" and are not required to be surrendered

Special attention is directed to the exceptions allowed under Section 2 of the Executive Order

CRIMINAL PENALTIES FOR VIOLATION OF EXECUTIVE ORDER
$10,000 fine or 10 years imprisonment, or both, as provided in Section 9 of the order

Secretary of the Treasury.

Fig. 1.1 U.S. Executive Order No. 6102

States.[1] Throughout the Great Depression, the Roosevelt administration continually expanded their executive power by declaring emergencies, asserting that it was the president's duty "to do anything that the needs of the Nation demanded unless such action was forbidden by the Constitution or by the laws."[2]

In a country governed by rule-of-law, such a massive deprivation of property rights is unimaginable, such as the prosecution of those by the U.S. government who failed to turn in their gold stocks in time and endorsing the confiscation of any gold that was withheld. The Supreme Court, subdued by Roosevelt, affirmed these acts of deprivation, ruling that the forced exchange and confiscation did not violate the U.S. Constitution.[3]

During the Great Depression, the Roosevelt administration threatened to expand the size of the Supreme Court in order to curb its power. Although the U.S. Constitution defines the powers of the Supreme Court and has expanded its power of judicial review through the landmark decision of *Marbury v. Madison* (which allowed the Supreme Court to declare acts of Congress and executive orders unconstitutional), the Constitution does not specify the number of Supreme Court justices. Historically, this has been stable at nine, but Roosevelt threatened to appoint additional justices to "dilute" the influence of existing justices if the Supreme Court obstructed his "New Deal." This was a classic case of a crisis forcing a dangerous move against the rule of law. The Patriot Act passed after 9/11 was a similar notorious example.

The U.S. government had ample reasons of public interest for forcing the exchange of gold: in face of the Great Depression and because of the existing gold standard at the time, the public's habit of hoarding gold prevented the Federal Reserve from expanding its monetary supply. Thus, forcing the returning of gold for U.S. dollars could "activate" gold assets, turning the gold in people's hands into base money. However, the seizing and purchase of gold took place at $20.67 per ounce (at the 1932 price), which was immediately raised to $35 per ounce for international trade, causing the public's gold assets to depreciate by over 40% overnight.[4]

1975—The year the U.S. government finally allowed its citizens to own gold again.

Since 1933, U.S. presidents have normalized the use of extraordinary powers by limiting them to emergency declarations. In the early 1970s, U.S. presidents declared two domestic emergencies: by President Nixon in 1970 regarding the U.S. postal

---

[1] To understand the legal foundation of executive presidential powers, the reader is referred to Ouyang, Yu, and Michael A. Morgan. "The Contemporary Presidency: How Presidents Utilize Their Emergency Powers." *Presidential Studies Quarterly*, 2019, 718–732.

[2] "Special Committee on the Termination of the National Emergency" of the 93rd Congress. "The Report of the Special Committee on the Termination of the National Emergency (Senate Report 93-549)." November 19, 1973, 2. https://ia902207.us.archive.org/24/items/senate-report-93-549/senate-report-93-549.pdf.

[3] The Supreme Court upheld the constitutionality in a series of cases, including *United States v. Bankers Trust Co,* 294 U.S. 240 (1935); *Nortz v. United States*, 294 U.S. 317 (1935); and *Perry v. United States*, 294 U.S. 330 (1935).

[4] Locascio, Vincent R. *The Monetary Elite Vs. Gold's Honest Discipline.* Weltanschauung Financial Pr, 2005, 106–107.

workers' strike and in 1971 over the floating exchange rate system. The misuse of extraordinary powers by U.S. presidents has in fact raised alarms in Congress, which created "the Special Committee on the Termination of the National Emergency" in 1973, also known as "Senate Report 93–549", to clear up the state of emergency persisting since 1933 and began to limit the President's emergency powers. Only when one looks into this report they realize the shocking revelations of Congress—the Senate discovered that the presidential order banning gold hoarding since the Great Depression, the 1950 deployment of troops to Korea under the guise of the Korean War (the U.S. has never declared war on Korea, considering it a conflict and the deployment a "police action"), as well as the aforementioned Nixon emergencies, had still been in effect.

Subsequently, on August 14th, 1974, the U.S. Senate passed a law declaring that the ban on the storage of gold by individuals would be lifted on December 31st, 1974.[5]After a lengthy ban, **in 1975, the American people were finally able to legally own gold.**

However, by this time, the price of gold had reached $140 per ounce.

1.1.2 The Default of US Dollar as the World's Gold Standard: The Collapse of the Bretton Woods System

For millennia, gold has been the single universally accepted symbol of wealth across civilizations. Although Keynes the economist called it a "barbarous relic," his academic authority could not ease the reality of the World War II era: even Britain had to settle payments for the American war supplies in gold. To sustain the military activities against Hitler, Britain had to transport gold by train from Canada to the U.S. in exchange for war equipment. When France surrendered to Nazi Germany, the German occupiers rushed to the French central bank only to find that gold had been moved away; not only were the Germans unable to seize it but also Churchill's attempt to "borrow" the French gold was mercilessly denied. Thus, the preserved wealth of generations of French citizens played a significant role in the post-war recovery and rebuilding efforts.

In 1944, as World War II was drawing to a close, the United States held more than half of the world's gold reserves. At this juncture, the U.S. assumed the role of the world's central bank: the U.S. dollar was pegged to gold and, vice versa, other currencies were pegged to the dollar. As promised by the U.S. government, any foreign government could exchange their U.S. dollars for gold, solidifying the dollar's "as good as gold" status.

[5] U.S. Congress. "An Act to Provide for Increased Participation by the United States in the International Development Association and to Permit United States Citizens to Purchase, Hold, Sell, or Otherwise Deal with Gold in the United States or Abroad." Pub. L. No. 93–373, 88 Stat. 445. 1974.

In 1971, however, in Executive Order 11,615, President Richard Nixon shockingly announced the suspension of gold conversions for foreign governments, breaking the promise of U.S. to the world. This meant that the dollars that countries had long exchanged for gold could no longer be redeemed for this commodity. By 1973, the Bretton Woods system had officially collapsed.

1.1.3 The Denationalization of Money: Reflections on Liberalism

Timeline:

- 1933: U.S. government confiscates people's gold at $20.67/oz.
- 1934: U.S. government sells gold in the international market at $35/oz.
- 1944: Bretton Woods Agreement pegs U.S. dollar to gold at $35/oz.
- 1971: U.S. government stops gold withdrawals for foreign governments.
- 1973: Bretton Woods system ends, with U.S. dollar no longer tied to gold.
- 1975: American people can buy gold at $140/oz.
- 1980: Gold price escalates to $590/oz.

Looking at the above figures, any rational and ethical scholar will ponder about this stark deprival of people's properties. What actions have the U.S. government implemented? Could a government-managed currency be superior to a privately managed one? How did the United States, proclaimed to be the grandest experiment in human governance, exhibit such behavior that is essentially different from historical regimes, that is, debased currencies and robbed their own people of their wealth?

At the above historical crossroads, two opposing voices emerged. One involved various models proven by mainstream economists, and the other included the profound reflections of a minority of economists. Post-WWII saw a trend toward the mathematization of economics, where the distinction between introductory, intermediate and advanced economics was no longer marked by the depth of thought or the complexity of concepts but rather by the difficulty of the mathematical tools employed. Economic textbooks have subsequently shifted away from or rather looked down upon discussions of the nature of money, preferring to indulge in complex monetary equations.

In contrast to the above, the Austrian School of Economics still maintained a deep engagement with economic, social and philosophical issues. These works were exemplified by Friedrich Hayek who delved into social and philosophical aspects, often finding greater resonance beyond economics in legal, political and philosophical circles. Emerging from debates with the collective perspective of the German Historical School, his school advocated methodological individualism and individual choice.

Hayek was awarded the Nobel Prize in Economics in 1973 for his theories on social evolution and the use of knowledge in society, arguing against central planning and in favor of individual choice and market economies. His skepticism towards state nationalism contrasted sharply with the nationalistic economic studies of German Historical School.

Albeit he won the Nobel Prize for his work on monetary theory and business cycles, Hayek became more widely known for his theories of social evolution. His seminal works, "The Road to Serfdom" (1944) and "The Use of Knowledge in Society" (1945), criticize central economic planning and emphasize the importance of the role of price mechanism in a market-based economy in synchronizing diverse market information. He asserted that well-ordered societies arise from the spontaneous and often unpredictable outcomes of individual human actions instead of centralized planning, and that failures in such planning can lead to significant societal costs.

In response to the collapse of the Bretton Woods system, Hayek published "The Denationalization of Money" in 1976, arguing for the private issuance of currency rather than government monopoly. In harmony with his established beliefs, Hayek maintained in this work that governments had historically proven unreliable in monopolizing commodities, leading to inefficiencies. Thus, he postulated that governments' monopoly on currency issuance can be no more efficient than private currency issuance.

In Hayek's model of private currency competition, creditors naturally gravitate toward currencies that tend to appreciate in value, while debtors prefer those that depreciate. The interplay of these preferences leads to the selection of a currency with a stable value as the common choice. He believed that competition between private issuers would be superior to a government monopoly, stating that [money] "*would be better supplied by competition between private issuers than by a monopoly of government.*"

However, in a modern legal system, with the state being the exclusive issuer of currency, private money issuance faces formidable challenges. The state's prerogative over coinage is a deeply entrenched aspect of its sovereignty, fiercely protected by criminal laws against any private encroachment. This monopoly extends to the regulation of financial services, such as deposits, loans and foreign exchange, all of which require government authorization and operate under strict state supervision.

Anonymity in the exchange of scholarly ideas is a deeply rooted academic tradition. A prime example is the famous "t-distribution" in statistics, published under the pseudonym "Student" by the Englishman William S. Gosset.

Akin to Zorro's iconic "Z," Satoshi Nakamoto stated his birthday to serve as a cryptic clue to their true identity. This seemingly insignificant detail, combined with the pivotal Bitcoin white paper, suggests his strong belief in the advantages of private currency competition over government monopoly, similar to Hayek's libertarian philosophy.

1.2 Overview of Bitcoin Technology[6]

The invention of Bitcoin solved two pivotal issues in peer-to-peer transactions. Firstly, asymmetric encryption confirms the proof of ownership, ensuring that ownership can be verified even if the user's identity is anonymous. Secondly, to address the issue of double spending, that is, the same digital currency could be spent twice, Bitcoin uses a consensus mechanism known as Proof of Work (PoW). This system requires network participants, called miners, to perform complex calculations to validate transactions and record them on the blockchain, thus creating a secure and immutable ledger and negating the need for centralized authority.

1.2.1 The Double Benefit of Asymmetric Encryption Signatures: Proof of Ownership and Privacy Protection

Unlike in physical money or gold, in Bitcoin, monetary value is stored in transaction records. Bitcoin as such is not a tangible coin but a record of transactions, specifically called "Unspent Transaction Outputs" (UTXO), which are transferable electronic proofs of ownership.

UTXOs are established using an asymmetric encryption for signing that authenticates the identity of the owner. The Elliptic Curve Algorithm is used for this purpose, which generates a public key and address from a private key. This process is irreversible to ensure that the private key is not deduced from the public key or address, yet the two can mutually authenticate each other.

The public key, derived from the private key, serves as the public receiving address and the means by which others can verify one's assets. The private key, however, remains confidential and is effectively the "ultimate identity card." In essence, in a fully anonymous environment, one's private key is their credential in a completely anonymous environment. With asymmetric cryptographic signing, Bitcoin protects the identity of the user while verifying ownership rights in peer-to-peer transactions.

The earliest form of cryptocurrency, eCash, was launched in 1994, bringing to life the concept of "untraceable electronic cash", as envisioned by Chaum, Fiat and Naor in 1988. This system preserved customer privacy using cryptographic blind signatures, allowing anonymous transactions without bank involvement.[7] In 1998, Wei Dai introduced B money to the cryptographic community, emphasizing its anonymity feature to protect user privacy. Similarly, Bitcoin's white paper in 2008 clearly defined its privacy protection method as "anonymity", using public key strings to receive payments without recording any user information in the system.[8]

---

[6] The technical principles of Bitcoin will be explained in more detail in Sect. 5.3 of this book.

[7] Chaum, David, Amos Fiat, and Moni Naor. "Untraceable electronic cash." *Advances in Cryptology—CRYPTO'88: Proceedings 8*. Springer New York, 1990, 319-327

[8] Nakamoto, Satoshi. "Bitcoin: A Peer-to-Peer Electronic Cash System." 2008, 6. https://bitcoin.org/bitcoin.pdf.

1.2.2 Construction of Bitcoin Transaction Data: Transactions, Blocks and Chains

The relevant literature generally suggests that blocks form a chain, so this technology can be aptly called "blockchain." In fact, transactions within bitcoin blocks are linked by transaction records, forming a continuous chain of transactions or a "transaction chain." Let us now explore the characteristics of a "block" and the process of blocks forming a "chain."

A "block" is a data entity formed by packaging multiple transaction data together; it can be thought of as a ledger that records many transactions. A single transaction in its simplest form is sized approximately 250 bytes, although actual transactions are typically larger. The maximum size of each block was limited by Satoshi Nakamoto at 1 megabyte (1024 kilobytes), which means that a single block can contain up to 4096 (1024000/250) transactions. Using the ledger analogy, Nakamoto maximized a single ledger at 1024 pages, with each basic transaction occupying a quarter of a page, such that a ledger can contain a maximum of 4096 transactions.

As blocks join to form a chain, the transactions they contain align to create a unique sequence. A bookkeeper, following protocol rules, records transactions in a block until it is full. Then, the block is sealed with a timestamp and linked to the previous block by recording its number on the cover, creating an unbroken chain of ledgers. There is a notable tendency in this blockchain: the "deeper" a block is in the chain, the more immutable its transactions become. To change a transaction, such as one from 2015 in block height 363,270, every subsequent block would have to be changed and reconciled, which is a nearly impossible task.

This prompts the important question of how ledger manipulation can be prevented. Bitcoin innovatively uses the Proof of Work (POW) mechanism, in which miners compete in hash computations to win the right to record transactions, preventing block tampering. Bitcoin operates without a central server, relying on miners in the network to provide computing power, who in turn compete for the right to record transactions with bitcoins. The system rewards the miner who has won this right, a process known as "mining." As for the mining operation, it involves performing two rounds of SHA256 hash calculations on the "block header" data, resulting in a 256-bit hash value.

Computing a hash value typically takes only a few seconds; however, Bitcoin's protocol increases the difficulty level by requiring certain conditions, such as the first 19 digits must be zeros. To tackle this challenge, miners engage in a trial-and-error process by continuously entering random numbers (known in the trade as "nonce," short for "number only used once") to generate a hash that meets Bitcoin's stringent criteria. Due to the unpredictable nature of the SHA256 algorithm, finding the correct hash involves both computational power and chance. Moreover, Bitcoin dynamically adjusts the mining difficulty to maintain an average block time of about ten minutes, striking a balance between security and efficiency.

The above principles of Bitcoin may seem overly complex to those without a technical background; however, understanding the following three key points can provide a basic understanding of the core principles of Bitcoin, regardless of the finer details:

Firstly, Bitcoin's blockchain is an intricate design in which transactions are collected into blocks, and these are linked together, forming a blockchain with a ledger-like chain of transactions. By design, each block can hold up to 4096 transactions due to the system's capacity limits.

Secondly, block chaining ensures the immutability of transactions by creating a sequential link to previous blocks, making it computationally impractical to alter historical data through the Proof of Work system.

Thirdly, the mining difficulty adapts to keep the average block creation time at around ten minutes, which is critical for network stability and efficient transaction verification.

1.3 Governance Mechanism[9]

1.3.1 Autonomous Community

The innovation behind Bitcoin is not only technical but also reflected in the design of its community ecosystem. It advocates the use of blockchain technology by fostering a "decentralized" community that operates autonomously, with no central authority to govern or manage its processes. This pioneering approach has set a new paradigm for how communities can self-organize and function without the need for a central organizing node.

From an operational perspective, Bitcoin has introduced a unique "mining" process that allows self-regulation and the maintenance of operations through the ecosystem. Unlike centralized networks that rely on a central server to provide computing power, this power requirement in Bitcoin's mining process is decentralized, where participants called "miners" contribute computing resources to the network. In exchange for their efforts, the system rewards them with bitcoins. This not only incentivizes participation but also ensures the continued operation of the network. Ownership and transaction validation in this system does not depend on a single authoritative node (like a bank verifying an account balance) but rather on a consensus mechanism recognized by the majority of miners, also known as the "longest chain principle."

By utilizing mining for decentralized consensus, and based on blockchain technology, Bitcoin introduced a remarkable novel payment method based on trustless interactions and decentralized governance. Specifically, when numerous nodes across the network run identical codes and follow the same protocols or smart contracts,

---

[9] For further information on governance, Sect. 5.8 contains a comparative analysis of the governance models of Ethereum, EOS, and Bitcoin, along with their respective advantages and disadvantages.

they inherently adhere to a unified set of rules and logic. This creates a form of governance that is executed autonomously by the code itself. As a result, this entire system operates organically and free from the oversight or intervention of any centralized authority, exemplifying a self-sustaining model of the community ecosystem.

1.3.2 Governance Code

At the governance level, the highest principle within the Bitcoin ecosystem is the maxim "code is law", where governance ultimately manifests through modifications and updates to the code. Bitcoin has spontaneously formed a governance mechanism. characterized by shared decision-making among maintainers, core developers, and miners.

In the early stage of Bitcoin, the authority to make decisions regarding the development of Bitcoin rested solely with Satoshi Nakamoto. Later, he delegated this power to Gavin Andresen, who assumed the role of "maintainer." Andresen then distributed this power to four others, creating a system in which five people share the maintainer's authority, and only a consensus among them grants the final authority to change the code. Typically, these five maintainers solicit and consider the views of all developers in the open source community before making decisions.[10]

However, the support of miners is crucial, as without their computing power, the overall computing capacity of the network could degrade or even collapse. Therefore, while a group of five has the authority to change the code, their power is by no means absolute. In an autonomous community, command-style authority is likely to be rejected by other miners, resulting in a fork, meaning that if miners refuse to run the new code and they continue to use the original code, this can lead to the coexistence of two separate systems operating on different code bases.

Through empirical learning, Bitcoin has naturally established rules for code modification: core developers propose changes, known as Bitcoin Improvement Proposals (BIPs), based on consultations within the Bitcoin open source community, and develop new versions of the Bitcoin software. Miners then vote on these changes, and once 90% of the blocks are agreed on, the changed code automatically takes effect.

In the autonomous and self-regulating governance model of Bitcoin, maintainers and developers have the right to propose initiatives, while miners have the right to reject them. Thus, the two groups provide checks and balances on each other, with miners having the ultimate ability to "vote with their feet," which acts as a constraint on maintainers and developers.

[10] The term "developers" refers to individuals who are active within the Bitcoin community and contribute to its codebase. At the time of writing, there were approximately 400 such contributors.

1.4 Summary

Satoshi Nakamoto conceived Bitcoin as a peer-to-peer payment system that operates independently of any centralized authority. This groundbreaking approach positioned Bitcoin as an open-source, decentralized, peer-to-peer, anonymous digital currency.[11] The ideological underpinnings of Bitcoin appear to be heavily influenced by Friedrich Hayek's advocacy of private money, reflecting a broader desire to conduct a social experiment in private currency.

Despite Hayek's thought of private money inspired Bitcoin, the adversaries and challenges that Hayek and Nakamoto sought to address were different. Hayek challenged the government's monopoly on issuing currency, whereas Nakamoto targeted the inherent need for third-party trust, which included the commercial banks that Hayek supported, even if those banks competed in a free market.

Hayek was concerned with the political and economic challenges of how to facilitate the marketization and free competition of money. Nakamoto, on the other hand, addressed the technical challenge of creating a virtual currency system that operates without relying on trusted third-party servers, thus eliminating the need for a centralized server.

Such technical challenge is inextricably linked to economic aspects. By eliminating centralized servers, Bitcoin inherently frees its monetary system from the need for third-party trust. In this way, the innovation of Bitcoin extends beyond the technological realm to revolutionize the social structure of its community ecosystem: it has catalyzed the creation of a "decentralized" ecological governance model, facilitated by blockchain technology, where everything is spontaneous and there is no need for a central node to organize, manage or adjudicate.

---

[11] Nakamoto, Satoshi. "Bitcoin: A Peer-to-Peer Electronic Cash System." 2008. https://bitcoin.org/bitcoin.pdf. (page 1 and page 8)

Chapter 2
Evolution of Digital Currencies

What constitutes money and how has Bitcoin reshaped it? Why do we say that digital currencies represent not only new ways of payment but also an entirely new form of money? How will digital currencies challenge conventional financial systems and theories?

This Chapter examines the chronicle of money, focusing on the impact of Bitcoin on redefining currency. We explore how Bitcoin, through its decentralized nature and blockchain technology, has greatly challenged traditional notions of money. We further delve into digital currencies as more than just new payment methods, highlighting their role as a new form of money. This evolution signifies a considerable shift in the financial landscape, as digital currencies offer alternative transaction methods and embody a totally new monetary concept, reshaping existing financial theories and systems.

2.1 Overview

In a contemporary sense, the birth of Bitcoin in January 2009 unequivocally established the realm of "digital currency." The novel concept of "peer-to-peer electronic cash" introduced by Bitcoin greatly expanded people's comprehension of the form of money. In contrast to conventional currencies, like banknotes or coins, a digital currency has no tangible entity but is stored and transacted as digital data. Therefore, its novelty lies not only as a payment method but also a type of currency.

Prior to the era of Bitcoin, early virtual currencies referred only to tokens used in specific online spaces. Back then, the term "virtual" was the opposite of "real", and the literal meaning of virtual currency was "tokens in the non-real world." Typical examples of virtual currency, such as Q coins issued by Tencent for online games, were exclusive to specific online spaces. The latter can be purchased with legal currency (e.g., Chinese yuan) and then used to buy virtual goods, such as in-game

Y. Wu and W. Zhu, *The Fundamentals of Digital Currency*,
https://doi.org/10.1007/978-981-97-8261-1_2

items, avatars, themes, and virtual gifts. These "virtual currencies" were not transferable between users and thus could not be considered as "money." International regulators refer to these types of virtual currencies as "closed" or "inconvertible", which do not possess financial attributes and are not subject to financial regulation.

Emergence of Bitcoin: Reshaping the Concept of "Virtual Currency"

Firstly, from a technological perspective, the newly introduced Bitcoin adopted asymmetric encryption technology and possessed the characteristics of decentralization and distribution. It also became known as a "cryptocurrency"; thus, the concept of virtual currency expanded to include Bitcoin, and the term "virtual" became the antithesis of "real" legal tender. With this stage, the meaning of virtual currency had changed to privately issued digital currency.

Secondly, Bitcoin was novel among virtual currencies, as it obtained the functions of "money", such that it could be transferred between individuals, extending beyond limited online spaces. In practice, it could serve as a store of value, a medium of exchange and a unit of account, fulfilling the three major functions of money. The meaning of virtual currency had thus transformed into "non-legal tender token/ currency." As Bitcoin surpassed the single-purpose nature of specific online spaces, international regulators began to refer to this type of virtual currency as "open" or "convertible." As Bitcoin-like virtual currencies possessed the functions of money, they inevitably became subjects of financial regulation.

Thirdly, the emergence of cryptocurrencies spurred the idea of issuing a new type of "central bank digital currency" via blockchain technology; central banks worldwide began to investigate how to leverage blockchain technology to enhance the efficiency of legal currency payment settlements. Along this path, the concept of "digital currency" gradually evolved into a higher-level concept that encompassed both central bank digital currency and privately issued digital (virtual) currency. Digital currencies had also diversified along a binary division based on the creditworthiness of the issuer (refer to Fig. 2.1).

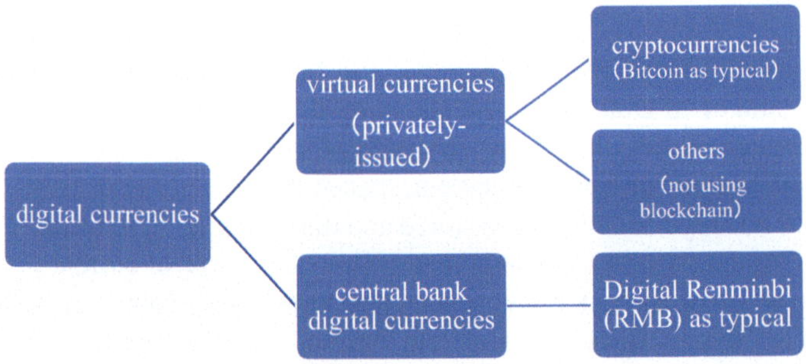

Fig. 2.1 Overview of Digital Currency Types

2.2 Virtual Currency: De Facto Money/Currency

Virtual currencies, including cryptocurrencies, are often labeled as "currency", but this does not by default make them eligible to be recognized as "legal tender" or "fiat money" by authorities. In fact, they are called currencies because they fulfill the three main functions of money to an extent: acting as medium of exchange, unit of account, and store of value. Over time, the term "currency" has misleadingly become almost interchangeable with "legal tender" in daily conversations. This confusion can make discussions about the monetary nature of digital currencies challenging, as it blurs the line between legal recognition and functional use. Henceforth, when we talk about "currency" in the context of "virtual currency" or "cryptocurrency", we refer to its functions, not its legal status as money.

In other words, "currency" discussed in relation to virtual currencies does not mean that these are legally recognized types of money. Instead, this term refers to the ability of such currencies to function as money in practice (refer to Fig. 2.2). This distinction is crucial for a deep understanding and discussion of the evolution of digital currencies.

"What does money constitute?" is probably one of the most difficult questions to answer in economics, much like "What is law?", perplexing most legal philosophers. As a start, the commodity theory of money holds that money is a commodity and its value comes from being a commodity. The historical basis of this notion lies in the use of gold and silver currencies during human civilization, followed by the establishment of gold and silver standards. The credit theory of money offers a different view: it proposes that money functions primarily as an accounting tool to measure the credit-debt relationship. This theory gained prominence after the U.S. dollar was decoupled from gold in the early 1970s, offering a compelling explanation for the nature of money in modern financial systems. Recent anthropological research supports the credit theory by providing evidence that challenges traditional views and enriches our understanding of the evolution of money.

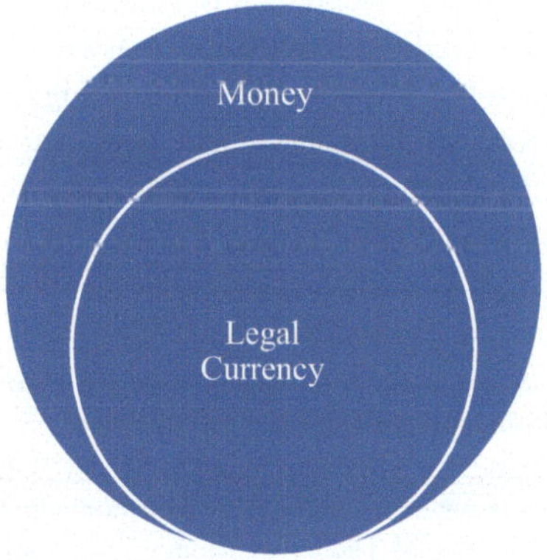

Fig. 2.2 The relationship of money and legal currency

From Commodity Theory To Credit Theory: Barter Or Credit Relations—Which One Came First?

A high school student in China would likely agree without hesitation that "gold and silver are not inherently money, but money inherently consists of gold and silver."[1] This insightful statement, made by Karl Marx in 1859, has become a frequently cited quote in all political economics textbooks in China. These works claim that barter came first, and from barter emerged money with the property of being a universal equivalent. Gold and silver came to be money because they themselves were commodities with value. In the long history of the human exchanges of things, "banknotes" gradually appeared, which were originally certificates of gold and silver issued by commercial banks, guaranteeing that they could be redeemed for these previous metals. Under the gold or silver standard currency systems, the legal currency issued by central banks (i.e., banknotes issued by them) is also a certificate representing gold and silver, promised by central banks to contain a certain amount of them.

After the collapse of the Bretton Woods system in the 1970s, the legal currencies of major countries were neither tied to gold or silver nor they specified the amount of gold or silver they represented; moneys in the world as we know it became purely fiat currencies. Obviously, this means that the commodity theory of money cannot explain the current credit-based monetary system.

The credit theory of money appeared before World War I, which does not discuss the value of money itself but purely its functions as medium of exchange and unit of account. Alfred Mitchell-Innes, a British economist and a pioneer of the credit theory of money, pointed out in his 1913 article "What Is Money" that credit and debt are two aspects of the same legal relationship, and creditors and debtors are the parties in this legal relationship. It follows that when credit and debt are created, money is created. In his 1914 paper, he further argued that money is merely a measure of this credit-debt relationship, much like feet and hours are used to measure distance and time.[2] Unsurprisingly, the credit theory of money is more suited to explaining today's fiat currency system.

Recent theoretical developments go even further, with some scholars proposing that credit relationships existed before barter relationships. In his work, David Graeber, a renowned anthropologist, attempted to prove the credit theory of money from an anthropological perspective. He pointed out that early humans engaged in exchange through credit-debt relationships, and that credit-debt relationships preceded barter.[3]

---

[1] Marx, Karl. *A Contribution to the Critique of Political Economy.* Chicago: Charles H. Kerr& Company, 1904, p.212.

[2] Innes, A. Mitchell. "What Is Money?" *The Banking Law Journal*, 1913, 377–408, p.392. http://www.newmoneyhub.com/www/money/mitchell-innes/what-is-money.html.; Innes, A. Mitchell. "The Credit Theory of Money." *The Banking Law Journal* 31 (1914): 151–168, p.155. http://www.newmoneyhub.com/www/money/mitchell-innes/the-credit-theory-of-money.html.

[3] Graeber, David. *Debt: The first 5000 years*. Penguin UK, 2012, 21-23.

Although different schools of thought stirred up a great deal of controversy over the true meaning of money, there are at least two consensuses. First, money has the three major functions of store of value, medium of exchange, and unit of account.[4] Second, money is a universally accepted means of payment that forms a common belief in purchasing services and goods between transacting parties.[5] In fact, these two consensuses are the standards for judging money: the former is an objective factor, while the latter is subjective, with a dynamically evolving interplay between the two.

Cigarettes In The Trench Of World War I

During World War I, under the tremendous war pressure, cigarettes became a "necessity" for frontline soldiers in the trenches, so they would also exchange them for other goods. Cigarettes in the battlefield in fact had even more advantages than legal currencies. As a result, soldiers from different countries had complex currency exchange rates. Importantly, even if legal currency was available, it might not be immediately consumable; therefore, cigarettes gradually became the "hard currency" exchanged among soldiers. It can be safely said that cigarettes were the "*de facto* money " for this particular group at that particular time.

Let us establish that **legal currency is highly likely to be *de facto* money**: as long as a country's monetary system does not collapse, the force of the state will always ensure that legal tender currency will be accepted in social transactions. However, **not all *de facto* money is legal currency**. A good example is the fate of the legal currency in China in the period before 1949, the year when the People's Republic of China was established. In 1948, the legal tender currency system in the area governed under the Kuomintang party collapsed completely, which brought the phenomenon in rural areas of China where rice served as a medium of exchange. Rice, being a basic necessity of life in this region, although not possessing the exclusive attributes of gold and silver, was still relatively easy to divide and store. Therefore, it became *de facto* money at that time in certain areas.

Financial regulators worldwide generally recognize that virtual currencies, or at least Bitcoin, are able to perform the functions of money. A typical case happened in 2016 when Mark Carney, the Governor of the Bank of England (the central bank of the United Kingdom) at the time, stated in a speech that virtual currencies such as Bitcoin are indeed able to perform the functions of money.[6] Moreover, as many sources have argued, Bitcoin has developed into a widely accepted means of payment within certain domains, such as the "dark web."

[4] These are the major functions of money as defined in mainstream textbooks. For example, the same viewpoint is conveyed by Mankiw, N. Gregory. *Principles of Economics*. 8th ed. Cengage Learning, 2018, p.605. The authoritative textbook of Marxist political economics in current China, Pang, Jinju, et al. *Political Economy*. 5th ed. Higher Education Press, 2014, 50-52. This textbook also lists two additional functions of money: means of payment (deferred payment) and world currency.

[5] Greco, Thomas. *Money: Understanding and creating alternatives to legal tender*. Chelsea Green Publishing, 2001, p.22.

[6] Carney, Mark. "The future of money." *Scottish Economics Conference. Edinburgh: Edinburgh University*. 2018.

Currency, in its essence as a form of money, is primarily recognized for its role as medium of exchange rather than as store of value. It embodies the principle of being a universally recognized instrument for conducting trades and transactions. The concept of currency is revolving around: historically, the role of money has been filled by tangible assets like banknotes and coins, yet the advent of virtual currencies, including cryptocurrencies, has expanded this traditional view. These digital forms, despite lacking official legal tender status, have gained certain acceptance as valid payment methods within certain boundaries. Therefore, it is both logical and appropriate to categorize them as "currencies", acknowledging their role as parallel to that of conventional banknotes and coins in enabling economic activities.

2.3 Evolution of Virtual Currency

The concept of virtual currency first appeared in the late 20th and early 21st centuries, initially manifested in the form of tokens within online games. At this stage, they were essentially digital assets existing within the digital realm, lacking the full attributes of conventional currencies. However, the introduction of Bitcoin significantly redefined the landscape of virtual currency. Its creator(s) sought to revolutionize the traditional financial system by introducing a decentralized digital currency, challenging the prevailing dominance of state-issued currencies.

As other game-changing effects in monetary systems, the advent of Bitcoin catalyzed the development of a myriad of other virtual currencies and stimulated the conceptualization of central bank digital currencies (CBDCs). The trajectory of virtual currency branched into another technical path, with Bitcoin marking a major milestone on this path. This pivotal event led to the proliferation of various cryptocurrencies modeled after Bitcoin, among which Ethereum (ETH) stands out as a notable advancement, embodying the next generation of blockchain technology. The nuances and implications of these technological advances are further explored in Chap. 5.

2.3.1 *The Era Leading up to Bitcoin: Virtual Currencies as Tokens Used in Specific Online Spaces*

Virtual currencies first appeared on gaming platforms, which issued their own tokens for pre-paid recharging in online games. Taking Tencent's Q coins as an example, users can purchase Q coins from Tencent with fiat currency and use them for specified purposes in designated online spaces, such as buying game equipment or props on the Tencent gaming platform. In this context, "virtual" refers to the virtual world

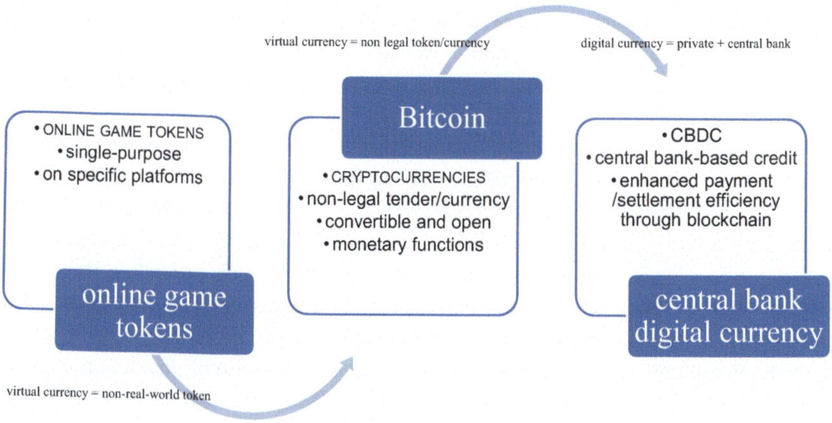

Fig. 2.3 The evolution of monetary concepts: virtual currency and digital currency

corresponding to the real world, and virtual currencies generally denote game tokens in a specific space.[7]

Virtual currencies like Tencent do not possess financial attributes and are not subjects of financial regulation (refer to Fig. 2.3).

In Everyday Life, "Token" Can Be Understood As A Form Of Value Certificate. Grammatically, "token" is a common and widely used English word. For example, coins used for public transportation, game tokens at amusement parks, or airline mileage points, all can be considered as tokens. The term "token" is also used in computer programming, referring to a proof of access to computer permissions. In this context, it is a string of characters that grants access to a computer system. The use of "token" in computer systems was borrowed from the concept of transportation tokens and game tokens: when one uses a transportation token, they get the right to take the bus, and when one inserts a game token into a gaming machine, they earn the right to play the game. Similarly, in a computer system, if one provides the appropriate token, they can access the computer system.

2.3.2 *Redefining the Essence of Virtual Currency: The Impact of Bitcoin*

Bitcoin, known as a cryptocurrency due to its use of asymmetric encryption technology, reaches beyond specific online spaces and functions, as it embodies the three

---

[7] For the early meaning of "virtual currency," refer to the relevant studies of the time, such as: Li, Chong. "The Development of Virtual Currency and the Reconstruction of Monetary Theory and Policy." *The World Economy* 8 (2003); Shuai, Qinghong. "Q Coin, U Coin, POPO Coin, and Electronic Currency." *E-Commerce* 1 (2007); Fu, Zhu. "Analyzing the Impact of Virtual Currency on the Current Monetary System from the Perspective of Q Coin." *Financial Economics* 4 (2008).

major attributes of money: store of value, transaction medium, and unit of account. It thus represents a typical open and convertible virtual currency, which paved the way for the evolution of "virtual" as in virtual currency, contrasting with "real" fiat currencies.[8]

The concept of "virtual currency" is initially introduced in non-financial regulatory documents in relation to gaming tokens. As an illustration, the Chinese Ministry of Culture, in its departmental regulation known as "The Provisional Measures for the Administration of Online Games" (2010), defines virtual currency as in-game tokens within online spaces, representing the prevalent interpretation preceding the era of Bitcoin. This document refers to these tokens as "virtual currencies in online games", specifying that they can only be utilized for exchanging products and services within the game itself, and are not allowed for payment, the purchase of physical goods, or conversion to other units. According to this definition, game tokens are considered closed and non-convertible virtual currencies.

However, with the emergence of Bitcoin, the meaning of virtual currency has transformed significantly. In 2017, the People's Bank of China, together with six other ministries, issued the "Announcement on Preventing the Financing Risks of Token Offerings", which explicitly prohibited virtual currency financing activities using terms such as bitcoin and ether.

"Virtual currency" has entirely distinct interpretations in the "Provisional Measures for the Administration of Online Games" and the "Announcement on Preventing the Financing Risks of Token Offerings." The definition in the former refers only to game tokens, while the latter denotes privately issued digital currencies with financial regulatory significance. The fundamental difference lies in the former being closed and non-convertible while the latter being open and convertible. "Virtual currency", discussed herein as a financial phenomenon, pertains to the one mentioned in the "Announcement on Preventing the Financing Risks of Token Offerings."

Notably, there are major technological differences between online platform tokens and cryptocurrencies. Cryptocurrencies utilize completely different techniques, involve asymmetric encryption, and possess characteristics of decentralization and distribution. These new types of privately issued tokens are commonly referred to as "cryptocurrencies" from a technological perspective. Since both cryptocurrencies and game tokens are privately issued and not "real" (legal) currencies, the emergence of cryptocurrencies inexorably expanded definition of virtual currency. After the birth of Bitcoin, numerous virtual currencies adopting similar asymmetric encryption techniques appeared, leading to a remarkable boom in the crypto market

---

[8] Financial Action Task Force. "Virtual Currencies, Key Definitions and Potential AML/CFT Risks", June 2014. http://www.fatf-gafi.org/media/fatf/documents/reports/Virtual-currency-key-and-potential-aml-cft-risks.pdf, p.26.

and sparking a social experiment of private currencies.[9] Therefore, virtual currency is often used interchangeably with cryptocurrencies without further clarification.

Private Digital/Electronic Currencies Before Bitcoin

It is worth noting that prior to the rise of Bitcoin, various private digital/electronic currencies had already been devised. These are all centralized and do not employ the blockchain technology. One notable example is "WebMoney", introduced by a Russian private enterprise in 1998. This was initially designed as an intermediary solution for prepaid cards and remittance services. Upon reassessing its significance with the advent of Bitcoin and stablecoins, it becomes evident that, like stablecoins, WebMoney and similar private tokens used for remittance services possess characteristics beyond mere payment functionality: they not only facilitate the storage and transaction of value but also act as independent units of account. Since its conception, WebMoney has developed to offer different units of accounting for a range of currencies, such as WMZ (WebMoney Dollar), WME (WebMoney Euro), WMR (WebMoney Ruble), and more. This evolution marks a substantial forward step, elevating these tokens from mere payment instruments to distinct forms of currency. Private currencies like WebMoney exhibit three key characteristics: they are virtual (private) in nature, possess general payment functionality that is not limited to a specific scope, and are electronic but not encrypted. In this book, we regard WebMoney and similar private currencies as virtual currencies, but we must admit that WebMoney or similar private currencies are indeed merely transitional species and lack the advanced attributes typically associated with "digital", such as being encrypted and programmable. In Sect. 3.3 of this book, we further discuss the essence and classification of centralized or non-crypto virtual currencies like WebMoney.

2.3.3 Birth of the Concept of Digital Currencies

The concept of digital currencies emerged and solidified with the advent of cryptocurrencies. Interestingly though, the idea of central bank digital currencies (CBDCs) dates back to over three decades ago. In the early 1980s, the Federal Reserve Bank of Kansas City began organizing an annual economic policy symposium in Jackson Hole (Wyoming, U.S.). Attended by the Chair of the Federal Reserve and senior officials from major central banks around the world, this event evolved into a significant global central banking venue. James Tobin, the 1981 Nobel laureate in economics, introduced the early vision of CBDCs at this symposium in 1987, presenting his paper in the proceedings.

Amid the US savings and loan crisis of 1985-1986, Tobin proposed a solution to address the risks associated with commercial bank deposits. He suggested that the central bank could offer "deposited currency" directly to the public.[10] According to

[9] Wu, Yun, and Wei Zhu. "Virtual Currencies: A Failed Social Experiment of Private Currencies?" *Financial Regulatory Research*, no. 6 (2020). https://www.researchgate.net/publication/373111648_Virtual_Currencies_a_Failed_Social_Experiment_of_Private_Currencies. Accessed on 24 Aug 2023.

[10] Tobin, James. "The Case for Preserving Regulatory Distinctions." *Restructuring the Financial System: A Symposium Sponsored by the Federal Reserve Bank of Kansas City*, 1987, 167–183.

this concept, the central bank would open accounts to provide electronic money (e-money) and electronic payment services directly to the public and businesses. This can be considered as the groundwork for what would later become the concept of a central bank digital currency (CBDC). At the time, however, Tobin's ideas remained theoretical. Subsequent research mainly focused on how central banks issuing money directly to the public might affect the financial system.[11]

The introduction of Bitcoin sparked new discussions on using blockchain technology to overhaul the existing fiat currency system. In 2014, J.P. Koning proposed the concept of "Fedcoin" on his blog, envisioning the issuance of US dollars using Bitcoin technology.[12] The formal proposition of CBDCs originated from Ben Broadbent, the Deputy Governor of the Bank of England, in 2016. Broadbent advocated that central banks could leverage Bitcoin's underlying technology to issue digital forms of fiat currencies. Furthermore, he argued for an expanded understanding of digital currencies, stating that they should encompass not only privately issued digital currencies like Bitcoin but also digital fiat currencies issued by central banks.

Although CBDCs employ asymmetric encryption technology like Bitcoin, they are typically not classified as cryptocurrencies because their issuance is backed by central banks. With these concepts gradually entrenched in the financial landscape, the international community has standardized terminology over time for digital currencies, distinguishing between central bank digital currencies and private digital currencies. The latter, often called "virtual currencies", are further divided into encrypted and non-encrypted types, based on their technological features.

A detailed explanation of the classification of digital currencies will be provided in the next chapter.

2.4 Technological Forms and Financial Characteristics of Digital Currencies

Regularly used online banking and third-party payment methods, such as Alipay, WeChat Pay and PayPal, possess a significant degree of electronic or digital functionality; however, these should not be confused with "digital currencies." Digital currency signifies a new breed of currency and payment method, which is originally digital and designed to function as peer-to-peer digital cash that facilitates direct payments, clearing and settlements, potentially bypassing financial intermediaries and thereby transforming the foundation of the existing financial system.

It should be noted that the terms "electronic currencies" or "electronic payments" are often used but do not equate to digital currencies. The concept of digital currency was introduced to highlight a distinction from the simple or primitive digital payment methods such as "electronic currencies" and "electronic payments" (online banking

[11] A typical example: Bank for International Settlements. "Implications for Central Banks of the Development of Electronic Money," October 1996. https://www.bis.org/publ/bisp01.pdf.

[12] Koning, J. P. "Fedcoin," October 19, 2014. http://jpkoning.blogspot.com/2014/10/fedcoin.html.

and third-party payment). "Digital" currencies embody a more advanced and fully digitized form of electronic payment or currency. While the existing monetary system already allows for the digital storage, transfer, and settlement of funds, and we regularly use electronic means like online banking and third-party payments for transactions, these means are not what we refer to as digital currencies. As such, **the transition from "electronic currencies" and "electronic payments" to "digital currencies" is not merely a matter of increased digitization but marks a conceptual leap, signifying a move towards a more sophisticated and higher level of digitization. In other terms, digital currencies introduce an innovative currency and payment paradigm.**

2.4.1 From "Electronic" to "Digital": The Semantic Differences Indicating the Degree of Digitization

In certain contexts, the terms "electronic" and "digital" can be used interchangeably. Currently, "digital" is always a subset of "electronic"; however, the distinction between "electronic" and "digital" implies a nuanced difference in the degree of digitization.

From a technological standpoint, "electronic" encompasses both "analog" and "digital", with the former representing the early stage of electronic technology and the latter signifying a more advanced stage.

Obviously, analog technology simulates physical world parameters. For instance, in electrical and electronic systems, analog signals continuously represent physical quantities such as sound, light and temperature. Early mobile communication devices, like the analog signal-based "brick" phones, along with equipment such as fax machines, film cameras, cassette players, and conventional TVs exhibiting snowflake noise, all operate on analog signals.

Conversely, digital signals convert analog signals by attributing them discrete values. The widespread adoption of computers and networks has made digital signals preferable in communication processing, establishing them as the mainstream technology. Modern computers utilize a binary system, which is the predominant method of digital computation. Devices like smartphones, digital televisions, and IoT devices also operate on digital signals.

Although analog signals can carry a high density of information, they are prone to noise interference. Digital signals, on the other hand, are resilient to environmental noise during transmission and processing. Moreover, they enable complex computations and operations, along with a more extensive programmable space.

Nowadays, most "electronic" devices rely on digital signals. However, **regarding digital economy, using "electronic" and "digital" implies a premeditated distinction, with "digital" suggesting a higher level of digitization. This distinction denotes enhanced computational and programmable capabilities.**

The definition of "electronic money" (e-money) by the European Union, as per the Electronic Money Directive 2009/110/EC, well illustrates the above subtlety.[13] Therein, the typical form of "e-money" is a general-purpose prepaid card, essentially an electronic counterpart to traditional legal tender cash. Indeed, the term "electronic" in this context refers to electronic payment services based on legal tender, encompassing methods such as online banking and innovative payment solutions like third-party payments.[14] **The term "electronic" in this context simply refers to a simple digital "image" of cash.**

Electronic Money In Practice

"Electronic money" (e-money) in the European Union is a simple digitization of legal tender. Even the European Commission states on its official website that "electronic money (e-money) is the digital alternative to cash."[15] The European Banking Authority also clarifies that electronic money is in the form of prepaid value, where buyers use legal tender to purchase electronic money, which represents the digital form of legal tender.[16] Specifically, buyers obtain electronic money worth the same value in exchange for the payment of legal tender. Holders of electronic money can use it for payments and have the right to request the issuer to redeem electronic money for equivalent legal tender at any time.[17]

According to Article 2(2) of the 2009 EU Electronic Money Directive, the requirements for defining electronic currency include the following: electronic storage of monetary value; the holder's right to claim monetary value from the issuer; issuance by the issuer based on received funds; acceptance by parties other than the issuer as a means of payment.

Referring to the above EU requirements, China's UnionPay prepaid card can be considered as a type of electronic money. However, commonly used cards for transport, such as subway or bus cards and shopping cards, are not considered electronic money as per the EU definition, since they can only be accepted by their respective issuers.

When referring to existing electronic payments and currencies, we continue to use the modifier "electronic" to indicate a relatively simple feature of digitization of an analogue form of money. In contrast, "digital currency" implies a rich and advanced level of digitization, including the use of cryptographic and consensus algorithm technologies, the description of value on shared ledgers, the assurance of ownership of each value using asymmetric encryption and digital signatures, and the ability to trace the historical flow of value. Thus, "digital currency" signifies a

---

[13] Directive 2009/110/EC of the European Parliament and of the Council of 16 September 2009 on the taking up, pursuit and prudential supervision of the business of electronic money institutions amending Directive 2005/60/EC and 2006/48 and repealing Directive 2000/4.

[14] For the scope of electronic payments, the reader can also refer to footnote 12 of the People's Bank of China. "2020 Overall Operation of the Payment System Report," March 24, 2021. https://www.gov.cn/xinwen/2021-03/24/content_5595427.htm.

[15] Source: "E-Money," https://ec.europa.eu/info/business-economy-euro/banking-and-finance/consumer-finance-and-payments/payment-services/e-money_en. Accessed on 27 May 2021.

[16] European Banking Authority. "EBA Opinion on 'Virtual Currencies,'" July 2014. https://eba.europa.eu/file/44764/download?token=DeE-57CM, p.12.

[17] For specific processes of pre-issuance and redemption, refer to Article 11 of the 2009 EU Electronic Money Directive.

higher degree of technological richness compared to simple digitalization seen in "electronic payments" and "electronic currencies."

2.4.2 *Digitization of Currency and Payments in Existing Legal Currency Systems*

Digital currency is a concept first introduced to augment existing issuance and settlement systems. Within the present global currency system, central banks issue currency in two forms: cash (physical) and commercial bank reserves at the central bank (electronic). Correspondingly, there are two distinct electronic accounting systems for legal currency.

The first system operates between the central bank and commercial banks. Commercial bank reserves at the central bank are not physical cash but in electronic form, which are recorded exclusively on the central bank's ledger. Settlements between commercial banks are facilitated through the central bank, causing an increase or decrease in the commercial bank reserves at the central bank. Within the existing legal currency framework, an electronically issued legal tender by the central bank circulates only between the central bank and commercial banks.[18] Settlement in the **original** form of electronic currency occurs solely between commercial banks via the central bank (refer to Fig. 2.4).

The second system functions between commercial banks and their customers. Commercial banks maintain records of customer deposits in electronic form, enabling transfers and transactions through electronic means. However, this system is simply an electronic accounting and transactional platform developed by commercial banks. Essentially, commonplace electronic payment methods, such as online banking and third-party payment services, are electronic or digital representations of currency transfers fabricated by financial intermediaries. They signify the digitization of cash by various commercial banks through their proprietary electronic systems, essentially representing a **derivative** form of physical cash.

Electronic Payments As A Derivative Form Of Physical Cash

Regulations regarding legal currency are comparable across countries, with the legal tender usually comprising both banknotes and coins. Legal tender is the designated means of payment. In China, Article 16 of the Law of the People's Bank of China states that "The legal tender of the People's Republic of China is the Renminbi. All public and private debts within the territory of the People's Republic of China shall be paid in Renminbi, and no entity or individual may refuse to accept it." Regulations on the Administration of Renminbi further

---

[18] The Committee on Payments and Market Infrastructures, Bank for International Settlements. "Digital Currencies," November 2018. https://www.bis.org/cpmi/publ/d137.pdf. p.6.

Commercial bank deposits at the central bank serve three functions: firstly, they fulfill the requirement for legal reserve deposits; secondly, they represent positions for interbank settlements; and thirdly, they enable commercial banks to earn interest on their deposits from the central bank.

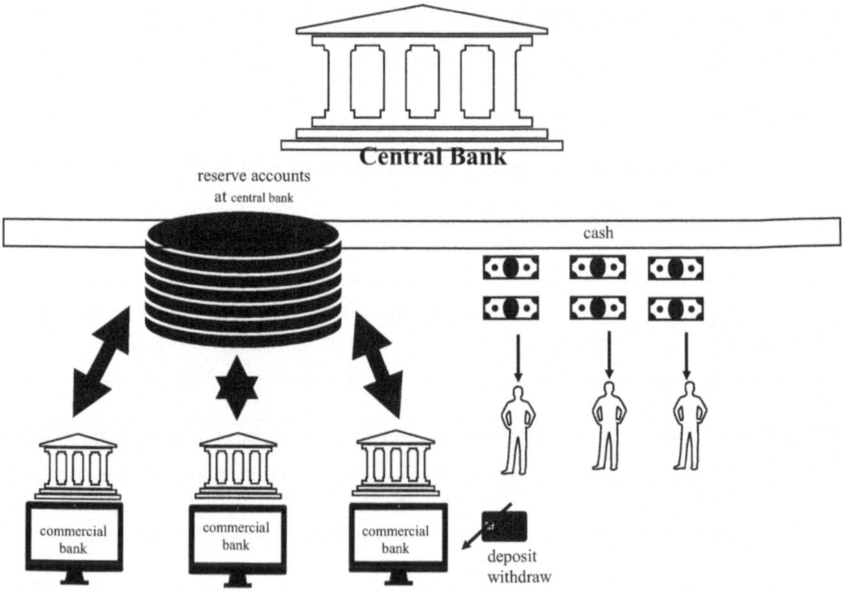

Fig. 2.4 Cash and reserve accounts at the central bank

clarify that Renminbi includes both banknotes and coins, which are collectively referred to as "cash" in this work.

Yet, our society has gradually entered a "cashless society" where cash is increasingly replaced by electronic payment methods. From online shopping to physical grocery shopping, and even to paying parking fees or utility bills, people generally use card payments or third-party payments (Alipay, WeChat Pay, PayPal, etc.).

What added value do these electronic payment methods actually have for users? On what grounds can we trust these electronic payments? Instead of representing the physical cash itself they only embody the right to cash. When one receives an electronic transfer, it signifies that they have obtained the right to cash and can unconditionally withdraw the corresponding cash from financial institutions.

In the context of the existing legal currency system, let us consider the example of interbank retail customer transfers executed by commercial banks. A single transfer comprises three stages: payment (encompassing payment instructions and the actual fund transfer), interbank settlement (conducted through clearing institutions), and final settlement (executed via the central bank). The entire process necessitates the collaborative efforts of commercial banks, clearing houses, and the central bank to be completed. For instance, when Customer Alpha of Bank A initiates a fund transfer to Customer Beta of Bank B, even though the payment instructions and fund transfer may conclude within seconds, the subsequent clearing and settlement processes take longer to complete. Clearing establishes the credit and debit relationships between financial institutions, while settlement finalizes the transfer of funds and assets based on the clearing outcome, thereby resolving the credit and debit relationships between the interacting financial institutions.

The Process Of Interbank Remittance

Initially, an "advance payment" is made for the customer's transaction. Customer Alpha sends a transfer instruction through Bank A, and Bank B immediately transfers the specified amount to Beta' account at Bank B upon receiving the instruction.

After the processing of the "advance payment", a creditor-debtor relationship is formed between Bank A and Bank B. At this point, Bank B has effectively "advanced" the funds, with Bank B being the creditor and Bank A being the debtor.

Third, the creditor-debtor relationship is affirmed through clearing. The existence of multiple "advance payment" activities between different banks every day leads to multiple creditor-debtor relationships. Clearing institutions function to determine the NET creditor-debtor relationship between banks, where multiple creditor-debtor relationships are offset to produce a net value, thus determining the net creditor-debtor relationship between banks.

Finally, the creditor-debtor relationship is terminated through a concluding settlement step. Commercial banks need to send instructions to the central bank to transfer the deposits therein held by commercial banks, thus completing the settlement and closing the creditor-debtor relationship.

The seemingly simple process of interbank remittance requires complex clearing and settlement processes to be completed after the payment instruction is sent, requiring a robust financial infrastructure to support it.

China has established a "modernized payment system" to ensure accurate and efficient clearing and settlement processes. The interbank fund transfers in Chinese daily life are cleared through different systems. The clearing of fund transfers between commercial banks is handled by the Clearing House of the People's Bank of China, whereas the clearing of interbank card transactions, such as domestic debit card payments, is managed by card settlement organizations such as China UnionPay.

Remarkably, the People's Bank of China has taken the lead in establishing the "China National Advanced Payment System" (CNAPS), which includes six payment clearing subsystems, including "Real Time Gross Settlement System", "Batch Payment System for Small Amounts", "Online Payment Interbank Clearing System", among others. The "Real-Time Gross Settlement System" is aimed at processing large-value payments between financial institutions, where funds are transferred directly between the reserve accounts of financial institutions at the central bank, with clearing and settlement occurring in real time and on a per-transaction basis. Meanwhile, the "Batch Payment System for Small Amounts" and the "Online Payment Interbank Clearing System" provide clearing services for retail interbank transfers, with batch and periodic clearing, i.e., net settlement.[19]

2.4.3 Cryptocurrency as a Novel Form of Currency and Payment Method

1. The Three "New" Dimensions Of Cryptocurrency

---

[19] Regarding the history of CNAPS, see Yang, Wenjie. "Development of China's Modernized Payment System." *China Finance*, no. 14 (2017): 18–20. For further information on the six subsystems, see Wang, Wei. "Modernized Payment System: China's Payment and Clearing Expressway." *Financial Electronization*, no. 10 (2019): 63–64.

To understand cryptocurrency as a new form of currency and payment method, it is helpful to distinguish it from and compare it with existing fiat currencies across three dimensions (refer to Table 2.1).

Firstly, from the perspective of currency form, cryptocurrency is originally digital. In contrast, the original form of currency within the existing monetary system is cash, with the electronic form reserved exclusively for commercial bank reserves at central banks.

Secondly, regarding the payment process, cryptocurrency operates as peer-to-peer digital cash, which allows for payment, clearing and settlement to occur simultaneously. Conversely, electronic transactions between retail customers in the existing monetary system require separate processes for these stages and depend on the centralized databases of commercial banks, clearing institutions and central banks.

Thirdly, in terms of the financial system structure, the peer-to-peer cash potential of cryptocurrency opens up the possibility of bypassing traditional financial intermediaries. This could potentially revolutionize the credit creation pattern of the current financial system.

2. The Two Fundamental Transformations Of Cryptocurrency: Source Of Trust And Pattern Of Credit Expansion

In the current financial system, customers deposit their money into commercial banks to earn interest. These banks then lend this money to others, creating new loans, which turn into new deposits, helping the banking system create more credit. This process is possible because cash as legal tender is interchangeable or generic. When a customer deposits money in a bank, it mixes with other people's deposits. Although a bank can

Table 2.1 Digital characteristics of existing legal currencies and digital currencies

Type of money		Issuer	Original form	Store and transaction	Higher Levels of digitization
Digital currencies	CBDC	Central bank	Digital	Digital	Yes
	Virtual currencies/ cryptocurrencies	Private	Digital	Digital	Yes
Existing legal currency		Central bank	Physical cash (banknote, coin)	Derivatively electronic (common customers through commercial banks)	No
			Originally electronic (Commercial banks hold reserves at central bank)	Originally electronic (among commercial banks)	

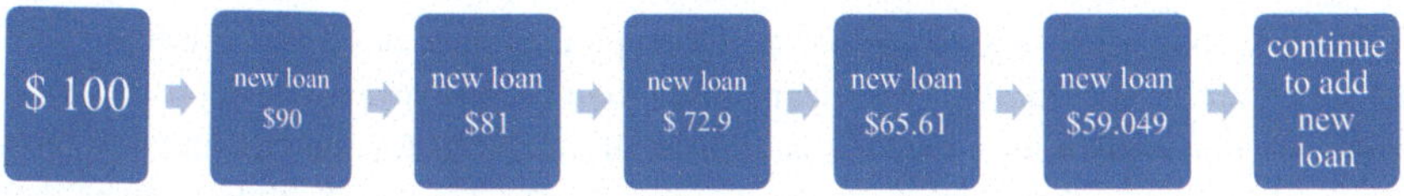

Fig. 2.5 How commercial banks expand money supply through loans

lend this money to someone else, this customer can always withdraw their deposit. However, they cannot ask for the exact same bills deposited. The expansion of credit relies on the trust customers place in their banks.

At present, there are four prevailing theories regarding money supply: the deposit creation theory[20], the money multiplier theory[21], the modern monetary theory of government creation[22], and the "loanable funds theory" or "credit creation theory."[23] Among these, the fourth theory, which proposes that money is created through the expansion of bank assets, primarily via loans, has gradually gained consensus.[24] It posits that money originates from the expansion of bank assets, with loans being the most representative bank asset. Consequently, in the modern monetary system, banks serve as the nexus of money creation and monetary policy primarily targets the behavior of banks creating money through loans.

Drawing from introductory-level economics knowledge (e.g., Economics 101), when a customer deposits cash into a bank, these funds become intermingled with that bank's other cash holdings, establishing a debtor-creditor relationship between the customer and the bank. The bank then lends out this cash under its own name. When borrowers deposit the loaned amount back into the bank, this initiates a cycle that expands the total money in circulation through the deposit-loan process conducted by the bank (refer to Fig. 2.5).

As can be seen in the figure, when a government mandates that banks can lend out only 90% of the deposited cash, holding 10% in reserve (as reserve requirements), the deposit reserve ratio stands at 10%. Under this condition, banks can generate a total money supply of 1000 yuan from an original deposit of 100 yuan. Similarly, if the deposit reserve ratio is 5%, an initial deposit of 100 yuan can lead to the creation of a total money supply of 2000 yuan. This calculation uses the limit of a geometric sequence method, a concept typically studied in high school mathematics.

[20] Gurley, John G., and Edward S. Shaw. *Money in a Theory of Finance*. Brookings Institution Press, 1960.

[21] Friedman, Milton, and Anna J. Schwartz. *Monetary Trends in the United States and United Kingdom: Their Relation to Income, Prices, and Interest Rates, 1867–1975*. University of Chicago Press, 1982.

[22] Wray, L. *A Primer on Macroeconomics for Sovereign Monetary Systems*. UK: Palgrave Macmillan, 2012.

[23] Werner, Richard A. "Can banks individually create money out of nothing? — The theories and the empirical evidence." *International Review of Financial Analysis*, no. 36 (2014): 1–19.

[24] McLeay, Michael, Amar Radia, and Ryland Thomas. "Money Creation in the Modern Economy." *Bank of England Quarterly Bulletin* Q1 (2014): 14–27.

In stark contrast to exchangeable cash, cryptocurrency possesses a unique trait that sets it apart: specificity. This means that when cryptocurrency is deposited with an intermediary, such as a bank, it is technically feasible for the customer to later request the return of the specific units they originally deposited. It also means that banks may find it challenging to lend out one's cryptocurrency to others, effectively impeding the traditional process of credit creation.

Digital currencies are poised to introduce two fundamental changes concerning the source of trust and the mechanism of credit creation:

(1) The trust in digital currencies does not hinge on financial intermediaries. In the conventional monetary system, trust in a fiat currency is ultimately derived from the central bank, while customer confidence in conducting financial transactions is placed in financial intermediaries. Conversely, for fully decentralized private digital currencies like Bitcoin, trust is established without reliance on any third party. For central bank digital currencies (CBDCs), regardless of whether a "double-layer issuance system" is employed or not, the credibility of digital cash is directly backed by the central bank, which reflects a direct relationship between currency owners and the central bank, bypassing financial intermediaries.

Understanding Trust No Longer Comes From Financial Intermediaries

Due to their different issuance methods, virtual currencies have significant differences in their credit basis for fulfilling their monetary function. It can be argued that the credit basis of Bitcoin relies largely on people's trust in algorithms and machines. Certainly, for asset-backed stablecoins like Tether (USDT), where the issuer ensures sufficient dollar reserves, credit comes from a combination of algorithms, machines, supported assets, and issuer credit. However, even for asset-backed stablecoins, trust is no longer dependent on financial intermediaries (readers will have a more comprehensive understanding of different types of virtual currencies after reading Chaps. 3, 4 and 11 of this book).

The fact that central bank digital currencies no longer rely on financial intermediaries like commercial banks has two implications. The first is that it is technically possible for central banks to directly issue digital currencies to end customers and eliminate the need for financial intermediaries for transactions. Of course, this would eliminate the conventional role of central banks. Therefore, China's digital yuan adopted a "a double-layer issuance system", where the People's Bank of China does not directly interface with customers. Customers can open a "digital wallet" with commercial banks or other financial intermediaries and conduct transactions through this wallet. The second implication is that even if the storage and transactions of central bank digital currencies are conducted through financial intermediaries (such as in a "double-layer issuance system"), the credit of customers' digital cash comes directly from the central bank, representing the relationship between currency owners and the central bank. In contrast, in the current fiat currency system, customer deposits and credit come from commercial banks.[25]

(2) Digital currencies feature traceability and unique, identifiable "labels", rendering them legally distinct assets. This means that even when multiple digital currencies are deposited with financial intermediaries, each customer's digital

---

[25] Regarding an authoritative introduction to the "dual delivery system" of the Chinese central bank digital currency, see Fan, Yifei. "Analysis of Policy Significance Regarding the Positioning of Digital Currency M0." *Financial Times*, no.001(15 Sept. 2020).

currency deposit remains distinct and traceable, which technically allows for the clear differentiation of one customer's digital currency from another's.

Owing to the shift in the trust foundation of currency away from financial intermediaries and the inherent nature of digital currencies as "specific assets", new questions emerge regarding the relevance of financial intermediaries and the future of credit expansion. Digital currencies hold the technical potential to revolutionize the traditional financial framework of "money creation by loans."

3. Why Cryptocurrencies Might Not Create Credit?—Differentiating Between Generic And Specific Property

In legal terms, a distinction must be drawn between "generic property" and "specific property." For example, let us suppose one purchases a mass-produced art print. If it becomes damaged, the law allows for compensation through the acquisition of another identical print that will have the same value. As mass-produced prints are treated as generic property, identical items can serve as replacements. In contrast, if the artwork is an original Picasso, it qualifies as specific property; even a new painting by Picasso could not replicate the original, as original paintings are unique, irreplaceable and can have no substitutes.

In a similar vein, cash deposited in a bank is typically considered generic property—it is a fungible and interchangeable thing. When it comes to cryptocurrency, however, each unit can be distinctly specified: once it is deposited with an intermediary, it is technically feasible to demand the return of the exact unit deposited. This specificity is the exact reason that challenges the bank's ability to lend out cryptocurrency, as the creation of the same credit may be hindered or rendered impossible.[26]

The surge of new cryptocurrencies thus prompts a pivotal dilemma: can financial intermediaries continue to expand credit in the face of this new technology, and if so, in what manner? The implications of a solution could be profound for the entire financial system.

In essence, the term "digital currency", as discussed herein, entails the complete digitization of issuance, storage and transactions, eliminating the need for physical forms of money such as paper or coinage. The digitization of a currency confers it the potential to bypass financial intermediaries, making this form of currency a digitized equivalent to cash. As digital currency is originally digitized from its inception, its entire organizational ecosystem differs significantly from the existing monetary systems that rely on commercial banks as intermediaries (refer to Table 2.2).

[26] See Committee on Payments and Market Infrastructures and the Markets Committee, Bank for International Settlements. "Central Bank Digital Currencies," March 2018. https://www.bis.org/cpmi/publ/d174.pdf, p.6. See also Beermann, Johannes. "Cash and Cryptocurrencies from the Perspective of Central Banks." *Financial Market Research*, no. 12 (2019): 109–112.

Table 2.2 Comparative summary of electronic money systems and digital currencies

Characteristics	Electronic money	Digital currency	
		Virtual currency	CBDC
Form	Digital "image" of cash	Originally digital	Originally digital
Manifestations	Account-based	Token-based	Token-based
	Database-based balance	Digital description of value	Digital description of value
	Generic	Specific	Specific
Realizable Transaction Methods	Centralized accounting; payment, clearing and settlement completed in separate steps	Peer-to-peer transaction, payment, clearing, and settlement completed simultaneously	Peer-to-peer transaction, payment, clearing, and settlement completed simultaneously

Chapter 3
The Logical Categorization of Digital Currencies

How did digital currencies evolve from gaming tokens to cryptocurrencies and CBDCs? How can be digital currencies efficiently categorized, and what sets virtual currencies apart from CBDCs? What are the key technologies forming the basis of digital currencies? What are the differences and applications of wholesale versus retail CBDCs? What are the main regulatory concerns for virtual currencies?

This chapter aims to provide a comprehensive overview of digital currencies, tracing their development from simple gaming tokens to complex forms such as cryptocurrencies and Central Bank Digital Currencies (CBDCs). Digital currencies can be divided into two main categories: virtual currencies and CBDCs, with the distinction rooted in their underlying credit systems. While the hallmark technologies of digital currencies include asymmetric encryption and decentralization, it is crucial to recognize the presence of non-cryptocurrency-type virtual currencies. Wholesale CBDCs are noted for enhancing the efficiency of the financial clearing and settlement processes, whereas retail CBDCs represent a novel form of currency. The convertibility of virtual currencies plays a pivotal role in defining their financial characteristics and acts as a crucial element in activating their financial regulation.

For a deep understanding of social phenomena, it is vital to comprehend their evolutionary process and analyze them from an abstract view. Failing to grasp the historical context of these phenomena may lead to conceptual confusion, while focusing only on the phenomena themselves limits cognitive development. In Chap. 2, readers could learn about the unique meanings of the terms "money/currency", "virtual", "crypto" and "digital", along with the historical evolution of digital currencies from gaming tokens to cryptocurrencies like bitcoin, and finally to central bank digital currencies. In this chapter, we seek to classify digital currencies from the perspective of their financial attributes, enabling readers to grasp the essential characteristics of different types of digital currencies.

Y. Wu and W. Zhu, *The Fundamentals of Digital Currency*,
https://doi.org/10.1007/978-981-97-8261-1_3

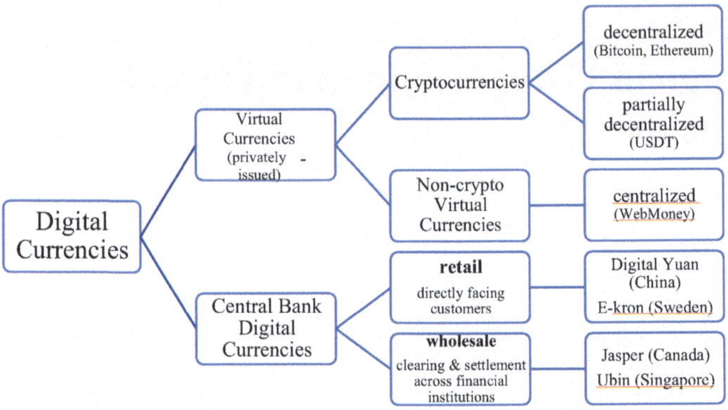

Fig. 3.1 Classification of digital currencies

3.1 Classification of Digital Currency Based on Credit: Virtual Currency and Central Bank Digital Currency

According to the origins of credit, digital currencies can be categorized into two types: "central bank digital currencies" (CBDC) and "private digital currencies." The main difference is that CDBCs obtain their credit from central banks, whereas private digital currencies rely on private sources of credit. Furthermore, private credit can be derived solely from algorithms and machines (as in the case of Bitcoin), or from a combination of algorithms, machines, support assets, and issuer credit (as seen in stablecoins).

CBDC refers to the digital or digitalized form of fiat currency. It has also become a specific term that describes the issuance and transaction of fiat currency in digital form, utilizing blockchain technology, cryptography, and distributed ledgers. Despite the technological innovations of CBDC, it remains a form of fiat currency with the same legal tender status as central banks' physical banknotes and coins. Conversely, virtual currency refers to privately issued digital currencies or digital tokens. The concept of "virtual currency" has been proposed to contrast with "fiat currency." As previously mentioned, since the advent of Bitcoin, the term "virtual" corresponds to "real" and "virtual currency" corresponds to "real currency", that is, fiat currency.[1] Meanwhile, the term "cryptographic" emphasizes the technological aspect and "virtual" focuses on the nature of credit.

CBDCs can be further classified into wholesale currencies and retail currencies[2] (see Fig. 3.1).

---

[1] See Financial Action Task Force. "Virtual Currencies, Key Definitions and Potential AML/CFT Risks", June 2014. http://www.fatf-gafi.org/media/fatf/documents/reports/Virtual-currency-key-and-potential-aml-cft-risks.pdf, p.26.

[2] Committee on Payments and Market Infrastructures and the Markets Committee, Bank for International Settlements. "Central Bank Digital Currencies," March 2018. https://www.bis.org/cpmi/publ/d174.pdf, p.6.

Wholesale CBDC is not intended for individual retail users but rather serves as a means of clearing and settlement between financial institutions. In Sect. 2.4, we have examined the complex process of payment, clearing and settlement within the existing fiat currency system by using cross-bank remittance as an illustrative example. This seemingly simple cross-bank remittance transaction relies on a substantial centralized financial infrastructure for clearing and ultimately achieves centralized settlement within the central bank. Wholesale CBDC involves the transformation of deposits by commercial banks from electronic to a digitized format. Given its decentralized characteristics, this type of currency allows for the seamless integration of payment, clearing and settlement, ultimately enhancing the efficiency of these processes.

Prominent examples of wholesale currency can be observed through initiatives like the Jasper project by the Bank of Canada and the Ubin project by the Monetary Authority of Singapore. These projects aim to streamline and enhance the process of large-scale clearing and settlement among commercial banks and selected financial institutions (where periodic settlement currently still involves the participation of central banks). Wholesale currency, by its essence, is not intended for individual users but rather focuses on facilitating inter-institution clearing and settlement. It can also be perceived as a technological advancement in the clearing and settlement methods within the existing financial system. This transformative currency is founded on the fact that the above institutions already engage in electronic clearing through their reserves held in electronic form with central banks.

Clearing & Settlement Using Wholesale Central Bank Digital Currency: A Distinctive Approach Compared To The Existing Monetary System. Currently, banks rely on centralized clearing organizations like "UnionPay", Visa and Mastercard to centrally record and confirm the creditor-debtor relationships (clearing) among them. Subsequently, debt settlement between banks is accomplished through transfers facilitated by the central bank. The Jasper and Ubin projects, however, eliminate the dependence on centralized clearing organizations by adopting a decentralized distributed ledger to record transactions between participating entities. In this new framework, transactions are directly recorded and accounted for among the involved parties, eliminating the need for a centralized clearing organization. This strategy not only enables more efficient settlement but also mitigates the reliance on central authorities for clearing and settlement processes.

Retail CBDC is specifically designed for general use by public individuals and represents a fully-fledged form of digital currency issued by the central bank. It enables peer-to-peer digital cash transactions and functions as a form of digital currency. Crucially, **the value of retail CBDC is backed by the central bank's digital signature, serving as proof of ownership.** This type of CBDC, as exemplified by China's digital yuan (e-CNY), is typically recorded on both the central bank's electronic ledger and the distributed ledgers maintained by commercial banks.

The "Digital Yuan" Pioneered By China Is Currently The Most Widely Used Of All Central Bank Digital Currencies. At the end of 2019, e-CNY began its trial run in cities like Shenzhen and Suzhou, allowing public individuals to use it for red packet giveaways and small-scale payments in various scenarios, such as transportation. As of June 30, 2021, the digital yuan trial had involved over 10 million whitelisted users, with 20.87 million personal wallets and 3.51 million corporate wallets created. The cumulative transaction volume had reached 70.75 million transactions, totaling 34.5 billion yuan, with over 1.32 million trial scenarios.

Notably, China's CBDC, although inspired by blockchain technology, does not fully embrace decentralization or distribution. Instead, Qian Yao, the then director responsible for developing CBDC, clarified that China's central bank digital currency "draws on the concepts of blockchain technology to establish a relatively balanced centralized/distributed ledger registration center."[3]

In Chapter 6, we expand on the inherent technical limitations of blockchain technology, such as its low capacity and slow speed, making virtual currencies (bitcoin, for example) unsuitable for large-scale daily use as a means of payment. These factors are deemed a decisive factor behind China's decision to not simply adopt blockchain technology for its e-CNY.

Importantly, CBDCs, despite adopting blockchain technology, cryptography and distributed ledgers, remain fundamentally fiat currencies and should not be confused with private virtual currencies.

The key to distinguishing whether a digital currency is a CBDC or a virtual currency lies in their associated credit system. For instance, some private entities issue digital currencies fully backed by fiat currency reserves, known as stablecoins, and these may be fully backed by fiat currency reserves, yet they do not represent the national credit led by central banks but are based on private promises. Similar to bank-issued promissory notes, even if fully backed by fiat currency reserves, stablecoins only represent private commitments (this will be further elaborated later).

3.2 Classification of Virtual Currency Based on Stable Value Arrangements: Stablecoins and Non-stablecoins

Satoshi Nakamoto, the pseudonymous creator of Bitcoin, under the strong influence of Hayek's ideas on private currencies,[4] set the ambitious goal of conducting a social experiment with private currencies from the very beginning. He even went a step further by challenging not only the monopoly of national currencies but also any form of third-party trust, including commercial banks that Hayek believed could provide sufficient competition. In his new virtual currency, Nakamoto envisioned credit to be derived solely from algorithms and machines. The challenge in this approach is that the intrinsic value of Bitcoin becomes difficult to understand, and it can fluctuate significantly when measured against fiat currencies. This volatility and uncertainty in value can pose challenges for individuals and investors in determining the true worth and stability of Bitcoin. Even renowned investor Warren Buffett has expressed skepticism towards Bitcoin, referring to it as a "gambling tool" and "rat

[3] Yao, Qian. "Prototype Concept of China's Legal Digital Currency." *China Finance*, no. 17 (2016): 13–15.

[4] Fantacci, Luca. "Cryptocurrencies and the Denationalization of Money." *International Journal of Political Economy* 48.2 (2019): 105–112.

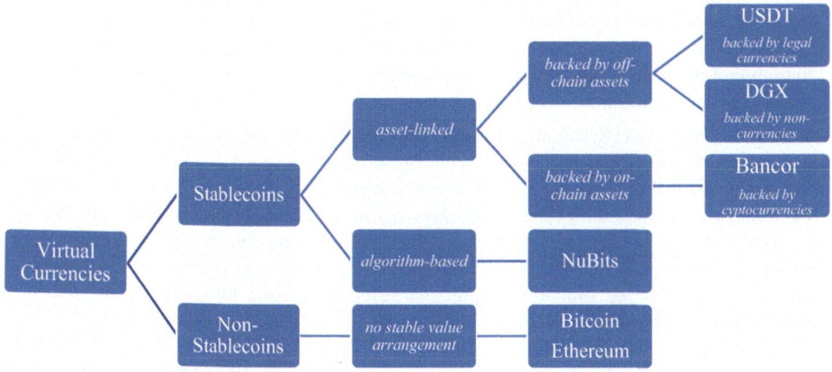

Fig. 3.2 Classification of Stablecoins

poison."[5] One might argue about the correctness of Buffett's understanding, but at least it highlights the controversy about the intrinsic value of Bitcoin even among top professional global investors.

To mitigate the issue of uncertainty in intrinsic value based on machine and algorithm trust and the significant value fluctuations, stablecoins backed by fiat currencies or physical assets have emerged. Also known as "asset-linked stablecoins", these currencies have a hybrid credit foundation that includes algorithms, machines and supported assets, backed by the credibility of the issuer (Please recall "Understanding that trust no longer comes from financial intermediaries" in Sect. 2.4.3 of this book). Figure 3.2 depicts the classification of stablecoins.

USDT, which is backed by the US dollar, stands as the most typical and extensively used stablecoin.[6] It is issued by Tether Limited and entrusted to banks as custodians to manage the US dollar assets. When Tether Limited receives a sum of US dollars, it gives the assets to the custodians for safekeeping and simultaneously issues an equivalent value of USDT. As another asset-linked stablecoin, Facebook's announced stablecoin "Libra" (now renamed as "Diem") was initially planned to be backed by a "basket" of currencies but has since been changed to be backed only by the US dollar. There are other commodity-backed virtual currencies, such as DGX (Digix Gold Token) that is backed by gold as the supporting asset. However, these types of stablecoins require the custody of the supporting assets, creating significant investor protection issues.

CAN STABLECOINS BE TRUSTED? Do they represent a stable value? Some studies have raised doubts about the claims made by Tether Limited. Griffin et al. (2018) questioned the

[5] Li, Yun. "Warren Buffett Says Bitcoin Is a 'Gambling Device' with 'a Lot of Frauds Connected with It.'" CNBC, May 4, 2019. https://www.cnbc.com/2019/05/04/warren-buffett-says-bitcoin-is-a-gambling-device-with-a-lot-of-frauds-connected-with-it.html.

[6] See FSB Financial Stability Board. "Regulation, Supervision and Oversight of 'Global Stablecoin' Arrangements: Final Report and High-Level Recommendations," 2020, 9–10. See also Bullmann, Dirk, Jonas Klemm, and Andrea Pinna. "In Search for Stability in Crypto-Assets: Are Stablecoins the Solution?" *ECB Occasional Paper* 23, no. 230 (2019).

adequacy of asset backing for USDT and uncovered that Tether had employed an unidentified Chinese accounting firm to audit its US dollar assets. Other researchers noticed a significant "month-end effect" in USDT, wherein Tether engaged in substantial bitcoin selling for USDT prior to the accounting firm's asset audit.[7]

In October 2021, The U.S. Commodity Futures Trading Commission (CFTC) settled charges against Tether Limited and its affiliated stablecoin issuer, Tether International Limited.[8] This settlement entails that "Tether held sufficient fiat reserves in its accounts to back USDT tether tokens in circulation for only 27.6% of the days in a 26-month sample time period from 2016 through 2018." It further discloses that, in an attempt to create a misleading perception of sufficient reserves, Tether intentionally moved funds into accounts prior to the designated audit date. This finding supports the previous revelations made by Griffin et al. (2018) regarding the "month-end effect."

Furthermore, there are stablecoins backed by other cryptocurrencies, known as on-chain asset-backed stablecoins, which derive their value from the stability of the underlying cryptocurrencies on the blockchain. Thus, stablecoins backed by real-world assets are referred to as off-chain asset-backed stablecoins, like USDT mentioned earlier. The value of on-chain asset-backed stablecoins depends on the stability of the supporting cypto-assets. If these assets are solely on-chain assets, achieving stability between them may be challenging when measured against fiat currencies. BANCOR is a notable example of an on-chain asset-backed stablecoin, which will be addressed in more detail in Chap. 5.

In a broader sense, the stablecoin classification also covers algorithm-based stablecoins, which aim to maintain price stability by adjusting the total token supply through algorithms. In this currency design, when the token value decreases, a portion of the tokens is destroyed to uphold price stability, and vice versa. Nonetheless, algorithm-based stablecoins, such as NuBits, have not been able to practically achieve the desired stable value. As a result, these stablecoins have consistently collapsed[9] and are considered less reliable in terms of value compared to non-stablecoins like Bitcoin.

---

[7] Griffin, John M., and Amin Shams. "Is Bitcoin Really Untethered?" *The Journal of Finance* 7, no. 4 (2020): 1913–1964. This paper was first published on the SSRN website on June 25, 2018, and was updated on November 5, 2019.

[8] CFTC. "CFTC Orders Tether and Bitfinex to Pay Fines Totaling $42.5 Million," October 15, 2021. https://www.cftc.gov/PressRoom/PressReleases/8450-21.

[9] Bullmann, Dirk, Jonas Klemm, and Andrea Pinna. "In Search for Stability in Crypto-Assets: Are Stablecoins the Solution?" *ECB Occasional Paper* 23, no. 230 (2019).

3.3 Technical Classification of Virtual Currency Based on Asymmetric Encryption Technology and Decentralized Features

Bitcoin is a well-known cryptocurrency that uses "encryption" to secure transactions. This is specific to digital currencies as a special type of encryption called "asymmetric encryption", adding a digital signature for transaction validation. While traditional electronic payment systems also use this asymmetric encryption technology, it mainly serves the purpose of secure communication rather than as a transaction signature. The predecessor of digital currencies, eCash also used this encryption, which Bitcoin took a step further by combining it with a consensus mechanism, allowing for peer-to-peer transactions and removing the need for central servers. On this account, Bitcoin is "distributed" and "decentralized."

Symmetric Encryption Is The Counterpart Of Asymmetric Encryption. In the movie "Eternal Wave", the radio stations in Shanghai and Yan'an share a prearranged codebook. Both parties reach a consensus on the corresponding information in advance, which is a typical example of symmetric encryption. Meanwhile, asymmetric encryption does not require the parties to agree on a password beforehand but rather uses key exchange for verification.

Even though asymmetric encryption technology can facilitate peer-to-peer payments, it does not guarantee complete decentralization. The precursor to digital currencies, eCash, also used asymmetric encryption technology to achieve peer-to-peer transactions but could not achieve complete decentralization in areas such as issuance, payment, clearing, and settlement: the final ledger of eCash is still held by banks, and the confirmation of transaction results still relies on the centralized ledger of the bank (eCash is discussed further in Chapter 5).

The greatest technological contribution of Bitcoin lies in the combination of asymmetric encryption technology using the "proof-of-work" mechanism to achieve peer-to-peer and decentralization, creating what we refer to as blockchain technology. Proof-of-work is the core principle of the Bitcoin mechanism, which will be discussed specifically in Chapter 5.

Cryptocurrencies possess unique characteristics that make them decentralized, but the degree of decentralization varies (see Table 3.1). To understand this proposition, we need to analyze the detailed aspects of issuance, payment, clearing, and settlement. Bitcoin is entirely decentralized, as it exhibits decentralization across all the three aspects. On the other hand, a cryptocurrency like USDT is centralized in its issuance but decentralized in payment and settlement, thus has a limited degree of decentralization.

Looking at the history of virtual currencies, non-cryptographic private electronic tokens, which do not use asymmetric encryption technology, are also classified as virtual currencies. This classification is explicitly acknowledged by the Financial Action Task Force (FATF), an international anti-money laundering organization.[10] Most of these virtual currencies emerged before Bitcoin, which rely on a centralized ledger system and are managed by centralized entities to record the rights of each

[10] Financial Action Task Force. "Virtual Currencies, Key Definitions and Potential AML/CFT Risks", June 2014. http://www.fatf-gafi.org/media/fatf/documents/reports/Virtual-currency-key-and-potential-aml-cft-risks.pdf, pp.4–5.

Table 3.1 Technological features and decentralization level of virtual currencies

Types	Asymmetric encryption	Highly digitalized	Decentralized	Examples
Cryptocurrencies	Yes	Yes	Entirely decentralized	Bitcoin
			Partially decentralized	USDT
Non crypto virtual Currencies	No	No	Entirely centralized	PerfectMoney WebMoney

user, making them entirely centralized. Q-coins, purchased by legal currencies and used within the online platforms and services of Tencent, are a typical example. Some non-encrypted virtual currencies even go beyond the scope of purely utility tokens and possess monetary functions similar to Bitcoin, such as Russia's WebMoney and Panama's "Perfect Money"; they are widely used for commercial payments, remittances, and person-to-person payments.[11]

Importantly, fully centralized virtual currencies do not (at least currently) possess advanced digital characteristics like Bitcoin. These purely centralized virtual currencies are typical transitional species, akin to "platypuses." These mammals exhibit both the egg-laying characteristic unique to birds and the milk-feeding characteristic of mammals. We classify them as mammals, but we also acknowledge that they partially lack the primary characteristics of mammals. **If we consider electronic currency and payments as birds and typical digital currencies as mammals, then purely centralized virtual currencies are much like platypuses.**

Classifying transitional species has always been a challenge in traditional morphology-based taxonomy, and the same difficulty applies to the classification of centralized private electronic tokens. Taking WebMoney as an example, which was created in 1998 and has a technological path similar to electronic currencies, fully utilizes a centralized database while it lacks the advanced technical features of digitalization. In this sense, classifying it as an electronic currency is perfectly appropriate. The common feature among early virtual currencies like WebMoney is their use of centralized databases and their ability to link with bank cards. Therefore, external observers have often considered the issuers of these virtual currencies to be engaged in remittance or non-bank third-party payment services, and the tokens issued were seen as an intermediate link in remittance or payment services or a form of prepaid card service (i.e., the electronic currency business in the European Union).

Indeed, WebMoney has obtained "electronic currency" and "electronic payment" licenses in countries of the EU. However, this does not imply that WebMoney is identical to existing electronic currencies and payments but rather indicates that these licenses provide the best match for WebMoney within existing legal frameworks. In

[11] Keatinge, Tom, and David Carlisle. "Virtual Currencies and Terrorist Financing: Assessing the Risks and Evaluating Responses," 2018. https://www.europarl.europa.eu/RegData/etudes/STUD/2018/604970/IPOL_STU(2018)604970_EN.pdf, p.18.

Table 3.2 Centralized Private Electronic Tokens as transitional species

	e-money	Centralized private electronic tokens	Cryptocurrencies
Typical examples	Pre-paid card	WebMoney	Bitcoin, USDT
Medium of exchange	Yes	Yes	Yes
Store of value	Yes	Yes	Yes
Independent unit of account	No	Yes	Yes
High level of digitalization	No	No	Yes
Transfer object	Corresponding fiat currency	Ownership of the token itself	Ownership of the token itself

a similar fashion, the U.S. law specifies that virtual currency transfer services must apply for a "money services business" (MSB) license.

The major distinction between WebMoney and "e-money" lies in the fact that the former has substantially evolved beyond being a mere substitute for legal tender. Electronic money, on the other hand, solely facilitates the settlement and transfer of prepaid legal tender to the recipient, acting as a mere substitution for legal tender during the payment process. WebMoney possesses its own independent units of account, tied to the Russian ruble, US dollar, euro, and gold, denoted as WMR, WMZ, WBE, and WME respectively. Moreover, when transferring WebMoney between payers, the ownership of WebMoney is also transferred.[12] This specific characteristic of WebMoney as a new form of currency became more apparent in terms of functionality with the introduction of stablecoin USDT in 2014. Both WebMoney and USDT functionally rely on legal tender as the underlying asset while also serving as independent units of account that represent ownership of the currency (Table 3.2).

Therefore, we can acknowledge that centralized private electronic tokens (excluding those used within platforms such as gaming or similar tokens) do not carry the advanced digital features of digital currencies. However, given the development history of digital currencies and virtual currencies, we classify this as a distinct category of transitional "species", which partly steps into a "new species." In particular, we place these fully centralized private electronic tokens into the realm of virtual currencies.

[12] See Webmoney. "WebMoney Transfer Code," https://www.wmtransfer.com/eng/legal/codex.shtml, paragraph 1.3.1. Accessed on 27 May 2021.

Table 3.3 Classification by FATF and ECB based on convertibility

By FATF	By ECB	Convertibility	Typical examples
Non-convertible virtual currencies	Fully closed	Obtaining from and used in specific platform	World of Warcraft gold, credit card rewards
	One-way	Purchased by legal currencies but can't be converted back; used in specific platform	Q-Coin
Convertible virtual currencies	Bi-directional	Converted with legal currencies and other virtual currencies	Bitcoin

Source ECB, FATF[13]

3.4 Categorization of Virtual Currencies Based on Regulatory Necessity: Convertibility

The convertibility of virtual currencies, which is the primary focus of the international regulatory community, refers to their ability to be transformed into legal tender or other forms of virtual currencies. According to this logic, virtual currencies that possess convertibility or openness are termed convertible or open virtual currencies, while those lacking convertibility are referred to as non-convertible or closed virtual currencies. A common example of a convertible virtual currency is Bitcoin, which can be transferred directly between users, enabling exchanges with legal tender and other virtual currencies.

Other virtual currencies are specifically designed for use within a particular community and have limited utility outside of these environments. Q-Coins, for instance, can only be used within Tencent's gaming world and cannot be transferred to third parties. When users purchase Q-Coins with Chinese yuan or use them to buy virtual goods within the game, Tencent adjusts the Q-Coin balance accordingly in the user's account. However, transferring Q-Coins between user accounts is not possible; the reason is not a technical burden, but rather a function that Tencent has not provided. If this function was allowed by Tencent, Q-Coin would no longer be a token with limited usage in a specific closed virtual space, but rather a medium of exchange in any open setting. In terms of financial regulation, if Q-Coin was made to have the capability for cross-account transfer, it would no longer be different from centralized virtual currencies like WebMoney (Table 3.3).

The European Central Bank further categorizes non-convertible virtual currencies into two types. The first one encompasses in-game currencies generated within completely closed online communities, such as rewards obtained in online games (e.g., World of Warcraft gold) or various forms of reward points (e.g., flyer miles

[13] European Central Bank. "Virtual Currency Schemes," October 2012. https://www.ecb.europa.eu/pub/pdf/other/virtualcurrencyschemes201210en.pdf; Financial Action Task Force. "Virtual Currencies, Key Definitions and Potential AML/CFT Risks", June 2014. http://www.fatf-gafi.org/media/fatf/documents/reports/Virtual-currency-key-and-potential-aml-cft-risks.pdf.

and credit card rewards). Virtual currencies in the second type involve those that can be purchased with legal tender but only in a one-way process, as they cannot be converted back into legal tender. Such is Tencent's game currency, Q-Coin, which can be acquired using Chinese yuan. Both types represent electronically traded goods within closed ecosystems and do not fall within the purview of financial regulation concerns.[14]

Non-Convertible Virtual Currencies Are Only A Step Away From Transitioning From Closed To Open Systems. To illustrate this potential transition, we can examine the example of Q-coin. Introduced by Tencent in 2002, it was initially used to purchase game time, items, and value-added services on their gaming platform. Users would pay Chinese yuan to Tencent's bank account through various online payment methods, and in return, Tencent would credit the corresponding amount of Q-coins to their account.

However, unlike with online banking, credit cards and third-party payments, Q-coin has not allowed for the transfer of funds between accounts. This is not due to technical limitations but rather a deliberate feature omission by Tencent. By enabling the transfer of value between accounts, Q-coins would have supported open payment services, transforming them from a prepaid usage system to a more general payment method.

Technically, Q-coin is similar to other centralized payment systems as it relies on a 'centralized database for accounting purposes. However, the lack of transferability and the absence of a conversion option to fiat currency classifies Q-coin as "a utility token" rather than a fully convertible virtual currency. Consequently, it does not require regulation by financial authorities. Whether Tencent might introduce bi-directional conversion functionality for Q-coins will depend on the setting of their payment software.

Due to certain vulnerabilities in the system, unofficial and non-compliant channels and markets may arise, allowing for the trading of Q-coins. For example, they could be exchanged for point cards, which could then be transferred between players in games, indirectly facilitating the trading of Q-coins and enabling bi-directional exchanges with Chinese yuan. However, such activities would not be compliant with regulations. If Tencent were to offer bi-directional conversion functionality for Q-coins, effectively transforming them into a universal payment tool, they would need to obtain a payment license and abide by financial regulations.

To summarize, even though administrators may initially restrict the transferability and convertibility of "non-convertible" currencies to specific virtual environments, unofficial secondary markets could still emerge, offering opportunities to convert these into fiat currencies or other virtual currencies. Usually, administrators implement control measures, such as terminating memberships, to discourage the creation or use of secondary markets that violate currency rules. Consequently, the non-convertible characteristic of a virtual currency is not necessarily fixed.

In the next chapter, we specifically discuss how centralization is a matter of degree influenced by technology that does not determine the regulatory attributes of virtual currencies. The question of whether convertibility is the key criterion triggering regulation will be examined in Chap. 8.

---

[14] European Central Bank. "Virtual Currency Schemes," October 2012. https://www.ecb.europa.eu/pub/pdf/other/virtualcurrencyschemes201210en.pdf, p.5.

Chapter 4
Decentralization and Centralization: The Two Facets of Digital Currency

How does the decentralization of Bitcoin differ from that of other cryptocurrencies? How does the decentralization level influence financial regulation in digital currencies? In what ways do CBDCs like the Digital Yuan vary in decentralization from Bitcoin? Why and how can the U.S. government sanction transactions with the so-called decentralized cryptocurrencies?

In this chapter, we delve into the intricacies of decentralization of cryptocurrencies, specially focusing on Bitcoin among other digital currencies. We explore the principles of technology neutrality and functional equivalence in the context of digital currency regulation. We also examine the impact of varying degrees of decentralization on financial regulation and highlight the differences between Central Bank Digital Currencies (CBDCs) like the Digital Yuan (e-CNY) and Bitcoin. This chapter reveals a fact often neglected by non-professionals: while cryptocurrencies are decentralized, their transactions heavily rely on centralized exchanges, allowing governments to enforce legal measures on these virtual currencies.

While Bitcoin does indeed have characteristics of decentralization, one must not generalize decentralization as a characteristic of all virtual currencies and cryptocurrencies without qualification. The degree of decentralization in digital currencies can be measured by three dimensions: issuance, payment, and clearing and settlement (hereinafter referred to as settlement in this chapter). Newspaper articles commonly claim that digital currencies have characteristics of decentralization, and even some serious academic journals accept this premise without making distinctions.

The fact whether a virtual currency is decentralized or not is not the decisive factor regarding its financial regulation, whereas decentralization does present new challenges for regulatory methods and monitoring tools. Virtual currencies adopt different technological arrangements, influencing their degrees of decentralization. To assess the specific impact of decentralization on financial regulation from a regulatory perspective, we should closely focus on the specific degree of decentralization and analyze which technological features have changed the key concerns of regulation.

Y. Wu and W. Zhu, *The Fundamentals of Digital Currency*,
https://doi.org/10.1007/978-981-97-8261-1_4

4.1 How Should Regulation Treat New Technologies? Technology Neutrality and Functional Equivalence

When the Internet emerged as a new technology in the 1990s, the United States was the first to propose the principle of "technology neutrality" as a fundamental principle for regulating and legislating new technologies. In practice, this principle gradually evolved into the principle of "functional equivalence."[1] Technology neutrality implies that regulation and laws should not discriminate against or favor certain technologies, while functional equivalence refers to achieving the same regulatory goals for activities with the same functions. The latter principle is driven by a goal-oriented approach, which does not require the same regulatory rules to be uniformly applied but considers the characteristics of new technologies and adopts differentiated rules, ultimately achieving the same regulatory goals for different technological activities. In its anti-money laundering guidance for virtual currencies, the Financial Action Task Force (FATF) has integrated the principles of functional equivalence and objective-based approach, calling it the "functional equivalent and objective-based approach."[2]

The decentralization of cryptocurrencies is a matter of extent, such as the position on a sliding scale, rather than a binary question of YES or NO. We can measure the (de)centralization degree of digital currencies from at least three aspects: issuance, payment, and clearing and settlement. If Bitcoin represents a "thorough" or complete decentralization, then virtual currencies like WebMoney represent complete centralization. There are many cryptocurrencies that fall between these two extremes, demonstrating limited degrees of decentralization or centralization; different virtual currencies employ different technological arrangements, resulting in varying degrees of centralization. In this context, the use of asymmetric encryption technology is merely a technical factor instead of being a defining criterion for virtual currencies. From the regulatory aspects of virtual currencies, the presence of centralization is also a matter of degree and not the core question. It is important to closely examine the specific degree of decentralization and analyze which technological features change the key regulatory criteria, allowing for an assessment of the specific impact of decentralization on financial regulation. Some literatures emphasize the decentralization characteristics of Bitcoin; however, the uncritical attribution of decentralization as an essential characteristic of virtual currencies requires further detailed analysis and evaluation.

---

[1] Reed, Chris. "Online and Offline Equivalence: Aspiration and Achievement." *International Journal of Law and Information Technology* 18, no. 3 (2010): 248–273.

[2] Financial Action Task Force. "Guidance for a Risk-Based Approach to Virtual Assets and Virtual Asset Service Providers," June 2019. https://www.fatf-gafi.org/media/fatf/documents/recommendations/RBA-VA-VASPs.pdf.

4.2 Bitcoin: A Completely Decentralized Cryptocurrency

As covered earlier, cryptocurrencies specifically refer to private digital currencies (virtual currencies) that use asymmetric encryption "signatures." Bitcoin achieves peer-to-peer transactions by combining these signatures with proof-of-work consensus mechanisms, thus freeing itself from reliance on centralized servers and possessing the commonly mentioned characteristics of "distributed" and "decentralized." The precursor to cryptocurrencies, eCash, had already used asymmetric encryption "signatures", but Bitcoin's implementation of asymmetric encryption technology combined with the proof-of-work consensus mechanism has achieved trustworthy transactions in a peer-to-peer environment, eliminating reliance on a centralized system. Bitcoin has developed into a complete and influential system that can operate independently. It thoroughly achieves decentralization, freeing itself from centralized servers in all processes, including issuance, payment and settlement. It enables free peer-to-peer payments in a decentralized environment, and accomplishes settlement at the same time during the payment process.

4.3 Decentralization: A Matter of Degree

As we have seen in Sect. 4.1, the decentralization of digital currencies is a matter of degree, which can be measured from at least three aspects: issuance, payment and settlement. Existing electronic payment systems are managed based on an account system and utilize centralized servers to store data and run the business logic code.[3] They do not employ a decentralized and public architecture like blockchain; therefore, their issuance, payment and settlement processes are centralized, thus can be considered as "completely centralized." In contrast, Bitcoin represents a "completely decentralized" approach. Certainly, there are other influential digital currencies that fall between these two extremes (see Table 4.1).

In the case of asset-backed stablecoins like USDT, payment and settlement processes are decentralized, while issuance is centralized. USDT is recognized as a cryptocurrency that has surpassed Bitcoin in terms of trading volume, becoming the largest virtual currency in terms of transaction volume.[4] However, it only achieves decentralization in the payment and settlement processes, while its issuance process remains completely centralized. The technical architecture of USDT is based on public blockchains like Bitcoin and Ethereum. During payment, the wallet software constructs transactions, information is submitted onto the blockchain, and miners package the transactions into blocks to complete settlement. The whole process does not require a centralized institution to provide account and ledger services. However,

[3] For information of the current mainstream IT systems and structures of banks, see Jin, Panshi, et al. "SOA-Based New Generation Banking System Architecture for Banking Group." *Computer Systems and Applications* 25, no. 12 (2016): 42–52.

[4] Source: coincapmarket.com. Accessed on 20 October 2022.

Table 4.1 Technologies and levels of (DE) centralization of E-Payments and digital currencies

	Electronic money/ payment	Centralized virtual currencies	Digital RMB	USDT (asset-linked)	Bitcoin
Blockchain	No		No	Yes	Yes
Distributed ledger	No		Yes	Yes	Yes
Asymmetric encryption	No		Yes	Yes	Yes
Cryptocurrency	–		–	Yes	Yes
Issuance	Centralized		Centralized	Centralized	Decentralized
Payment	Centralized		Decentralized	Decentralized	Decentralized
Clearing and Settlement	Centralized		Centralized	Decentralized	Decentralized
Degree of decentralization	Completely centralized		Limitedly	Limitedly	Completely decentralized

being a stablecoin, the issuance of USDT still follows a traditional centralized model. It is issued by Tether Limited and (at least outwardly) promises a 1:1 redemption against the US dollar. In other words, USDT no longer requires the support of Tether Limited servers in the payment and settlement processes, while the issuance process of asset-backed stablecoins remains centralized.

In the case of central bank digital currencies (CBDCs) like Digital Yuan (digital RMB), payment is decentralized, while issuance and settlement are centralized. The concept of Bitcoin has inspired central bank digital currencies in various countries, but central banks' interest in Bitcoin and blockchain mostly draws on their decentralized settlement and payment characteristics, to improve efficiency. However, as legal tender, the degree of decentralization in central bank digital currencies is lower than that of asset-backed stablecoins. Digital Yuan adopts a "double-layer issuance system" in which the central bank does not directly serve end-users but provides services through commercial institutions, mainly commercial banks, which open "digital RMB wallets" for customers. In the issuance process, the centralized database of the central bank controls and manages the quota for commercial banks to issue digital currency. Commercial banks in turn distribute the digital currency to users through their currency issuance and quota management systems.[5] Once the

[5] Regarding the issuance model of the digital currency of People's Bank of China, refer to Fan, Yifei. "China's Central Bank Digital Currency Should Adopt a Double-Layer Issuance System." *Financial View*, no. 3 (2018). For technical details regarding the issuance of the digital currency (CBDC) of People's Bank of China, the reader can refer to the following patents owned by the Digital Currency Research Institute of the People's Bank of China: 1) "A Method and System for Generating Digital Currency" (Chinese Invention Patent CN110751467A, Public Release Date: Feb. 4, 2020); 2) "A Method and System for Recalling Digital Currency Quotas" (Chinese Invention Patent CN110619567A, Public Release Date: Dec. 27, 2019).

transactions between end customers are completed, they are submitted to the transaction repository of the commercial bank, finalizing the process of transferring digital currency and ultimately achieving final clearing and settlement.[6]

In 2017, Qian Yao, The Then- Director To Develop Chinese CBDC, Pointed Out In "Some Thoughts On Central Bank Digital Currency" That Blockchain Technology Has Limitations, And Central Banks View It As A "Reference For New Thinking." The Digital Yuan does not fully adopt blockchain technology but relies on centralized databases, cryptographic digital signatures, distributed ledgers, and other technologies.[7] Therefore, Chinese CBDC developers often quote that Digital Yuan only "draws on the concept of blockchain technology."

Under the double-layer issuance system, users can open a "digital RMB wallet" at designated commercial banks. From their perspective, there seems to be no difference between transferring funds between digital wallets and directly between regular bank accounts. However, direct transfer between digital wallets involves the direct transfer of encrypted strings of digital RMB, whereas performing this between regular bank accounts involves corresponding balance adjustments on the central ledger of the bank.

Furthermore, the highest degree of decentralized payment is represented by the dual offline mode for digital RMB, which is being developed by the People's Bank of China. Upon closer examination, it can be argued that the offline payment feature of digital RMB is even more decentralized in the payment process compared to Bitcoin. Bitcoin payments require an online connection, and the decentralization of Bitcoin in the payment process refers to its shift from relying on a single server to multiple servers. In comparison, the offline payment feature of digital RMB does not rely on any server.

4.4 Centralized/Non-crypto Virtual Currencies and Cryptocurrencies: Similarities in Design and Function

Bitcoin has led the revolution of private digital currencies through asymmetric encryption technology. However, a large number of Internet-based private digital/electronic currencies had emerged before its birth, some of which achieved great success in business. "WebMoney" is a typical example of a successful centralized

[6] For the process and technical principles of digital RMB transactions, the reader can refer to the following patents owned by the Digital Currency Research Institute of the People's Bank of China: "A Method and System for Circulation of Digital Currency" (Chinese Invention Patent CN110659889A, Public Release Date: January 07, 2020).

[7] Some articles, written by senior officials of the People's Bank of China, are considered to convey the fundamental design principles of digital currency to the society, such as Xu, Zhong, et al. "Exploration of Central Bank Digital Currency Theory." *China Finance*, no. 17 (2016): 33–34; Fan, Yifei. "The Theoretical Foundation and Architectural Choice of China's Legal Digital Currency." *China Finance*, no. 17 (2016): 10–12; Yao, Qian. "Some Thoughts on Central Bank – Issued Digital Currency." *Journal of Financial Research*, no. 7 (2017): 78–85; Fan, Yifei. "Several Considerations on Central Bank Digital Currency." *First Financial Daily*, 26 Jan 2018, A05; Di, Gang. "Analysis of Digital Currency." *China Finance* 17 (2018): 52–54.

Table 4.2 Comparison of Non-crypto Virtual Currencies and Stablecoins

	Non-crypto Virtual Currencies	Stablecoins	
Examples	WebMoney	USDT	DGX
Backed Assets	legal currencies (including USD) Gold	USD	Gold
Functions of value store and exchange medium	YES	YES	
Unit of account	YES	YES	
Transfer object	ownership of the token itself	ownership of the token itself	
Asymmetric encryption and High level of digitalization	NO	YES	
Centralization	completely centralized	centralized issuance, decentralized payment, clearing and settlement	

virtual currency.[8] WebMoney Transfer Ltd., a network payment company founded in Russia, issued and began to operate WebMoney in 1998. It conducted extensive operations in Europe and Asia with over 43 million registered users in 2022. As a result, WebMoney became a popular method for cross-border payments.[9]

As discussed in Sect. 3.3, WebMoney does not possess the same level of digitization as cryptocurrencies, and can only be considered as a transitional species between electronic payment systems and digital currencies. However, we can retrospectively categorize it as a digital currency, much like how a platypus is classified as a mammal. In this section, we further compare WebMoney and two typical stablecoins, USDT and DGX, to illustrate their similarities in design and function, as shown in Table 4.2.

As the comparison demonstrates, the financial design concept of WebMoney is very similar to asset-backed stablecoins like USDT and DGX, as indicated by the similarities in issuance arrangements and redemption guarantees. WebMoney Transfer Ltd. serves as the issuer and manager of WebMoney. In the issuance process, users exchange legal tenders or gold for WebMoney, and WebMoney Transfer Ltd. entrusts the received legal tenders to designated custodians for management while guaranteeing the conversion of WebMoney into legal tenders or gold.

Similar to USDT and DGX, WebMoney serves not only as a store of value and a medium of exchange but also as an independent unit of account. It offers different units tied to specific currencies, such as WMR (tied to the Russian ruble), WMZ (tied to the US dollar), WME (tied to the euro), and WMG (tied to gold). It should also be

[8] See Mullan, P. Carl. *History of Digital Currency in the United States*. New York: Palgrave Macmillan, 2016'. This book provides a comprehensive review of privately issued digital currencies that were commercialized between 1996 and 2004, and offers detailed insights into nine influential virtual currencies, discussing their technological as well as operational aspects.

[9] See its official website, https://www.wmtransfer.com/. Accessed on 4 May 2021.

noted that, like USDT and DGX, the transfer of WebMoney concerns the ownership of the tokens themselves and not the underlying reserve of legal currency or gold.

Furthermore, WebMoney also achieves real-time clearing and settlement, with payments resulting in direct adjustments to account balances in a centralized database system. The operations of payment, clearing and settlement with WebMoney can be completed simultaneously (Mullan 245–260).[10]

4.5 Virtual Currency Transaction Methods

4.5.1 Introduction: Can Virtual Currency Be Sanctioned?

On March 7, 2022, Bloomberg reported that the US would expand its sanctions against Russia into the realm of virtual currencies.[11] Upon a careful analysis of Bloomberg's report, it appears that this US sanction on virtual currencies is not much different from common financial sanctions: freezing Russian users' virtual currencies and prohibiting virtual currency transactions with these users.

It is understandable that the US leverages the role of dollar as the global reserve currency to implement financial sanctions, but how can it impose sanctions in the realm of virtual currencies?

Juan Zarate: A Player In U.S. Financial Sanctions

Juan Zarate, a former member of the US Treasury between 2001-2005, personally took part in implementing targeted financial sanctions against foreign countries, and has a step-by-step account of how the United States unleashed the immense power of targeted financial sanctions. In his book, "Treasury's War: The Unleashing of a New Era of Financial Warfare", Zarate provides firsthand insights into how the United States implemented financial sanctions to target and dismantle the economic systems and weapons development capabilities of adversarial nations. He coined the phrase "financial death penalty" to highlight the harsh and severe nature of such sanctions.[12]

Financial sanctions usually involve the freezing of financial assets and the denial of transactions. Freezing financial assets typically involves the suspension of access to bank accounts. For example, if an individual holds US dollars in a US-based bank, the US government can take over the authority to freeze those assets; once effective, the owner is prevented from accessing or utilizing the funds. The denial of transactions refers to financial institutions refusing to engage in any financial activity with the sanctioned entities. The inability to

[10] It is important to note that such payment and settlement processes within WebMoney are limited to transactions between its platform users. Similar to synchronous payment and settlement between two accounts within a commercial bank, it does not imply any technological advantage implemented by WebMoney. For specific technical details and operational methods, refer to pages 245–260 of the aforementioned book by P. Carl Mullan (2016).

[11] Yang, Yueqi. "Coinbase Blocks 25,000 Crypto Wallets Linked to Russian Users." Bloomberg News, March 7, 2022. https://www.bnnbloomberg. ca/coinbase-blocks-25–000-crypto-wallets-linked-to-russian-users-1.1733821?ms.

[12] Zarate, Juan. Treasury's War: The Unleashing of a New Era of Financial Warfare. Hachette UK, 2013.

conduct transactions in US dollars equates to being cut off from the international financial system. This exclusion effectively isolates the sanctioned country, rendering it akin to a financial island. Similarly, targeted individuals become financial outcasts, facing severe limitations in conducting financial affairs altogether.

Is virtual currency not supposed to be decentralized? How could it possibly be sanctioned? To understand this issue, we need to grasp the essence of the trading methods of virtual currencies.

First, virtual currencies, represented by Bitcoin, are indeed decentralized in principle. However, in reality, a considerable number of transactions need to be conducted through centralized virtual currency exchanges (such as Coinbase). Since such exchanges must comply with the same anti-money laundering regulations as banks, transactions conducted through exchanges require at least real-name verification. In this way, governments can freeze individuals' virtual currencies in exchanges, just like freezing personal bank assets.

Second, virtual currencies symbolized by Bitcoin go through anonymous transactions on the blockchain. However, all transaction records on the blockchain are public and transparent, making virtual currency transactions traceable even on blockchains.

4.5.2 Decentralization and Centralization

According to almost all media reports, cryptocurrency transactions are peer-to-peer and free from any third-party institution. While this statement is generally correct, it is incomplete. Most cryptocurrencies are indeed decentralized, such as Bitcoin; however, Bitcoin has two methods of transaction: on the blockchain and through centralized exchanges.

The Two Transaction Methods Of Bitcoin

In order to understand blockchain transactions, we can tentatively compare Bitcoin private keys to physical cash. Whoever possesses the private key possesses the bitcoin just like whoever holds the physical cash owns it. In blockchain transactions, the private key is stored by the user in a non-custodial wallet (also known as "unhosted wallet"), and the user can transfer the cryptocurrency from one non-custodial wallet address to another solely on the blockchain.

As for the transaction going through centralized exchanges, storing cryptocurrency within centralized virtual currency exchanges is similar to depositing physical currency in a bank. When using centralized exchanges for trading, users store their cryptocurrency in a custodial wallet (also known as a hosted wallet) provided by the platform, which facilitates trading by transferring the cryptocurrency between different "custodial wallets" based on user instructions (a further analysis of centralized trading will be provided in Chapter 5, Section 4.5).

Bitcoin transactions on the blockchain are unquestionably fully decentralized and can be understood as the original form of transactions. This is why Bitcoin is referred to as "electronic cash." Just like with physical cash, transactions with bitcoin on the blockchain can be anonymous, obviating the need for a bank or any an intermediary institution. Bitcoin wallet addresses are completely open and can be registered at any time without a verification of identity (hence they are anonymous), allowing users to transfer bitcoin from one address to another on the blockchain. Technically, it is also impossible to freeze bitcoin on the blockchain.

However, the issue lies in the fact that bitcoin can also be traded through centralized exchanges, and the trading volume through this channel far exceeds that on the blockchain. This is the reason why the sanctions imposed by the US on virtual currency owned by Russia are equivalent to those on banking assets owned by Russia; the US can demand banks to freeze Russian assets, and likewise, it can demand virtual currency exchanges to freeze Russian-held virtual currencies.

Traditional financial sanctions are implemented through financial institutions, and in the field of virtual currency, these sanctions are implemented through controlling virtual currency exchanges. When a government freezes an individual's bank assets, it effectively terminates the individual's account transactions. As a result, he/she cannot transfer money to other accounts or withdraw funds. Similarly, when customers store their bitcoin private keys in a virtual currency exchange, transactions between customers are recorded within the exchange's different "wallets", and this accounting measure is achieved by tapping into the exchange process. Therefore, exchanges can also freeze customers' assets, prohibiting the transfer of virtual currency from their wallets to other wallets and preventing customers from withdrawing virtual currency to non-custodial wallets on the blockchain (see Fig. 4.1).

Given the current technological conditions and the need for exchange between currencies, centralized exchanges are unavoidable. For example, one can transfer

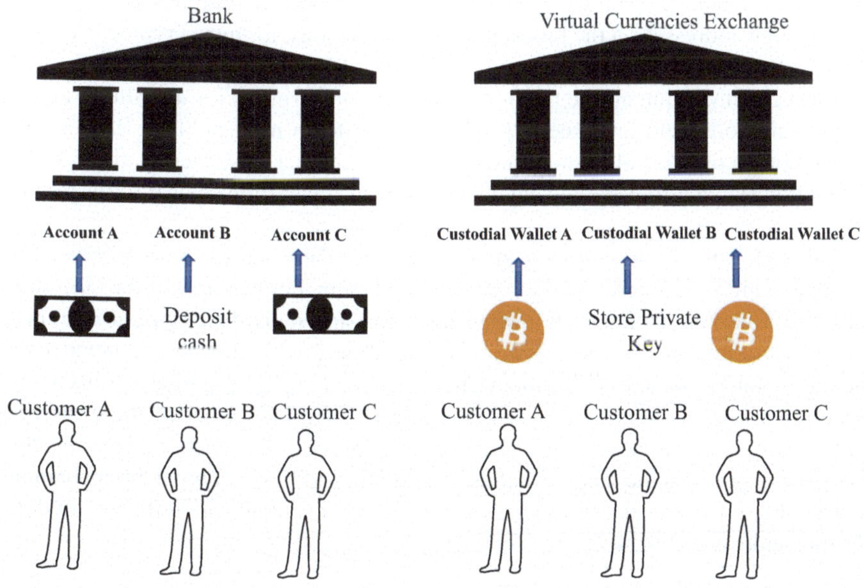

Fig. 4.1 Comparison: commercial banks versus virtual currency exchanges

bitcoin on the blockchain, but should they wish to exchange it for fiat currency or ether, the only feasible technology currently available is throughs centralized exchanges. One of the challenges in cross-currency transactions is the "**Sophia's Dilemma**", which is discussed in Sect. 5.5 of this book. Additionally, there are inherent flaws in using virtual currency as a payment method. On the blockchain, the maximum theoretical transaction processing speed for bitcoin is 6.83 transactions per second. This technological limitation prevents it from becoming a widely used payment method for the general public, while centralized exchanges for trading are a practical solution.

4.5.3 Anonymity and Traceability on the Blockchain

During the action of imposing sanctions on Russian virtual currency activities, the well-known US virtual currency exchange Coinbase publicly stated that they identified Russian addresses on the blockchain through blockchain analysis technology and prohibited these addresses from transacting on their platform. This clearly implies that the US has extended sanctions to the blockchain itself.

As mentioned before, it is not technically feasible to freeze cryptocurrencies on the blockchain. However, US virtual currency exchanges can prohibit these addresses from transacting on their platform, that is, once these addresses on the blockchain have been labeled as Russian addresses, the exchange will no longer accept cryptocurrencies transferred to these addresses (deposits) and will not allow the exchange of cryptocurrencies to be transferred from these addresses (withdrawals).

Although addresses on the blockchain are anonymous, for most cryptocurrencies (such as Bitcoin), these addresses are traceable. Taking Bitcoin as an example, in a peer-to-peer environment, the method to prevent tampering is for all mining nodes to maintain consistent bookkeeping. Therefore, Bitcoin must publicly disclose all transaction records for all mining nodes for verification. Consequently, the Bitcoin transaction ledger is transparent; anyone can link the transaction chain through public data.

Although Bitcoin addresses are anonymous, once these addresses are labeled, it is possible to infer the identity of the person behind them. For example, if the custodial wallet in a certain exchange is owned by a Russian individual (virtual currency exchanges require real-name registration and comply with anti-money laundering standards similar to banks), and this wallet frequently engages in transactions using a particular address, it can be reasonably inferred that the owner of the custodial wallet also owns the deposit and withdrawal addresses. By further analyzing the relationship between the labeled addresses and other addresses on the blockchain, it is possible to discover the transaction network and potentially identify the holders of more addresses (Fig. 4.2).

BLOCKCHAIN DATA ANALYSIS CAN BE PERFORMED USING VARIOUS SOFTWARE (COMMONLY KNOWN AS BLOCKCHAIN EXPLORERS) THAT DIRECTLY CONVERT TRANSACTION ADDRESSES AND AMOUNTS IN BLOCKCHAIN TRANSACTION DATA INTO

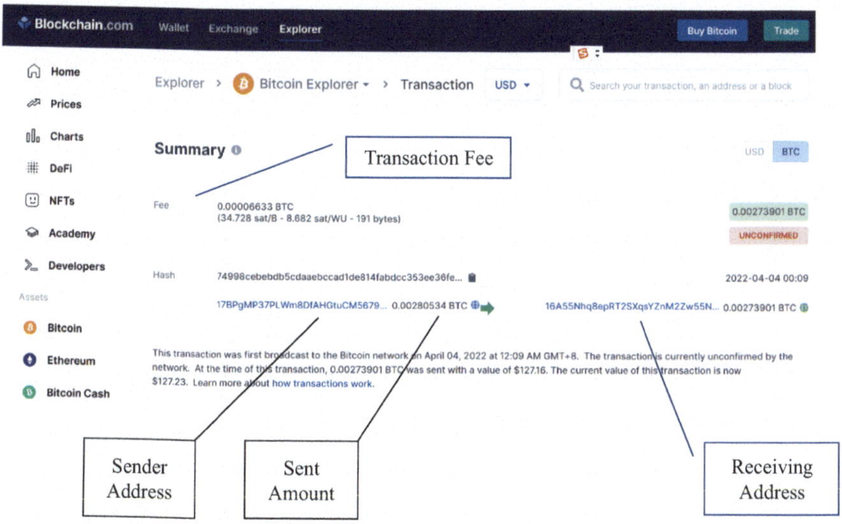

Fig. 4.2 Analysis of bitcoin Transactin records on the Blockchain.com Website[13]

READABLE FORMATS. By using these software coupled with visualization tools, it is easy to identify transaction networks. For example, one can visit the Blockchain.com website, which timely decodes transaction records for various mainstream cryptocurrencies such as Bitcoin. Figure 4.2 shows bitcoin transactions recorded at Beijing time, April 4, 2022, 00:09, where an address starting with 17 transferred 0.000280534 bitcoin to an address starting with 16.

[13] In the figure, "sat" represents the smallest unit of bitcoin called "satoshi", where one satoshi is equal to one hundred millionth of a bitcoin; "sat/B" represents the amount of bitcoin corresponding to each byte in the blockchain ledger; "wu" stands for "weight unit," indicating a new unit obtained by subtracting the weight of signature data from the total weight when calculating bytes, combined with non-signature data.

Part II
Social Experiment of Digital Currencies

Chapter 5
The Milestones of Private Digital Currencies

In light of the pioneering direction established by Bitcoin, what are the various development paths virtual currencies are taking? Which currencies are deepening the innovative concepts of Bitcoin, and which ones are charting new territories by reversing its course? How do these differing approaches impact the stability, adoption and technological progress of virtual currencies in the context of the broader financial ecosystem?

In this Chapter, we analyze the divergent paths that virtual currencies have taken since the inception of Bitcoin. We discuss those that have traced the revolutionary footsteps of Bitcoin, followed by others that have chosen to explore the opposite direction, suggesting a spectrum of advancement and innovation in the realm of digital currency. This heralds a focus on the dynamic nature of cryptocurrency evolution, including both improvements to and alternative explorations of the original Bitcoin concept.

5.1 Overview

DigiCash, a company founded by cryptographer David Chaum, filed for bankruptcy in 1998, just nine years after its inception. Chaum, who was living in the Netherlands at the time, devised an algorithm known as "blind signature" and used it to develop an anonymous digital currency payment system called "eCash." He viewed the Internet as a boundaryless and unprotected environment that leaves people's privacy and financial security exposed and fragile like lambs in the wilderness. Chaum firmly believed that the anonymous payment system of eCash could shield individuals and preserve order on the Internet. He founded his company to promote his product and philosophy, and indeed, a handful of banks endeavored to follow his idea by adopting eCash. However, after nine years of effort, DigiCash still went bankrupt, and Chaum attributed this failure to a general disregard for privacy among members of the public.

Y. Wu and W. Zhu, *The Fundamentals of Digital Currency*,
https://doi.org/10.1007/978-981-97-8261-1_5

In 2009, programmer Hal Finney received 10 bitcoins on his laptop, marking the first Bitcoin transaction. This transaction, sent by an individual using the pseudonym Satoshi Nakamoto, also the inventor of Bitcoin, remains recorded in the Bitcoin ledger to this day. Back then, 10 bitcoins were worth relatively little. However, over a decade later, their value peaked at around 670 thousand US dollars. This was also a time of financial crisis, causing widespread global insecurity and anxiety. Nakamoto inscribed his dissatisfaction with the global financial system and the prevailing order in Bitcoin's genesis block, stating that "The Chancellor is on the brink of the second bailout for banks." His creation enabled peer-to-peer payments over the Internet without the need for central servers, proving that the traditional prerequisites of the Information Age—wealth custodianship and third-party trust—were no longer necessary.

The development of digital currency has spanned a full 20 years from Chaum's initial proposal of the technological principles of eCash in 1988 to Nakamoto's publication of the Bitcoin Whitepaper in 2008, a remarkably long period in the evolution of digital currency.

Technically, eCash is considered the first cryptocurrency or private digital currency for it was pioneer in using asymmetric cryptography for signatures, enabling the direct transfer of encrypted character strings representing monetary value between transaction parties without the need for a bank server. This innovation allowed for peer-to-peer electronic payments for the first time. However, eCash was still tied to the conventional banking system. Although it was considered "untraceable electronic cash," it relied on commercial banks for clearing and settlement to finalize the transfer of value.

It was not until the advent of Bitcoin that virtual currency fully managed to escape the need for third-party trust. The design philosophy of Bitcoin is such that any server in a peer-to-peer network can become a ledger-keeping server with "transaction verification" authority. In a peer-to-peer network, Bitcoin does not rely on a fixed centralized server to validate transactions, nor does it depend on a single server to prevent double-spending fraud.

If eCash is considered to have achieved "peer-to-peer electronic payment," then Bitcoin can be regarded as "peer-to-peer electronic cash," being not only a new payment method but also a new form of currency. It combines asymmetric encryption technology with proof-of-work to conduct the issuance, payment and settlement of currency in a distributed environment, enabling cryptocurrencies to operate independently from trusted third parties and achieve truly decentralized systems.

The birth of Bitcoin genuinely marked the beginning of cryptocurrencies, virtual currencies, and digital currencies, an epochal moment in history. While numerous virtual currencies have emerged since then, only a few are considered real landmarks in the history of digital currency (refer to Table 5.1).

Upon examining these milestone virtual currencies, some seem to follow the "revolutionary" or forward direction established by Bitcoin, while others are exploring the opposite direction (refer to Fig. 5.1).

Table 5.1 Milestones in private digital currencies

Virtual currencies	Launch year	Core Tech	Milestone	Objective
eCash	1994	Blind signature	Peer-to-peer electronic payments (privacy protection)	Decentralized peer-to-peer electronic payments, eliminating the need for intermediaries such as banks
Bitcoin	2009	Blockchain	Peer-to-peer electronic cash	Issuance, payment, settlement, and clearing are facilitated in a distributed environment, wholly eliminating reliance on third-party trust
Ethereum	2015	Smart contract	Smart contract platform, fully programmable currency	Built on blockchain technology, enabling the complex contract and automated execution of contracts within a peer-to-peer network
BANCOR	2017	BANCOR Algorithm	Automatic issuance Automatic trading	Token supply is auto-adjusted based on algorithms, and transactions no longer rely on matched trading but are traded against liquidity pools using algorithmic trading
USDT	2014	Layer 2 protocol and ERC20, etc	Price stability	Returning to centralized trust, token value is backed by the Issuer's reserve of USD. Issuance is centralized, while payment, clearing and settlement are decentralized
DGX	2016	ERC20	Asset circulation	Uses ERC20 to digitally represent the value of gold, facilitating rapid circulation of gold value while still depending on centralized institutions
EOS	2018	POS	Community governance	Community governance relies on voting mechanisms based on proof-of-stake (POS), along with protocols governed by a combination of code and written agreements

(continued)

Table 5.1 (continued)

Virtual currencies	Launch year	Core Tech	Milestone	Objective
Diem (Libra)	2019 (whitepaper)	Consortium blockchain	Compliance	Complies fully with existing financial regulations, allowing for cross-border payments and global financial integration
Grin and Zcash	2019	Zero-knowledge proofs	Complete privacy protection	Virtual currency trading data is stored securely and privately using cryptographic proofs, ensuring advanced privacy protection beyond that of Bitcoin, enhancing user privacy even further

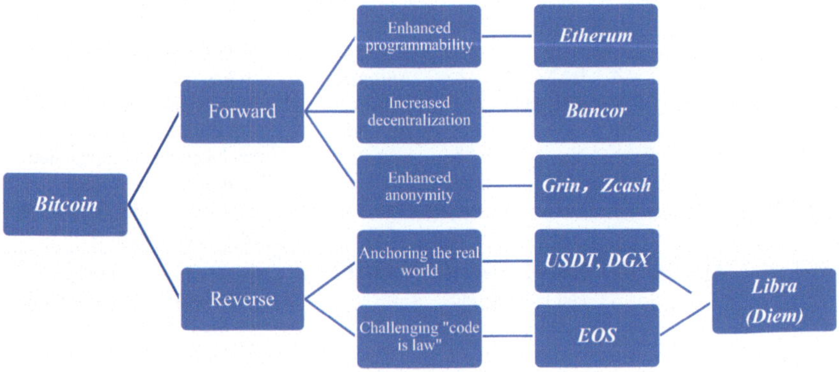

Fig. 5.1 The two main developmental directions of virtual currencies

Nature always maintains balance through the interaction of opposing forces, such as electrons and protons, matter and antimatter, and so on. Similarly, the concept of Yin and Yang has long been recognized in Chinese philosophy. Interestingly, this concept is also widely rooted in the deep spiritual world of the Indo-European language family, including modern Romance languages like French, Italian and Spanish, where nouns have masculine and feminine genders.

Confucius believed in the concept of the Constant Mean (中庸, zhongyong). This idea concerns the highest moral state, as stated by Confucius in the *Analects*: "Perfect is the virtue which is according to the Constant Mean." As further elaborated by Cheng Yi, a prominent Confucianist of the Song Dynasty: "Not being extreme is called the Mean; not changing is called 'constancy'. The Mean is the righteous path of the world, and constancy is the established principle of the world."[1] F. Scott Fitzgerald also touched on this concept

[1] Legge, James. "The analects," in *Sacred Books of the East*, vol. 1, Chinese Text Project, https://ctext.org/analects/ens. Accessed on 6 September 2023.

in the opening of his book *The Crack-Up*: "The test of a first-rate intelligence is the ability to hold two opposed ideas in mind at the same time and still retain the ability to function."[2]

Following the emergence of Bitcoin, the trajectory of virtual currencies did not strictly align with the innovative path blazed by Bitcoin; they also ventured in the opposite direction. The authors of this book believe that the progression of virtual currencies adheres to the principle of the "Constant Mean"; in other words, it manifests the "first-rate intelligence" in humanity. Embracing this viewpoint helps the reader to gain valuable insights into the "digital currency phenomenon."

Major Developments Along the New Direction Pioneered by Bitcoin:

1. *Enhanced programmability: Ethereum.* Ethereum inherits the blockchain concept from Bitcoin but significantly enhances programmability. Unlike Bitcoin, which features restricted scripting capabilities for security reasons (offering only 179 opcodes executed on a stack-based virtual machine and lacking support for loops), Ethereum is fully programmable. While Bitcoin functions purely as a currency system, Ethereum also operates as a decentralized application platform. Currently, Ethereum stands as the world's largest blockchain platform, hosting the majority of decentralized applications.
2. *Increased decentralization: Bancor.* Prior to Bancor, trading between different tokens was reliant on centralized exchanges for price discovery, liquidity provision, and matchmaking. Bancor, utilizing the smart contracts of Ethereum, enabled flexible token issuance based on market demand and facilitated token exchanges within smart contracts, eliminating the need for centralized exchanges. Bancor is an on-chain liquidity protocol that is founded on blockchain smart contracts. It enables users to issue new tokens and create liquidity pools by staking mainstream currencies such as Ether, which supports automated token-to-token transactions. The supply and pricing of Bancor tokens are automatically adjusted by algorithms in response to market demand. For instance, if one wishes to trade their USDT, an Ethereum-based token, for Ether, they can utilize BNT as an intermediary within the Ethereum network. (Note: at present, Bancor only permits token transactions on the Ethereum network and is unable to facilitate cross-chain exchanges.)
3. *Enhanced anonymity: Grin and Zcash.* Bitcoin transactions comprise transferring bitcoins between blockchain addresses that are pseudonymous rather than fully anonymous. Although the addresses are not directly tied to identities, they are public, potentially allowing for the tracing of transactions (this topic is further explored in Sects. 4.5 and 9.5). Grin and Zcash advance privacy protection by encrypting address information and facilitating signature verification within cryptographic zero-knowledge proofs. This measure effectively conceals transaction addresses.

[2] Fitzgerald, F. Scott. "The Crack-Up." *The Crack-up*. New York: New Directions, 1993, 69.

Reverse Explorations of Bitcoin's Pioneering Direction:

1. *Anchoring the real world: Tether (USDT) and Digix (DGX).* Since trust in Bitcoin is solely based on trust in the code, the mechanism of Bitcoin eliminates the need for trust in third parties in the real world. However, Bitcoin's value is inherently ambiguous since it stems from mining and lacks clear value foundations. To address the issue, Tether introduced USDT, a stablecoin with its reserves tied to the US dollar and using the "OMNI protocol" on Bitcoin. In 2016, Digix issued DGX, a stablecoin backed by gold reserves. Both of these stablecoins were aimed at stabilizing value through reserve assets; however, they relied on centralized issuers and custodians, deviating from decentralization.
2. *Challenging "code is law": EOS.* While Bitcoin aspires to achieve a governance order where "code is law," this system has its limitations. In this model, the developer community, including maintainers and developers, identifies needs and writes a code. After consensus among the miners, this code is executed unalterably on the blockchain. However, this governance system is not immune to "computational despotism," where mining pools with significant hash power can influence voting outcomes. In contrast, EOS has adopted a "representative democracy" model, where the EOS community elects super nodes with the authority to arbitrate contentious transactions, which means that outcomes generated by the EOS blockchain code can be altered.

In 2019, the social media giant Facebook introduced Libra, which compromised the existing order by combining the trends of anchoring in the real world and challenging the notion of "code is law." In 2020, Facebook rebranded Libra to Diem, but its basic architecture remained unchanged. In the 2019 whitepaper, Libra aimed to anchor a basket of currencies, while Diem shifted to anchor solely to the US dollar. Diem planned to establish super nodes to oversee governance. Although Diem retained some aspects of Bitcoin's decentralization ideals, it only achieved decentralization in the payment aspect.

5.2 eCash: The Innovator of Peer-to-Peer Electronic Payments

A pioneer initiative in the use of asymmetric encryption technology, the concept of eCash was invented by David Chaum, initially intended to develop a payment system that would prevent banks from tracing users' payment information. However, eCash did not gain popularity as it still relied on a balance in a centralized bank database to manage accounting. The technology for describing digital assets using asymmetric encryption remained dormant for 20 years until the emergence of Bitcoin.

In 1982, cryptographer David Chaum published his paper 'Blind Signatures for Untraceable Payments,' in which he first introduced the concept of "blind signatures."

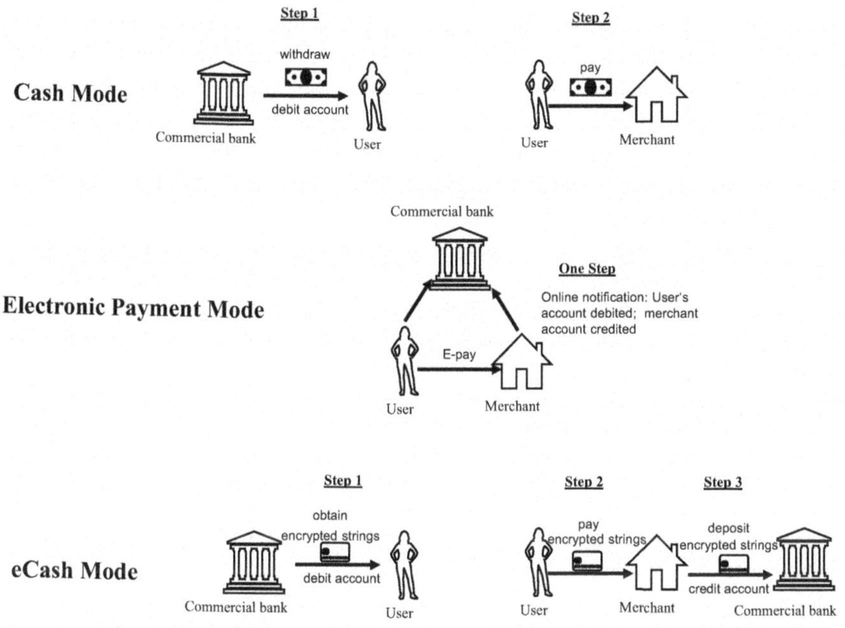

Fig. 5.2 The privacy-protection payment model initiated by eCash

This technology allowed banks to act as trusted third parties and sign payment data without knowing the detailed payment information of the payers.[3]

In 1988, along with Amos Fiat and Moni Noar, David Chaum published "Untraceable Electronic Cash," which described the algorithm for implementing "blind signatures" using RSA asymmetric encryption. This protocol enabled the exchange of "untraceable electronic cash" between banks, users and merchants.[4]

Chaum's electronic cash utilizes "blind signature" technology to ensure untraceability and protect user privacy. This means that banks cannot access consumer spending data, and merchants cannot acquire personal details of consumers. This form of eCash not only mirrors the transactional nature of tangible cash but also secures the confidentiality of personal information in a similar manner.

Compared to traditional cash transactions and electronic payments, eCash seamlessly integrates the anonymity advantage of cash and the convenience advantage of electronic payments (Fig. 5.2).

In cash mode, cash circulation becomes independent from the bank once users withdraw cash. The payment process only verifies the authenticity of the currency but not the user's identity, ensuring privacy protection. However, cash payments lack the convenience of electronic payment.

[3] Chaum, David. "Blind Signatures for Untraceable Payments." *Springer EBooks*, 1983, 199–203. https://doi.org/10.1007/978-1-4757-0602-4_18.

[4] Chaum, David, Amos Fiat, and Moni Naor. "Untraceable Electronic Cash." *Lecture Notes in Computer Science*, 1990, 319–327. https://doi.org/10.1007/0-387-34799-2_25.

In electronic payment mode, the payment process involves communication with the bank to verify the identity of the payer and the merchant using an account and password. Payment involves debiting the funds from the payer's account and crediting the payee's account. For a successful transaction, the bank must possess the identity information of both parties involved. Electronic payments offer great convenience for customers, but they compromise privacy protection as the bank has access to customer identity and transaction information.

In the eCash mode, eCash is a form of electronic payment that offers great convenience without the bank having access to customer information. Upon withdrawing cash, users receive a digital string representing currency that is digitally signed by the bank. Privacy protection is ensured by the transfer of this digital string in the payment process.

Technical analysis of the eCash payment process:

An eCash payment can be outlined as follows: User Alice opens an account with Bank Beta and installs an eCash client on her PC. When Alice needs to withdraw money and sent it to another user, the following sequence is initiated:

1. Alice sends a request x to Bank Beta in the form of an encrypted message $c(x)$ that cannot be decrypted by Bank Beta.
2. Upon receiving Alice's request, Bank Beta deducts the requested amount from Alice's account and performs "blind signing" on the encrypted message, resulting in $s(c(x))$.
3. Alice performs a deblinding operation on the signed message $s(c(x))$, deriving $c\prime(s(c(x))) = s(\mathrm{x})$, which is the bank's signature on the request x.
4. Alice pays $s(\mathrm{x})$ to Bob.
5. Bob notifies the bank of $s(\mathrm{x})$, and the bank credits the amount to Bob's account.

The above process has been simplified compared to the actual protocol and will not be detailed here. It is worth noting that in step 3, the deblinded value $s(\mathrm{x})$ obtained by Alice allows her to go offline from the bank. The bank has no knowledge of the trace of $s(\mathrm{x})$, which no longer depends on the banking system. Alice can save $s(\mathrm{x})$ on a floppy disk, USB drive (although USB drives did not exist conception of eCash in 1994), send it via email, or simply make a paper note in ASCII code. In any form, $s(\mathrm{x})$ represents the value of the dollar.

The digital format of $s(\mathrm{x})$ in eCash is the first true digital currency as it eliminates the need for a centralized server in the payment process. In eCash, it is the digital entity that holds value.

Note: In the actual eCash protocol, the representation of digital currency is given as $C = \prod_{1 \leq i \leq k/2} f(x_i, y_i)^{\frac{1}{3}} mod n$.[5]

Let us now explain the operating principle of eCash. Back in the 1990s, if a user (let this be Sophia) used eCash, she would still need to go to an ATM or a bank every week to withdraw 1000 yuan from her account. However, instead of receiving physical cash, Sophia would be given encrypted strings, which would be stored in her ATM card. At that time (as USB drives were not yet available), these strings essentially represented cash, and once stored in her card, she could use them for payment at the mall. For example, if she bought a bag at a store, the merchant would

[5] Chaum, David, Amos Fiat, and Moni Naor. "Untraceable Electronic Cash." *Lecture Notes in Computer Science*, 1990, 319–327. https://doi.org/10.1007/0-387-34799-2_25. p.3.

read the strings from her card, similar to accepting cash. After receiving the encrypted strings amounting to 500 yuan, the merchant would then go to an ATM or a bank to deposit these encrypted strings into their own account. The key point here is that these strings representing cash would not contain Sophia's name, ID number or any personal information about her. Neither the bank nor the merchant would know that Sophia was making the payment. This is the greatest difference between eCash and current electronic payments. In the latter, when making a purchase by card, although the merchant can only access customer information that their payment processor allows them to see (usually the so-called "track data" that includes card number and expiry date, card holder's name, and sometimes—for card-not-present transactions—address details for shipping/billing purposes), the specific transaction immediately becomes known to the card holder's bank that holds personal data such as name, billing address, etc.

In this way, eCash separated the payment process from the banking system, while it still relied on banks for issuance and final acceptance/redemption (clearing, settlement) functions. Banks were only responsible for converting fiat currency into eCash and vice versa. Upon receiving eCash, the merchant would deposit the received digits into the bank, eventually converting them into fiat currency.

David Chaum founded DigiCash in Amsterdam, the Netherlands, in 1990. He launched the eCash system in 1994, based on the original concept of untraceable electronic cash that received support from numerous internationally renowned banks in the following years. However, due to poor management and other factors, Chaum left the company in 1999 and eCash gradually declined.

Among the multiple reasons for the failure of eCash, the most significant one appears to be that user privacy was not a widespread concern in society at the time. While banks obtained our fictional Sophia's identity and transaction information, she did not mind this as there were no transactions she needed to conceal. The significance of personal privacy only became a prominent issue after the rapid development of the Internet.

5.3 Bitcoin: The Generator of a Paradigm Shift

In eCash, asymmetric encryption was used for digital signatures, providing proof of ownership. However, it relied on the banking system to facilitate encrypted value transfers between users. Bitcoin inherited the asymmetric encryption signature technology from eCash and combined it with a proof-of-work mechanism. This allowed operating independently of central servers, embodying the often discussed "distributed" and "decentralized" characteristics. While eCash achieved a certain degree of peer-to-peer payment, its value generation and final verification still depended on the banking system. In contrast, Bitcoin established a new value system, where the creation, validation and transaction of value are completely free from centralized servers, and peer-to-peer transactions are enabled under distributed conditions.

Table 5.2 Features of cash and electronic payments

	Cash	Electronic payment	Bitcoin (P2P electronic cash)
Form	Inherently physical (statutory form of legal tender)	Derivatively electronic (originated from cash)	Inherently electronic
Source of Trust	Credit of issuer (trust on central bank)	Credit of financial institutions (trust on FIs)	Credit of "issuer" (Trust on machine and algorithm)
Circulation	Decentralized	Centralized (relies on banking system)	Decentralized
Payment process	P2P direct payment (payment, clearing, and settlement completed simultaneously)	Three separate processes of payment, clearing and settlement	P2P direct payment (payment, clearing, and settlement completed simultaneously)

5.3.1 From "Peer-to-Peer Electronic Cash" and Beyond

Cryptographers had been able to protect and transfer value using asymmetric encryption algorithms since eCash; however, the issue of trust in third parties remained unsolved for over a decade. In 2008, Satoshi Nakamoto introduced the idea and technical path of Bitcoin in his paper "Bitcoin: A Peer-to-Peer Electronic Cash System."[6] The phrase "peer-to-peer electronic cash" clearly highlights the fundamental breakthrough Bitcoin accomplished in the modern payment system: *By utilizing a peer-to-peer environment, it achieved electronic cash payments without relying on trusted third parties and solved the problem of value proof in a trustless scenario* (refer to Table 5.2).

Those familiar with modern payment systems will understand that "peer-to-peer electronic cash" is not feasible within the existing legal currency system; payment systems are either in the form of physical cash or electronic transactions. If the latter are chosen, they must rely on financial institutions, primarily banks.

In the legal systems of various countries today, "cash" (including both coins and banknotes) is the statutory and native form of legal tender. If it is substituted for electronic payment, reliance on the financial system (primarily banks, but now also including third-party payment providers) is necessary to digitize the native form of cash. Bank accounts record the income and expenses of individuals, and individuals transfer assets by instructing banks. Electronic payments, in essence, are the promise of financial institutions to deliver cash. Therefore, current electronic payment methods inevitably revolve around financial institutions, while the clearing and settlement steps between these institutions are centralized around central banks. (Please refer to Sect. 2.4.2 of this book for examples of interbank payments.)

[6] Nakamoto, Satoshi. "Bitcoin: A Peer-to-Peer Electronic Cash System." *Decentralized Business Review*, 2008.

From the perspective of the form of currency and means of payment, the fundamental breakthrough of Bitcoin lies in it being a peer-to-peer electronic cash, combining the two seemingly incompatible forms "cash" and "electronic."

- ***Native form***: Both Bitcoin and cash exist and transact in their native forms. While Bitcoin takes the form of digital tokens, cash takes the form of coins and banknotes. In contrast, electronic payments only exist as a derivative form of cash.
- ***Direct credit***: Both Bitcoin and cash derive their credit from the issuer. Credit in Bitcoin can be attributed to the operation of machines and algorithms, which function as its "issuer," while cash credit comes from central banks. Bitcoin represents currency value directly in the form of tokens, while cash represents this value in the form of banknotes and coins. In contrast, credit for electronic payments comes from banks, and users must have trust that these banks can redeem the equivalent cash.
- ***Decentralization***: Bitcoin and cash, being representative of value themselves, both exist in a decentralized manner without relying on any third-party for proof of value.
- ***Peer-to-peer direct payments***: Bitcoin enables direct payments between parties, with the three processes of payment, clearing and settlement completed simultaneously. In contrast, current electronic payments rely on the financial system and require completing these three distinct processes separately. Peer-to-peer direct payments are an example of decentralization, and the concept of decentralization is exemplified by this payment system.

It is frequently stated that everything that exists has a reason for its existence, which raises the question: Why, in the era of the Internet, does the proof and transfer of value still rely on financial institutions? The simple reason is that electronic data lacks uniqueness and cannot serve as a medium for the transfer of value. In the world of computing, data can be infinitely replicated, that is, it falls short of being scarce or unique, leading to the potential for double spending. In the Internet age, the only solution to this issue is through verification by a trusted third party.

> To understand the concept of double spending, let us bring the example of a promissory note as a debt instrument. Let Alexander be the issuer of this note and Sophia being the holder. The note text includes payment of 100 yuan upon presentation three months later. Now, this text can be processed using a computer, but proof of value cannot. (For readers who are not familiar with promissory notes, imagine it as a loan note.)
>
> If Alexander writes a promissory note using a Word document on a computer, could Sophia use the same file to demand acceptance from Alexander? Of course not. This would be dangerous because Sophia could make 10,000 copies of the Word version of the promissory note, and Alexander would then owe her 1 million yuan. This is known as the "Double Spending" problem.

Prior to the emergence of Bitcoin, two methods had been derived for addressing the double spending problem.

Method 1: Creating a paper IOU ("I owe you") that is signed by both parties. This paper ensured uniqueness and, in legal terms, photocopies or scanned copies could not be considered as IOUs. At most, they could be regarded as evidence that the IOU once existed (due to the uniqueness of the paper).

Method 2: If Alexander and Sophia opt to use an electronic form of the loan note, it is necessary to have a trusted third party as a witness to ensure the immutability and uniqueness of the data. For instance, some banks now act as trusted third parties and provide electronic signature services. The common method is for bank customers to use a U shield and sign an electronic contract through facial recognition. (Electronic form requires third-party certification.)

Simply put, the "Double Spending" problem is the primary challenge to achieve trustworthy payments in a peer-to-peer network without relying on a third party's trust. In computer networks where data can be duplicated indefinitely, a proof of value (such as a promissory note) can be duplicated and reused without a centralized server for verification. The peer-to-peer electronic cash system of Bitcoin emerged as a powerful solution by addressing the issue of proving the uniqueness of value.

5.3.2 Technical Implementation of Bitcoin

The technological solution of Bitcoin is revolutionary in that it uses asymmetric encryption technology for signatures and combines it with the Proof-of-Work (PoW) mechanism to achieve peer-to-peer transactions, eliminating the need for reliance on central servers. This allows it to possess the characteristics of being both distributed and decentralized. From a technical perspective, let us explain how Bitcoin achieves peer-to-peer electronic cash.

1. The Form of Bitcoin: Unspent Transaction Outputs (UTXOs)

Like traditional electronic payments, Bitcoin abandons physical forms such as paper money or gold. In addition, to ensure trusted payments in a peer-to-peer environment, Bitcoin utilizes transaction records as the carrier of the currency. Despite the word "coin" in the name Bitcoin, there is no physical "coin" shining brightly in the Bitcoin system (despite being suggested by several attractive digital image representations one can find online).

Satoshi Nakamoto's Bitcoin is represented purely by transaction records. **When claiming ownership of a bitcoin**, one is **actually claiming ownership of a transaction record** that shows the transfer of bitcoin from Address A to Address B. This record is known as an "Unspent Transaction Output" (UTXO), which **can be thought of as a transferable electronic voucher of rights**.

> UTXO in Bitcoin can be understood by comparing it to the endorsement of a promissory note. For example, if a bank issues a promissory note to Alexander, stating that it will pay him 100 RMB in three months, he can use this promissory note to buy the *Textbook of Abstract Algebra* from Sophia. As a general rule of commercial law in most countries, when Alexander transfers a promissory note to Sophia, he must write "Transferred to Sophia" on the back of the note, along with his signature and the date. In legal terms, this recording of transfer on the back of the note is called "endorsement transfer."

Fig. 5.3 The Generation of Public Key and Address from Private Key as a One-Way Process[7]

Sophia can then pay Chloe with this promissory note to purchase the *Textbook of Field Theory*, also completing an endorsement transfer. Afterwards, Chloe can endorse and transfer the note to Jonathan as payment for the *Textbook of Noncommutative Algebra*.

As we have seen in the above example, in the case of Bitcoin, UTXO refers to the unspent output of a transaction, similar to the promissory note, representing the rights or ownership of a specific amount of bitcoin and a record of its origin. Each UTXO is used as input for future transactions, similar to the promissory note being transferred from one person to another.

2. Signature Verification by Asymmetric Encryption

In the Bitcoin system, the transfer of bitcoin from address A to address B is recorded in the form of UTXOs. But how can a user prove that they are the true owner of address B?

In the real world, users can use their identification card to prove that "I am myself" or provide a signature as proof of identity. However, in a peer-to-peer environment, there is no third party for identity verification. Bitcoin solves this problem by utilizing asymmetric encryption technology (refer to Fig. 5.3).

Bitcoin uses the Elliptic Curve Algorithm, wherein users possess a private key that can be set arbitrarily, and can derive a public key and address through the algorithm. This is a one-way and irreversible algorithm, meaning that users cannot derive the private key from the public key or address. However, the private key, public key and address can all be mutually verified. The private key acts as the users' "ultimate identification" instrument. The transfer and verification processes of Bitcoin can be described as follows:

Bitcoin Transfer Process:

- Transfer to the recipient's "address"
- This address can be made public

Bitcoin Verification Process:

- Validate the "address" using the "public key"
- Verify the "private key signature" using the "public key"

For example, during a transaction, when payer Alice wants to transfer bitcoin to payee Bob, Alice specifies Bob's public key address (or a wallet address generated from the public key). This information is then submitted to the network, where miners package and create blocks, forming a public ledger.

If recipient Bob wants to spend the bitcoin received from Alice, he uses his corresponding private key to sign the transaction and then publishes it on the network. Any miner that receives this transaction uses Bob's public key to verify the signature using Bob's private

[7] Andreas, M. Antonopoulos. "Mastering Bitcoin: Unlocking Digital Cryptocurrencies." *O'Reilly Media*, 2016, 63.

key. If the verification is successful, it confirms that Bob is the legitimate owner of the digital currency.

3. Block Chaining and Transaction Chaining

Many studies and reports corroborate that blocks are chained together, hence we metaphorically refer to this technology as "blockchain." In the case of Bitcoin, transactions within a block are also "chained" together, forming a continuous transaction chain or transaction chaining.

A "block" is a data structure that packages multiple transaction data together; it can be understood as a ledger that records multiple transactions.

As blocks are "chained" together, transactions are also linked. Miners, while following the rules, fill up the ledger (block) with transactions, then a time seal is placed on the block and the identification number of the previous block is also recorded. This process creates a cohesive chain of linked blocks, forming a continuous ledger system (refer to Fig. 5.4).

4. Proof of Work (PoW): Maintaining System Operation

The blockchain created by this process has a characteristic: the older the ledger, the more difficult it is to tamper with the transactions within it. If one wants to change a transaction in block 363,270 recorded in 2015, they would need to change all the subsequent blocks in the ledger since 2015 in order to do so.

Bitcoin creatively utilizes the Proof of Work (PoW) mechanism, where every miner participates in the process of keeping records, commonly known as "mining." This activity is the source of the system's computational power. This prompts the

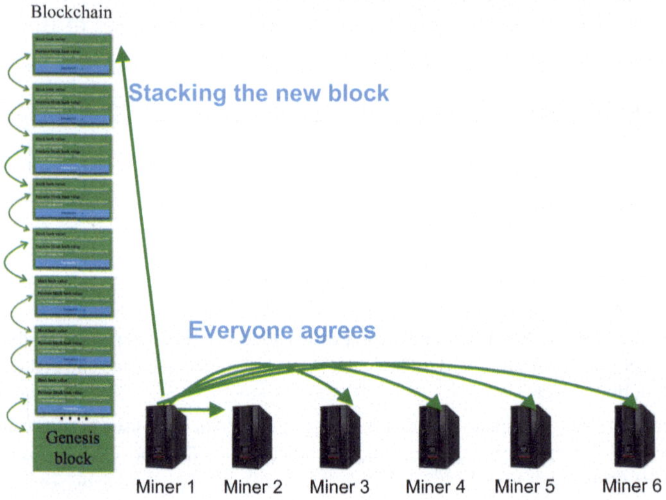

Fig. 5.4 Block chaining

question of why miners consume electricity and invest in hardware devices to partizcipate in mining. It is because Bitcoin sets up a reward mechanism, where miners can receive system (mining) rewards and transaction fees (Fig. 5.5).

System rewards are the native source of Bitcoin. When the records of a miner are validated by the system, bitcoin rewards are given. Bitcoin has a fixed total supply of 21 million coins, which are distributed in a fixed proportion and will gradually decrease over time (Fig. 5.6).

Apart from rewards from record keeping, miners can also collect transaction fees from traders. For example, if Alex wants to transfer bitcoin to Sophia, he must pay a transaction fee to the miner who records the transaction.

Transaction fees in Bitcoin are not fixed but rather determined through negotiation between users and miners. During the process of transferring bitcoin, users propose a fee and miners will prioritize and accept transactions based on this fee, creating a system of centralized price quoting and transaction matching. Therefore, the quantity of trading activities in the market significantly affects bitcoin transaction fees.

Fig. 5.5 The sources of Miners' income

Fig. 5.6 The total supply decrease model of bitcoin

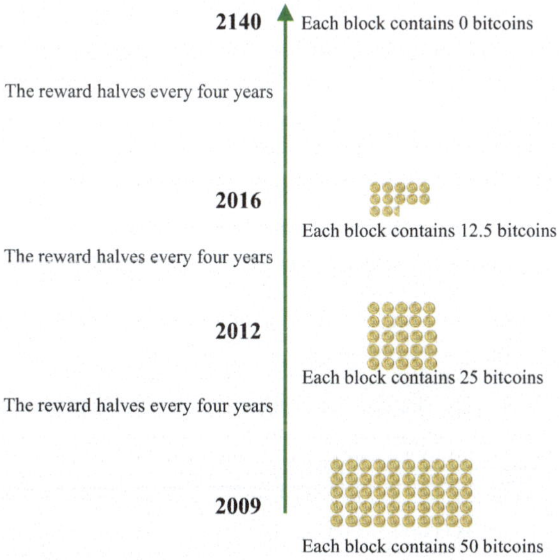

5. Proof of Work: The Prevention of Tampering through Expensive Hashing Competition

How does Bitcoin use mining to prevent ledger tampering? Miners compete for the right to keep records, but only the miner whose records are validated by the system receives rewards. This process is called "hashing competition."

Why is Hashing Competition a Significant Challenge?

After miners package the ledger, they must perform hashing calculations. Computing a hash value for a given set of data takes only a few seconds; however, Bitcoin places specific requirements on the resulting hash value. In order for a miner's record to be accepted by the system, they must compute a hash value that meets these requirements. This hashing competition involves a combination of computational power and chance.

Miners first use the SHA256 hashing algorithm to perform two rounds of hashing calculations on the "block header" data, resulting in a 256-bit binary hash value. Bitcoin sets specific criteria for miners to meet, such as the first 19 digits being zeros.

To compute the required hash value, miners utilize a trial-and-error approach. They continuously substitute a random number, referred to as "nonce" (an abbreviation for "number used once"), into the hash function to calculate a hash value that is smaller than the target value. Due to the highly random nature of the SHA256 calculation, the only way to find the desired hash value is by tirelessly trying different nonces. Therefore, successful mining depends on the miner's computational speed and a certain degree of luck. It may take just one attempt to find a valid hash value, or it may require billions of tries.

By setting an average time of around ten minutes for transaction packing and block creation, Bitcoin implements an automatic difficulty adjustment mechanism for the "hashing competition." This time setting strikes a balance between two crucial elements. If the time is too short, this will not enable sufficient computational power, making the network vulnerable to tampering attempts and potentially leading to synchronization issues. Conversely, if the time is too long, transaction confirmation times will be prolonged, negatively impacting miners' experience.

The Game of Hashing Competition in Bitcoin:

Hashing Calculation: The process of mapping an input data file of variable length to a fixed-length data file using a specific algorithm.

– *Bitcoin Hashing Calculation*: In Bitcoin, the SHA-256 algorithm is (repeatedly) used to calculate a hash value that is a 256-bit binary random number, with the objective of finding a hash value that meets specific requirements.

– *The Difficulty Adjustment Mechanism of Bitcoin*: Bitcoin employs a mechanism that automatically adjusts the difficulty level of the hashing competition to maintain an average calculation time of approximately 10 minutes.

As an example, below is the hash value of the 523,485th block on May 20, 2018:

0000000000000000000059554f757f7blde904220acb93675b5f4c34f8d9910e8

The winner of a hashing competition for a block can publicly announce their victory to gain recognition from other miners. Furthermore, the block hash of this block can be referenced by the next block. As long as this status is kept and remains on the longest chain, this indicates a highly secure record-keeping authority for this block (refer to Fig. 5.7).

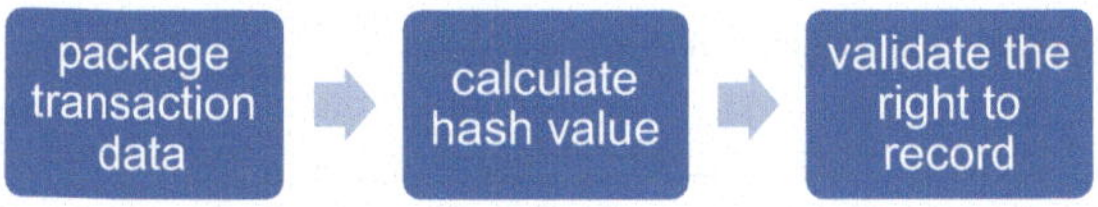

Fig. 5.7 The process of bitcoin ledger keeping

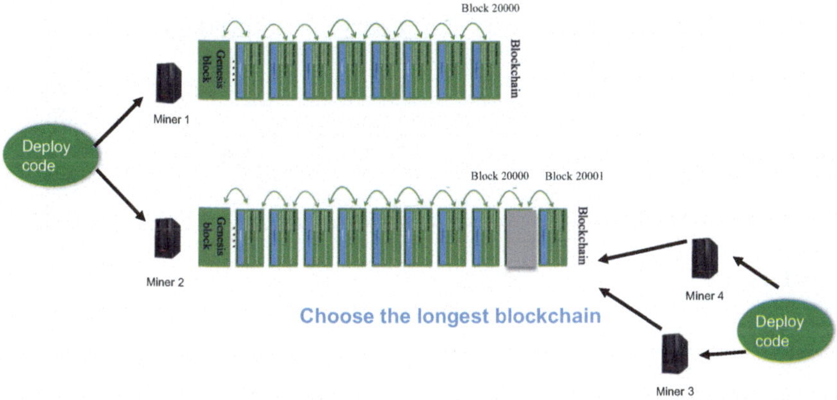

Fig. 5.8 The longest chain principle

What actions can be taken if someone tries to manipulate transaction records in a blockchain? Although it is technically feasible to modify records in a blockchain, doing so would require an enormous amount of computational power, making this kind of attack economically unfeasible. In fact, Bitcoin implements the principle of the longest chain, which means that if a participant has superior computational power, they have the potential to start from an older block and outpace the existing longest chain, allowing for tampering with blocks after that point (Fig. 5.8).

However, changing existing data on a blockchain requires surpassing the network's computational power by 50%. This type of tampering is mathematically possible but highly uneconomical. Spending such a massive amount of computational power would only result in block rewards, typically within a range of one million dollars or less (Table 5.3).

At the time of writing, the network's computational power is around 12.21 trillion trillion hashes per second. To manipulate Bitcoin blockchain data, one would need to surpass this computational power by 50%, which is equivalent to the computational power of 4 trillion normal Apple laptops or 2 million professional mining machines.

If successful in manipulating a block, the operator would receive a reward of 12.5 bitcoins. Given the highest price of bitcoin, which peaked at around $67,000 per unit, the potential earnings would not exceed $1 million.

A rational person with such immense computational power to alter blockchain data would find it more advantageous to utilize this resource for legitimate purposes,

Table 5.3 The computational power of mining machines

	Number of SHA256 hashes per second	Hashing power	Power consumption	Manufacturer	Price
Common MAC PC	300,000/s	0.3 M	–	–	–
Ant S17	62 trillion/s	62 T	3600 W	BITMAIN	14,000 RMB
Innosilicon T3 +	57 trillion/s	57 T	3600 W	Innosilicon	12,000 RMB
WhatsMiner M10	33 trillion/s	33 T	2145 W	WhatsMiner	8000 RMB
WhatsMiner M20S	68 trillion/s	68 T	3264 W	WhatsMiner	14,000 RMB
Global Hashing Power	1.221×10^{20}/s	122.1 E	–	–	–

such as direct mining; the profits obtained from this would far exceed any gains from tampering with the blockchain.

6. Summary of Technological Breakthroughs and Mechanism Innovations in Bitcoin

Bitcoin introduced a proof-of-work mechanism, creatively solving the double-spending problem. In a peer-to-peer network, Bitcoin does not rely on a fixed, centralized server to validate transactions and prevent fraudulent double-spending. Instead, in the Bitcoin design, countless node servers in the peer-to-peer network can each potentially become the transaction-validating ledger server. Approximately every 10 min, all node servers participate in a computational power competition to earn the right to keep the ledger. The outcome depends not only on the computational power of the servers but also on bare luck. As a result, the server with the authority in each 10-min ledger-keeping round is random and unpredictable.

The proof-of-work mechanism of Bitcoin is an innovation in the field of computer networking: it achieves practical data consistency among a large number of anonymous nodes that can freely join or leave the open network cluster. Prior to this strategy, various consensus algorithms existed, such as BFT, PBFT, PAXOS, RAFT, etc., but these were suited for closed networks with a limited number of nodes.

In summary, proof-of-work and incentive competition combine the confirmation of ledger recording rights with the issuance of currency. This deflationary automatic currency issuance mechanism is a significant advancement in the world of currencies.

5.3.3 Bitcoin: Redefining Currency

1. Redefining the Value of Currency

From a value perspective, Bitcoin is a direct digital representation of value. Similar to gold, it possesses intrinsic value, whereas its realization is completely independent of any trusted third party in the physical world.

- Bitcoin was created in the digital realm and functions as a native currency of this realm. Its issuance, storage, and circulation does not depend on trusted third parties.
  - Bitcoin is issued based on an algorithm, which determines the total supply and issuance rate.
  - Bitcoin enables peer-to-peer transactions on the blockchain.
- Bitcoin is no longer a mapping of commercial relationships in the physical world.
  - Bitcoin is not a tool for account keeping for banks or financial institutions.
  - Bitcoin is not anchored to any real-world asset and is not a computer record of the ownership and transfer of any physical currency or asset.
  - Bitcoin is not a liability declared by any individual or institution in the physical world.

2. Redefining the Technology of Currency

From a technological perspective, Bitcoin has reconstructed the technical form of currency. Cryptocurrencies, virtual currencies and digital currencies have become new social phenomena that have taken the stage in history. Subsequent digital currencies have more or less adopted the following technical features pioneered by Bitcoin:

- Electronic form: All digital currencies adopt an electronic form.
- Based on cryptography: Asymmetric encryption technology is used for signature verification (to protect privacy).
- Peer-to-peer payments.
- Programmable: Bitcoin opened the door for programmable currencies, and Ethereum took this novelty to new heights.

5.3.4 Bitcoin: Exploring a Machine Order that Does not Rely on Violence

The innovation of Bitcoin is reflected not only at the technical level but also in the design of community ecology. Bitcoin has opened up a decentralized governance model using blockchain technology where everything is spontaneous, and there is no need for a central node for organization, management and decision-making.

At the operational level, Bitcoin introduced the innovative process of "mining" to allow for self-sustained ecological operation. In any centralized network community, system computing power is typically provided by central nodes or servers to maintain system operation. However, Bitcoin avoids centralization by using mining machines to provide computational power to the entire system. In exchange, miners are incentivized with bitcoin through a sophisticated mechanism that maintains the self-operation of the entire system. The ownership and transfer of bitcoin no longer rely on proof from a central node, such as a bank proving the number of assets in a bank account, but they are mutually verified by all nodes based on the longest chain principle, which is the consensus of the majority of mining machines.

Mining machines not only enable a decentralized mechanism that creates a "trustless" and "decentralized" payment model for Bitcoin but also allow for a decentralized governance model using blockchain technology. When multiple nodes run the same code and implement the same protocol or smart contract, they all follow the same logical code and rules, achieving governance through machine or code execution. All of this occurs spontaneously without the need for a central node to organize, manage or make decisions.

5.3.5 *Conclusion: Bitcoin as the Pioneer of a Paradigm Shift*

Bitcoin revolutionized currency by redefining its value and technology, while it also explored a machine order that transcends dependence on human violence. Subsequent digital currencies will unquestionably embark on forward or reverse explorations of Bitcoin, whether by redefining value, harnessing technology, or adopting new governance models.

5.4 Ethereum: A Smart Contract Platform and Fully Programmable Currency

The inception of Bitcoin created a new prototype for digital currencies, revolutionizing the value and technological form of money. Subsequent to Bitcoin, many private digital currencies were created, either inspired by or directly copying its code. However, most of these currencies strongly resembled Bitcoin until Ethereum arrived. While Bitcoin aimed to establish a new monetary order, the objective of Ethereum was to create a distributed application platform known as "World Computer." As a result, the technical details of Ethereum markedly differ from those of Bitcoin.

5.4.1 *Overview: From a Monetary System to a Decentralized Application Platform*

In 2013, Vitalik Buterin, a Canadian computer programmer, published the Ethereum whitepaper titled "A Next-generation Smart Contract and Decentralized Application Platform," proposing the development of a new and more powerful blockchain platform: Ethereum. This new form of digital currency inherited Bitcoin's blockchain technology and principles, including:

- Maintaining a trusted distributed ledger through a competition of computational power among nodes
- Peer-to-peer networking
- Privacy protection through asymmetric encryption
- The native cryptocurrency (Ether, ETH) is issued algorithmically without being anchored to any real-world asset
- Programmability.

Despite the similarities, Ethereum is not merely an imitation of Bitcoin. It is rightfully referred to as Blockchain 2.0, because while Bitcoin positions itself as a monetary system, Ethereum aims to be a platform for smart contract and decentralized application. For Bitcoin, the "bitcoin" itself as unit of currency is the end goal of its background system and technology. In contrast, the primary purpose of Ethereum is the "smart contract," and Ether serves as a means of payment to support the operation of these contracts. Unlike Bitcoin, which is considered as "pure money," Ether has a functional purpose. It is used to purchase "fuel" (gas) required to "drive" smart contracts, essentially paying for the computing power provided by miners (Table 5.4).

1. Ethereum: The World's Leading Blockchain Application Development Platform

On the world's largest blockchain application development platform of Ethereum, comprehensive technology makes programming and development highly convenient. Its smart contracts host globally the greatest amount of distributed business logic and code, having the majority of decentralized applications deployed. As of November 13, 2021, stateofthedapps.com reported a total of 2880 decentralized applications (DApps) deployed on Ethereum. The largest category was games, accounting for 19%, followed by gambling at 14%, finance at 13%, and social apps at approximately

Table 5.4 Bitcoin and ethereum: the basics

	Bitcoin	Ethereum
Whitepaper	*Bitcoin: A Peer-to-Peer Electronic Cash System*	*A Next-generation Smart Contract and Decentralized Application Platform*
Positioning	Monetary system	IT application platform
Goal	"Bitcoin" itself	Smart contracts
Token	Bitcoin	Ether ("gas fee" to execute smart contract)

9%. Globally, Ethereum has a total of 2998 nodes and a developer community of 1.2 million registered users.

Using Ethereum smart contracts, virtual currencies can be developed and deployed in as little as 10 min at almost zero cost. This convenience has made Ethereum the primary platform for digital currencies within just a few years. According to data from etherscan.io on November 13, 2021, there were a total of 466,741 ERC-20 token smart contracts and approximately 176 million account addresses on Ethereum. The highest transaction peak was reached on May 9, 2021, with a daily transaction volume of 1.71 million.

Since its launch in July 2015, Ethereum has evolved into the world's largest decentralized application platform and the most prodigious blockchain ecosystem community. Besides, the developers of Ethereum have ambitious plans to develop their brainchild into a "world computer." Although this is an ambitious goal that may take time to accomplish, Ethereum has certainly paved the way towards achieving it.

2. The Role and Mechanism of Ether on the Platform

The issuance mechanism of Ether, Ethereum's native cryptocurrency, differs slightly from that of Bitcoin. Ethereum organized a pre-sale, where Ether, already present in the original code, was used to raise funds for the development team. This issuing act in the code beforehand is known in the industry as "pre-mining." Thus, a total of 71.88 million ethers were pre-mined in Ethereum. Subsequently, according to the code, an additional 15.6 million ether are generated each year to incentivize miners, that corresponds to approximately 43,000 ether per day. The reward for producing each block includes around 5 ether and gas service fees. (As Ethereum transitions to version 2.0, the mechanism of ether issuance and distribution is also changing.) Unlike Bitcoin, Ether is not deflationary, and its total supply continues to grow.

As a decentralized blockchain, Ethereum is also an economic ecosystem, with Ether playing a crucial role as its currency. Similar to the Bitcoin system, consensus in Ethereum is built on incentives provided to miners in Ether, ensuring the overall security of the blockchain.

Different from Bitcoin, Ethereum features smart contracts. The code for these contracts is stored in information fields associated with Ethereum addresses. Transactions sent to smart contract addresses trigger the execution of these contracts, which consume "gas." This gas is paid for in ether, making up the income for miners who process and package these transactions. Thus, the gas paid in ether can be viewed as a service fee within Ethereum. For example, storing the number "2022" in a smart contract might consume approximately 26,000 gas units, which is roughly 0.0013 ether.

The existence of gas service fees constrains developers to write a concise code, ensuring that the blockchain system does not get bogged down in complex and unending operations.

5.4.2 *Programmability: Smart Contracts and Blockchain 2.0*

1. Programmability: Blockchain 2.0

Let us first clarify what programmability entails: it is the capability of utilizing a code to perform operations on "digital objects." The degree of programmability can vary across virtual currencies, with even Bitcoin possessing a certain level of programmability. However, due to its non-Turing complete scripting language, programmability in Bitcoin is comparatively limited. In contrast, Ethereum has Turing complete scripting language, offering a higher level of programmability.

The concept of programmability focuses solely on the capability of using a code to operate on "digital objects" and can be understood in terms of degree:

• Smartphones (such as iPhones) are fully programmable, allowing any programmer to write and deploy codes on them.

• Early cell phones featured poor programmability as the code must be written directly into the hardware.

• Traditional automatic switching systems (dial-up telephone) have even lower programmability.

• Antique plug-and-switch exchanges, where operators physically plugged and unplugged connections, were completely non-programmable.

This concept can be likened to the learning capabilities of animals. Humans have excellent programmability as they can learn and adapt after birth, while ants have very limited programmability dictated by their innate genetic traits.

When designing Bitcoin, Satoshi Nakamoto also considered the need for programmability. As a result, Bitcoin includes over 100 commands that can be used to develop scripts for controlling payment behavior on UTXO. However, the primary focus was to serve as a currency, with security as the highest priority. Therefore, the programmability of Bitcoin's scripting language is strictly limited to being Turing incomplete. This design choice is intentional and aligns with Bitcoin's emphasis on security. In contrast, Ethereum aims to function as an application platform, rather than just a currency; therefore, it provides a robust virtual machine that supports the deployment of Turing complete "smart contracts." These are more powerful than Bitcoin's "scripts" and enable the development of a wide range of applications and the execution of any "computable" task. This significant distinction is the very reason why Ethereum has been referred to as "Blockchain 2.0."

In the evolution of blockchain, Bitcoin is commonly referred to as "Blockchain 1.0," while Ethereum is considered as "**Blockchain 2.0**." The term "blockchain" represents the decentralized computer technology architecture used in the Bitcoin system. However, Bitcoin was primarily designed to function as a currency system, so its creator, Satoshi Nakamoto, focused primarily on security and thus excluded robust programming capabilities from its design.

On the other hand, Ethereum aimed to be an application platform rather than just a currency. It provides a powerful virtual machine capable of deploying Turing complete smart contracts, enabling a wider range of programming options. This is why it is often referred to as "Blockchain 2.0."

The historical relationship between Ethereum and Bitcoin can be compared to that of early cell phones and smartphones. The invention of the first mobile phone facilitated voice communication and paved the way for the era of wireless communication. In contrast, modern smartphones incorporate various functionalities beyond voice calls, aided by the support of wireless communication. Similarly, Bitcoin was initially designed as a currency system and ushered in the era of blockchain technology. Ethereum, with the support of this technology, was designed to allow for the deployment of any code and extends beyond mere monetary functionalities.

The distinction between Turing complete and Turing incomplete is not a judgement of superiority or inferiority in terms of programming languages, but rather a design choice. Ethereum, as a development platform, has chosen to design its smart contract programming language as Turing complete.

Turing complete: The Turing machine, invented by Alan Turing, is a universal computational model capable of performing any task that is considered "computable." This term is in quotes because some tasks are inherently uncomputable. A programming language or set of data operation rules is considered Turing complete if it can perform the same computational tasks as a Turing machine.

To draw an analogy with humans, a person is considered Turing complete if they are capable of performing any job in the world. While this may sound commendable, it also creates a dilemma. For example, if a task like "catching up with one's own shadow" is considered, the person executing this may have to keep running until exhaustion. Therefore, not all rules or languages need Turing completeness. For instance, the scripting language of Bitcoin does not aim to be Turing complete.

Ethereum's smart contracts are Turing complete. However, to prevent programs from getting stuck in infinite loops, a gas mechanism was introduced, which puts a cost on the task of "catching up with one's own shadow." For instance, if each step demands a cost of $1, just like the gas fee on Ethereum, this limitation will effectively stop the task from being executed.

Chapter 2 of this book has emphasized that the term "digital" in "digital currency" highlights a higher level of digitization. For digital currency, programmability perhaps is the simplest and most practical criterion. If an electronic currency is programmable, it can be classified as a digital currency. On the other hand, if a digital currency is not programmable, its level of digitization is compromised. Certainly, there may be cases where the architecture of a digital currency is programmable but does not expose programming interfaces, which is merely a matter of permissions.

2. Smart Contracts: Blockchain Distributed Applications

Due to his admiration for Nick Szabo's "smart contracts" concept, Vitalik Buterin incorporated it into the design of Ethereum, where he referred to the distributed applications developed and run on the platform as "smart contracts." However, it is important to note that Ethereum's smart contracts differ from Szabo's original concept. The term "smart contracts" is often used as a tribute to Szabo's significant contributions to cryptography, but crucially, his definition describes these as "*a set of promises, specified in digital form, including protocols within which the parties perform on these promises.*" Therefore, in Szabo's, interpretation, a smart contract is a digital agreement with automatic execution.

As often mentioned in the crypto community, smart contracts on Ethereum are "neither smart nor contracts."[8] While they have been compared to Szabo's original concept, they are essentially decentralized applications developed on the Ethereum platform and can be referred to as "blockchain code" or "chaincode." For instance, applications developed on Fabric that are distributed are commonly referred to as "chaincode," which accurately reflects their essence and makes them easy to understand.

The term "smart contract" was first introduced by Nick Szabo in his 1994 paper "Smart Contracts: Building Blocks for Digital Markets."[9] Szabo defined smart contracts as "a set of promises, specified in digital form, including protocols within which the parties perform on these promises." He illustrated a basic form a smart contract using a vending machine, where the user inserts $5 and the machine executes the contract by dispensing a can of cola.

Szabo's concept of smart contracts emphasizes that they are commercial agreements written in code, with a focus on "code execution." The term "smart" in smart contracts refers to being "smart" as opposed to being "intelligent" in the context of artificial intelligence. "Smart" in smart contracts does not refer to artificial intelligence, but rather it signifies that the contract is code-based and capable of automatically executing rules. Instead of mimicking human intelligence, the purpose of smart contracts is to exhibit intelligence in the sense that they are code-based and capable of automatically executing rules. This makes smart contracts more efficient than traditional paper contracts in the real world.

Szabo proposed that smart contracts would be embedded in various hardware and software systems, eventually spreading throughout the world. Similar to vending machines, card readers, Electronic Data Interchange (EDI), and the SWIFT Network, smart contracts based on automated hardware and software would execute agreements between individuals and maintain business relationships between them. Due to its Turing completeness, the Ethereum Virtual Machine (EVM) supports smart contracts. This has made programming and developing tokens using Ethereum smart contracts highly convenient and practically cost-free; in just a few years, Ethereum became the foundation for various digital currencies, enabling the deployment of a token in as little as 10 minutes.

In traditional computing environments, deploying a program typically means running it locally on a single computer. However, smart contracts represent a fundamental theoretical shift. When deployed, the code is executed on millions of Ethereum nodes distributed across the network.

5.4.3 *The Three Elements of Internet Commerce*

In Wei Dai's vision of B-Money, virtual commerce on the Internet comprises three essential elements: digital identity, digital currency, and digital contracts. We believe

---

[8] State-Of-The-Dapps. "Sotd-Www/Pages/About.Vue at Master · State-of-the-Dapps/Sotd-Www." GitHub, n.d. https://github.com/state-of-the-dapps/sotd-www/blob/master/pages/About.vue. Accessed on 17 September, 2023. The original statement is "And remember… smart contracts are neither smart, nor contracts!".

[9] Szabo, Nick. "Smart contracts: building blocks for digital markets." *EXTROPY: The Journal of Transhumanist Thought, (16)* 18.2 (1996): 28.

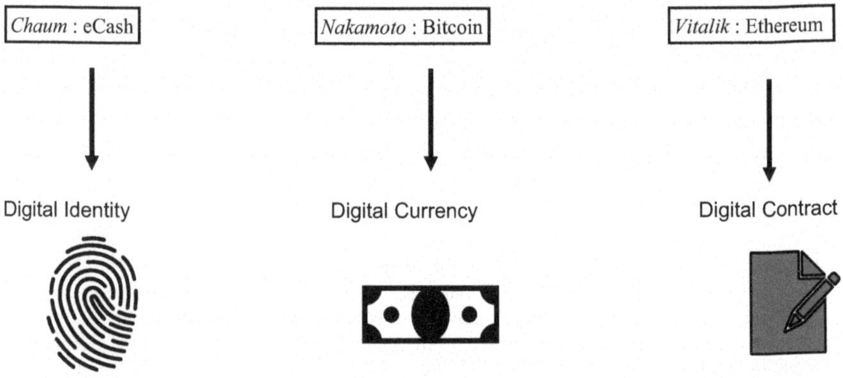

Fig. 5.9 The three elements of internet commerce

that these elements have been technologically realized through eCash, Bitcoin and Ethereum, respectively (refer to Fig. 5.9).

5.4.4 *Other Technological Breakthroughs*

Ethereum represents a technologically divergent route from Bitcoin in several key aspects. A primary difference lies in Ethereum's rejection of the Unspent Transaction Outputs (UTXOs) model, a foundational element of the Bitcoin architecture. The rigidity of Bitcoin's script, attributed to its reliance on UTXOs, limits the flexibility of its contracts, which can be likened to drafting a contract on a 100-yuan banknote, where the agreement pertains solely to the entirety of the 100 yuan, without the possibility of specifying individual units or any single yuan within that amount. In contrast, Ethereum employs a balance-based system, enabling the development of robust and adaptable smart contracts. This construct allows the results of smart contract computations to be incorporated directly into the balance of an address.

While Bitcoin primarily records the outcomes of computations and the system's current state via transaction and block data, Ethereum takes a different approach: its transactions activate smart contracts, the outcomes of which are logged in each node's state database. Essentially, a blockchain in Ethereum records the steps taken (the process), and the end results are stored in its state database. This design allows Ethereum to support a wider range of applications and interactions within its financial ecosystem.

Initially, Ethereum used a proof-of-work consensus algorithm, which has since transitioned to a revolutionary proof-of-stake algorithm represented by Ethereum 2.0. This has a block time of 15 s, making it much faster than Bitcoin. Ethereum features several unique technological innovations, including the Patricia tree and uncle blocks.

The technological innovations of Ethereum can be summarized as follows:

(1) The initial consensus mechanism has changed from proof-of-work to proof-of-stake, meaning that accounting rights and incentives are no longer based on computational competition but on the quantity of coins held;
(2) Sharding has been started, transitioning from a single chain to 64 virtual chains that are managed by a central chain called the "beacon chain," which greatly reduces congestion and lowers transaction fees on the Ethereum network;
(3) Ewasm has been adopted (Ethereum WebAssembly, an upgrade to the Ethereum Virtual Machine (EVM)), which enhances network capability to handle more complex applications;
(4) The economic model has changed, decoupling rewards from computational power and transitioning to a proof-of-stake model based on staked ether coins.

5.5 BANCOR: Decentralized Trading Network for Smart Tokens

5.5.1 The First Sophia Dilemma

If our Sophia wishes to exchange her Bitcoin for Ether, she must visit a cryptocurrency exchange. Although Bitcoin and Ethereum are decentralized, exchanges are centralized and rely on third-party trust. It is possible for exchanges to go bankrupt, and there is a risk of theft of Sophia's cryptocurrency held on the exchange. For instance, in 2014, Mt. Gox, the world's largest cryptocurrency exchange at the time, registered in Japan, declared bankruptcy after announcing the loss of 850,000 bitcoins belonging to its customers. More information on these issues and related cases will be provided in the next chapter (Fig. 5.10).

Following the launch of Bitcoin, online exchanges for convenient trading emerged rapidly. The earliest of these was Mt. Gox. As more cryptocurrencies surfaced,

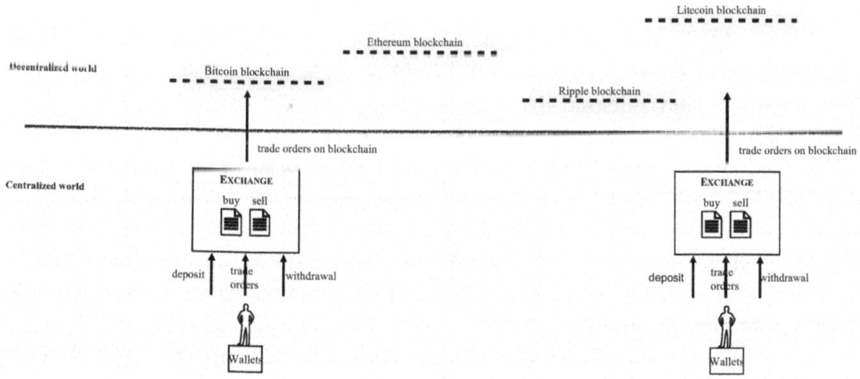

Fig. 5.10 The centralized world of virtual currency exchange

more exchanges appeared, facilitating the trades of cryptocurrency-fiat currency, cryptocurrency-cryptocurrency, and cryptocurrency finance transactions.

These exchanges are centralized and function similarly to a combination of a stock exchange and stock registry, facilitating cryptocurrency trades. Bitcoin and Ether can be traded on their respective blockchains without the need for centralized trust. However, to enable cross-blockchain transactions between the two, one must still rely on centralized exchanges to facilitate the transaction. This pattern can be described as "one step forward, half a step back." While Bitcoin itself does not rely on third-party trust, the trading of Bitcoin has this requirement.

What is the mechanism behind cryptocurrency exchanges? Once users deposit their virtual currencies into an exchange, the virtual assets come to be under the control of the exchange, similar to depositing cash into a bank. When users view their account balance on the exchange platform, such as having 1 bitcoin, they merely see a digital record in the exchange database; the exchange itself may not actually hold one bitcoin on the Bitcoin blockchain.

This is because exchanges can freely utilize the virtual currencies deposited by users, as the transactions solely occur within the exchange database. Only when a user initiates a "withdrawal" transaction, does the transaction need to be written onto the blockchain, transferring the virtual currency from the exchange's address to the user's specified address. (In the next chapter, we go on to discuss how "Mt. Gox" artificially inflated the amount of bitcoin in exchange accounts for manipulative reasons.)

During transactions, such as "cryptocurrency-fiat currency" or "cryptocurrency-cryptocurrency" pairs, the order book of the exchange plays a crucial role in matching buyers and sellers, ultimately determining the price through the matching mechanism.

While the security of virtual currencies relies on the robustness of blockchain technology, cryptocurrency exchanges are built on their own software code and databases, rendering them susceptible to external manipulation. Consequently, incidents of virtual currency theft often stem from attacks on the exchanges themselves rather than direct hacking of the underlying blockchain technology.

5.5.2 Decentralized Smart Solutions

In February 2017, Galia Benartzi, a US technology enterpreneur, and her team designed the Bancor protocol, a decentralized trading network, based on Ethereum's smart contract. They released the Bancor whitepaper and created the first "smart token," referred to as Bancor Network Token or BNT.

The fundamental idea behind the Bancor protocol is to issue a "smart token," BNT, which "holds" one or more other tokens as reserves. In this context, "holding" is different from "anchoring," in that the issued smart token actually locks a significant number of other tokens as reserves within the smart contract. In this sense, Bancor can also be considered as a type of stablecoin, that is on-chain asset-backed (refer to Chap. 3.2 for classification).

BNT serves as a central hub for exchanging various virtual currencies. The Bancor protocol uses algorithms to automatically determine the proportional relationship, or relative price, between BNT and other virtual currencies, allowing for exchanges between different virtual currencies through the buying and selling of BNT. Transactions occur through Bancor as the central counterparty, ensuring that buyers and sellers of different currencies do not directly transact with each other.

Bancor utilizes smart contract codes to facilitate the decentralized exchange of virtual currencies and eliminate the operational risks associated with centralized exchanges. The smart contract essentially holds reserves of multiple cryptocurrencies, ensuring liquidity for users. An algorithm written in the smart contract determines the issuance volume and relative price of Bancor tokens in proportion to other virtual currencies. Through smart contract control, Bancor maintains a fixed ratio between the total market value of issued "smart tokens" (measured in reserve tokens) and the total quantity of reserve tokens held.

Bancor is an innovative solution in the field of digital currencies as it provides an automated reserve mechanism between different cryptocurrencies via smart contracts. It anchors and collateralizes the value of digital currencies and introduces an automated protocol for the issuance and trading of digital tokens, making decentralized exchange networks feasible.

WHAT IS THE ALGORITHM MECHANISM FOR VALUE STABILIZATION IN BNT?

The algorithm mechanism design employed by BNT to maintain value intends to ensure a fixed ratio between the total market value of the "smart token" (measured in reserve tokens) and the overall supply of reserve tokens, known as the Constant Reserve Ratio (CRR). If the issued quantity of "smart tokens" is denoted as *Supply* with a total value represented as *Value*, and the reserved token balance is labeled as *Balance*, the total value of the "smart token" can be calculated as:

Therefore,

$$CRR = \frac{Balance}{Supply * Price}$$

In other words,

$$Price = \frac{Balance}{Supply * CRR}$$

In order to ensure a constant proportional relationship between the total value of reserves and the total value of "smart tokens," the Bancor protocol smart contract calculates the *Price* for each transaction based on the current *Balance* and *Supply*. This determines the price and supply for the transaction. According to the function equation, the reserve token price E required to buy a quantity T of "smart tokens" is given by:

$$E = R_0\left(\sqrt[F]{1 + \frac{T}{S_0}} - 1\right)$$

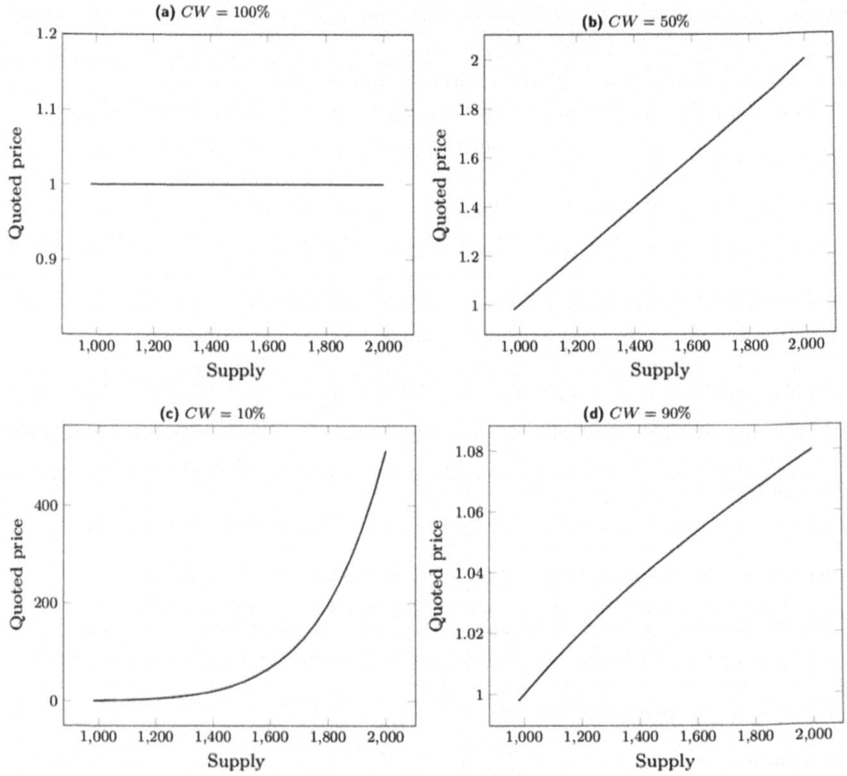

Fig. 5.11 Supply and price curves at different CRR values[10]

> The relationship between the price and supply of "smart tokens" varies depending on the value of CRR. When CRR is set to 100%, the actual mechanism in operation is the 100% reserve mechanism, making the "smart token" essentially a stablecoin.
>
> The curves below illustrate the relationship between supply and price for different values of CRR (see Fig. 5.11).

Overall, Bancor represents an innovation in the realm of digital currencies, establishing an automatic reserve mechanism through smart contracts between cryptocurrencies. Its setup anchors the value of digital currencies and provides collateralization, providing an automated protocol for the issuance and trading of digital currencies, and offering a viable solution for a decentralized trading network. Similar in principle, if we momentarily set aside considerations of regulatory compliance, Uniswap subsequently sparked the DEFI (Decentralized Finance) craze. This model of exchanges transacts with code and algorithms as the counterparty, along with currency issuance and pricing executed by algorithms, thus reducing the dependency on individuals

[10] Hertzog, Eyal, Guy Benartzi, and Galia Benartzi. *Bancor Protocol: Continuous Liquidity for Cryptographic Tokens through Their Smart Contracts*, 2017.

and organizations. This constitutes a push towards the distributed, decentralized ethos first pioneered by Bitcoin.

5.6 USDT: Stable Arrangement Anchored to Legal Currencies

5.6.1 The Second Sophia Dilemma

By holding bitcoin, Sophia will face a great challenge: this cryptocurrency shows high volatility in price against fiat currencies. Bitcoin and Ethereum are algorithmically generated and lack any underlying assets, which has led to significant disagreement among professional investors regarding their "intrinsic value" and how to assess this value. Well-known investor Warren Buffett has considered Bitcoin a "gambling device" or "rat poison squared." While Buffett's understanding may not necessarily be appropriate, it does highlight the great controversy surrounding the intrinsic value of Bitcoin among the world's top professional investors.[11]

It is noteworthy that on January 10, 2024, the U.S. SEC, after previously rejecting more than 20 filings since 2018, approved eleven spot bitcoin exchange-traded product (ETP) shares. However, on the same day, SEC Chair Gary Gensler stated, "While we approved the listing and trading of certain spot bitcoin ETP shares today, we did not approve or endorse bitcoin." He further emphasized that "*bitcoin is primarily a speculative, volatile asset.*"[12]

How Volatile is the Price of Bitcoin? The value of bitcoin is extremely volatile. In the early stages of its development (2011), its price surged 40 times in just two months, reaching $30 per bitcoin from $0.75. However, by February 2012, it had plummeted to under $2, a decline of over 93%. A significant fluctuation occurred on November 21, 2019, with a 7% price drop within 24 hours. In comparison, a daily fluctuation of 1% in major national currencies and 2%-3% in major stock market indices is considered substantial.

It will be seen in the next chapter that the volatility of Bitcoin, based on long-term analysis of various asset price fluctuations, is generally ten times higher than that of major currencies, three to five times higher than that of precious metals, three to five times higher than that of stock markets, and three times higher than that of crude oil. In other words, Bitcoin is extremely unstable, surpassing that of major existing currencies by an order of magnitude and significantly exceeding the extreme volatility of major risk assets. Consequently, Bitcoin seems to fail to properly serve as a reliable means of value store, and parties involved in transactions are unable to agree on future goods and services priced in bitcoin.

---

[11] Li, Yun. "Warren Buffett Says Bitcoin Is a 'Gambling Device' with 'a Lot of Frauds Connected with It.'" CNBC, May 4, 2019. https://www.cnbc.com/2019/05/04/warren-buffett-says-bitcoin-is-a-gambling-device-with-a-lot-of-frauds-connected-with-it.html.

[12] Chair Gary Gensler. "Statement on the Approval of Spot Bitcoin Exchange-Traded Products," January 10, 2024. https://www.sec.gov/news/statement/gensler-statement-spot-bitcoin-011023.

5.6.2 USDT: A Fiat Reserve Solution

While BANCOR followed the path paved by Bitcoin to address the challenges of unstable currency value and cross-currency transactions through a decentralized trading network, USDT took a contrasting approach. By utilizing real-world assets as reserves and issuing USDT in proportion to these reserves, USDT offers a solution to the Second Sophia Dilemma. This can be seen as a better solution in many ways:

- USDT is backed by the US dollar, resulting in near-zero volatility between USDT and the US dollar. From a real-world perspective, USDT no longer experiences price fluctuations when measured against the internationally accepted currency, the US dollar. In contrast, BANCOR only stabilizes the currency value within the virtual currency world, and in reality, BNT still experiences significant fluctuations against legal currencies.
- USDT bridges the gap between the virtual and real worlds, acting as a medium for value exchange between the two. BANCOR, on the other hand, remains limited to transactions within the virtual currency realm, requiring centralization for virtual-to-fiat currency exchanges.

USDT, however, represents a return to the traditional financial order and a significant departure from the decentralized paradigm set by Bitcoin from two aspects:

- USDT relies on real-world assets as reserves and on third-party credit. It needs to entrust its US dollar assets to financial institutions, and the issuer must honor its obligation to maintain sufficient reserves and prevent embezzlements. We find that this trust in human beings is unreliable, and the ongoing legal investigations and litigations involving USDT are a powerful illustration of this issue.
- USDT has reduced decentralization. If we consider the three aspects of issuance, trading, and clearing/settlement, the issuance process of USDT is centralized, while Bitcoin, Ethereum and BNT are all automatically issued by algorithms, thus achieving decentralization in all three aspects.

5.6.3 The Mechanism of USDT

1. Centralized Issuance Backed by the US Dollar as a Reserve

Tether Ltd. has issued USDT since 2014, which is currently the most widely circulated stablecoin. Tether claims that each USDT it issues is backed by one US dollar held in reserve at a bank, and Tether appoints a custodian bank to manage the US dollar assets. When Tether receives a USD deposit, it entrusts the assets to the custodian for safekeeping and simultaneously issues an equivalent amount of USDT.

During the issuance phase, USDT is centrally issued by Tether Ltd., and the company pledges its value – one USDT equals one dollar of Tether's liability.

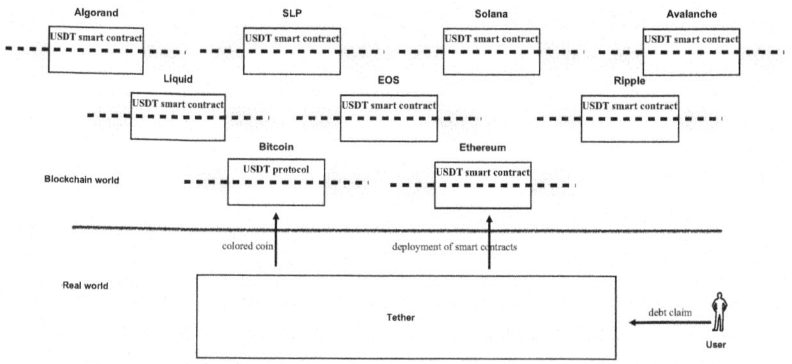

Fig. 5.12 The multi-chain issuance of USDT

However, in the trading phase, USDT remains decentralized, capable of undergoing peer-to-peer transactions in a distributed environment, where payment occurs simultaneously with clearance and settlement.

Tether also promises full redemption: at any time, it offers anyone holding USDTs the option to redeem one USDT for one US dollar from the company.

This type of stablecoin, compared to Bitcoin, represents a regression to traditional financial order. Unlike Bitcoin, which has no issuer, the issuance phase of USDT is centralized; Tether issues it based on credit, similar to a bank, and USDT represents a debt of Tether. However, in contrast to the significant fluctuations of bitcoin, the price of a stablecoin relative to fiat currency is fixed, providing advantages in virtual currency trading and payment activities, and making USDT a hedging tool and a general payment instrument for virtual currency users.

2. Multi-Chain Issuance

USDT does not have its own blockchain but is issued based on mainstream blockchains in the industry, such as Bitcoin and Ethereum. As a digital currency, USDT is peer-to-peer akin to the blockchains it resides on, and it supports smart contract programming, enabling functionalities like multi-signature (a feature both Bitcoin and Ethereum possess, which requires multiple signatures for payment authorization) and DEFI (Decentralized Finance). Taking the context where fiat currencies like the US dollar are not digitally supported and are under strict regulation, USDT finds a significant niche. Therefore, it is no surprise that, as of November 2021, the total USDT supply had reached approximately $75 billion.

As shown in Fig. 5.12, USDT is issued on 9 different blockchains. On November 14, 2021, the issuance figures of USDT on different blockchains were as follows:

- Bitcoin (via the Omni protocol)[13]: $1.335 billion

[13] The introduction of MasterCoin (later renamed as Omni) in the Bitcoin community in 2012 was a noteworthy innovation. It developed its own cryptocurrency by implementing a second-layer protocol on top of the Bitcoin protocol, a technique later referred to as colored coins. The issuance of USDT on the Bitcoin blockchain utilizes the colored coin technology pioneered by Omni.

- Ethereum: $37.833 billion
- TRON: $36.992 billion
- EOS: $85 million
- Liquid: $36.56 million
- Algorand: $74 million
- SLP: $6 million
- Solana: $1.14 billion
- Avalanche: $1 million

We should also note that USDT was initially built on the Bitcoin protocol and expanded to other chains later, primarily based on smart contracts. This allows USDT to facilitate transactions with various cryptocurrencies on different blockchains and to be used within the smart contracts of these chains.

3. Trust Crisis of USDT

USDT is issued in a centralized manner and therefore essentially represents the liability of its issuer, Tether Limited. Thus, the trustworthiness of USDT is based on users' trust in Tether Ltd. As previously mentioned, some studies have raised doubts about whether the issuer of this stablecoin has sufficient assets to back the currency. In fact, some issues surrounding Tether Ltd. have gradually come to light.

USDT has faced criticism for its opaque reserve holdings, arbitrary issuance, modification of user commitments, misappropriation of funds, and other concerns. Additionally, there are still various compliance issues with private digital currencies at this stage, and their interface with traditional banks is uncertain. USDT serves as a bridge for individuals to enter the digital currency field. If central banks of various countries launch their own digital currencies, the competitive advantage of stablecoins like USDT issued by private companies could diminish rapidly and significantly.

5.7 DGX: From Anchored Currency to Digitized Asset Ownership

5.7.1 Digitized Asset Ownership

In 2014, USDT was introduced as a stablecoin backed by US dollars, addressing the issue of price volatility, referred to as the "Second Sophia Dilemma" in this book (see Sect. 5.6.1). In 2016, Digix, a Singapore-based company, introduced DGX on the Ethereum blockchain, following a similar approach to USDT but with a different reserve asset: physical gold in equivalent proportions. With the support of this reserve asset, i.e., each unit of DGX representing a specific amount of physical gold, the problem of price volatility encountered in the "Second Sophia Dilemma" is mitigated. In this sense, DGX, like USDT, falls under the category of asset-backed stablecoins (as discussed in Sect. 3.2). It is noteworthy that while gold itself shows some degree of price fluctuation as an asset (since it is no longer considered a currency), this volatility is relatively low and gold still serves as a store of value (for more information on asset volatility, refer to Sect. 6.4 of this book).

Remarkably though, DGX's significance goes beyond being a stablecoin: it anchors assets in a physical form, enabling "asset blockchainization." Compared to fiat currency, physical assets rely more heavily on third-party credibility. Therefore, it is crucial to verify the authenticity of such assets, along with challenges associated with storage and delivery.

To establish DGX as a credible digital token of ownership, the most important task is to establish an indisputable connection between real-world assets and their "on-chain digital ownership." To fulfill this need, Digix has developed a "Proof of Provenance" for gold, which records all information related to the physical gold's production, logistics, storage, inspection, and auditing processes. The "Proof of Provenance" is distributedly executed by various stakeholders and recorded directly on the blockchain. While this still cannot solve the ultimate dilemma of "asset tokenization," it provides a partial solution that aims to minimize reliance on third-party trust. This approach has also been adopted by many similar projects.

5.7.2 Asset 'Blockchainization'

In 2016, DigixDAO issued the DGX token on Ethereum through a smart contract. Each DGX token represents one gram of gold, and the Singapore-based company Value Max provides certification, custody, and redemption of the gold provided on the platform.

DGX was one of the earliest stablecoins, predating Ethereum's ERC-20 token standard, which became one of the first successful applications on Ethereum. DGX is a stablecoin, with its value backed by physical gold and redemption guaranteed by an institution. This value guarantee requires the commitment of a credible third party, relying on their creditworthiness.

In contrast, Bitcoin and Ethereum are truly native digital currencies, whose value is not tied to any real-world assets. Stablecoins like DGX are pegged to tangible assets. Each DGX is a token within an Ethereum smart contract, yet it also represents one gram of gold held in Digix's vaults (refer to Fig. 5.13).

DGX represents physical gold, and the biggest challenge for such non-native digital assets is to prove their corresponding relationship with real-world assets. In other words, how can users holding DGX have trust in Digix that there is indeed one gram of gold stored in their vault? In traditional financial models, users rely on trust in third parties. If a reputable bank claims to have gold in their vault, users are inclined to believe it.

Now, in the context of blockchain, we have learned that minimizing reliance on third parties is a crucial aspect. The most important task in "asset blockchainization" is to establish an indisputable connection between physical assets and on-chain

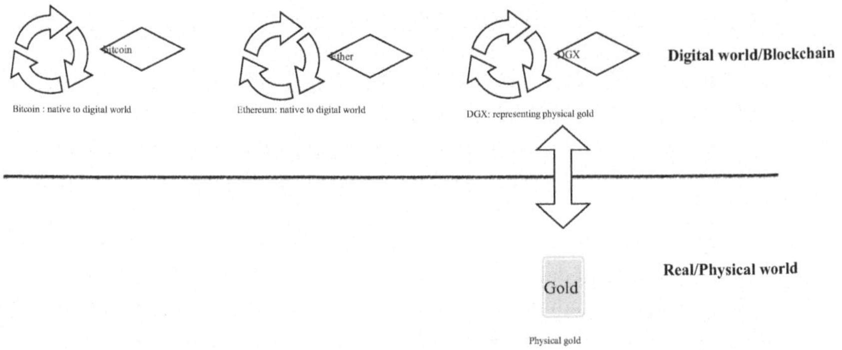

Fig. 5.13 DGX anchored to gold

digital ownership. Indeed, Digix has designed and developed a "proof of provenance" system for physical gold, recording all information related to the production, logistics, inventory, inspection, and auditing measures. This information is stored either as scanned copies of paper documents or as photos in a decentralized IPFS file system. The recording process is distributed, with different stages completing the records. Each stage is interconnected to ensure the integrity and coherence of the entire process, minimizing the possibility of fraudulent activities in any individual stage.

The types of information and documents in Digix's proof of provenance include:

- Gold asset information: details about gold bars, gold asset IDs, and historical information
- Gold inventory audit reports
- Gold inventory custody information: warehouse receipts, and gold quality inspection reports upon receipt
- Supplier information: supplier delivery receipts, photographs of physical gold, and analysis cards

Undoubtedly, despite the interconnected process that allows for mutual checks and supervision, these reports are still susceptible to falsification and collusion. If we continue to approach this issue with a blockchain mindset, the solution would be to expand the "on-chain" process. This means directly recording data from the gold production, logistics, and inspection phases onto the blockchain. The more processes that are recorded on the chain, the lower the possibility of collusion. Digix has stated that, to prevent collusion, they have implemented conflict of interest segregation among different participants in the supply chain. In other words, the same company can only be involved in one stage of the provenance process.

It is important to note that blockchain and digitization are not omnipotent. Even with detailed data recorded on the chain, "asset blockchainization" still faces a significant challenge. Physical assets must and can only be under the control of a third party. Regardless of the asset's value, a vault keeper always guards the entrance,

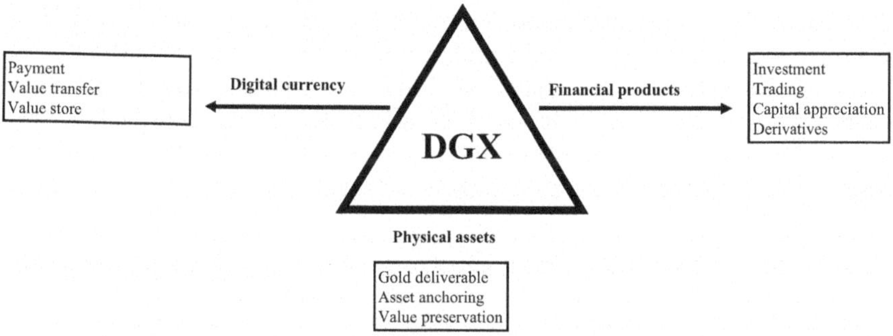

Fig. 5.14 The functions and attributes of DGX

exposing them to unforeseen risks such as theft, robbery, and fraud. In the blockchain context, we can borrow a phrase from Nick Szabo to explain the significance of asset blockchainization: "*While thugs can still take physical property by force, the continued existence of correct ownership records will remain a thorn in the side of usurping claimants.*"[14]

DGX indeed facilitates the purchase of gold, offering more convenience in the process than buying physical gold bars. Although it appears similar to "paper gold" or "gold ETFs" currently offered in the financial industry, DGX is more enriched in features and functionality in several ways:

- Transactions are more flexible, allowing purchases in quantities smaller than one gram.
- It offers the delivery of actual gold bars, fulfilling customer requests for physical gold. As of November 13, 2021, a total of 67 gold bars had been delivered to customers, as stated in DGX's asset listing.
- DGX can be freely transferred and exchanged for other virtual currencies on cryptocurrency exchanges.
- It can be used for payments, accepted at hundreds of businesses that support DGX.
- DGX is utilized in financial services like lending; Digix has developed lending and other financial services based on DGX.

DGX represents physical gold, but it is not simply a digital code for a set amount of gold. Rather, it is the digitization and abstraction of the value of gold. DGX, as a token, is a new creation with diverse functionalities and multiple attributes (refer to Fig. 5.14):

- It facilitates value transfer as a private digital currency.
- It corresponds to physical assets, allowing the acquisition of an equivalent amount of gold.
- It can be used as a financial product for investment purposes.

[14] Szabo, Nick. "Secure Property Titles with Owner Authority," 1998. http://szabo.best.vwh.net/securetitle.html. Also available at: https://www.fon.hum.uva.nl/rob/Courses/InformationInSpeech/CDROM/Literature/LOTwinterschool2006/szabo.best.vwh.net/securetitle.html.

As an attempt to meet the compliance requirement, Digix does not classify DGX as a security token, but has issued a separate token called DGD. It carries distinct equity features and represents ownership in Digix DAO, a decentralized autonomous organization founded by Digix. Investors can acquire DGD by investing in Ether, and holding DGD grants them entitlement to receive dividends from DGX transaction fees and participate in the governance of Digix DAO.

HOW TO UNDERSTAND THE SECURITY ATTRIBUTES OF DGX? Readers of Chapter 8 of this book may ponder whether DGX should be classified as a security token. This question raises concerns about variations in relevant laws across different countries. If we follow the analysis of the *Howey* test under US securities law, as discussed in Section 8.1, DGX would certainly be deemed a security. However, the official classification of DGX as a security token depends on the specific laws of each country.

For example, in Singapore, the regulatory authority has granted DGX a regulatory sandbox experiment license, allowing for a trial period before regulation. Based on our research of Singaporean laws up until December 2021, it remains unclear whether DGX should comply with securities regulation. Regarding this matter, interested readers may refer to the revised edition of "A Guide to Digital Token Offerings" issued by the Monetary Authority of Singapore (MAS) on May 26, 2020.

The idea of "asset blockchainization," as demonstrated by DGX, is crucial for unlocking the full potential of blockchain technology. It revolutionizes traditional assets by promoting faster transactions, improving circulation efficiency, and reducing trading costs. Yet, the major hurdle in advancing the blockchainization of assets lies in establishing trust and reliability for physical assets on digital platforms. Overcoming this challenge is a primary goal of digital technology. Furthermore, continuous efforts are needed to guarantee that business practices and functionalities align with regulations.

5.8 EOS: Not "Code is Law" but "Intent of Code is Law"

EOS has experimented with new governance models in two key areas. Firstly, it opposes the concept of "code is law," asserting that the "intent of code is law." EOS recognizes that code cannot perfectly capture the intentions of contract parties, and it emphasizes the need to articulate the intent of smart contracts in human language. Secondly, the system challenges the notion of "hashpower equals authority" by allowing token holders to vote for super nodes to govern the network.

5.8.1 The Issue at Hand: "Code is Law" Alone Cannot Solve the Challenges of Human Governance

The innovation of Bitcoin is manifested not only in its technological aspects but also in its design of community governance. This is best exemplified by the act of

Bhagwan Chowdhry, a finance professor at UCLA Anderson School of Management, who once nominated Satoshi Nakamoto for the 2016 Nobel Prize in Economics for the governance ideal of the Bitcoin community.[15]

1. Governance Ideal of the Bitcoin Community

Traditional Internet communities, regardless of size, always have an accountable entity - this may be a commercial company, a non-profit organization, or even an individual. This entity controls both the data generated within the community through Internet applications (such as social networking sites), and the code. As Tim Berners-Lee, the inventor of the World Wide Web, warns in his letter that users are losing control over their own data, while large Internet companies are establishing a hegemony over data.[16]

Bitcoin is not just a monetary system; it also explores the transformation of governance structures. The key distinction between cryptocurrency communities, such as Bitcoin, and Internet communities is that in the former, data produced by the community is collectively controlled by all participating nodes, with no single authority having power over it. As for the code, in most cryptocurrency communities, it is open-source and maintained by community developers in accordance with community rules.[17] Cryptocurrency communities are designed to achieve community autonomy, decentralize power, and form a community consensus to protect the property and fairness of users.

Regardless of political science or management science, establishing effective governance mechanisms is a perennial challenge for humans. Virtual currencies, represented by Bitcoin, attempt to achieve community self-governance. However, this ideal has not been fully realized and still faces various flaws that are continuously being explored and developed.

2. Bitcoin: The Game between "**Oligopolistic Politics**" and "**Dominance by the Powerful**"

The governance decision-making model of Bitcoin follows the principle of "code is law," where power equates to computational power. Maintainers and core developers hold the power of initiative, proposing code modifications, while miners possess direct voting power through their computational power and can ultimately influence maintainers and developers through voting. In this process, ordinary users (bitcoin holders) are excluded from direct voting and can only indirectly influence community governance by choosing to enter or leave the community.

---

[15] Coleman, Lester. "UCLA Finance Professor Nominates Satoshi Nakamoto For Nobel Prize." CCN.Com, 4 March 2021. https://www.ccn.com/ucla-finance-professor-nominates-satoshi-nakamoto-nobel-prize/.

[16] World Wide Web Foundation. "Three Challenges for the Web, According to Its Inventor." World Wide Web Foundation, 12 March 2017. https://webfoundation.org/2017/03/web-turns-28-letter/.

[17] Certainly, there are also some cryptocurrencies that are controlled by an entity such as a foundation or a company, which holds the power to develop the code. In such cases, from the perspective of code, cryptocurrency communities are no different from Internet communities.

The Group of Bitcoin "Maintainers." The decision-making power for the development of Bitcoin initially rested with Satoshi Nakamoto himself, who later transferred this authority to Gavin Andresen. Andresen first served as the "Maintainer" of the project. Subsequently, he decentralized the power by sharing it with four other individuals, creating a framework where the maintenance responsibilities were shared among the five members. Once a consensus was reached among the five individuals, they had the final authority to execute any code modifications. The earliest members include Gavin Andresen, Pieter Wuille, Wladimir van der Laan, Gregory Maxwell, and Jeff Garzik. However, in 2014, Gavin Andresen stepped away from his role, Wladimir van Der Laan taking over as the lead. From that time, the team changed again, with Wladimir van Der Laan, Jonas Schnelli, Marco Falke, and Samuel Dobson being in the maintainer group. In February 2023, Wladimir van Der Laan resigned and Michael Ford took over as the lead maintainer. Subsequently, the five members were Michael Ford, Hennadii Stepanov, Andrew Chow, Gloria Zhao, and Ryan Ofsky.[18]

In their decision-making process, the five maintainers consider the opinions of all developers in the open-source community to reach a consensus. Their power does not derive from a scepter or seal, but rather from a Trusted Key List document on GitHub.[19]

Bitcoin's 11-year development history has resulted in its current governance mechanism, which, although functioning smoothly, has experienced significant crises, controversies, and divisions. These issues stem from the gap between the ideal of self-governance and the reality of its implementation. The self-governance mechanism of the Bitcoin community faces two main concerns:

Firstly, the small group of maintainers and core developers can be influenced by vested interests, creating a characteristic similar to "**oligarchical politics**." Former maintainers, including Gregory Maxwell and Pieter Wiulle, were founders of the commercial company Blockstream, in which many core developers had vested interests. As a result, this company holds significant influence over the core developers, making it a key factor in triggering major controversies in Bitcoin's development, such as the "block scaling debate."

Bitcoin's blockchain scaling debate. So far, the greatest controversy in the Bitcoin ecosystem has been undoubtedly the debate over block size. The Bitcoin system set a block time of approximately 10 minutes per block, and the original "Bitcoin Core" version, created by Satoshi Nakamoto, set the block size limit at 1 megabyte, restricting Bitcoin's transaction capacity to a maximum of around 7 transactions per second. This limitation prevents Bitcoin from functioning as a retail payment system, and it forces to remain primarily an investment and store of value tool. (This limitation will be further analyzed in the next chapter.)

To address the above issue, two approaches have emerged within the Bitcoin community: one is to increase the block size, and the other is to use the Lightning Network for off-chain transactions. The second option seems to further increase the decentralization of the system.

These two approaches have sparked widespread debate within the Bitcoin ecosystem. A large group of mining operators support larger blocks because they allow for more transactions and rely on the increased computing power of larger mining machines (in a larger block scenario, running a full Bitcoin node on a regular home PC becomes excessively difficult).

[18] The history of maintainer changes can be found at https://github.com/bitcoin/bitcoin/commits/master/contrib/verify-commits.

[19] This document can be accessed at https://github.com/bitcoin/bitcoin/blob/master/contrib/verify-commits/trusted-keys.

In addition, larger blocks also generate higher transaction fees for miners. However, since the majority of mining operations were located in China at the time, with four of the world's five largest mining facilities located there, these mining facilities were concerned about potential disadvantages due to domestic and international network bandwidth limitations. As a result, while Chinese miners supported larger blocks, they welcomed only moderately sized block upgrade proposals and did not favor more radical approaches that would involve doubling the block size every two years.

Some core developers support larger blocks, too. For example, developers Gavin Andresen and Mike Hearn were strong advocates of larger blocks. In July 2014, Mike Hearn submitted BIP 64, a small P2P protocol extension that performs UTXO lookups given a set of outpoints, and followed up with an updated code version in October 2014. In July 2015, Gavin Andresen submitted BIP 101, which proposed an 8-megabyte block size in 2016, with the block size proposed to to double every two years until reaching 8 gigabytes in 2036. Core developer Jeff Garzik had actually proposed block size scaling back in 2010 during the Satoshi Nakamoto era. In 2015, he submitted BIP100, which set forth increasing the block size to 8 megabytes, which the operators of Chinese mining facilities were willing to accept.

However, Blockstream, a company with significant influence among Bitcoin developers, has focused on developing sidechain and lightning network technologies, both of which are competing scaling solutions to increasing block size. Core developers representing Blockstream, such as Gregory Maxwell and Pieter Wuille, along with Blockstream CEO Adam Back, opposed the large block proposal, and have put forward the "SegWit+Lightning" solution.

As Bitcoin's core developers split, supporters of larger blocks such as Gavin Andresen and Mike Hearn left the playing field. Eventually, this "civil war" within the Bitcoin community turned into a battle between mining operators and core developers, where miners demanded an increase in block size, while core developers opposed it.

Secondly, power is manifested in computing power. Similar to how large individual shareholders can influence the voting results at a publicly listed company's general meeting, some individuals who control a significant number of mining machines can play a prominent role in the voting process, creating a kind of "**dominance by the powerful**" characteristic.

3. Ethereum: The Game Between "Enlightened Despotism" and "Plutocracy"

After Bitcoin, Ether is the second largest cryptocurrency in terms of influence. Ethereum, the platform for Ether, operates under a founder dictatorship model, where the founder Vitalik Buterin holds the power to unilaterally modify the code, and no concept of "code is law" exists. Buterin did not choose to disappear; instead, he retains control of the Ethereum Foundation, which ultimately makes decisions within the Ethereum community. This effectively makes him the "monarch" of the community.

The Ethereum Foundation Changes the code unilaterally

In 2016, a smart contract called "The DAO" was launched on Ethereum. It functioned as an unmanaged venture capital fund where investors could contribute Ether to this smart contract. However, due to a vulnerability in the code, hackers gradually stole $160 million worth of Ether. The Ethereum community faced a significant dilemma: as the theft was the result of code execution, should they accept this outcome as part of the risk? Ultimately, the community decided to recover the massive loss by forking Ethereum. This can be essentially likened to abandoning an old contract and starting over. When two parties signing a contract, where party A inadvertently includes a clause that is disadvantageous to them, after incurring losses, party A unilaterally nullifies the contract to form a new one. This action significantly damaged the reputation of Ethereum and its leader, Vitalik Buterin, and also undermined the notion of "code is law."

However, Buterin does not rule with absolute power, but rather with an "enlightened despotism" approach. When making important decisions, the Ethereum Foundation generally "seeks public opinion," and users can cast votes based on the number of tokens they hold.

During the design phase, Ethereum deliberately addressed the risk of centralization of computing power. Its consensus algorithm, Ethash, requires a significant amount of memory, effectively nullifying the advantages of ASIC miners (which only compute SHA256 and do not require large amounts of memory). As a result, mining nodes within Ethereum become more decentralized, and the platform no longer relies on specialized mining equipment as Bitcoin does. Additionally, Ethereum's innovation lies in "smart contracts" and programmability. Using the Solidity language, developers can easily create new virtual currencies and contracts. Therefore, Ethereum is not only a "decentralized payment method" but also a "decentralized development platform," where "users" are more important than "computing power."

Under the "voting by token" structure, the influence on voting results depends on the number of tokens held. This allows wealthy entities, known as plutocrats or financial giants who possess a significant amount of ether, to exert control over voting outcomes. This method of voting by coin holdings, while different, does not address the issue of voter absence seen in the Bitcoin community. Instead, it introduces a new problem: the more ether one holds, the more influence they have. Therefore, in the Ethereum community, the modification of rules and regulations is ultimately decided by the plutocrats who own a significant number of tokens. Governance within the Ethereum community becomes a strategic game between the "monarch" (Vitalik Buterin) and the "plutocrats."

5.8.2 The Governance Mechanism of EOS

While Bitcoin and Ethereum use the Proof-of-Work (PoW) consensus algorithm where computing power determines authority, EOS adopts the Delegated Proof-of-Stake (DPoS) consensus algorithm that features representative democracy.

In the DPoS algorithm, all token holders cast votes to select 21 super nodes, which take turns in producing blocks. The consensus among these super nodes is achieved using the PBFT (Practical Byzantine Fault Tolerance) algorithm. If a super node fails to fulfill its responsibilities, it can be replaced by a backup node.

PROOF OF WORK (PoW). Similar to the direct democracy system of ancient Athens, this grants every node the right to participate in the governance of public affairs. In a blockchain, these affairs are centered around bookkeeping. Within PoW, the method to determine which node gets to record transactions is comparable to a dice-rolling contest. The node that "wins" the roll gets to do the bookkeeping, while other nodes supervise the compliance of the record keeping process. However, PoW has two flaws, as discussed earlier:

1. Voting in PoW is based on computational power, giving significant weight to large mining farms.

2. PoW adopts a competitive bookkeeping approach where all nodes repetitively engage in the competition, leading to excessive energy consumption.

PROOF OF STAKE (PoS). This sets an electoral process based on tokens held by participating nodes in the ecosystem. Mining rights are determined by election. This approach offers clear advantages, most notably the promotion of energy conservation, as it does not necessitate the participation of all members in competitive mining. However, a drawback is that individuals with greater holdings have a higher likelihood of being selected, potentially resulting in the concentration of power known as "plutocracy," where the wealthiest individuals hold the greatest authority. We can draw a parallel here with companies where PoS consensus enables shareholders to directly decide on production and operations, favoring the interests of major shareholders.

DPoS replicates the representative democracy model of political governance within the blockchain. Under the DPoS consensus, super nodes are elected to act as the management team in a company or as elected officials in representative democracy, such as a president and senators. In contrast, PoS enables direct governance by token holders based on their holdings, similar to shareholders and voters directly influencing governance matters.

The DPoS consensus mechanism of EOS involves all token holders voting to elect the 21 super nodes responsible for bookkeeping. The introduction of representative democracy in this process serves two purposes. Firstly, it improves efficiency by avoiding the need for direct democratic decision-making involving all participants, which may have been feasible in ancient city-states like Athens but is rather impractical in modern large-scale communities with millions of people, leading to low execution efficiency. Secondly, it guards against the lack of governance expertise among the general public or actions driven by the malicious manipulation of emotions (refer to Fig. 5.15).

When comparing consensus algorithms in blockchain, as previously analyzed for Ethereum, PoS (Proof of Stake) inherently tends to facilitate "plutocracy," where the wealthiest individuals have the greatest power. In contrast, DPoS (Delegated Proof of Stake) separates wealth from the right to keep records. Different consensus mechanisms lead to a variety of governance concepts and mechanisms:

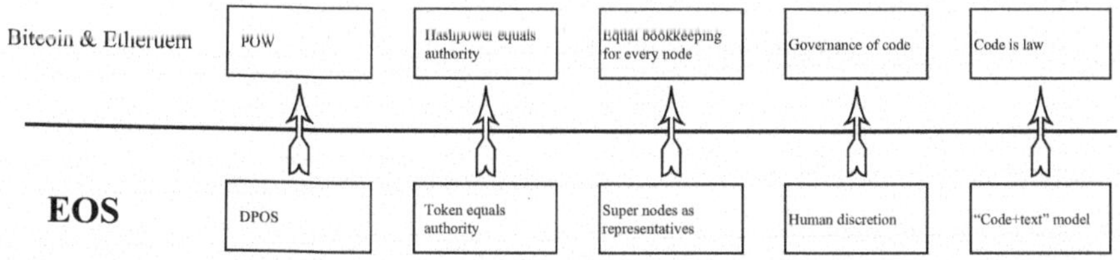

Fig. 5.15 The governance mechanism of EOS

First, the distinction between "hashpower equals authority" and "token equals authority." In the PoW (Proof of Work) mechanism of Bitcoin and Ethereum, hashpower equals authority, placing the right to keep records under the control of powerful mining operations. Developers also write code, while this requires miner voting to take effect. Critics of this mechanism argue that miners do not represent users, so why should they have such power? Meanwhile, proponents of PoS (Proof of Stake) and DPoS (Delegated Proof of Stake) prefer to give power to token holders, i.e., the users.

The power of token holders is not only reflected in the bookkeeping but also affects the use of EOS. In Bitcoin and Ethereum, the speed of transaction processing by miners is determined by the transaction fee, similar to prioritizing those who tip more. In EOS, the speed is determined by the CPU, memory and bandwidth owned by the token holders; simply put, the more you deposit, the faster your transaction.

Second, the method of bookkeeping. In the peer-to-peer networks of Bitcoin and Ethereum, all nodes are equal in record keeping based on a competition of hashpower and luck, sacrificing efficiency for decentralization. In contrast, DPoS entrusts record keeping to 21 super-nodes, focusing on collaboration rather than competition, which is more efficient but has been criticized for compromizing decentralization.

Third, human discretion. Bitcoin and Ethereum operate on a "code is law" principle. Once a need is identified, coded by the developer community and agreed upon by miners, it must be executed, and such transactions on the chain cannot be altered by anyone. However, EOS allows super-node arbitration of certain controversial transactions, which means that the results generated by the EOS chain code can be changed. Important parameters on the EOS chain, such as block size and block production speed, are adjusted through voting by "representatives" elected by token-holding users.

Fourth, dispute resolution. Bitcoin and Ethereum adhere to "code is law," but EOS does not believe that code can fully articulate human will. Therefore, it adopts a "code plus text" model, attaching Ricardian contracts to each smart contract code to represent human intent. In the event of a dispute, these Ricardian contracts can be used for community arbitration to be decided by arbitrators.

For example, if Sophia holds EOS cryptocurrency and loses her EOS private key, she can still recover it. In addition, if Sophia deploys a smart contract on EOS for air conditioner purchases and obtains agreements from community members, when disputes arise, such as the air conditioner does not meet the expected quality and the contract automatically executes payment, Sophia can file a lawsuit based on the Ricardian text contract attached to the smart contract.

5.8.3 Good Governance: The Perennial Dilemma in Political Philosophy

As we have seen, in terms of governance mechanisms, autonomous communities realized through blockchain technology still face significant challenges, such as the concentration of decision-making power and the difficulty for ordinary users to have a voice. However, it is still too early to discuss their successes, failures, advantages, and disadvantages. In the end, finding the right balance in governance mechanisms remains a perennial dilemma in political philosophy.

The self-governance of the cryptocurrency community lacks previous experience to draw on. Yet, over the past decade, spontaneously formed orders have helped Bitcoin and Ethereum become financial systems worth hundreds of billions of dollars. These are large global communities formed without coercive violence, supported by a spontaneously established order.

From a dynamic perspective of the monetary system, a decade may still be too short. One should not deny the power of competition and evolution because of temporary governance challenges. After all, cryptocurrency users have the right to "vote with their feet." The long-term presence of private competition can, through repeated trial and error, eventually lead to fortuitously successful governance models. A good example of the potential for improvement by voting with one's feet is the famous Bitcoin block size debate that led to a successful fork.

Economic communities based on cryptography and blockchain represent a new model of economic cooperation beyond the corporate model. The exploration of cryptocurrency communities targets a valuable accumulation of experience that challenges the data control rights of large Internet companies and provides an alternative model for the future development of the Internet.

5.9 Diem: Yielding to the Order of Reality

5.9.1 Diem: A Huge Potential Impact

In 2018, social media giant Facebook revealed that it was exploring and developing blockchain technology. On June 28, 2019, the American tech giant officially released a whitepaper on "Libra" (now known as Diem), announcing its foray into the realm of digital currency. Diem is a stablecoin that was originally planned to be pegged to a basket of fiat currencies but was later revised to be tied to the U.S. dollar. Amidst strong opposition from the U.S. Congress and regulators, Libra faced a rebranding to Diem in 2020, which is planned to be operated independently by the Diem Association and has yet to launch for the public.

Diem aims to become a global currency, provide inclusive financial services to its 2.7 billion (and potentially more) users, and build the world's largest financial infrastructure. The tech giant's grand ambition dwarfs private digital currencies such as Bitcoin and Ethereum, which began in the cryptography community initiated by cypherpunks with grassroots participation.

Facebook, a giant in the tech industry with a market value of over $500 billion and a global user base of 2.7 billion people, has a significant technological reservoir. Imagine a day when Facebook's all users transact with Diem, not only crossing international borders but also potentially replacing letters of credit in current international trade with smart contracts, thereby overcoming the uncertainties of cross-border trade; then, Diem could even replace international commercial arbitration in resolving customer disputes. Let us think about it: what other currency could be so widely and conveniently used, or what government could settle global trade disputes so effectively?

Chapter 10 of this book conceptualizes the "Republic of Supremacy" that wields a globally recognized digital currency. By controlling currency, this Republic has direct control over individuals transcending sovereign borders., and it essentially exerts coercive power through arbitration and judicial decisions Similarly, if Diem operates the monetary transactions of the 2.7 billion customers of Facebook, Facebook-Diem will be a new pontiff in the digital age, just like the Republic of Supremacy.

5.9.2 *The Centralized Path of Diem: Comprehensive Compromise with the Order of Reality*

If Bitcoin represents complete decentralization, then Diem has chosen a centralized approach, as a reflection on the failed monetary functions of Bitcoin (as will be discussed in Chap. 6) and a compromise with the order of reality (see Table 5.5).

1. Diem is Based on Fiat Currency Asset Reserves

In terms of the currency issuance mechanism, Diem is based on fiat currency as a backing asset, which gives it intrinsic value. Initially, Libra had a basket of fiat

Table 5.5 Comparison between bitcoin and diem

	Bitcoin	Diem	Issues to be addressed by Diem
Currency Creation	Mining (computing power contribution)	Collateral legal currency reserve	Volatile value
Participation Mechanism	Public chain (unlimited participating nodes)	Consortium chain (limited to 100 licensed nodes)	Insufficient capacity for everyday payments
Organizational Form	Autonomous community	Operated by Diem Association, managed and ultimately controlled by Diem Committee	Drawbacks of autonomous order

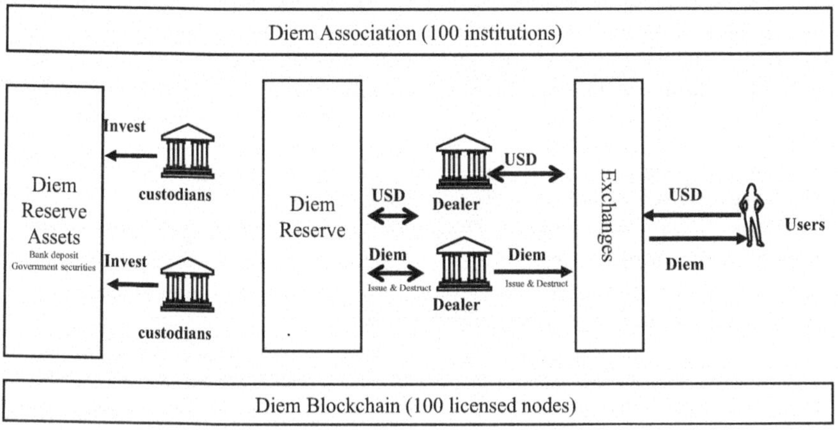

Fig. 5.16 The framework of diem

currencies such as the US dollar as reserve assets, with the value of Libra tied to the value of the respective fiat assets. However, following its rebranding to Diem, this approach shifted to issuing single-currency stablecoins, such as ≋USD, ≋EUR, and ≋GBP, in addition to a multi-currency coin, ≋XDX.

In contrast, Bitcoin is derived from mining or the contribution of computing power, where the more computing power provided to the system, the more bitcoin is earned. As such, Bitcoin's value is independent of fiat currency and has its own system. In contrast, the pegging of Diem to fiat currency reflects a realist approach and acts as a critique and self-reflection on the instability of Bitcoin's value. By pegging to fiat currency, Diem addresses the issue of the volatile value of virtual currencies. This is essentially the same approach as the previously mentioned USDT (see Fig. 5.16).

Regarding earlier stablecoins such as USDT, many questions have been raised by academics and industry about the adequacy of their reserve assets. It can be stated that the adequacy of a stablecoin's reserve assets is a critical element for its value stability. Consequently, Diem has established a dedicated reserve management policy.

5.9.3 Diem Adopts a Centralized Governance Mechanism

Unlike the autonomous governance mechanism of the Bitcoin community, the governance structure of Diem is centralized: decision-making and management authority is exercised by the Diem Committee, which was set to initially consist of 100 members with equal voting rights, and the Diem Association being responsible for operations.

In terms of the participation mechanism, Diem operates as a permissioned chain (consortium chain) with only 100 limited nodes possessing voting rights. This is similar to the decision-making mechanism of limited original shareholders in non-publicly listed companies. In contrast, Bitcoin operates as a public chain, allowing anyone to participate in the ledger and perform decision-making without restrictions. Therefore, in theory, any node contributing computing power to bitcoin becomes a shareholder, similar to buying shares in publicly traded companies where capital contributions grant shareholder status.

> Based on accessibility, blockchain can be categorized into three types: public chain, private chain, and permissioned chain (also known as consortium chain).
>
> A PUBLIC CHAIN, such as Bitcoin and Ethereum, can accommodate unlimited nodes, and unknown nodes can freely join.
>
> A PRIVATE CHAIN is a blockchain solely owned and operated by enterprises, organizations or individuals, with a limited number of known nodes.
>
> A PERMISSIONED CHAIN, also known as a CONSORTIUM CHAIN, requires permission and identity verification before unknown nodes can join. It adds a governance layer to the blockchain to govern the behavior of participating nodes.
>
> Permissioned chains are known for their high efficiency, data privacy protection, and regulatory advantages. If permissioned chains can balance the essential characteristics of blockchain, such as "unlimited nodes" and the "free joining of unknown nodes," and meet regulatory requirements, they may become the mainstream in the future development of blockchain.

From an organizational perspective, Diem is managed by a dedicated association responsible for daily operations, with decision-making and management authority exercised by a specialized committee. Conversely, Bitcoin's open participation mechanism forms a community-driven autonomous order without a fixed organizational structure or management institution.

The participation mechanism and organizational form of Diem represent a deep reflection on the shortcomings of decentralized governance in virtual currency communities. Diem's whitepaper states that although its visionary ideal is a public chain, the decentralized decision-making model of public chains fails to provide the necessary scale, stability and security for billions of people worldwide to engage in transactions.

Modern centralized settlement systems, such as electronic banking, have effectively addressed the security and speed requirements of electronic payments in retail transactions. To this end, Bitcoin's system currently lacks the capacity to support large-scale everyday retail transactions.

Given the present context, Diem's governance mechanism operates under a centralized management framework, jointly controlled by a select group of original members, often large companies. In this sense, Diem represents an extension of the power held by national fiat currencies, with these companies harnessing new technologies to facilitate transactions. While Bitcoin symbolizes an "autonomous order," Diem can be considered a "semi-autonomous order" that confines participation in governance to a limited number of original members.

5.9.4 Compliance Dilemma: The Key Challenges for Diem

Facebook was the first major Internet company to enter the world of virtual currency. While Diem may not have made significant advancements or innovations in its model and technology, it has exerted sufficient influence to spark a global financial revolution and transformation, attracting the attention of regulators in different countries. Whether it is regulators' concerns about compliance or the public's concerns about privacy, Diem is surrounded by skepticism. As a result, the initiators of Diem agree that ensuring compliance is their primary responsibility. By exploring effective ways to collaborate with regulators, they are determined to create a viable path towards digital currency compliance.

On October 23, 2019, the U.S. House Financial Services Committee held a hearing on Facebook that, to be accurate, rather resembled a critical assembly. Representatives delivered scathing criticisms of Facebook, highlighting its past transgressions such as racial discrimination and privacy violations, while raising questions about the potential impact of Libra's launch.[20] Committee chair Maxine Waters subsequently drafted the "Keep Big Tech Out of Finance Act," which aims to prohibit large platforms like Facebook from obtaining financial licenses or engaging in financial activities.[21]

Behind the strong opposition from lawmakers is a wariness of super-private corporations that is rooted in America's founding principles. The anti-trust laws of the twentieth century, for example, are a direct reaction from this caution. Second, despite their significant impact, Bitcoin and Ethereum have not altered the existing fiat currency system (either in terms of transaction speed or ability to shake the fiat system, as we will discuss in Chap. 6). In contrast, Diem has the daunting potential to become the "Republic of Supremacy," an entity that could supersede sovereignty.

Following Mark Zuckerberg's congressional testimony, senior U.S. government and Federal Reserve officials have also expressed concerns about Libra. As a result, several major partners (PayPal, Visa, Mastercard, eBay, Stripe, and Mercado Pago) withdrew from the project within months.

Libra had initially planned to obtain a payment system license from the Swiss Financial Market Supervisory Authority (FINMA). However, in late 2019, Swiss President Ueli Maurer stated that the central bank would not accept Libra's reserve system, which featured a basket of currencies. Thus, Libra's compliance plans in Switzerland failed and the project returned to the United States. It was subsequently rebranded to Diem to emphasize its independence, and the reserve scheme was modified to anchor only the U.S. dollar or a single currency.

The launch date for Diem has been pushed back several times due to regulatory challenges. The pilot launch of a stablecoin pegged to the US dollar, originally planned for 2021, has not been successful as of November 2021. In October 2021,

[20] The full text can be found on the House of Representatives website: https://docs.house.gov/Committee/Calendar/ByEvent.aspx?EventID=110136.

[21] The full text can be found on the House of Representatives website: https://financialservices.house.gov/news/documentsingle.aspx?DocumentID=404479.

Facebook launched a small pilot of its digital wallet Novi in the United States and Guatemala, but it used the digital currency Paxos and worked with Coinbase. Facebook has stated that Novi will be promoted alongside Diem once it receives regulatory approval. In response, some senators have called for a halt to the Novi pilot project.

Cryptocurrencies originated at the grassroots level when compliance was not a concern for the creators, some of whom openly challenged the authority of the existing monetary order. However, a trend towards the widespread adoption of new technologies often leads to a compromise between opposing forces. A multitude of cryptocurrencies will inevitably move towards compliance, a trajectory determined by the advanced technology inherent to cryptocurrencies. Their goal is not to challenge for the sake of challenge, but to bring better technology and innovative models. However, the road to compliance will be long and arduous, testing the patience of both innovators and regulators.

5.10 Grin, Zcash: The Peak of Anonymity

5.10.1 Dilemma in the Bitcoin Design: Anonymous User but Transparent Ledger

Bitcoin operates on a public blockchain, where any node can join the network anonymously. However, the blockchain ledger is transparent, making all transactions between nodes publicly accessible (see Fig. 5.17).

- To protect privacy, Bitcoin uses asymmetric encryption, with public keys designated for receiving funds and private keys for signing payments. This is referred to as cryptocurrency, where encryption is used for "signatures" rather than "data encryption."
- In order to prevent double-spending fraud in a peer-to-peer network, Bitcoin must make all transaction records available to all mining nodes for verification (maintaining consistent accounting through consensus algorithms). As a result, the transaction ledger becomes transparent and traceable through analysis.

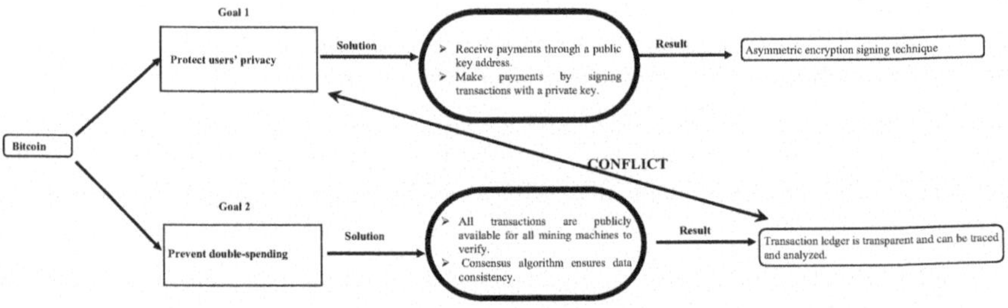

Fig. 5.17 The bitcoin design dilemma

- In other words, Bitcoin can protect the privacy of its users because it operates using public and private keys without requiring the collection of personally identifiable information, which is common practice in traditional banking. Bitcoin uses asymmetric encryption signatures to protect and circulate value in a peer-to-peer environment, rather than encrypting the information itself. Therefore, despite being called a cryptocurrency, Bitcoin does not provide complete privacy protection.
- Since the early days of Bitcoin, the digital currency community and researchers have both discovered that it is possible to analyze the transaction ledger of cryptocurrencies like Bitcoin to trace the owners and the flow of transactions.
- If Sophia owns bitcoin, no one would actually know that her public key address belongs to her. However, all of her bitcoin transactions are recorded in plain text on the blockchain, visible to everyone. By analyzing these transaction data, it is actually possible to trace the movement of bitcoin. In addition, centralized exchanges must comply with anti-money laundering regulations that require the disclosure of users' true identities. When Sophia transfers bitcoin from the blockchain to an exchange, a relationship is established between her and the public address she used. By consolidating Sophia's real identity information provided during the registration process on centralized exchanges, it becomes possible to link her actual identity to specific blockchain addresses. This makes it feasible to track Sophia's transaction activities on the blockchain.

Extensive efforts are being made to link anonymous public addresses to the real identities of users. A notable case is that of Satoshi Nakamoto, whose address contains approximately 1 million bitcoins. The fact that this address belongs to Nakamoto raises the possibility of uncovering his elusive identity if the bitcoins of this address are ever used. Similarly, when a cryptocurrency exchange is hacked, criminal investigators track the addresses that receive funds transferred from the centralized exchange. For this reason, some blockchain security companies extensively collect bitcoin addresses that are publicly available on the dark web. They make connections between these addresses and continuously monitor them to assist law enforcement in investigating cases and tracking criminal activities. In Chap. 8, we delve into further discussing the trend towards transparent blockchain under the pressure of global AML regulation.

5.10.2 Zero-Knowledge Proofs: Complete Anonymity

To reconcile the dilemma between user privacy and the prevention of double spending, cryptocurrencies such as Grin employ zero-knowledge proof technology to achieve user anonymity and an opaque ledger. In 2016, discussions about improving Bitcoin's encryption protocol were instigated within the Bitcoin community, led by figures such as Andrew Poelstra. This culminated in the release of the Grin Whitepaper in 2017, which detailed Grin's algorithms and protocols. The Grin

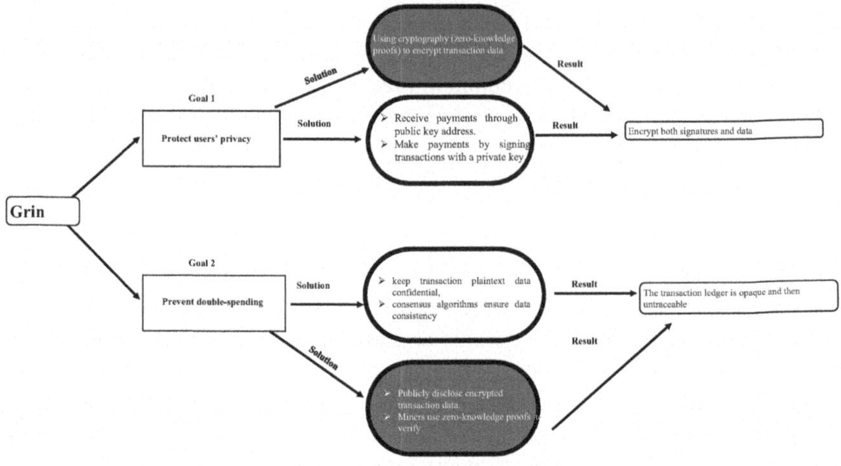

Fig. 5.18 The way of zero-knowledge proofs

mainnet went live on January 16, 2019. Cryptocurrencies such as Grin represent a complete form of encryption, addressing the privacy concerns inherent to Bitcoin and taking privacy protection to the maximum level.

As shown in Fig. 5.18, the core technology behind Grin is the zero-knowledge proof from the field of cryptography. Transactions processed using this technology result in ciphertext, which is then posted to the blockchain. Based on this ciphertext, miners can verify the balance and other transaction details. For example, if Sophia pays 2 Grin to Bob's address, the data submitted to the public ledger is encrypted; however, computing nodes can verify that Sophia's signature is correct and that no double spending has occurred.

> WHAT IS ZERO- KNOWLEDGE PROOF? In 1989, S. Goldwasser, S. Micali and C. Rackoff introduced the concept of zero-knowledge proof in a research paper, which later played a significant role in cryptography.
>
> In a zero-knowledge proof, two or more parties are involved: the prover and the verifier. The prover aims to demonstrate to the verifier that they possess a specific knowledge or statement without disclosing any information about it.
>
> For instance, let us consider an example involving our fictional Sophia and Alex. Sophia wants to prove to Alex that she knows the route from the Forbidden City to the Temple of Heaven. Instead of simply pointing at it on a map, which would instantly reveal the route to Alex, Sophia can use a different method. They both depart from the Forbidden City while Sophia drives to the Temple of Heaven, with Alex closing his eyes along the way. Upon reaching the destination, Alex can confirm that Sophia knows the route without gaining any knowledge of the specific route herself. In this way, Sophia successfully proves her knowledge without revealing any information about the route during the process.

In 2019, another cryptocurrency called Zcash was launched, setting similar goals as Grin but employing a more complex zero-knowledge proof protocol known as zkSNARK.[22] The zkSNARK protocol is based on the Bulletproof scheme released in 2017, offering a non-interactive and concise zero-knowledge proof solution.[23] However, compared to Grin, it relies more heavily on advanced cryptography.

Cryptocurrency technologies like Grin and Zcash address the limitations of transparent blockchain systems by significantly enhancing privacy protection during digital transactions. As an effective means to strengthen privacy in digital currencies, Zero-knowledge Proofs are expected to be widely adopted in the future.

Virtual currencies like Grin, which prioritize transaction privacy, pose challenges to supervision-evading regulatory efforts within the virtual currency community. However, it should be noted that virtual currencies employing Zero-knowledge Proofs are not inherently in conflict with regulation. In fact, those willing to comply with regulations can still implement measures to ensure regulatory compliance while addressing privacy concerns.

[22] See Hopwood, Daira, Sean Bowe, Taylor Hornby, et al., "Zcash protocol specification." GitHub: San Francisco, CA, USA, 4, 220(2016): 32.

[23] See Bünz, Benedikt, Jonathan Bootle, Dan Boneh, Andrew Poelstra, Pieter Wuille, and Greg Maxwell. "Bulletproofs: Short Proofs for Confidential Transactions and More." *2018 IEEE Symposium on Security and Privacy (SP)*, 2018, 315–334. See also Gennaro, Rosario. "Quadratic Span Programs and Succinct NIZKs without PCPs." *Advances in Cryptology–EUROCRYPT 2013: 32nd Annual International Conference on the Theory and Applications of Cryptographic Techniques, Athens, Greece, May 26–30, 2013*, Springer Berlin Heidelberg, 2013, Proceedings 32.

Chapter 6
Private Digital Currencies: A Failed Social Experiment?

Considering both their technological innovations and inherent limitations, can cryptocurrencies truly fulfill the roles and functions of a reliable and widely accepted medium of exchange for the public on a larger scale? If the answer is negative, does it mean that cryptocurrencies like Bitcoin have no value? Has the social experiment of private digital currencies failed?

Cryptocurrencies have made significant technological strides since their inception, whereas their potential to become reliable and widely accepted mediums of exchange has been hindered by slow transaction speeds, high costs, and substantial price volatility. These factors limit their practical use in everyday transactions, where they are more often viewed as speculative assets than feasible mediums of exchange.

Despite the inability of Bitcoin to serve as a public payment tool, as well as its current high volatility, it does not necessarily lack value in the long term. Often referred to as "digital gold," Bitcoin shares several of its characteristics with gold, such as scarcity and decentralization, which may allow it to serve as an effective store of value, particularly in an environment of excessive fiat currency issuance.

Private digital currencies may not have not succeeded as widely accepted payment tools for the public on a large scale, however, they have sparked a technological revolution through blockchain technology, significantly reshaping economic and social structures. This ongoing social experiment suggests that although virtual currencies may have failed as monetary instruments, they hold significant potential as technological innovations and stores of value.

6.1 Overview

Karl Popper argued that the main attribute of a theory for being scientific is its "falsifiability." Thus, physics is considered a "standard" and "true" science, because the scientific community can discover and test scientific theories through controlled

Y. Wu and W. Zhu, *The Fundamentals of Digital Currency*,
https://doi.org/10.1007/978-981-97-8261-1_6

experiments. Natural sciences are similar in this way. However, social sciences cannot treat society as a laboratory to verify a certain theory, so they often involve conflicting perspectives.

Nevertheless, human society occasionally "presents" us with unplanned social experiments. For example, the hyperinflation phenomena in the Weimar Republic of Germany after World War I and the Nationalist Government-controlled areas of China after World War II provided economists with exceptional real-life social experiments to verify the relationship between the money supply and inflation.

Certainly, these examples also teach us that if "social engineering" fails, the consequences can be disastrous. Therefore, our understanding of social phenomena often relies on observing, summarizing and analyzing existing historical phenomena, and that we should highly value spontaneous social experiments that social activities naturally present us with.

The birth of Bitcoin in 2009 marked the entry of virtual currency as a phenomenal event in the annals of history. To date, virtual currencies have reached a peak market capitalization of trillions of dollars, with daily trading volumes surpassing $160 billion in recent years. These figures far exceed the daily securities trading volume of China, the world's second-largest economy. Virtual currencies, as an experiment of private currency, have evolved from being isolated or sporadic occurrences into a grand social movement.

This chapter aims to scrutinize this social experiment and elucidate why virtual currencies have been deemed as failed "currencies." However, our ambition extends beyond discussing failure. We strive to explore how the advent of blockchain technology brought about by virtual currencies will reshape human society. We contend that while virtual currencies may have failed as an experiment in currency, they have nonetheless succeeded as technological innovations and can be regarded as elements of an ongoing social trial and error experiment that is yet to reach its conclusion.

6.1.1 A Failed Social Experiment of Private Currencies

The industry, academia and government once all had high hopes for virtual currencies, such as promoting inclusive finance and enabling smart contracts through their programmability. However, the original intention of virtual currencies to become an all-round form of currency has failed, rooted in their underlying technological means. After more than a decade of development, Bitcoin has neither become an effective currency nor a popular payment method; instead, it has developed into a speculative asset.

From the perspective of the functions of money, virtual currencies have been far from successful. Due to technical limitations such as limited capacity, they have slow transaction speeds and high costs, therefore cannot serve as a medium of exchange for the public and have not demonstrated the advantages of inclusive finance. For example, the average verification time for each Bitcoin transaction is 10 min, and during transaction congestion, it can take days or even longer to complete a transaction. Meanwhile, payment methods such as Alipay can complete payments within seconds. Bitcoin transaction fees range from a few cents to as high as 200 RMB during congested periods, while Chinese domestic online banking transfers have zero fees, and international remittance fees are only a few hundred RMB. Compared to existing online banking and third-party payment methods like Alipay and WeChat Pay, Bitcoin lacks convenience and the competitive edge of low cost.

On top of the above issues, due to speculation and severe price manipulation, virtual currencies have exhibited extremely high price volatility, with 3 to 5 times greater price fluctuations than typical risk assets, preventing them from becoming a reliable store of value. In the early stages of development, for instance, the price of a bitcoin rose 40-fold within two months in 2011, from $0.75 to $30. Meanwhile, in February 2012, its price plummeted at under $2, marking a decline of over 93%.

Having a bitcoin is akin to owning a small-cap stock without price limits, as its value fluctuates wildly on a daily basis. Imagine having a bitcoin worth $10,000 in the morning, only for it to drop to $8000 in the afternoon. Would you still consider it a reliable means of wealth storage?

Furthermore, the uncertainty surrounding the intrinsic value of virtual currencies has made them a prime target for various financial scams, turning them into a breeding ground for fraud. A glance at the registered or sentenced blockchain-related crimes in China reveals a shocking picture of the extent of this fraud. For example, the "Virtual Currency GGP Win–Win Points" project defrauded 320 million RMB within six months, while the "Blockchain Smart Arbitrage" scheme by PlusToken involved an astronomical amount of 20 billion RMB.

What is even more concerning is that virtual currencies possess a high risk of money laundering due to their anonymity and cross-border nature. It is no surprise that they have become essential tools for criminal and terrorist activities.

6.1.2 A Successful Technological Innovation

Although Bitcoin was created as a digital currency, it has also introduced a series of new technologies, including blockchain technology. While the idea of blockchain originated from virtual currencies, it is not limited to them and has expanded beyond their scope. **While virtual currencies themselves can be seen as a failed monetary experiment, they have given rise to a successful technological revolution that has influenced various aspects of economic and social structures, including value circulation, proof of rights, and business models.**

Firstly, the feasibility of value circulation is demonstrated by the success of the Bitcoin autonomous community that does not rely on trust in third parties and has allowed for the realization of decentralized commercial networks. Indeed, Bitcoin has spontaneously formed a market worth hundreds of billions of dollars without any external coercive intervention, proving its robustness.

Secondly, smart contracts running on blockchain technology have enabled data trustworthiness and strong consistency without the need for third-party involvement, making automated contract execution a possibility and enabling machine commerce to become reality. In a distributed and trustworthy operational environment like the blockchain, smart contracts written in code can be automatically executed by machines. These contracts can form virtual agreements, virtual business relationships and virtual enterprises, giving rise to a new form of business that allows machines to execute commercial contracts and facilitate value transfer according to trusted code rules.

We believe that the success of localized experiments in blockchain and smart contracts reflects the vast potential of this technology to transform business models and social structures, which is precisely the direction this book aims to explore and envision.

6.1.3 An Ongoing Social Experiment

From the perspective of dynamism, 10 years may be too short, and we cannot negate the power of competition and evolution based on temporary difficulties. Nevertheless, through repeated trial and error, unexpected successful governance models may eventually emerge.

To address the problems and deficiencies encountered in the virtual currency experiment, Facebook planned to launch Libra, attempting to mitigate the issues of intrinsic value insufficiency, low transaction capacity, and the drawbacks of autonomous communities through reserve assets and centralized management.

At the same time, many central banks are actively researching, demonstrating or experimenting with "central bank digital currencies" with the aim to strengthen the status of fiat currency while incorporating the advantages of virtual currency technology. In the field of currency, virtual currency represents an ongoing social experiment: it has led to a profound technological revolution with the potential to fundamentally disrupt existing business models and social structures. This provides the background for the introduction of central bank digital currencies, and we eagerly await to see what opportunities they will bring.

In conclusion, the ongoing social experiment with virtual currency provides us with excellent observation opportunities. Undoubtedly, we should not completely reject the innovations brought by virtual currencies and blockchain technology simply because of their failures in fulfilling the intended monetary function and the negative "side effects" they have produced. Instead, we should recognize that the technological innovations they have introduced possess the potential for revolutionary impacts on economic models and social structures.

6.2 Reflecting on the Original Intent of Bitcoin

As mentioned in Chap. 2 of this book, "currency" has generally become synonymous with "legal tender" or "legal currency." However, in reality, "currency" can refer to both legal tender and de facto currency, with the latter including both general equivalents (such as gold and silver) and ordinary tangible items (such as rice). The evolution of human currency has seen a transition from private to national currency, and national currencies have undergone a shift from the gold standard to pure credit currencies. With the development of modern nations, legal currency has become firmly established as the only recognized form of currency.

However, in the long history of currency development, legal currency is a relatively recent concept. In the early stages of civilization, general currency equivalents could be shells, gold, silver, etc., which later evolved into specially minted metal coins and printed paper banknotes. In the early stages of general equivalents and authorized minting, there were no fixed standards or official authorizations. The history of minting and printing currency has included stages of free minting, authorized minting, and unified minting. These early general equivalents and authorized minting can be considered different forms of private currency.

In the early Han Dynasty (206 BC to 220 AD) of China, private minting of coins was allowed, as seen under Emperor Gaozu (the founder and first emperor who reigned from 202 to 195 BC) with Han's policy of "permit the private minting." The "Edict on Counterfeit Coins" was issued during the reign of Emperor Hui (the second emperor who reigned from 195 to 188 BC), prohibiting the private minting of coins and taking back the government's coinage rights. During the reign of Emperor Wen (the fifth emperor who reigned from 180 to 157 BC), there was an attempt to open up private coinage again, which triggered a major discussion on the rights of coinage. After the Han Dynasty, hardly any authority was granted for private coinage. Between 1837 and 1866, it was completely allowed in the United States, inducing the widespread issuance of worthless "wildcat bank" currency. The regulation of banks began with the National Currency Act of 1863 and the National Bank Act of 1864, which restricted the right of banknote issuance to national banks. With the establishment of the Federal Reserve System in 1914 and the formation of the US dollar system, the private issuance of currency became illegal.

The Bretton Woods system set up in 1944 marked the inception of the first global monetary order in human history. Under this system, the value of the US dollar was tied to gold, while other currencies were linked to the US dollar as the global currency standard. However, in 1973, this system collapsed as a result of the escalating international imbalance of payments by the United States. Consequently, the US dollar could no longer redeemed for gold, leading to a worldwide era of credit-based currencies without an anchor. The disintegration of the Bretton Woods system coincided with a prolonged period of stagflation in capitalist economies, which sparked profound skepticism regarding the moral and rational aspects of capitalist currencies.

On the one hand, the unilateral decision of the US government to sever the link between the US dollar and gold was perceived as a major act of plunder against the global population. During the Bretton Woods era, individuals were inclined to hold US dollars due to it representing a value equivalent to gold. However, the defaulting US government shattered this notion, causing the US dollar to be devalued to mere green paper with no intrinsic worth. Under the Bretton Woods system, $35 equated to 1 oz of gold. By 1973, the collapse of this system resulted in the value of 1 oz of gold surging up to $140, and ballooning to as much as $590 within a span of 5 years.

On the other hand, the debasement of fiat currencies exacerbated the stagflation crisis in capitalist economies, leading to people questioning the ability of national currencies to maintain stable values and foster economic growth. This erosion of trust further challenged the moral legitimacy and effectiveness of capitalist monetary systems.

In this context, the renowned liberal thinker Friedrich August von Hayek (1899–1992) published "*The Denationalization of Money*" in 1976, which became an important source of ideas for virtual currencies today.[1] Following a consistent viewpoint, Hayek believed that governments were not to be trusted, as history had repeatedly demonstrated that government monopolies on goods led to inefficiency. He argued that government-monopolized currencies were no better than privately issued currencies. Hayek analyzed the history of government-issued currencies, all of which ended in government dishonesty and currency depreciation. He proposed that competition among private issuers of money was superior to government monopoly. In Hayek's model of private competition, creditors tend to favor gradually appreciating currencies, while debtors tend to prefer gradually depreciating currencies. The combined forces of both parties lead to the selection of a stable currency.[2]

The ideology behind Bitcoin is rooted in the Austrian School of Economics and was directly influenced by Hayek's "Denationalization of Money." According to Hayek's ideas, state intervention in currency leads to exacerbated economic cycles and widespread inflation. In his view, a competition among privately issued currencies would ultimately produce a stable currency, reducing economic fluctuations and inflation.

Amidst the countless challenges about the current fiat currency system, private currencies exist in various forms. However, they have limited impact mainly due to their inability to address the trust issue. For example, many cities in Scotland and Northern Ireland issue local currencies, but can only do so with the permission of the parliament. Canada also has forms of private currency being issued, such as "tire money" that can be earned and spent mostly within the framework of the loyalty program operated by the Canadian Tire Corporation. Additionally, value instruments in commerce, such as loyalty points, air miles and prepaid cards, could also be considered as corporate currencies.

---

[1] For insights into the influence of Hayek's ideas on virtual currencies, refer to: Fantacci, Luca. "Cryptocurrencies and the Denationalization of Money." International Journal of Political Economy, 48.2 (2019): 105–112.

[2] Hayek, F.A. *Denationalization of Money: The Argument Refined*. 3rd ed. London: The Institute of Economic Affairs, 1991, 51–53.

The original intent behind the design of Bitcoin, which proved to be its greatest breakthrough feature, was to solve the trust issue of private currencies through machines and algorithms. That is, Bitcoin does not require third-party trust, as it is issued by algorithms. Trust in Bitcoin no longer depends on any specific individual(s) or organization(s). Bitcoin is generated through mining, which reflects the direct value of resource input. Moreover, Bitcoin controls its total supply through algorithms, preventing excessive issuance. Other virtual currencies that followed in the footsteps of Bitcoin or were inspired by it took alternative technological paths that share fundamental similarities with Bitcoin.

6.3 Virtual Currencies: A Spectacular Social Experiment of Private Currencies

In 2009, Bitcoin was born. Not much later, as of November 30, 2021, the etherscan.io website reported the existence of 466,700 virtual currencies developed based on the Ethereum ERC-20 standard alone. According to CoinMarketCap.com, out of the 14,290 virtual currencies listed on 430 virtual currency exchanges, the highest market value reached $29.2 trillion on November 8, 2021, with a daily trading volume of $245 billion on September 8, 2021. On this day, Bitcoin itself had a market value of $12.7 trillion and a daily trading volume of $66 billion. Blandin et al. (2020) found that by the end of September 2020, there were over 101 million independent users with accounts (virtual currency "custodial wallets") opened at virtual currency service providers and a total account count of 191 million (see Fig. 6.1).

Let us now compare the trading volume of virtual currencies with that of the securities market. On April 7, 2020, the trading volume tracked by Coinmarketcap

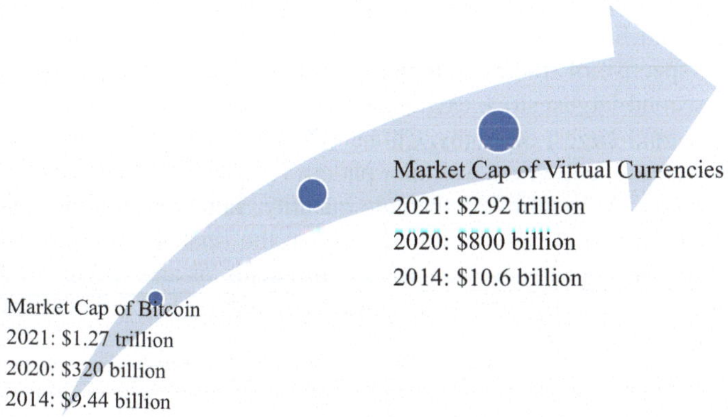

Fig. 6.1 The market capitalization of virtual currencies. *Note* Coinmarketcap.com retrospectively tracks the market capitalization of 10,045 virtual currencies. The data shown is as of November 30, 2021

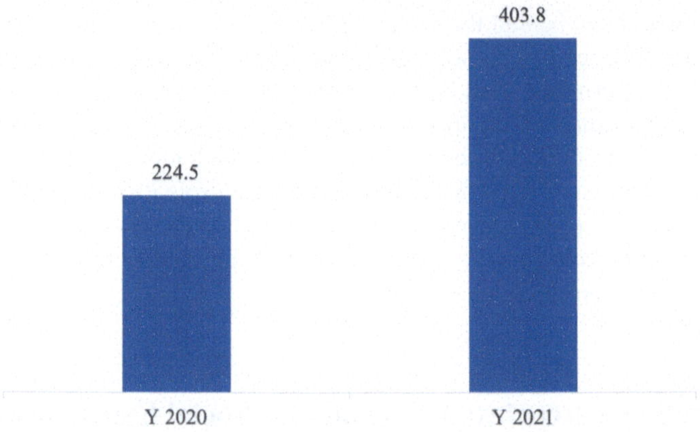

Fig. 6.2 The number of virtual currencies developed based on Ethereum ERC-20 (thousands)

Fig. 6.3 Comparison of trading volume of virtual currencies versus some large stock markets

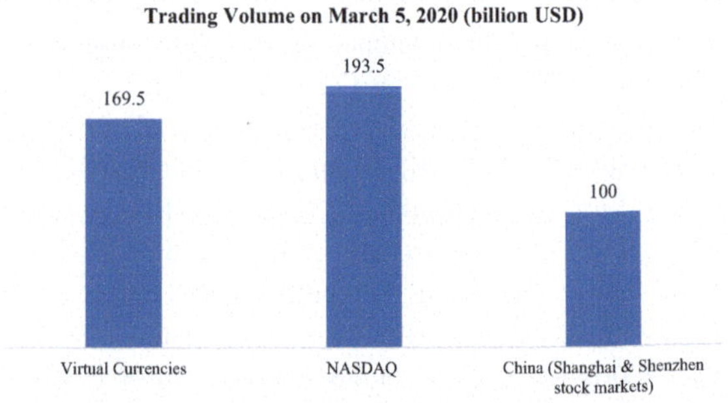

from 318 virtual currency exchanges was $169.5 billion.[3] On the same day, the trading volume of the US NASDAQ stock market was $193.5 billion, while that of the Shanghai and Shenzhen stock markets in China was only about $100 billion. From the perspective of trading volume, virtual currency is comparable to that of the world's second-largest stock exchange and exceeds the daily trading volume of the world's second-largest economy, China. When comparing the historical trading volumes of the past three years, a similar pattern is observed (see Fig. 6.2).

Virtual currencies, in terms of absolute quantity, value and trading volume, are massive and have become an important force in the financial market that cannot be overlooked. Thus, we believe that virtual currencies, as an experiment in private currency, are no longer isolated or sporadic phenomena, but rather a spectacular social movement (Fig. 6.3).

[3] The data source is Coinmarketcap.com, as of April 7, 2020. It is important to note that the website may have duplicate calculations for transactions between cryptocurrencies. For example, if there is a transaction worth $100 between Bitcoin and Litecoin, the website may count it as a $200 cryptocurrency transaction.

6.4 Why Cannot Virtual Currencies Effectively Fulfill the Functions of Money?

In Chap. 2 of this book, the basic concepts of "money," "digital currency" and "virtual currency" have been outlined. Virtual currencies are referred to as "money" not because they are recognized as "legal tender," but as they can, to some extent, perform the three main functions of money: store of value, unit of account and medium of exchange.

As previously stated, different schools of thought agree on at least two questions on what constitutes money: firstly, it has the three basic functions outlined above; secondly, it is a widely accepted means of payment that forms a common belief between transacting parties, allowing them to purchase services and goods by using it. In reality, these two consensuses are the criteria for judging money, with the former being an objective factor and the latter being a subjective factor. They interact with each other in dynamic evolution.

Complying with the main functions of money, virtual currencies are digital tokens that can perform the functions of value storage, medium of exchange, and unit of account, where the latter function is a derivative of the first two functions. A currency can only become a unit of account when it has the function of value storage and can effectively serve as a means of payment.

6.4.1 The Technical Limitations of Bitcoin for Public Use as Payment

1. Limited System Load Capacity: Unsuitable for Large-Scale Payments

The decentralized nature of Bitcoin inevitably brings drawbacks in efficiency and capacity. The technical design of Bitcoin limits its average transaction capacity to around 7 transactions per second, while Alipay recorded a peak transaction volume of 256,000 transactions per second on November 11, 2019.[4] As of November 23, 2019, Bitcoin had approximately 605,000 blocks, theoretically supporting around 2.478 billion transactions. This just falls short of the three-day clearing volume of China's third-party payment systems. In contrast, existing centralized electronic payment systems (banking electronic payment systems or third-party payment systems) can achieve unlimited capacity expansion through software and hardware upgrades.

Despite subsequent attempts to make improvements upon Bitcoin, other virtual currencies have not fundamentally overcome Bitcoin's inherent technical limitations. For instance, according to the Ethereum Whitepaper, the theoretical maximum

[4] "Double Eleven" is a shopping day with sales promotions in China, similar to Black Friday in the United States. Therefore, throughout the financial year, November 11th is the day with the highest volume of online payments in China.

Table 6.1 Comparison between bitcoin and existing currencies

	Legal currencies	Bitcoin	Consequences
System Capacity	Theoretically unlimited expansion (for the existing electronic payment system)	Upper theoretical limit present	Bitcoin cannot become a widely used payment method for the general public on a large scale
Payment speed	Only a few seconds (for existing electronic payments)	Average of 10 min for a batch of transactions	
Value volatility	Relatively stable (for major currencies)	Exceeding major currencies by 10 times	Bitcoin cannot serve as a store of value and a reliable unit of account
Payment cost	Domestic bank transfer in China: no cost Int'l wire transfer in China: 200–300 yuan	0.58–224 yuan (2016)	Bitcoin has not demonstrated the inclusive financial benefits it was anticipated to bring
Technical security	High	Low	

capacity of ether is only 15 transactions per second.[5] EOS claims a potential capacity of up to 3996 transactions per second,[6] but it is primarily used for smaller-scale national, regional or industry-specific payments. The recently proposed "Lightning Network" hopes to achieve low-cost and instant bitcoin transactions through off-chain technology (using bitcoin as a collateral for transactions within the Lightning Network, with final settlement on the Bitcoin system). However, it currently has a payment capacity of only 895 bitcoins[7] and faces several technical shortcomings[8] (refer to Table 6.1).

2. The Extremely Slow Transaction Speeds Prevent a Virtual Currency from Being Used for Daily Payments

From the perspective of individual transaction processing speed, Bitcoin lags behind existing widely-used electronic payment methods by several orders of magnitude,

[5] According to the Ethereum Whitepaper, Ethereum has a block time of 15 s, and ideally each block can accommodate 476 transactions. Therefore, Ethereum can theoretically handle 31 transactions per second. Based on data from etherscan.io, let us take November 27, 2019 as an example. On that day, from block 9,009,897 to block 9,009,921, a total of 25 blocks were generated and 3,694 transactions were completed, averaging 10 transactions per second.

[6] Please refer to the official website, https://eosnetworkmonitor.io/.

[7] The Lightning Network was launched on the Bitcoin main net in January 2018. As of March 6, 2020, there were a total of 11,624 Lightning Network nodes and 36,289 payment channels, with an overall payment capacity of 895 bitcoins. The data was sourced from the 1 ml website, specifically, accessed on March 6, 2020, at https://1ml.com/statistics.

[8] As the Lightning Network structure tends towards centralization, its operational efficiency increasingly relies on the payment capacity of large central nodes, rather than the scale expansion of a peer-to-peer network.

Table 6.2 The volatility of different asset prices

Asset category	Assets	Volatility (60-day) (%)
Cryptocurrency	Bitcoin	85.7
Major currencies	US dollar index	7.5
	Chinese Yuan versus US Dollar	1.65
	British Pound versus US Dollar	8.64
	Euro versus US Dollar	9.19
	US Dollar versus Japanese Yen	9.4
Precious metals	Gold (COMEX)	14.4
	Silver (COMEX)	25.7
Stocks	Standard and Poor's 500 Index	16.5
	Shanghai composite index	22.5
Oil	Brent crude (ICE)	28.5

Note The data provided above is valid as of November 29, 2019. The start dates for the various assets are as follows: June 1, 2000 for major currencies, stocks and oil; April 19, 2010 for gold; October 25, 2010 for silver; and July 18, 2010 for Bitcoin. The information was sourced from Wind and blockchain.info

making it unsuitable for everyday public use. In practice, the average confirmation time for a bitcoin transaction is 10 min (even longer for high-value transactions). In contrast, Alipay completes a transaction in less than 3 s, while for commonly used contactless card payments, this takes less than 1 s. In December 2017, the increase in bitcoin transactions due to the price surge caused congestion in the Bitcoin system, resulting in an average waiting time of 2 days and 2 nights per transaction.[9]

For the above reasons, from the standpoint of exchange medium, Bitcoin and subsequent virtual currencies cannot be used for widespread public payments due to their small capacity and slow transaction speeds, but is only suitable for large-scale transactions with lower time constraints.

6.4.2 *Excessive Volatility Prevents Virtual Currencies from Serving as Store of Value and Unit of Account*

From the perspective of being a store of value, the volatility of Bitcoin is significantly higher than that of fiat currencies, making it unsuitable as a means of storing value and a reliable unit of account.

For a more illustrious understanding of Bitcoin's instability, its extreme volatility can be quantified by comparing it with other assets over the long term (refer to Table 6.2).

[9] Data source: https://btc.com/stats.

Taking Bitcoin as an example, during its early development in 2011, it experienced a remarkable 40-fold surge within two months, soaring from $0.75 to $30. However, in February 2012, its price plummeted below $2, witnessing a decline of over 93%. The most recent significant fluctuation occurred on March 12, 2020, when the price of a bitcoin dropped by 38% within 24 h.[10] In contrast, the daily price fluctuation of major fiat currencies in sovereign states rarely exceeds 1%, and the daily fluctuation in major stock market indices typically ranges from 2 to 3%; it is rather unusual to observe price fluctuations of more than 10% within a single day.

Comparing the volatilities of different asset prices over the long term, bitcoin is 10 times volatile than major fiat currencies, 3 to 5 times than precious metals, 3 to 5 times than the stock market, and 3 times than crude oil (see Table 6.1). This extremely high volatility prevents Bitcoin from serving as a consistent store of value, and it also hinders people from entering into contracts for goods and services priced in bitcoin. From the perspective of monetary functions, due to the aforementioned flaws in the two core functions, a system based on a virtual currency unit of account also struggles to maintain stability and effectiveness.

6.4.3 The High Technical Requirements and Transaction Costs Prevent Virtual Currencies from Realizing Comprehensive Financial Advantages

Bitcoin does not require a standard registration process like a bank account and can transfer value without the need for financial intermediaries. Accordingly, supporters of Bitcoin have repeatedly proclaimed that decentralized virtual currencies can improve financial access for those who are unable to obtain services from the existing financial system, such as people in remote areas without bank branches or those who struggle to access such services. However, this is merely a theoretical deduction and does not align with the actual situation.

Firstly, consumers who possess the requirements to use virtual currencies already fulfill the prerequisites to enjoy existing financial services. For instance, to use virtual currencies, one must have Internet access or the ability to connect to the Internet. Being able to use virtual currencies also means the capacity to exploit existing Internet financial services, such as online payments and remote bank account access. This also presents a paradox in inclusive finance: users who can securely deal with virtual currency for payments must possess electronic devices and the corresponding technical capabilities, and such individuals often have ample access to services within the existing financial system.

Secondly, the security requirements for virtual currencies are often too high and exceed the technical capabilities of ordinary individuals. There are two forms of storing virtual currencies: "custodial wallets" (where the private keys are managed by service providers such as exchanges) and "non-custodial wallets" (where the

[10] For historical Bitcoin prices, the reader is suggested to refer to blockchain.info.

private keys are managed by users themselves). Numerous virtual currency exchanges have introduced custodial wallets, allowing users to conveniently view their assets and transfer virtual currencies to others, similar to using a bank account. However, custodial wallets still have significant security deficiencies. In 2013, Mt. Gox, a virtual currency exchange that accounted for 70% of global bitcoin trading volume, announced that $450 million worth of bitcoin belonging to its customers had been stolen by hackers (Vigna, 2014). In August 2016, Bitfinex, a well-known virtual currency exchange (also responsible for issuing USDT), announced the loss of $70 million worth of bitcoin belonging to its customers (Baldwin, 2016). For users with larger holdings, it is necessary to use "non-custodial wallets" to enhance the security of virtual currencies by storing private keys on personally owned media. This requires such high technical proficiency that is difficult for ordinary people to master.

Furthermore, virtual currency transfers are not cost-free, and due to limited capacity and slow speed, the transaction costs are often excessive. When transferring virtual currencies such as bitcoin and ether, a certain proportion of virtual currencies must be paid as compensation to the mining machines that provide computational power. As the value of virtual currencies increases and the transaction activity rises, the transfer fees are also becoming higher. Taking bitcoin as an example, in 2016, the average transaction fee for bitcoin in Chinese yuan was 0.58 yuan, but by December 2017, it had reached as much as 224 yuan.[11] In comparison, domestic online transfers in China have already accomplished zero transaction fees, and major banks usually charge between 200 to 300 yuan per transaction for overseas remittances. Therefore, bitcoin transfers do not offer any cost advantages.

6.5 The Inherent Technological Flaws that Make Virtual Currencies Unfit for the Functional Role of Currency: The Case of Bitcoin

As a result of the preeminent media hype, we often perceive Bitcoin as a new and advanced "high-tech" innovation. Nonetheless, as mentioned in the previous section, technological flaws prevent virtual currencies like Bitcoin from being used for daily payments. In this section, we specifically delve into the underlying technological flaws using Bitcoin as an example.

As for the technological efficiency of a system, the difference between Bitcoin and existing electronic payments (such as Alipay) is vast, akin to the difference between a horse carriage and a rocket. We can confidently state that "Bitcoin is the horse carriage." In fact, as a payment tool, the gap between these two systems is hundreds

[11] Data source: https://btc.com/stats. Please note that the transaction fees for Bitcoin are not fixed but are determined through negotiations between users and miners. Users propose a fee quotation when transferring Bitcoin, and miners "accept orders" based on the fees, forming a decentralized system where users offer quotes and miners freely accept orders. Therefore, the level of trading activity in the market greatly affects the transaction fees.

of times greater than the difference in speed between a horse carriage and a rocket. The reader should, however, be mindful of the fact that this discussion solely pertains to the aspect of payment tools and does not negate the innovation and application value inherent to the blockchain technology brought about by Bitcoin.

As the popular Chinese proverb goes, 'the development of novelty often follows a tortuous path.' This holds true for Bitcoin and numerous other virtual currencies. While Bitcoin offered a novel approach to prevalent currency and payment systems, at least for now, along with various other virtual currencies, it has not demonstrated any significant advantages as payment method. In fact, these currencies can be considered to be "lagging behind" in key technological indicators, making them incapable of becoming widely used payment methods for the general public. But why is there such a stark contrast between reality and expectations? This brings us to the subtleties of the underlying technology of Bitcoin.

6.5.1 The Structure of Bitcoin Data: Transactions, Blocks, and the Blockchain

In order to achieve trusted payments in a peer-to-peer environment, Bitcoin creatively uses transaction records as the carrier of currency. Although the name Bitcoin includes the word "coin," there is no physical entity within the Bitcoin system. The model that Bitcoin constructs is vastly different from the traditional banking system's balance-based approach, and even more divergent from the ancient systems of gold and silver coins and paper money (although it is similar in terms of circulation and privacy protection). Satoshi Nakamoto's Bitcoin design appears in the form of transaction records: instead of owning a bitcoin, one owns a record of someone else transferring bitcoin to them. This record is called an "Unspent Transaction Output" (UTXO), which can be understood as a transferable electronic voucher (readers can review Chap. 5, Sect. 6.3 for more information).

Blocks are connected to form a chain, hence this technology is called "blockchain." Transactions within Bitcoin blocks are also linked together through the form of unspent transaction outputs, forming a chain of continuous transactions. Let us take a closer look at the characteristics of "blocks" and the process of forming the "chain."

A "block" can be understood as a ledger that records multiple transactions; it is a data structure formed by packaging multiple transaction data together. In the simplest case, a single transaction is approximately 250 B in size, although in reality, transactions can exceed this value. The size of each block was limited by Satoshi Nakamoto to a maximum of 1 MB (1024 kB), so one can easily infer that a block can accommodate a maximum of 4096 (1,024,000/250) transactions. Using the metaphor of a physical ledger, Satoshi Nakamoto has stipulated that a ledger can have a maximum of 1024 pages. Each basic transaction occupies 1/4 of one page, so a ledger can contain a maximum of 4096 transactions.

As blocks form a "chain," so do transactions. The accountants (so-called "miners") follow the rules and record transactions on the ledger (block). Once the ledger has been filled with transactions, a time seal is placed on its cover and the number of the previous ledger is also recorded on the cover, creating a connected chain of ledgers. A prominent characteristic of this ledger chain is that the older the ledger, the more difficult it is to tamper with the transactions within it. For example, to modify a transaction in a block at height 363,270 in the year 2015, all the ledgers after that year's ledger must be modified and re-recorded.

To prevent tampering with the ledger, Bitcoin creatively uses a mechanism called proof-of-work, where miners compete through hash computations to obtain the right to record transactions and prevent block tampering. Bitcoin does not have a central server but is powered by the computational power provided by miners of all nodes. Miners compete to earn the right to record transactions, and the system rewards the winning miner with Bitcoin, often referred to as "mining." Miners perform proof-of-work computations by hashing the data in the "block header" twice (Bitcoin uses the SHA-256 hash computation), resulting in a 256-bit hash value.

Calculating the hash value takes only a few seconds, and miners can complete it instantaneously. To make mining more challenging, Bitcoin imposes requirements on hash computations, such as finding a hash value with the first 19 digits as zeros. To find the required hash value, miners must use a trial-and-error approach, continuously inputting random numbers (referred to as "nonces") to compute a hash value below a certain threshold. Since the output of SHA-256 is highly random, the only way to find a specific hash value is to continuously try different random values. Hence, whether a miner can successfully mine a block depends on both the miner's computational speed and luck. It is equally possible to find a suitable hash value on the first attempt or after billions of attempts. Bitcoin automatically adjusts the time for hash computations, setting it to an average of 10 min and dynamically adjusting it. This time setting strikes a balance between two factors: if the time is too short, it consumes insufficient computational power, making it easy for tampering attempts to continue and causing network synchronization instability. On the other hand, if the time is too long, the transaction confirmation takes too long, resulting in a poor mining experience. (The comprehensive explanation of complex hash computation extend beyond the scope of this work. Interested readers can refer to Chap. 8 of "A Brief History of Blockchain").

Understanding the operational efficiency of Bitcoin can be delineated in three aspects for non-technical individuals:

Firstly, each Bitcoin transaction validation process can be seen as a "block creation," where multiple transaction data files are organized together, packaged, and sealed with data hashes and timestamps, ensuring that they remain unaltered thereafter.

Secondly, the Bitcoin block size is set at 1 MB, theoretically capable of recording up to 4096 transactions.

Thirdly, the block creation time represents the time taken by miners to validate transactions, package blocks, and compete for hashes. According to the Bitcoin code, the target difficulty of hash competition adjusts dynamically to maintain an average block creation time of 10 min.

6.5.2 Extremely Low System Processing Speed

Bitcoin sets the block creation time to an average of 10 min, which means that the verification time for a "batch" of transactions is also around 10 min. Besides, the average confirmation time for each transaction is also approximately 10 min. This speed is clearly unacceptable for everyday public payments. Just imagine, if someone in front of a customer at a supermarket uses Bitcoin for payment and it takes 10 min for the transaction to be confirmed by the merchant: the queue would stretch for kilometers. Let us do a simple calculation: if it takes 10 min to process a payment at each cashier counter in a supermarket, only 6 transactions can be completed every hour, equivalent to a maximum of 48 transactions during an 8-h business day.

Now, let us reflect on the time we typically spend for electronic payments in our daily lives. From empirical evidence, Alipay processes each transaction within 3 s (referring to system processing time only and excluding time for opening the app, entering passwords, and other user operations). Network bank transfers can also arrive within seconds. According to the technical specifications of China UnionPay, contactless card transactions should take less than 500 ms.

Transaction Confirmation Times:

Bitcoin vs. Alipay=10 minutes vs 3 seconds = 200× slower

Bitcoin vs. Contactless IC Bank Cards=10 minutes vs. 500 milliseconds = 1200× slower

6.5.3 Excessively Low Concurrent Processing Capability

The processing speed of a system also depends on its concurrent processing capacity. For example, the number of cars that can travel on a highway depends both on its length and its width, as it determines how many cars can pass through at once. Bitcoin can process a maximum of 4096 transactions every 10 min, which is equivalent to a maximum of 6.83 transactions per second.

The concurrent processing speed of Bitcoin:

4,096 transactions/10 minutes = 6.83 transactions/second

Conversely, according to data released by Alipay during the 2017 "Double 11" event, Alipay's peak transaction processing volume per second reached 256,000 transactions. This signifies a huge difference in processing speed between the two, with a gap of 37,000 times! In comparison, the difference in speed between a rocket's first cosmic velocity and a carriage is only 474 times (see Table 6.3).

To give an analogy, consider the "Bitcoin Expressway" where 4096 transactions are processed in 10 min, equivalent to only 6.83 transactions per second. Meanwhile, the "Alipay Expressway" processes an astounding 256,000 transactions per second.

Now, consider a total of 4097 transactions globally, where processing the 4097th transaction would have to wait until the completion of the previous 4096 transactions and another 10 min. This situation is similar to the long queues of cars extending

Table 6.3 Speed comparison

	Speed	Difference
First cosmic velocity	7.9 km/s = 28,440 km/h	[Speed] First cosmic velocity: Carriage = 474×
Carriage	60 km/h	
Alipay	256,000 transactions per second	[Processing speed] Alipay: Bitcoin ≈ 37,481×
bitcoin	4096 transactions per 600 s = 6.83 transactions per second	

for several kilometers or even tens of kilometers at a single toll station during peak travel seasons.

6.5.4 Limited System Load Capacity

By doing further simple mathematical calculations, we can discover that, theoretically, Bitcoin can only process 590,000 transactions per day and 212 million transactions per year. Looking at actual transaction processing speeds, taking data from the third quarter of 2019 as an example, daily Bitcoin transactions numbered around 300,000. From January 9th, 2009 to April 12th, 2019, Bitcoin had accumulated approximately 400 million transactions in its history.

In comparison, China's National Internet Payment Clearance Platform (China UnionPay) handles an average of 1.18 billion transactions per day, that is, nearly three times the total transaction volume in Bitcoin's history. It is important to note that this number only represents a portion of China's Internet third-party payment transaction volume, as some transactions are settled through China UnionPay, while others are settled through other online payment platforms or within major payment companies' internal cycles (see Table 6.4).

Theoretically, under full load, the Bitcoin system can only handle approximately 2.12 billion transactions per year, equivalent to about 1/5 of the daily settlement volume through UnionPay. The cumulative transaction volume of Bitcoin over almost 10 years is only about 1/3 of the daily settlement volume through UnionPay.

6.5.5 The CBDC Architecture Implies the Limitations of the Current Blockchain Technology

The blockchain technology set in motion by Bitcoin originated from the grassroots cryptography community but quickly gained the interest of governments, especially central banks, in various countries. Central banks from China, the UK, Canada, Japan, and Singapore have all conducted subsequent experiments with blockchain

Table 6.4 System capacity comparison

Bitcoin	Third-party payments in China
The maximum number of transactions that Bitcoin can theoretically handle: [Per Hour] 60 min × (4096 transactions/ 10 min) ≈ 24,600 transactions [Per Day] 24 h × transactions Per Hour ≈ 590,000 transactions [Per Month] 30 days × transactions Per Day ≈ 17.7 million transactions [Per Year] 12 months × transactions Per Month ≈ 2.12 billion transactions	Alipay: 256,000 concurrent transactions per second during "Double 11" in 2017
As of November 23, 2019, there had been a total of 605,026 blocks. Thus, the maximum number of transactions it can handle is 2.478186496 billion transactions (605,026 blocks × 4096 transactions), which actually amounts to around 400 million transactions	Chinese third-party payment settlement volume (via UnionPay): 1.18 billion transactions per day in the third quarter of 2019

technology. However, most of them only applied this technology to wholesale transactions (clearing and settlements between financial institutions) rather than retail transactions (daily payments and transfers for the public). The pressures faced by wholesale transactions are certainly much lower than those faced by retail transactions. This choice and positioning, although primarily driven by considerations in the financial industry, also reflects a certain degree of attitude towards blockchain technology. Countries conducting CBDC experiments, such as the UK and Canada, have both stated that their interest in blockchain technology lies mainly in clearing and settlement efficiency. In other words, clearing and settlements between financial institutions can be preferably achieved on a blockchain, eliminating the need for central bank intermediation. This efficiency refers specifically to clearing and settlement efficiency, rather than the technical efficiency discussed earlier (transaction speed, scalability, etc.).

According to publicly available information, China's digital currency, the Digital Renminbi or Digital Yuan, was the world's first CBDC to enter the experimental stage in the retail sector. However, it did not fully adopt blockchain technology, but instead introduced distributed ledger technology for transaction tracing, similar to the "transaction chaining" mentioned earlier. In the issuance, settlement, payment, and redemption processes, the Digital Renminbi adheres to a centralized system revolving around the central bank.

The technology choices made through the experiments with CBDCs by central banks around the world indirectly indicate that current blockchain technology is not the preferred choice for mainstream official currency and payment systems.

6.5.6 *Summary: The Limitations of Bitcoin and Virtual Currencies as Payment Methods*

Bitcoin, as a revolutionary technological innovation, holds great significance. However, its slow transaction confirmation speed and limited concurrent processing capacity has prevented its widespread adoption, making it difficult to replace the existing fiat currency system as a mainstream currency. The achievements of Bitcoin-like technologies in payment and settlement processes are only applicable to wholesale businesses with low time sensitivity and limited transaction volumes.

Subsequent virtual currencies have attempted to improve upon Bitcoin, but they have yet to serve as widespread payment methods used by the general public on a large scale. Bitcoin and many other virtual currencies still cannot function in this role. While future technological developments may enable blockchain to be used as a high-capacity payment system, the intrinsic limitations of virtual currencies such as value, transaction costs, and compliance persist, making it challenging for them to assume the role of mainstream currency. These limitations of Bitcoin and other virtual currencies as private currencies remains a highly debated topic, inviting further exploration.

6.6 The Manipulation of Virtual Currency Prices in an Unregulated Market

As pointed out by Wobach in "*Trust, but Verify: Why the Blockchain Needs the Law*," distributed ledger technology, which underpins trust in blockchain, should not be confused with trust in specific individuals and institutions.[12] Notwithstanding this proposition, in the world of virtual currency trading, certain dominant exchanges have emerged that manipulate prices by taking advantage of their unique position. This has also been seen in the history of Bitcoin, where exchanges have controlled and caused significant price increases, and such actions have led to distorted prices and rampant speculation within the virtual currency market.

As discussed in Sect. 2.5 of this book, for cryptocurrencies like Bitcoin, which are based on asymmetric encryption technology, two methods of trading exist. The first is directly on the blockchain, where transactions occur between different addresses (similar to cash transactions). The second involves trading through centralized cryptocurrency exchanges, which operate in a similar way to traditional banking transactions.

Despite the decentralized nature of Bitcoin that can be sustained through community self-governance, the reality of trading allows cryptocurrency exchanges to

[12] Werbach, Kevin. "Trust, But Verify: Why the Blockchain Needs the Law." *Berkeley Technology Law Journal*, 33 (2018): 489–553.

manipulate bitcoin prices using their unique positions. Numerous studies have highlighted the involvement of exchanges in manipulating bitcoin prices during the two most significant price surges in the history of this digital currency.

6.6.1 Mt.Gox Manipulated Bitcoin Price in the First Surge

In the first major price surge, from October 3, 2013, to November 30, 2013, the price of one bitcoin rose from $116 to $1150, a tenfold increase in just two months. According to reports and research presented in a Tokyo District Court ruling, the price manipulation during the end of 2013 surge was attributed to Mt.Gox Exchange, the largest global trading platform at that time.

> HOW DID MT. GOX MANIPULATE BITCOIN PRICE THROUGH ARTIFICIALLY INFLATED USD FUNDS AND BITCOIN IN SPECIFIC ACCOUNTS? In 2017, three researchers from Tel Aviv University in Israel and The University of Tulsa in the United States conducted an academic study using rigorous data and logical analysis to prove that Mt. Gox artificially inflated USD funds and bitcoin in specific accounts, and then manipulated the price of bitcoin through transactions between these accounts.[13]
>
> When trading through virtual currency exchanges, users deposit their bitcoin private keys into the exchange, which holds custody of these keys. When users engage in transactions, the bitcoin is only reflected in their wallet accounts within the exchange, and the actual transfer of bitcoin occurs when users withdraw the bitcoin to the blockchain.
>
> As long as users do not withdraw the bitcoin, the exchange can freely increase the amount of bitcoin in their accounts. This is similar to an unregulated bank being able to arbitrarily increase the amount of deposits in customer accounts, as long as the customers do not withdraw the funds.
>
> The above study pointed out that the Mt Gox Exchange fraudulently credited several accounts with bitcoin and manipulated its price from $150 to $1,000.
>
> However, this inflated bitcoin will eventually need to be redeemed, while Mt Gox Exchange cannot provide these bitcoins. This is similar to a bank artificially increasing the amount of deposits and later unable to provide the funds when customers come to withdraw. The study estimated that the Mt Gox Exchange credited and inflated the value of at least 600,000 bitcoins in these accounts.
>
> Under immense external pressure, in February 2014, Mt Gox Exchange announced that "We were hacked, 850,000 bitcoins are missing!" (valued at $450 million at the time). Later, they also announced that they had "found" 200,000 bitcoins. Interestingly, the price of bitcoin skyrocketed afterwards, reaching $20,000 in 2017. According to market value, these "found" bitcoins were sufficient to compensate the victims' losses (calculated based on the end-of-2013 market price).

In March 2019, the Tokyo District Court ruled that the CEO of Mt Gox, Mark Karpelès, was guilty of tampering with records and inflating assets. The prosecutor also accused him of embezzling bitcoin but lacked sufficient evidence and therefore

---

[13] For detailed analysis on this topic, refer to Gandal, Neil, et al. "Price manipulation in the Bitcoin ecosystem." *Journal of Monetary Economics* 95 (2018): 86–96. The initial draft of this paper was made public on May 23, 2017, and underwent revisions based on peer review before publication.

did not receive court support.[14] During the investigation by law enforcement authorities in Japan, the New York Attorney General's Office initiated an investigation into price manipulation and the loss of bitcoin.[15]

6.6.2 *Tether Manipulated Bitcoin Price in the Second Surge*

A second surge took place from March 27, 2017, to December 17, 2017, during which the price of one bitcoin soared from $1046 to a peak of $20,089, a 20-fold increase in nine months. In the longer term, the market capitalization of bitcoin witnessed a remarkable growth from around $9.4 billion on January 1, 2014, to its historical peak of $320 billion on December 17, 2017. In June 2018, an academic study revealed how Tether Limited manipulated the price of bitcoin by issuing the stablecoin USDT and controlling the Bitfinex exchange, the largest global cryptocurrency exchange.

> In 2018, two researchers from the University of Texas at Austin and Ohio State University, respectively, published a rigorous academic paper exposing how Tether Limited manipulated the price of bitcoin by artificially inflating "money."[16] The company played two roles in this venture: issuing the stablecoin USDT and controlling the Bitfinex exchange. USDT, backed by US dollars, acted as a bridge between the virtual world of dollars and virtual currencies, enabling transactions to take place in the virtual realm.
>
> By studying 200GB of transaction data, the two experts established several key assumptions in their paper: (1) When the price of bitcoin fell, a large amount of USDT was used to purchase bitcoin. (2) When the price of bitcoin neared whole number levels, a large amount of USDT was used to buy bitcoin. (3) An "end-of-month effect" was noticeable, where auditors examining the USDT asset status prompted selling a significant amount of bitcoin for USDT.
>
> In the updated version of the paper in 2019, the researchers added a new finding: traders from one account demonstrated a "clairvoyant" ability to anticipate the timing of trading and exerted "extremely large" influence on bitcoin prices, manipulating much of the price increase between March 1, 2017 and March 31, 2018.

As a result of these strange events, in November 2018, the US Department of Justice and the Commodity Futures Trading Commission (CFTC) launched a joint investigation into the potential price manipulation behind bitcoin.[17]

---

[14] Furukawa, Yuki. "Former Mt. Gox CEO Mark Karpelès Gets Suspended Jail Term." Bloomberg, March 15, 2019. https://www.bloomberg.com/news/articles/2019-03-15/former-bitcoin-baron-mark-karpeles-gets-suspended-jail-term. Accessed on March 5, 2021.

[15] Del Castillo, Michael. "New York Attorney General Warns That Kraken Cryptocurrency Exchange Could Be Violating Regulations." Forbes, September 18, 2018. https://www.forbes.com/sites/michaeldelcastillo/2018/09/18/new-york-attorney-general-warns-kraken-cryptocurrency-exchange-could-be-breaking-the-law/#6ff8ef67380f. Accessed on March 5, 2021.

[16] Griffin, John M. and Amin Shams. "Is Bitcoin Really Un-Tethered?" *The Journal of Finance*, 75.4 (2020): 1913–1964. This paper, also available on the SSRN website: https://ssrn.com/abstract=3195066, which was first published online on June 25, 2018 and updated on November 5, 2019.

[17] Robinson, Matt, and Tom Schoenberg. "Bitcoin-Rigging Criminal Probe Focused on Tie to Tether." Bloomberg, November 20, 2018. https://www.bloomberg.com/news/articles/2018-11-20/bitcoin-rigging-criminal-probe-is-said-to-focus-on-tie-to-tether. See also Rooney, Kate. "As

The status of Bitcoin as the progenitor of cryptocurrencies and its significant price surges triggered a wave of investment in virtual currencies, leading to the emergence of numerous "altcoins" and the popularization of initial coin offerings (ICOs). Subsequently, the skyrocketing prices of various "coins" became a hot topic worldwide.

6.7 The Proliferation of Counterfeit and Air Coins: A Disaster Area for Fraud

6.7.1 The Spread of Altcoins

In the early days, "altcoins" only referred to virtual currencies imitating Bitcoin and this was a neutral term. However, with the advent of Ethereum in 2015, the technical barriers for altcoins were completely eliminated, resulting in a flood of altcoins saturating the market. They have since become synonymous with virtual currencies lacking both technical innovation and value. In China, altcoin is sometimes translated as "competitive coin" or "replacement coin," but more commonly as "shanzhai coin" using the term "shanzhai," to imply a shoddy or inferior imitation. With the substantial expansion of scams associated with these virtual currencies, Chinese people often refer to "shanzhai coin" as "air coin," implying that these coins hold neither value nor technological innovation.

In the early days, "altcoins" often had innovative technical features and did not necessarily have a derogatory meaning. In October 2011, Litecoin became the earliest Bitcoin imitator by adapting several parameters of Bitcoin.[18] Other virtual currencies, such as Mastercoin, were designed to be sophisticated and unique, which became classic examples of Bitcoin's second-layer protocols.[19] However, many of them simply copied the code to run an independent chain or forked from a specific block of Bitcoin, resulting in forked coins such as BCH and BSV.[20] The operations of these

Bitcoin Nosedives, Regulators Said to Be Investigating Whether It Was Propped Up Illegally." CNBC, November 20, 2018. https://www.cnbc.com/2018/11/20/regulators-investigate-whether-bitcoin-price-was-propped-up-illegally.html. Accessed on March 5, 2021.

[18] For information about Litecoin, please refer to its official website, https://litecoin.info/index.php/Litecoin. To understand its code, please read the publicly available code on their GitHub page, https://github.com/litecoin-project?page=2.

[19] Mastercoin, which later became Omni Protocol, was released in January 2012. The interested reader can refer to their protocol documentation at https://www.omnilayer.org/. For more detailed information about the Omni Protocol, study the Omni Protocol Specification at https://github.com/OmniLayer/spec or directly access the code on their GitHub page at https://github.com/OmniLayer/.

[20] The term "fork" originally comes from software engineering to describe creating a separate branch or version of software. Eric Allman defined it in a technical paper in 1980. His concept was borrowed by the cryptocurrency community, and each time changes are made to the code of a cryptocurrency, a new version is created, resulting in a "fork." This gives rise to a new cryptocurrency that is different

early altcoins varied in terms of the required technical skills and costs, depending on the developers' level of pursuit of technical innovation. However, they still had certain technical and cost investment needs.

> The exact origin of the term altcoin is difficult to trace, but the earliest known altcoin, "Namecoin," was released in April 2011. This was followed by "Litecoin" in November 2011 and "Dogecoin" in December 2013. These cryptocurrencies, based on the Bitcoin source code with minor modifications, are referred to as alternatives of Bitcoin, or altcoins for short.
>
> Upon its release, Litecoin made some parameter adjustments to the Bitcoin code, reducing the block time from 10 minutes to 2.5 minutes and changing the proof-of-work algorithm to sCrypt. As the earliest Bitcoin imitator, the technical principles of Litecoin were similar to Bitcoin and its code was based on it with small modifications, making it unnecessary to write a separate whitepaper for this altcoin.
>
> In the beginning, the definition of altcoin was inconsistent. In an article for The Wall Street Journal, Paul Vigna first defined it as "alternative versions of Bitcoin."[21] In an article for MarketWatch, Aaron Hankins believed that all cryptocurrencies except Bitcoin were altcoins.[22] In the early cryptocurrency community, Bitcoin's design inspired all other cryptocurrencies, hence the term altcoin to refer to alternatives to Bitcoin. With the advancements of cryptocurrencies and blockchain technology, later cryptocurrencies were no longer based on the Bitcoin source code but developed from scratch, presenting significant differences in principle and mechanism. As a result, the term "alternative version of Bitcoin" was no longer fit, but people had already become accustomed to using altcoin to refer to all cryptocurrencies other than Bitcoin.

The emergence of Ethereum in 2015 eliminated the technical barriers for creating altcoins. Ethereum's smart contracts use the Solidity language, allowing developers to easily create new virtual currencies by deploying a standard ERC20 code. This process is as simple as registering a domain name and can be completed in less than 10 min. According to etherscan.io, as of June 12, 2018, there were a total of 90,738 ERC20 token smart contracts on the Ethereum network. By March 5, 2020, this number had increased to 245,504, and by November 30, 2021, it had reached 438,000. Truly valuable tokens are rare among this large number of tokens. Ethereum's development surpasses Bitcoin in terms of convenience and flexibility, and its reputation as Blockchain 2.0 has attracted a large network community of developers and virtual token creators.

Altcoins flourished after the emergence of Ethereum, transforming the virtual currency market from Bitcoin's dominance to a proliferation of various altcoins. According to Coinmarketcap's rankings based on market capitalization, there were 5164 virtual currencies in January 1, 2014, with a total market capitalization of

---

from the original, such as BCH and BSV being forks of Bitcoin. For reference, see Allman, Eric. "An introduction to the source code control system." *University of California at Berkeley, Working paper* (1980).

[21] Vigna, Paul. "Which Digital Currency Will Be the Next Bitcoin?" The Wall Street Journal, December 19, 2017. https://www.wsj.com/articles/which-digital-currency-will-be-the-next-bitcoin-1513679400.

[22] Hankins, Aaron. "Bitcoin Begins the Week with a Stumble; SEC Announces Adviser for Digital Assets." MarketWatch, June 4, 2018. https://www.marketwatch.com/story/bitcoin-begins-the-week-on-a-sour-note-2018-06-04. Accessed on March 5, 2021.

$10.6 billion (with bitcoin accounting for $9.4 billion). However, by December 17, 2017, the total market capitalization of virtual currencies had reached $800.3 billion (with bitcoin accounting for $320 billion). At the end of 2017, Bitcoin's share in the total market capitalization of virtual currencies decreased from about 90% to about 40% and has since remained stable at that level. Thus, the virtual currency market transformed from Bitcoin's supremacy to a proliferation of various altcoins.

6.7.2 *Bitcoin and Other Mainstream Virtual Currencies: A Hotbed for Speculation and Fraud*

Since its emergence, the uncertainty surrounding the value of Bitcoin has made it difficult for ordinary investors to understand and easy for fraudsters to exploit. Virtual currencies, represented by Bitcoin, lack a value anchor and thereby their intrinsic value is ambiguous. Not only do ordinary investors struggle to grasp the value of virtual currencies, but professional investors also find it hard to explain the corresponding prices between Bitcoin and fiat currencies. Furthermore, due to the extremely high volatility of Bitcoin (as discussed in Sect. 6.1.2), it is not fit to become a sound investment asset.

Around 2013, regulatory agencies in the United States and Europe began to pay attention to the significant risks of virtual currencies, such as Bitcoin, being used for financial fraud, and took relevant enforcement measures. In 2013, the Securities and Exchange Commission (SEC, 2013) issued a risk alert to investors titled "Ponzi Schemes Using Virtual Currencies," pointing out that virtual currencies were easily exploited by Ponzi schemes. These include enticing investors with new cutting-edge technologies, convincing them of a rare investment opportunity to make them lower their guard, and using the benefit of anonymity and lack of regulation of virtual currencies for fraudulent activities. The SEC (2014) issued a further risk alert titled "Bitcoin and Other Virtual Currency-Related Investments," not only highlighting the vulnerability of virtual currencies like Bitcoin to fraud but also stating that even without fraud, virtual currencies like Bitcoin were not suitable for ordinary investors due to their high volatility and lack of regulation. Besides, the European Banking Authority (EBA), the Consumer Financial Protection Bureau (CFPB), the Financial Industry Regulatory Authority (FINRA), and other institutions have also issued investor alerts over time.

The world of virtual currency has seen a rise in various fraudulent activities using Bitcoin and other mainstream virtual currencies as a facade. In addition to issuing risk alerts, US regulatory authorities have also published numerous cases. For example, in the Shavers case in 2013, the issuer claimed to have issued a fund backed by Bitcoin assets, and through complex algorithms for arbitrage trading, they guaranteed a weekly return of 7%. This was a typical Ponzi scheme using virtual currencies as a cover. In the Garza case in 2015, the defendant lured investors to invest in their Bitcoin mining products, claiming that they could obtain "hashlets" by investing, which would allow them to receive mining benefits from Bitcoin at no cost for a lifetime. In just four months in 2014, the defendant deceived 10,000 victims in the amount of $19 million. In this case, the fraudster promoted the concept of "hash," widely used in the blockchain, in a misleading manner, successfully juggling investors out of their assets.

The characteristics of fraud cases in the United States, as listed above, typically involve complex schemes targeting individuals who belong to the middle class or above and have received a certain level of education.

IN THE CASE OF HOMERO JOSHUA GARZA, the main character in the Garza case, he operated two mining companies called GAW Miners and Zen Miner. He publicly announced that his two mining companies were dedicated to bitcoin mining, and that investors could purchase "hashlets" from these companies to obtain lifetime mining profits from bitcoin without any cost. In this case, the fraudster exploited the concept of "hash," a widely used element of blockchain technology, and successfully tricked investors with plausible but false claims. This scheme was relatively complex, requiring victims to have heard of "hash" and "hash calculations." Therefore, we can speculate that the victims were individuals who regularly read financial newspapers and magazines. However, compared to the complex "arbitrage trading" scheme in Shavers, this fraud idea is not too intricate, making it much more successful from the perspective of the fraudster; within four months, Garza swindled more than 10,000 people and fraudulently obtained $19 million.

THE CASE OF TRENDON T. SHAVERS is another prime example of complex fraudulent schemes. Shavers founded an entity called Bitcoin Savings and Trust (BS&T). From February 2011 to August 2012, BS&T claimed to issue a fund backed by bitcoin assets, which would generate a weekly return of 7% through complex algorithmic arbitrage trading. Just think about it: achieving a weekly return of 7% translates to an annualized return of 3641%! The only way to gain such returns would be through a Ponzi scheme using newly acquired funds to pay returns to previous victims. In August 2012, BS&T was unable to fulfill its obligations and announced its closure, falling subject to an investigation by the U.S. Securities and Exchange Commission. This scheme was quite intricate, making it difficult for investors without a financial education to fall victim to it. The most enticing aspect was the combination of "bitcoin" and "arbitrage trading." In legitimate arbitrage trading, it is indeed possible to control returns (or losses) within a certain range. If we were to paint a portrait of victims of this scheme, it would likely feature middle-class individuals who frequently learn investment techniques through the Internet and best-selling books. As a result, the total number of victims in this scheme was only 100, with a collective investment of $4.5 million in bitcoin.

6.7.3 The Rampant Spread of "Altcoins" Using Blockchain and Cryptocurrency as a Cover to Become Tools for Fraud

The emergence of Ethereum has completely eliminated the technical barriers for virtual currencies. The price fluctuations of altcoins have become entirely detached from operational profits or technological achievements, relying solely on marketing strategies and market manipulation. In China, altcoins that lack any technical substance or value support are commonly referred to as "air coins." Both domestically and internationally, numerous altcoin-related scams have emerged under the

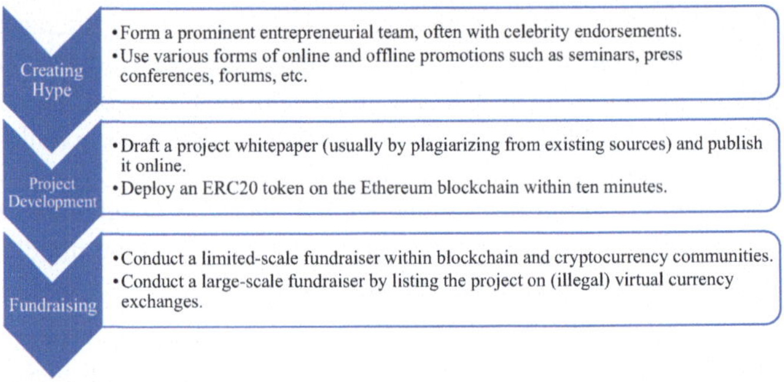

Fig. 6.4 The typical fundraising process of aircoins in China

guise of "blockchain" and "virtual currencies," making them a breeding ground and high-risk zone for fraud, with a wide range of fraudulent schemes.

If we consider that virtual currency fraud cases in the United States have a certain level of technological complexity, such fraud cases in China are more straightforward and aggressive. Virtual currency fraud here primarily involves the issuance of altcoins that lack any technological substance. The key to the success of these altcoins lies in publicity and hype, making celebrity endorsements and marketing impact crucial (see Fig. 6.4).

Due to the lack of government regulation and self-regulatory responsibilities similar to the securities market and stock exchanges, virtual currency exchanges do not fulfill self-disciplinary regulation duties. In these exchanges, project teams themselves or third parties can act as market makers and directly manipulate the prices of virtual currencies; fundraising for virtual currencies is no longer based on technological competition, but rather relies on celebrity endorsements and the guise of high technology. In summary, three common strategies are used in fraudulent exchanges:

The first strategy is the issuance of worthless or unoriginal aircoins for the purpose of fundraising. A particularly infamous aircoin known as "Space Chain" gained significant popularity upon its initial release, with many influential figures in the industry endorsing it. Within a day, it managed to raise 1 billion of funds. However, during the limited-scale fundraising stage, several scandals emerged, including allegations of plagiarized whitepapers. Once listed on exchanges, the value of Space Chain plummeted, causing the previously endorsing figures to distance themselves from it. As a result, on March 8, 2018, the Development Zone Branch of the Yangzhou Public Security Bureau filed a case against Space Chain for suspected fraud.[23]

The second strategy is conducting pyramid schemes using altcoins. These schemes are started by offering attractive returns during lock-up periods but eventually transform into pyramid schemes. They employ multi-level marketing strategies, targeting

[23] Feng, Yingzi, and Wei Jin. "Prominent Figures Hurriedly Dissociate Themselves as Space Chain Plunged 90%." *Huaxia Times*, 9 April 2018, 13. (冯樱子和金微, 太空链破发90% 大佬纷纷撇清关系, 华夏时报, 2018年4月9日, 第13版).

investors with popular cryptocurrencies like Bitcoin. They promise high monthly or yearly returns and incentivize investors to recruit more participants. One notable case was the "GGP Win–Win Points" scheme, where popular individuals such as Lu used virtual currencies to create a pyramid network spanning over 30 levels and involving more than 10,000 people. The total amount involved in this scheme surpassed 320 million RMB. The significance of this case is marked by the fact that it was acknowledged as a typical case by the Supreme People's Procuratorate of China in 2019.[24]

In the third form of scam, projects offer high dividends for aircoins that they issue themselves, with a lock-up period involved. In this scheme, investors use popular virtual currencies like bitcoin or ether to purchase aircoins and hold them for a designated lock-up period. The project teams then promise investors attractive dividends in the form of additional aircoins during this period. To maintain the illusion of real profits, they manipulate and control the prices of these aircoins on a specific exchange. This tactic aims to retain existing investors and attract new ones.[25] One example of such scheme is the "Baer Chain" project, where investors exchanged Ethereum for the clone coin "BRC" issued by Baer Chain. These invested BRC coins were then locked for a specified period, and investors were rewarded with new BRC coins through a supposed wealth game.[26]

The Massive Fraud Scheme: PlusToken

In recent years, projects like "Blockchain Pig Farming" and "Smart Dog Brick Laying" have emerged, enticing unsuspecting users to join with the promise of quick wealth through blockchain. While many people dismiss these projects with laughter, they have still managed to deceive investors. They key to this success is that they leverage the power of blockchain and the Internet, employing tactics that far exceed traditional financial fraud.

On July 30, 2020, the Ministry of Public Security of China published news of a major cross-border pyramid scheme case, titled "Ministry of Public Security Leads

---

[24] The case was appealed and received its final ruling in 2019. Later, it was recognized as a typical case by the Supreme People's Procuratorate in the same year. For more information, please refer to the official website of the Supreme People's Procuratorate: https://www.spp.gov.cn/xwfbh/wsfbh/201912/t20191203_440338.shtml.

[25] Wang, Yang, and Ye Pan. "Beware of Blockchain Becoming a 'Golden Signboard' for Scams." *Economic Reference News*, 11 November 2019, 5. (王阳和潘晔, 警惕区块链成行骗 "金字招牌", 经济参考报, 2019年11月21日, 第5版).

[26] For information related to Baer Chain, please refer to the article titled "Beware! Baer Chain: A Fundraising Scheme Packaged as Listing" on the Sohu website: http://www.sohu.com/a/334138228_120131663.

On June 15, 2020, the official WeChat account of Haizhou Branch Bureau of Public Security in Lianyungang City, Jiangsu Province, published a notice titled "Announcement on Verification and Registration of Investment Membership Information in Baer Chain Case." This stated that suspects Cheng and Zhang, among others, were involved in organizing and leading a pyramid scheme. The case has been transferred to Haizhou District People's Procuratorate by Haizhou Branch Bureau of Public Security for review and prosecution. The victims were requested to register at designated locations by June 30th.

Crackdown on the Largest-ever Multinational Ponzi Scheme Using Digital Currency: PlusToken Illegal Trading Platform Completely Destroyed, Involving Over 40 Billion Yuan."[27] A final judgment on this virtual currency fraud case, the largest in the world so far, was delivered on November 26, 2020, by the Intermediate People's Court of Yancheng City in Jiangsu Province.

The mastermind of this case, Chen, along with his accomplices Ding, Peng and others, established the PlusToken platform in 2018, promoting it as a "decentralized smart brick-laying wallet" and promising users an annual return of up to 700% if they invested in their virtual currency. In just one year, this clear-cut scam swept through 170 countries worldwide, victimizing 2.69 million people and defrauding over 50 billion Chinese Yuan worth of virtual currency (calculated based on the market value during the time of the 2019 incident). It can be stated that PlusToken is the epitome of recent large-scale virtual currency scams.

THE DECEPTIVE TACTICS OF PLUSTOKEN: "SMART DOG BRICK-LAYING" SCHEME

Deceptive lure: The project token, PlusToken, promotes itself with the gimmick of "smart dog brick-laying." It claims to generate token income on the blockchain through this activity, guaranteeing monthly returns of 6% to 18%.

Illusion of wealth: Dividends during lock-up period. Customers invest in PlusToken using mainstream virtual currencies like Bitcoin and Ethereum, and in return, they receive new PlusToken tokens periodically. Meanwhile, the criminals manipulate the market price of PlusToken, providing customers with the illusion of increased token value and quantity. This scam follows a similar pattern as the aforementioned "Baer Chain."

Business model: Utilizing a pyramid scheme approach, the scheme incentivizes participants to recruit others. Members are ranked, in increasing order, as "members," "big holders," "experts," "gurus," and "founders," respectively, with corresponding amounts of PlusToken awarded as rewards and rebates. This scheme has resulted in the development of a 3,293-layer pyramid network.

Organizational structure: Within the scheme, different tasks are assigned to various groups, including technical team, marketing team, customer service team, and coin transfer team. These teams respectively handle the tasks of technical maintenance, promotional activities, customer inquiries, and the verification and distribution of withdrawals.

International propaganda: The scheme employs tactics such as recruiting international students as the face of the operation, arranging seminars, training sessions, and tourism activities to enhance credibility and authority. Additionally, substantial on-site and online promotional activities are organized in South Korea, Japan, and China.

In early 2019, public security organs in Yancheng, Jiangsu Province established a special task force to investigate the PlusToken project. To evade legal sanctions, the criminals relocated personnel and servers overseas and continued their fraudulent activities. In June 2019, Chinese police officers were dispatched to multiple countries and regions to cooperate with local law enforcement and successfully apprehended 27 key suspects hiding abroad. Additionally, one main suspect was captured within China. With this operation, the PlusToken case was essentially figured out.

In March 2020, public security organs arrested a total of 82 core members suspected of participating in pyramid schemes. The seized virtual currencies in this

[27] The Ministry of Public Security's report can be found at the following website: https://www.mps.gov.cn/n2253534/n2253535/c7293348/content.html.

Table 6.5 Seized criminal proceeds in the PlusToken case

Virtual currencies	Seized quantity/ coins	Unit price in February 2021/ USD	Total value/ USD	Unit price at peak in May 2021/ USD	Total value/ USD
BTC	314,200	38,395.69	12,063,926,523	62,654	19,685,886,800
ETH	9,174,200	1602.308	14,699,891231	3909	35,861,947,800
BCH	117,500	440.4615	51,754,231	1542	181,185,000
DASH	96,000	117.0769	11,239,385	411	39,456,000
DOGE	11,060,000,000	0.070154	775,901,538	0.716	7,918,960,000
LTC	1,847,700	148.6154	274,596,646	383	707,669,100
EOS	51,363,300	3.230769	165,942,969	14.37	738,090,621
XRP	92,800	0.421538	39,119	1.77	164,256
Total			28,043,291642		65,133,359,577

case can be considered as constituting China's largest financial fraud. According to the court's judgment, the total value of the seized virtual currencies, taken at the lowest price from May 1, 2018 to June 27, 2019, exceeded 14.8 billion RMB. Calculated using the market price at the time of the case in June 2019, the total value surpassed 50 billion RMB. Even considering price calculation with the lowest figures, this fraudulent amount would rank among the greatest in the history of financial fraud cases in modern China (see Table 6.5 for reference).

Considering the market prices in 2021, the illegal gains from this case are even more shocking: the total value of these virtual currencies ranged between 28 to 65 billion US dollars, equivalent to approximately 182 billion to 422.5 billion RMB (calculated at a rate of 1:6.5). In comparison, the GDP of Yancheng, Jiangsu Province in 2020 was 600 billion RMB, with fiscal revenues of only 40 billion RMB.

6.8 Virtual Currency as a Money Laundering Tool

6.8.1 Virtual Currencies Becoming a Payment Tool for Cybercrime

Virtual currencies have gained considerable popularity and have been widely adopted as a prevalent payment method within the darknet community, serving as a means of conducting transactions among cybercriminals. Thus, they have become an essential tool for facilitating illicit transactions between criminal entities. In fact, almost all transactions conducted on darknet markets exclusively rely on virtual currency (Fig. 6.5).

Fig. 6.5 The layers of internet[28]

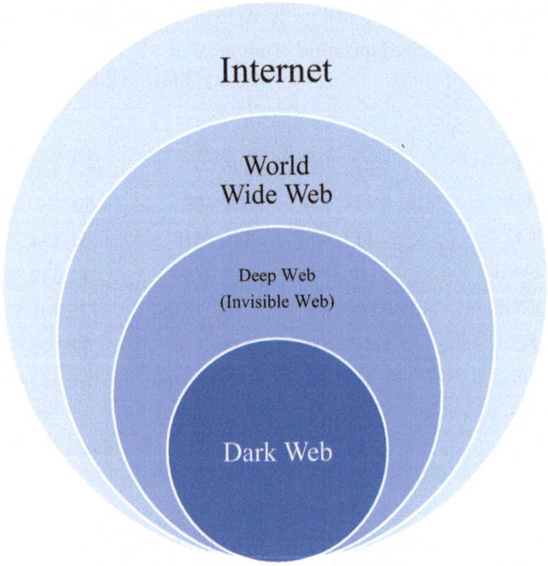

THE LAYERS OF INTERNET: The current World Wide Web is part of the Internet, which can be divided into two parts: the surface web and the deep web. An ordinary person can only access the surface web in their daily lives, which can be indexed by search engines and accessed directly through regular browsers. On the other hand, the deep web, also known as the invisible web, consists of content that cannot be indexed by search engines, including email, paid databases, or company intranets. The scope of the deep web is estimated to be at least 4,000 to 5,000 times larger than the surface web.

The "Dark Web" is a part of the "Deep Web" that deliberately hides content, web addresses, etc., using encryption technology, requiring special software, authorization, or settings to access. The most common Dark Web addresses are those supported by the Tor network, which appear as "onion" in Tor clients and browsers that support the Tor protocol. In addition to Tor addresses, Dark Web addresses include I2P, Freenet, and other types.

Due to its strong anonymity and confidentiality features, the Dark Web can be used to protect privacy and engage in legitimate activities such as personal encrypted communication. However, it is also exploited by criminals and terrorists, serving as a platform for illegal activities, coordination, and actions encompassing various crimes.[29] For instance, the infamous Dark Web marketplace "Silk Road," which was shut down by the U.S. government in 2013, facilitated transactions totalling $1.2

[28] Finklea, Kristin. "Dark Web," *Congressional Research Service*, R44101 (2017), 3, https://fas.org/sgp/crs/misc/R44101.pdf. Accessed November 15, 2021.

[29] Of course, the intention is not to stigmatize the Dark Web, just as the author does not intend to stigmatize virtual currencies. Here, the author's intention is solely focused on the "inherent risks" associated with the Dark Web being exploited for criminal activities or, more precisely, its characteristics making it susceptible to such exploitation. According to research conducted by the "Terbium Labs" in the United States, approximately 47.7% of domain names on the Dark Web were engaged in legal activities, while 52.3% were involved in illegal activities, approximately an equal split.

billion between January 2011 and September 2013. It offered not only weapons, drugs, counterfeit passports, child pornography, and sex slavery materials but also organ trafficking services. As the founder of the website proclaimed, "I am creating an economic simulation to give people a first-hand experience of what it would be like to live in a world without the systemic use of force."[30] Furthermore, the Dark Web is also utilized for terrorist activities. For example, a post in 2014 widely circulated on the dark web titled "How to Support ISIS Anonymously", providing instructions on how to fund ISIS through Bitcoin without being detected.[31]

The emergence of virtual currencies has supplied matching anonymous payment tools for the Dark Web, creating a closed-loop system for financial transactions that can efficiently evade existing anti-money laundering monitoring. Nearly all Dark Web markets conduct transactions using virtual currencies, with approximately 76% utilizing Bitcoin and 7% employing Ethereum.[32] Bitcoin has consequently earned the moniker "King of the Dark Web."

6.8.2 Virtual Currencies to Cover Various Criminal Payment Activities

According to a 2015 report by the European Police Organization, virtual currencies were no longer limited to transactions on the dark web; they were already being exploited by various forms of cybercrime and used for transactions between criminal entities. For example, there has been a recent rise in various forms of online extortion, such as ransomware attacks, server breaches, and privacy breaches, which demand

---

This research randomly captured 400 onion addresses and analyzed their activities using tracking technology on a specific day. The research's merits lie in the random selection of addresses, avoiding any bias caused by manual selection. However, its limitations include being limited to the statistics of single-day activities and only encompassing onion routing addresses.

The research conducted by "Terbium Labs" holds significant weight in recent efforts to present a more accurate portrayal of the Dark Web, as it was even reviewed by the International Monetary Fund (IMF).

See Gollnick, Clare, and Emily Wilson. "Separating Fact from Fiction: The Truth about the Dark Web." *Terbium Labs*, 2016, https://dsimg.ubm-us.net/envelope/385643/510233/The%20Truth%20About%20The%20Dark%20Web.pdf. Accessed on November 25, 2021.

See also Kumar, Aditi, and Eric Rosenbach. "The Truth about the Dark Web." *Finance & Development* 56, no. 3 (2019): 22.

[30] Dewey, Caitlin. "Everything We Know About Ross Ulbricht, the Outdoorsy Libertarian Behind Silk Road." Washington Post, October 3, 2013. https://www.washingtonpost.com/news/the-switch/wp/2013/10/03/everything-we-know-about-ross-ulbricht-the-outdoorsy-libertarian-behind-silk-road/. Accessed on November 25, 2021.

[31] Stalinsky, Steven. "The Cryptocurrency-Terrorism Connection Is Too Big to Ignore." Washington Post, December 17, 2018. https://www.washingtonpost.com/opinions/the-cryptocurrency-terrorism-connection-is-too-big-to-ignore/2018/12/17/69ed6ab4-fe4b-11e8-83c0-b06139e540e5_story.html. Accessed on November 25, 2021.

[32] Ciphertrace. "Q2 2019 Cryptocurrency Anti-Money Laundering Report - CipherTrace," February 10, 2020. https://ciphertrace.com/q2-2019-cryptocurrency-anti-money-laundering-report/.

victims to pay a ransom using virtual currencies. This shift towards digital crime has boosted the usage of virtual currencies for payments.

In 2017, ransomware outbreaks occurred on a large scale in China and various parts of the world.[33] Infected computers were required to pay a ransom in the form of Bitcoin in return for restoring normal functionality. This marked the public's first encounter with using Bitcoin for ransom payments. The European Police Organization also observed that an increasing number of criminal activities had no longer been using traditional financial systems for payments but had begun exploiting the anonymous nature of virtual currencies to evade surveillance and law enforcement agencies.

Looking at the usage of virtual currencies themselves, at least half of them are involved in illegal criminal activities. According to a study conducted in 2018, one-quarter of Bitcoin users and half of bitcoin transactions were associated with illegal activities. This translates to an estimated annual volume of around $72 billion between 2015 and 2017, which is equivalent to the total annual drug crime expenditure in the United States and Europe.[34] These figures, both in relative and absolute terms, are astounding. It is no wonder that the then-president of the Financial Action Task Force (FATF), Marshall Billingslea, emphasized in a public article in October 2018 the importance of countries recognizing the severity of virtual currencies being exploited for criminal activities, that is, "virtual assets and financial crime now go hands in hand."[35]

[33] Ransomware is a type of computer virus that primarily operates by encrypting infected computers and demanding a ransom. Victims a corresponding password to unlock their files. One notable example of ransomware is WannaCry, which erupted in 2017. Hackers deployed this virus to extort affected users, typically demanding payment in virtual currencies like Bitcoin. Once the payment is made, the hackers provide a decryption password allowing users to restore their files.

[34] See Foley, Sean, Jonathan R. Karlsen, and Talis J. Putnins. "Sex, Drugs, and Bitcoin: How Much Illegal Activity Is Financed Through Cryptocurrencies?" *Review of Financial Studies*, 32.5 (2019): 1798–1853.

Some studies have also suggested that the number of illicit activities involving Bitcoin may not be significant. The IBM Watson AI Lab at the Massachusetts Institute of Technology (MIT) conducted in-depth learning using artificial intelligence on 230,000 payment flows and 166 features from 200,000 Bitcoin nodes. They found that only 2% of these nodes were engaged in illegal activities, while 21% were involved in legitimate activities. However, due to the inability to effectively identify the remaining 77%, the persuasive power of this study is limited. (Weber, Mark, et al. "Anti-money laundering in bitcoin: Experimenting with graph convolutional networks for financial forensics." *arXiv preprint arXiv:1908.02591* (2019), submitted on July 31, 2019, available at https://arxiv.org/abs/1908.02591).

[35] Billingslea, Marshall. "Virtual Assets and Financial Crime Now Go Hand in Hand." Financial Times, October 29, 2018. https://www.ft.com/content/8e26bba2-d91f-11e8-aa22-36538487e3d0.

6.9 What is the Real Value of Bitcoin? An Unavoidable Question

Any reliable prediction about future bitcoin prices is a perilous endeavor, just like our stock analysts who are often contradicted by the market itself: many even argue that letting investment analysts pick stocks is no better than having a monkey do it. Neither can we predict the price fluctuations of bitcoin in the next minute, nor can we say whether it is currently overvalued or undervalued, just as we cannot predict the temperature in Beijing on a specific date in January 2030. However, we can safely argue that the average temperature in Beijing in January 2030 will be much colder than that in July 2030. Even in terms of the financial market, such broad trends seem obvious. Here, we merely venture to outline (not predict) the broad developmental trends of Bitcoin. Given that Ethereum's mechanism is more complex—it acts as gas on its application platform and has practical uses—we limit this discussion to Bitcoin alone as a reflection on the value of cryptocurrencies.

In Sect. 6.4, we argued that under the current technological conditions, Bitcoin cannot become a mass public payment method. Despite this fact, Bitcoin's value has been widely accepted. This cryptocurrency has surpassed a market capitalization of one trillion dollars, operating as a self-sustaining community without the need for enforced control, representing a remarkable creation in human institutional design.

The substantial value and transaction volume of Bitcoin are the result of countless investors casting their "votes" with real money, making it hard to dismiss Bitcoin's worth outright. Even if Bitcoin held no inherent value, once a consensus on its value was established, that consensus itself would impart value to it. This is the peculiar nature of value. Similar to diamonds, if the global consensus shifted to view diamonds as a curse rather than a blessing to marriage, they would be quickly deemed ordinary stones.

6.9.1 *The "Digital Gold" Metaphor*

Bitcoin is often referred to as "digital gold" because it shares several characteristics with gold, particularly as a store of value. This metaphor is signified by the following aspects:

- **Scarcity**: The total supply of Bitcoin is capped at 21 million coins, mimicking the finite availability of gold.
- **Decentralization**: Just like gold, Bitcoin operates independently of any central authority, maintained and verified through a decentralized network, which is part of its value proposition.
- **Value Preservation**: Many investors buy gold as a hedge against economic uncertainty and inflation. Similarly, Bitcoin is seen by some as an asset to hedge against inflation.

However, there are obvious limitations to the above metaphor, which is especially apparent in the current context:

- **Price Volatility**: The price of bitcoin is much more volatile than that of gold, which is generally viewed as a stable asset. Bitcoin prices can undergo severe fluctuations in a very short period.
- **Market Maturity**: Gold has been used as an investment and industrial product for thousands of years, whereas Bitcoin has only been around since 2009 and its market is still evolving.

6.9.2 The Dynamic Evolution of Bitcoin's Value

From the perspective of dynamic evolution, Nikolay Gertchev believes that the legitimacy of Bitcoin as money is similar to that of gold, possessing "money-ness."[36] Initially, Bitcoin was merely for personal amusement within the cypherpunk community (similar to the decorative use of gold in ancient times). However, as Bitcoin mining involves costs, it holds primitive value. Moreover, Bitcoin's decentralized ledger allows for the transfer of value, while its algorithmically determined finite supply (unlike unrestrained issuance of fiat currency) and the increasing cost of mining contribute to its rising value. As the value of Bitcoin increases, its acceptance also expands, promoting mutual enhancement that ultimately establishes Bitcoin as a trustworthy, appreciating currency. Although Gertchev's article was published in a concise format, it has had significant influence, which is considered a comprehensive exposition of Bitcoin's monetary attributes by many quantitative studies endorsing this viewpoint.

From the perspective of demand or utility, gold has extensive ornamental and industrial uses. Bitcoin proponents argue that its innovative decentralized ledger system, which records ownership and transfers, and its blockchain technology contributions (like proof of work and tamper resistance) are inherently valuable.[37]

In terms of transactional attributes, supporters believe that Bitcoin offers better transactional qualities than gold, allowing infinite divisibility and unrestricted transactions regardless of the geographical location of the parties involved. Some studies have even suggested that these transactional attributes themselves represent a technological contribution, enhancing the unique demand or utility value of Bitcoin.[38]

From a value perspective, supporters believe that the computational power invested in mining is an indicator of the costs of Bitcoin. While these costs cannot

---

[36] Gertchev, Nikolay. "The Money-Ness of Bitcoins." Mises Daily, April 4, 2013. https://mises.org/mises-daily/money-ness-bitcoins.

[37] Van Alstyne, Marshall. "Why Bitcoin Has Value." *Communications of the ACM* 57, 5 (2014): 30–32. https://www.researchgate.net/publication/273609426_Why_Bitcoin_Has_Value.

[38] Polasik, Michal, Anna Iwona Piotrowska, Tomasz Piotr Wisniewski, and Radosław Kotkowski. "Price Fluctuations and the Use of Bitcoin: An Empirical Inquiry." *International Journal of Electronic Commerce* 20, no. 1 (2015): 9–49. https://www.researchgate.net/publication/280570108_Price_Fluctuations_and_the_Use_of_Bitcoin_An_Empirical_Inquiry.

be directly linked to fiat currency prices, mining costs represent a lower bound for Bitcoin's price, similar to gold. Further studies concluded that while the price of virtual currencies, priced in fiat money, does not strongly correlate with mining costs, there is a statistically significant correlation between the price system of virtual currencies (the exchange rate among virtual currencies) and their mining costs.[39]

As for the mining costs and prices of Bitcoin (marked in legal currencies), we can observe that there exists a mutually reinforcing relationship between them, involving both positive and negative cycles. The Bitcoin mining market can be seen as fully competitive. When Bitcoin prices rise, the market sentiment boosts, leading to the addition of many new mining machines and driving up mining costs. This usually occurs during an extremely optimistic market phase, where the increased mining costs further drive up prices. However, when Bitcoin's price reaches a certain high level, and the market lacks the momentum to further elevate prices, mining becomes unprofitable, and latecomers (often those who purchased expensive mining equipment) may go bankrupt and leave the playing field. Likewise, when Bitcoin prices fall below a critical threshold, it makes mining unprofitable, which may lead to a mass exodus of mining rigs, causing costs to plummet. This scenario occurred after the high of September 2021 during a prolonged period of low Bitcoin prices. Such interplay miraculously maintains Bitcoin prices at certain levels, then forms new price expectations, leading to price increases and creating a spiraling upward cycle, as can be seen in Fig. 6.6.

Summarizing the supportive views on Bitcoin, since its total supply is fixed, Bitcoin's intrinsic value will gradually increase as mining becomes increasingly difficult (and costs keep rising), stabilizing its value over time.

6.9.3 A Future Store of Value?

In recent years, we have seen Bitcoin become a popular choice as value preservation tool in countries experiencing currency devaluation or economic instability, serving as a tool against inflation. The network effect could showcase the value of Bitcoin in more extensive transactions. This value is also significantly influenced by Bitcoin's user base and acceptance. As more people and businesses recognize and accept Bitcoin's value, the consensus on this value will gradually solidify and grow, likely reducing price volatility.

Moreover, as governments successively clarify regulations on cryptocurrencies, Bitcoin's role as a legal transaction and investment vehicle may be further consolidate, enhancing its value and the stabilization of its price.

Overall, with the major world currencies experiencing unusual monetary policies, such as unlimited easing, not only is the credit of fiat currencies being overdrawn

[39], Adam Hayes,"Cryptocurrency Value Formation: An Empirical Study Leading to a Cost of Production Model for Valuing Bitcoin." *Telematics and Informatics* 34, 7 (2017): 1308–1321. https://papers.ssrn.com/sol3/papers.cfm?abstract_id=2648366.

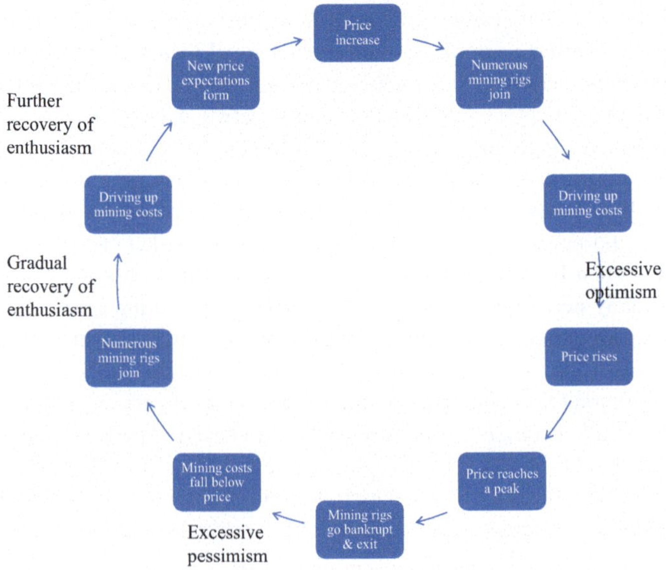

Fig. 6.6 The upward spiral of bitcoin prices and mining costs

but also their value. Bitcoin, as a competitive alternative to fiat currencies (at least as a store of value), might be pricing in the overdrawn value of legal tender.

From a broader trend perspective, Bitcoin may not be a practical payment tool but could very well serve as an effective store of value, although it seems inevitably to suffer high volatility in the foreseeable future.

Chapter 7
The Deeper Inner Workings of Digital Currencies: Central Bank Digital Currency

How did the concept of CBDC emerge as a response to Bitcoin and blockchain technology? What are the two distinct developmental paths set for CBDCs and their respective focal points and impacts? How has blockchain technology influenced the development of CBDCs, particularly in terms of payment technologies and models? What global experiments have been conducted that involve CBDCs? What are the details and significance of China's retail and wholesale CBDC model experiments?

In this chapter, we discuss the development and potential of CBDCs, with a focus on their responses to Bitcoin and blockchain technology. We identify two main driving forces behind CBDCs: financial crises leading to digital legal tender issuance by central banks and the advent of blockchain technology through Bitcoin. These also delineate two paths for CBDC development: efficiency-focused "wholesale" and public-oriented "retail" models. We further highlight the role of blockchain in CBDCs, particularly in innovative payment technologies.

Moreover, we examine China's CBDC experiments, emphasizing the importance of their dual approach incorporating both retail and wholesale models, that is strongly connected to China's significant role in the global development of digital currencies and its exploration of technological and regulatory aspects.

The author's fundamental perspective is the revolutionary potential of CBDCs, especially in the context of cross-border payments and the international monetary system. He believes that while domestic applications of wholesale CBDCs primarily enhance the settlement efficiency, international applications could lead to significant structural changes in the global financial system.

Y. Wu and W. Zhu, *The Fundamentals of Digital Currency*,
https://doi.org/10.1007/978-981-97-8261-1_7

7.1 Overview

7.1.1 The Conception of Central Bank Digital Currency (CBDC) as a Response to Bitcoin

The world's first concept of Central Bank Digital Currency (CBDC) inspired by Bitcoin and blockchain technology was Fedcoin in 2014. After that, RScoin in the United Kingdom became the first CBDC to undergo experimental operation in 2015. Since then, countries such as Canada, Singapore, Hong Kong, Thailand, and Japan have carried out their own experiments on CBDCs for various purposes using different technologies.

The concept of CBDC as a standalone idea was first proposed by Ben Broadbent in 2016. He emphasized the innovation of blockchain in settlement as the key aspect of CBDC worth studying.[1] Broadbent associated the concept of CBDC with cryptocurrency technology.

In 2017, Ole Bjerg defined money as having gone through three stages: minting, printing, and digital. In the present era of digital currency, CBDC, which is a universal electronic currency issued by central banks, falls into this category. In Bjerg's classification of currencies based on whether they are issued by central banks, electronic, and universal, CBDC satisfies all three criteria. The article analyzes the functions and potential effects of CBDC from the perspectives of currency users, managers, and issuers in different scenarios.[2]

In their 2017 internal report, Walter Engert and Ben S. C. Fung of the Bank of Canada defined CBDC as central bank-issued "digital currency that could be used by the general public." Their report provided a thorough analysis of the motivations and purposes of central bank-issued digital currencies, pointing out that some motivations were not urgent while others were not feasible. It stated that improving the efficiency of retail payment systems was the most meaningful motivation for CBDC at the time.[3]

In a 2017 paper on central bank cryptocurrencies (CBCC) by Morten Bech and Rodney Garratt, the concept of the "money flower" was introduced to classify currencies based on four dimensions: issuer, electrification, peer-to-peer architecture, and accessibility.[4] Building upon this classification, the Bank for International Settlements (BIS) proposed a widely accepted categorization of digital currencies in 2018. According to the BIS, Central Bank Digital Currencies (CBDCs) are defined as digital forms of currency issued by central banks, which can be further classified

---

[1] Broadbent, Ben. "Central Banks and Digital Currencies." *Speech by Deputy Governor for Monetary Policy, Bank of England to the London School of Economics*, 2 March 2016.

[2] Bjerg, Ole. "Designing New Money—The Policy Trilemma of Central Bank Digital Currency." *Copenhagen Business School Working Paper*, 2017.

[3] Engert, Walter, and Ben Siu-Cheong Fung. "Central Bank Digital Currency: Motivations and Implications." *Bank of Canada Staff Discussion Paper*, no. 2017-16, 2017.

[4] Bech, Morten L., and Rodney Garratt. "Central Bank Cryptocurrencies." BIS Quarterly Review, September 2017. https://ssrn.com/abstract=3041906.

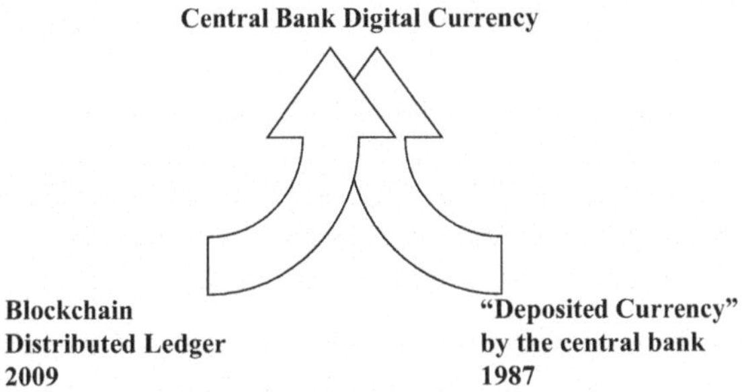

Fig. 7.1 The two driving forces of central bank digital currencies

into wholesale (limitedly accessible) and general-purpose (universally accessible) groups. For CBDCs with general-purpose functionality, they can be distinguished as either token-based or account-based.[5]

7.1.2 The Two Driving Forces of Central Bank Digital Currencies (CBDCs)

Historically, the First Driving Force Behind Today's CBDCs Was the Concept of Central Banks Directly Issuing Digital Legal Tender to the Public

In the early 1980s to the early 1990s, the United States faced a severe savings and loan crisis, which led to the collapse of numerous savings and loan associations. In response to the escalating crisis in 1985–1986, James Tobin proposed the concept of "deposited currency." The public could open "deposited currency accounts" directly with the central bank, with "deposited currency" referring to electronic cash issued by the central bank. Similar to physical cash, "deposited currency" represented the direct credit of the central bank. Through this concept, the public could enjoy perpetually secure electronic payment services without relying on financial intermediaries (banks).[6] The direct issuance of "deposited currency" by a central bank to the public can be seen as the earliest prototype concept of "central bank digital currency" (see Fig. 7.1).

At the time, the Internet was not widely accessible, physical cash still being the main form of currency. Thus, the concept of "deposited currency" may have been ahead of its time and lacked a significant social impact. In Sect. 5.2, we have discussed another cutting-edge private digital currency called eCash. Similarly, the pursuit of personal privacy protection by eCash did not garner significant social concern in the 1990s as it does today, which resulted in the failure of eCash.

[5] Committee on Payments and Market Infrastructures and the Markets Committee, Bank for International Settlements. "Central Bank Digital Currencies," March 2018. https://www.bis.org/cpmi/publ/d174.pdf, p. 6.

[6] Tobin, James. "The Case for Preserving Regulatory Distinctions." *Restructuring the Financial System: A Symposium Sponsored by the Federal Reserve Bank of Kansas City*, 1987, 167–183.

During the 1980s, the concept of "deposited currency" did not generate significant response. It was nearly a decade later, in 1996, when the Bank for International Settlements briefly analyzed the potential impact of central banks directly issuing electronic currency to the public in its report, although Tobin's paper was not referenced.[7] It was only after the emergence of Bitcoin that the possibility of central banks directly issuing electronic currency was brought up once again; people suddenly rediscovered Tobin's brilliant concept from over thirty years ago.

The Emergence of Blockchain Technology Through Bitcoin Became the Second Driving Force and the Most Direct Catalyst for CBDCs

In 2009, the creation of Bitcoin sparked a breakthrough phenomenon in virtual/cryptocurrencies, triggering a social movement of experiments with private currencies. While cryptocurrencies like Bitcoin have shortcomings in fulfilling the three functions of legal tender, therefore not displayed any potential to undermine existing fiat currency systems, major central banks have cautiously observed the development of virtual currencies and have not expressed concerns about their replacement of fiat currency.

However, Bitcoin technologically inspired the concept of transforming the fiat currency system using blockchain technology. In 2014, Canadian financial writer and blogger JP Koning proposed the idea of issuing a digitized US dollar called Fedcoin based on Bitcoin technology in an online article. In 2016, the Deputy Governor of Bank of England, Ben Broadbent, introduced the notion of developing a CBDC using Bitcoin technology, thus first mentioning the concept of "central bank digital currency" and associating it with blockchain technology.

By 2019, Facebook announced the Libra project, which triggered widespread concern among major nations regarding private digital currencies. As discussed in Sect. 5.8, the US Congress and monetary authorities openly expressed their concerns about Diem; furthermore, Switzerland and the United States did not grant the necessary permissions to this currency. Diem also stimulated major nations to accelerate research and development of CBDCs to a certain extent.

7.1.3 The Two Paths of Central Bank Digital Currencies

Bitcoin inspired the transformation of the existing fiat currency system, leading to two distinct development paths. The first involves leveraging blockchain technology in the financial institution's clearing and settlement processes to enhance efficiency, commonly referred to as "wholesale" CBDC. The second entails issuing electronic/digital fiat currency to the public, often known as "retail" CBDC or "general-purpose" CBDC. The first path primarily represents a technological improvement, which,

[7] Bank for International Settlements. "Implications for Central Banks of the Development of Electronic Money," October 1996. https://www.bis.org/publ/bisp01.pdf.

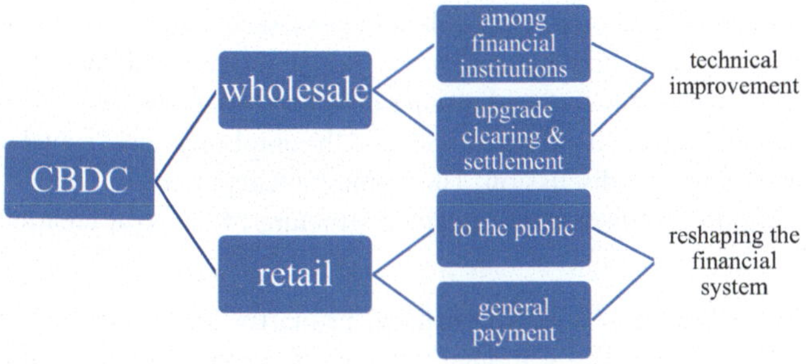

Fig. 7.2 The two paths of central bank digital currency

although considered as CBDC, merely enhances the efficiency of the existing electronic clearing and settlement processes without fundamentally altering the financial system (please refer to Sect. 2.4 of this book, where it is explained that financial institutions achieve clearing and settlement through central banks in the current monetary system, albeit at a lower level of electronic integration and with lower efficiency) (see Fig. 7.2).

Nowadays, the true potential for fundamental change in the financial system lies in the second path, namely, retail CBDC or general-purpose CBDC. In November 2019, the former Governor of the People's Bank of China, Xiaochuan Zhou, pointed out in his speech that "Central bank digital currency is more focused on the domestic market and may pay more attention to wholesale operations between central banks and third-party payment institutions in terms of digital currency provision in the wholesale and settlement process. In theory, central bank digital currency can also be used for retail services, but due to the significant impact it would have on the existing financial system, everyone is very cautious."[8]

As discussed in Sect. 2.4 of this book, by issuing digital fiat currency directly to the public, central banks are set to change the traditional path of money and exert at least the following impacts on the financial order:

- Currency form: The native form of digital currency becomes digital, transforming money from physical form to digital form.
- Payment efficiency: Digital currency functions as peer-to-peer digital cash, where payment is equivalent to clearing and settlement.
- Financial system: Digital currency gains the potential to operate independently of financial intermediaries and alter the credit creation framework in the existing financial system.
- Trust in digital currency no longer comes from financial intermediaries (e.g., electronic banks, third-party payment platforms), but directly from central banks, reflecting the relationship between currency holders and central banks.

[8] On November 8, 2019, at the 10th Caixin Summit; the speech video is available at: http://photos.caixin.com/2019-11-08/101480405_3.html#picture, and the transcript can be found at: https://www.sohu.com/a/352512170_481890.

- As digital currency becomes traceable and possesses unique identifiable "tags," with each unit deposited by customers being unique and identifiable, it is technologically possible to avoid mixing currencies together.
- The existence of financial intermediaries and the amplification of social credit will become new topics for discussion. The technological potential of digital currency has the capability to disrupt the financial structure of "deposit creation through lending."

Wholesale CBDC, in a domestic setting, primarily focuses on improving the efficiency of the clearing and settlement processes among financial institutions. It can be seen as a technological upgrade that streamlines transactions between banks. On the other hand, retail CBDC not only enhances payment efficiency but also has the potential to transform the general-purpose currency and reshape the entire financial system. Therefore, when discussing the impact of central bank digital currency, we generally refer to retail CBDC.

In the case of trans-border payments, wholesale CBDC, such as mBridge, aims to facilitate the clearing and settlement processes through collaboration between different central banks. This implies a fundamental shift in the current international financial system, which has traditionally relied on systems like SWIFT and the corresponding banks of US dollar. The introduction of wholesale CBDCs could potentially challenge the reliance on these systems and reshape the way cross-border payments are conducted.

7.2 How Has Blockchain Technology Inspired the Current Financial Landscape?

Bitcoin has demonstrated the feasibility of peer-to-peer electronic cash, and blockchain has timely introduced innovative technology and models, reigniting the idea of "cash deposit." However, central banks around the world need to make choices regarding these technologies and models, and they may not accept them all.

7.2.1 Payment Technologies and Models

The payment technologies and models of Bitcoin can be seen in Table 7.1.

It can be seen that, Bitcoin's innovations in payment technologies and business models are demonstrated in three aspects:

- A peer-to-peer payment, which facilitates direct transactions between parties, eliminating the need for intermediaries in clearing and settlement.

Table 7.1 Innovations in Payment Technologies and Models Brought by Bitcoin

Technological features	Innovations	Attitude of Central Banks	Choices by Central Banks
Asymmetric encryption signatures	Peer-to-peer payment	Recognize and accept	Elimination of intermediaries in clearing and settlement – Streamlining of payment process – Increased efficiency of the current electronic payments
	Registration of digital asset ownership under decentralized conditions	Recognize and accept	Declaration of ownership through digital signatures to achieve digitalized registration of asset
	Privacy protection	Cautious but accepted to an extent	– Protection of user privacy, but this requires measures against money laundering risks – Making use for inclusive finance in microtransactions, but needs to balance with regulation

- Decentralized digitalized ownership registration, which allows users to declare the ownership of digital assets through digital signatures, ensuring the verification of ownership rights in a decentralized condition.
- Privacy protection, which enables anonymous payment through electronic means.

1. Peer-to-peer payment

From the perspective of monetary transactions, it is easy to understand that asymmetric encryption technology enables peer-to-peer payments. This is the most easily noticeable technological innovation of Bitcoin that is most likely to be accepted by central banks. It can be argued that, from the beginning of the proposal of central bank digital currency, central banks have placed great emphasis on the characteristics of Bitcoin's peer-to-peer electronic cash, hoping to achieve payment and settlement through blockchain technology.

2. Registration of digital asset ownership under decentralized conditions

If we further consider the essence of Bitcoin beyond peer-to-peer payment technology, in a decentralized network, the ownership of rights can be determined by using asymmetric encryption technology for signature verification. In Chap. 5, Sect. 7.3, we have mentioned that bitcoin owners possess private keys to prove their ownership rights. In other words, the payment and transfer process of Bitcoin is a process of proving ownership.

Prior to the advent of Bitcoin, Nick Szabo had discussed how to use digital signatures to declare user ownership in a decentralized network in his 1998 paper titled "Secure Property Titles with Owner Authority." The birth of Bitcoin has truly provided a suitable solution to this problem. Subsequently, protocols such as Mastercard and BitShares were developed for asset registration purposes.

Blockchain technology provides a new way of holding and settling assets. In a famous speech in 2016, the Deputy Governor of the Bank of England, Ben Broadbent, highlighted that Bitcoin offered a sophisticated settlement method and a unique way of holding assets. He described its essence as a "decentralized virtual clearinghouse and asset register."

Before pursuing comprehensive testing of central bank digital currency, the People's Bank of China successfully conducted a pilot test of a blockchain-based digital bill trading platform in 2017.[9] Each validating node represents a reputable entity that securely stores its public and private keys. All participants on the bill platform require authentication and data encryption using private keys for transactions, queries and other business operations.

3. Privacy Protection

When it comes to payments with bitcoin, addresses on the public blockchain are open and do not require identity verification. This payment approach emphasizes customer privacy protection; however, the anonymity of such transactions can be potentially exploited for money laundering and criminal activities. Therefore, central banks and regulatory authorities generally approach this payment means with caution, aiming to strike a balance between privacy protection for customers and promoting inclusive finance. For instance, in the pilot process of China's Digital Yuan (renminbi), limited anonymity was allowed for small-value transactions.

7.2.2 Issuance Mechanism

The innovative Proof-of-Work (PoW) mechanism of Bitcoin combines the confirmation of transaction records with the issuance of currency through competitive incentives, thus creating an automatic deflationary currency issuance mechanism. This is deeply rooted in Hayek's concept of private currency, reflecting extreme distrust towards central banks. As Hayek pointed out, throughout history, central banks issuing currency in capitalist systems have always ended up with government

[9] Zhou, Lei, and Jie Chen. "Study of Use of Blockchain Technology in National Digital Currency." *Journal of Hangzhou Insititute of Financial Studies*, no. 6 (2018): 27–31. (周雷、陈捷,《国家数字货币应用区块链技术初探》, 载《杭州金融研修学院学报》2018(06):27–31).

Table 7.2 Innovations in the issuance mechanism brought by bitcoin

Technical features	Innovations	Attitude of Central Banks	Choices by Central Banks
Decentralized issuance	Decentralized issuance of currency	Strong opposition	Adhere to centralized issuance of currency
POW (proof-of-work)	51% honest computing power ensures payment security	Strong opposition	Insist on centralized ledger
	Competition for bookkeeping rewards	Strong opposition	– Oppose to algorithm-adjusted currency issuance – Adhere to flexible currency issuance
	Fixed-quantity deflationary currency		

insolvency and currency devaluation. In contrast, Bitcoin entrusts the issuance of currency to machines that strictly follow algorithms and predefines the transaction pace and total supply of bitcoin.

This mechanism fundamentally challenges the authority of central banks, which they cannot accept under any circumstances. To maintain their monopoly over currency, central banks have to reject the decentralized issuance of bitcoin and its proof-of-work mechanism. Currently, in the ongoing pilot phase of the Digital Yuan (renminbi), the model adopted is centralized issuance by the People's Bank of China (Table 7.2).

7.2.3 *Programmable Currency*

The currency form of Bitcoin is "token-based," where each bitcoin is a unique string of code. In contrast, the existing financial system operates on an "account-based" model, where currency is commingled and stored in centralized ledgers of financial institutions.

The fundamental feature of the digital form of currency lies in the distinction between "token-based" and "account-based" systems. In the "token-based" form, electronic/digital currencies are represented as a string of code, which is traceable. Traceability is not only crucial for anti-money laundering measures but also a prerequisite for programmability and intelligence.

The "token-based" nature of a currency enables its programmability, opening up a range of intelligent features. For example:

- Central banks can better achieve their goal of penetrative supervision and monitor the effectiveness of monetary policies through central bank digital currencies.
- The use of central bank digital currencies allows access to automated finance.

- The current 7-day payment feature provided by e-commerce platforms relies on a trusted platform. With central bank digital currencies, the payment terms can be defined in smart contracts, eliminating the need for third-party accounts.
- Deposit and prepayment used in businesses can be locked in smart contracts rather than being handed over to the merchant or third party, and automatic payment can be made based on the agreed terms.
- Central banks can designate a batch of currency to flow exclusively into green industries when issuing digital currencies.

Currently, the only implemented and tested large-scale pilot of central bank digital currencies is China's digital yuan. The country has witnessed experiments in payment technologies, models, and issuance mechanisms; however, the Digital Yuan has not yet opened up its smart contract interface. Our understanding in this regard is speculative: the extent to which smart contracts are open depends on the overall positioning of the central bank digital currency. As stated in the "Progress of Research and & Development of Digital RMB in China" (hereinafter referred as The Whitepaper of Digital RMB of 2021) programmability in Digital Yuan is realized by adding smart contracts that do not affect the currency's functionalities. This allows the Digital Yuan to facilitate automatic payment transactions based on conditions and rules agreed upon by the transacting parties while ensuring safety and compliance, thereby promoting business model innovation (Table 7.3).

7.3 Exploring Central Bank Digital Currency: From Early Practices to Blockchain

7.3.1 Four Potential Models of Central Bank Digital Currency

In the existing fiat currency system, central banks issue physical cash to the public, and the interaction between central banks and commercial banks occurs in electronic form. The reserve management and settlement systems of commercial banks rely on the centralized databases of central banks. If no specific technological pursuit is present other than digitization, it can be considered that the current reserve system already functions as a central bank digital currency, since reserve systems are based on database technology, which is electronic in nature (the term "digital" is an advanced form of "electronic," as discussed in Chap. 2).

Based on the existing fiat currency system, combined with blockchain and distributed ledger technology, there are logically four potential models for central bank digital currency (see Fig. 7.3):

1. **Wholesale CBDC (Type I)**: This involves blockchain technology to improve the efficiency of existing reserve systems through distributed ledgers. It is also

Table 7.3 Programmability of currency enabled by bitcoin

Technical features	Innovation	Attitude of Central Banks	Potential Choices by Central Banks
Token[a]	Traceability	Recognize and accept	Reforming the account-based system for the convenience of traceability
	Providing foundational support for programmability	Recognize and accept	Central banks expect programmability to bring regulatory innovation, issuance innovation, and financial business innovation
Script and smart contracts	Smart traceability	Recognize and accept	Improved regulatory efficiency in areas such as anti-money laundering and crime prevention
	Programmable currency	Recognize and accept	Regulatory innovation, financial business innovation – Penetrative supervision to monitor the effectiveness of monetary policies – Facilitating payments and transactions of financial assets – Automation in finance

[a] Based on scientific rigor, it should be "UTXO and Token" here. Cryptocurrencies can achieve traceability through various implementation methods, including UTXO + script, Ethereum's account balance + smart contracts, and Ethereum tokens. Different implementation methods imply different granularity, resulting in differences in traceability accuracy. In terms of traceability precision, Bitcoin's token is not as advanced as Ethereum's token. This table is a simplified discussion. Readers can refer to Chap. 7, Sect. 7.5 of this book for further details.

known as wholesale CBDCs, examples of which include Canada's CADcoin and Singapore's Ubin.

2. **Direct CBDC (Type II)**: This involves a centralized database where the central bank's balance sheet is accessible to the public. Individuals can open accounts with the central bank and transact on its electronic ledger. While this type may not strictly meet the criteria of a "digital currency" without using decentralized databases, it can still be called a CBDC. Examples include James Tobin's concept of "deposit cash" and Ecuador's Dinero Electrónico, the world's first central bank digital currency based on traditional account models.

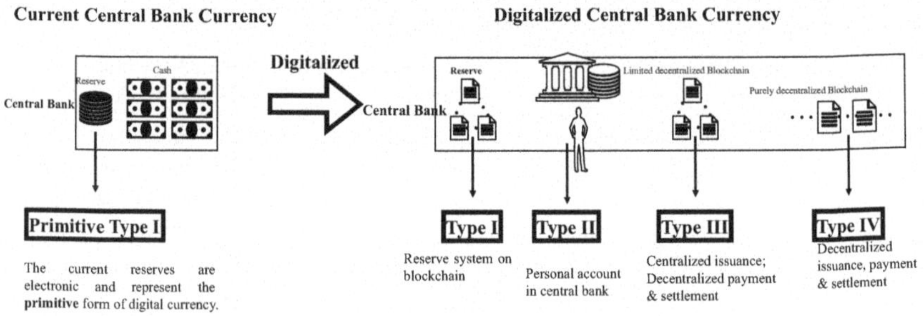

Fig. 7.3 Four potential models of Central Bank digital currency

3. **Retail CBDC with Limit Decentralization (Type III)**: This type is used for consumer payment purposes. It is an electronic form of currency issued by the central bank for retail transactions, based on blockchain-like distributed ledger technology and asymmetric encryption. This comprises the strict definition of a CBDC, also known as retail CBDC or general-purpose CBDC. Currently, general-purpose CBDCs are typically issued on centralized databases (to maintain the central bank's issuance monopoly), whereas settlement and payment processes utilize distributed technologies that support peer-to-peer transactions. An example is China's digital renminbi.
4. **Decentralized Retail CBDC (Type IV)**: This type is also used for consumer payment purposes, and is an electronic form of currency issued by the central bank based on blockchain-like distributed ledger technology and asymmetric encryption. However, its issuance process also operates on a decentralized system executed by algorithms. This is a fully decentralized form of digital currency similar to Bitcoin. Currently, very few central banks seriously consider this approach, with El Salvador being the only known case of a country using Bitcoin as legal tender.

It should be noted that the second type of CBDC cannot be considered a true "digital currency" and has proven to be impractical. The fourth type, which involves complete decentralization, amounts to relinquishing currency sovereignty and has no practical significance for general adaptation. Therefore, when discussing CBDCs, we generally refer to wholesale and retail CBDCs, with retail CBDCs considered the true forms of CBDCs.

7.3.2 Central Bank Digital Currency Experiments

1. Dinero Electrónico: Failure of the Central Bank Providing Services Directly to the Public

Dinero Electrónico in Ecuador was the world's first central bank digital currency based on a traditional account-based model. It was planned and launched in 2014, falling under the category of the second type of central bank digital currency, also known as "direct" central bank digital currency (more accurately termed as "central bank electronic currency" due to its low level of digitization). In this system, citizens directly opened accounts with the central bank and conducted transactions such as payments and transfers on their mobile phones. However, due to its failure to attract a large number of users and generate significant transaction volumes (with only 5000 users in 2015 and a total transaction value of only $800,000 by the end of 2016), this system was discontinued in 2017 and replaced by mobile payment systems provided by commercial banks.[10]

Dinero Electrónico was an unsuccessful attempt, indicating that both from the perspective of currency issuance and the operation of the payment system, a central bank operating an entire currency payment system independently without relying on commercial banks poses significant challenges.

Dinero electrónico in Ecuador

- Issuer: The Central Bank of Ecuador
- Technology: Centralized
- Model: Account-based system (centralized issuance, settlement and payment)
- Objective: The central bank provides account services directly to users
- Currency Type: Retail/General purpose
- Status: Operational but failed
- Digital Currency: Not strictly a digital currency, but a central bank electronic currency

2. Fedcoin: a Conceptual Prototype of a Standard CBDC

JP Koning, a financial writer and blogger from Canada, has published a series of articles on his blog discussing Bitcoin and how the existing central bank system could be transformed using Bitcoin's technological architecture. In 2014, he first came up with the idea of issuing fiat currency using blockchain technology in an article titled "Fedcoin." Therein, he suggested that the Federal Reserve issue a new currency called "Fedcoin", that incorporates similar blockchain technology as Bitcoin but is anchored in the value of existing US dollar banknotes and electronic reserves to address the volatility issue of Bitcoin.[11]

It should be clarified that some subsequent studies refer to Fedcoin as the concept of the first CBDC. This is based on the premise that the definition of CBDC includes technological elements, specifying that a CBDC must be built on new technologies like blockchain and distributed ledger and serve as a retail currency issued to the public.

Although JP Koning's Fedcoin has not been implemented, it received support for the concept from David Andolfatto, Vice President of the St. Louis Federal Reserve.[12]

[10] Please refer to White, Lawrence H. "The World's First Central Bank Electronic Money Has Come–and Gone: Ecuador, 2014–2018," n.d. https://www.alt-m.org/2018/03/29/the-worlds-first-central-bank-electronic-money-has-come-and-gone-ecuador-2014-2018/.

[11] Please refer to Koning, J. P. "Fedcoin," October 19, 2014. http://jpkoning.blogspot.com/2014/10/fedcoin.html.

[12] Please refer to "Bitcoin and Beyond: An Overview of Bitcoin," March 30, 2014. https://www.stlouisfed.org/dialogue-with-the-fed/the-possibilities-and-the-pitfalls-of-virtual-currencies/videos/part-2-an-overview-of-bitcoin.

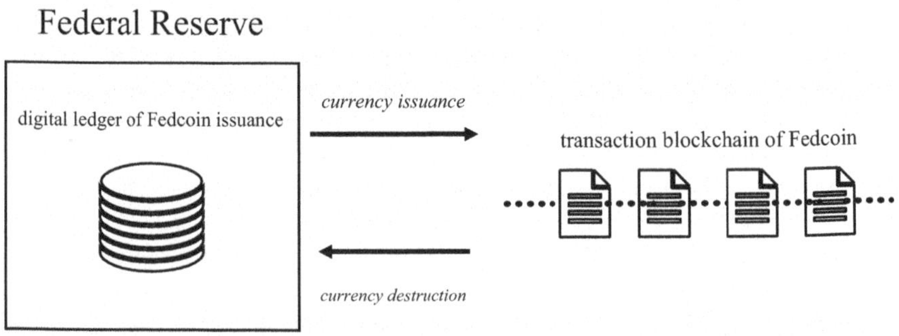

Fig. 7.4 The limited decentralization of fedcoin

Nonetheless, the subsequent design and experiments on CBDCs conducted by various countries have more or less learned and referenced the ideas of Fedcoin.

The blockchain technology used in Fedcoin is rather similar in pattern to Ripple and USDT, where the issuance and destruction of currency are executed by a single centralized institution, the Federal Reserve. However, the execution and verification of transactions are shared among numerous distributed nodes of banks and institutions, collectively maintaining the ledger data.

As can be seen from Fig. 7.4, after issuance, like US dollar banknotes, Fedcoin enters a state of free circulation and is no longer under the control of the Federal Reserve and commercial banks.

Fedcoin is an independent form of currency but can only be exchanged for US dollar cash and reserves at a fixed exchange rate of 1:1. When exchanging for a unit of Fedcoin, an equivalent amount of cash or reserves is destroyed, and when a unit of Fedcoin is disposed, an equivalent amount of cash or reserves is issued. Therefore, the issuance of Fedcoin is executed by the central bank, but its supply is determined by market demand.

Although Fedcoin is a third liability form for the central bank, its supply volatility is the same as that of cash, so it does not affect the monetary policy of the central bank. There is only one exception—Fedcoin allows the central bank to implement negative interest rates, something that was not possible in the past monetary system. From this perspective, Fedcoin provides a new tool of monetary policy for the central bank.

According to JP Koning, the main purpose of issuing Fedcoin is to reduce costs and provide a more economical payment method. US dollar cash incurs issuance costs, while Fedcoin can be issued at zero cost. Fedcoin achieves this by eliminating the process of settlement and achieving payment settlement simultaneously.

Undoubtedly, the issuance and operation of Fedcoin is going to impact the position of commercial banks, making them seemingly redundant. JP Koning believes that the way forward for commercial banks is to issue their own digital currencies, similar to today's bank deposits. Commercial banks can compete with Fedcoin through interest rates and services, thus finding a way to survive in the new model.

JP Koning predicts that, after the emergence of Fedcoin, bank deposits, commercial banks, credit card systems, cash, Fedwire, and even Bitcoin will be unable to compete and will gradually decline.

FEDCOIN

- Issuer: Federal Reserve (hypothetical)
- Technology: Blockchain (for transactions) and centralized database (for issuance)
- Model: Combination of an account-based system and blockchain (centralized issuance, decentralized payment and settlement)
- Objective: Digitization and blockchainization of the Federal Reserve's monetary system
- Currency Type: Retail/universal
- Project Status: Concept exploration only, not tested or implemented
- Digital Currency: CBDC in the strict sense (universally accessible CBDC)

3. Rscoin: An Experiment with Standard CBDC

The Bank of England, as the central bank of the United Kingdom, commenced the research of virtual currencies quite early. In 2015, they first introduced the concept of CBDC (Central Bank Digital Currency) and delved into the discussion and research of its technical and design aspects. As soon as a year later, they began collaborating with the University of London to design and develop RSCoin, which included experimental tests. While Fedcoin remained in the conceptual discussion stage, RSCoin became the first central bank digital currency to be developed and tested on a technical level.

RSCoin adheres to the same principles as Fedcoin: fiat currency is issued by the central bank while transactions are executed on a distributed ledger. RSCoin is an experimental project with a focus on the technological aspects. While its intention is to retain some of the technical features of Bitcoin, its two-phase transaction submission protocol is completely different from Bitcoin's Proof-of-Work protocol. The similarities between RSCoin and Bitcoin are limited to the digital signatures, addresses, and UTXO ledger structure. Such a design of RSCoin maintains the key role of the central bank; however, it significantly enhances capacity and scalability, reaching up to 2000 transactions per second during the experimental phase.[13]

From the working report of the Bank of England, it is evident that the bank's interest in Bitcoin technology lies in its clever settlement method and property holding mechanism. The Bank of England refers to Bitcoin as a "decentralized virtual clearinghouse and asset registry."[14] The original intention of Bitcoin was to eliminate the need for third-party trust and enable issuance and settlement without the involvement of a central bank. However, the Bank of England believes that central banks can use Bitcoin's technology but with a different purpose: to make more institutions, including individuals, rely more on and trust the central bank. In the traditional currency model, the central bank only opens its balance sheet to

[13] For details on RScoin, please refer to Danezis, George, and Sarah Meiklejohn. "Centrally Banked Cryptocurrencies," February 2016. http://dx.doi.org/10.14722/ndss.2016.23187.

[14] Please refer to Broadbent, Ben. "Central Banks and Digital Currencies." *Speech by Deputy Governor for Monetary Policy, Bank of England to the London School of Economics*, 2 March 2016.

commercial banks. With the support of distributed ledger technology, the Bank of England aims to explore whether central banks can provide access to their balance sheet to more commercial institutions and even individuals, which constitutes the experimental objective of the RSCoin project.

RSCoin maintains the anonymity and transparency of transactions. After the issuance of Fedcoin and RSCoin, the central bank no longer controls them; they circulate freely, anonymously, and utilize public–private key transactions that are impossible to monitor. However, their transaction ledgers are completely transparent, similar to Bitcoin.

The successful experiment of RSCoin serves as convincing proof that, at the technical level, blockchain technology can improve the efficiency of payment, clearing & settlement. It further demonstrates the technological neutrality and that decentralization and centralization can coexist harmoniously. While Bitcoin aims to achieve decentralized issuance and settlement, becoming a non-debt currency like gold, central bank digital currencies represented by Fedcoin and RSCoin reinforce the role of central banks, where currency remains a liability of the central bank and the position of centralized entities, such as commercial banks, is weakened.

RSCOIN

- Issuer: Bank of England (in collaboration with the University of London)
- Technology: Blockchain (for transactions) and centralized database (for issuance)
- Model: Combination of an account-based system and blockchain (centralized issuance, decentralized payment and settlement)
- Objective: Experimental access to the central bank's balance sheet for individual users.
- Type of currency: Retail/universal
- Project status: Experimental, not implemented
- Digital currency: CBDC in the strict sense (universally accessible CBDC)

4. CADcoin: An Experiment with Wholesale CBDC

In 2016, the Bank of Canada (the Canadian central bank), Canadian Payments Association, six commercial banks, and the R3 consortium collaborated on the initial trial of CADcoin, a digital fiat currency system. The experimental project was named Jasper, and its purpose was to explore the use of CADcoin in wholesale markets, rather than retail consumer transactions. The model involved that participating institutions deposited collateral with the Bank of Canada in exchange for CADcoin, which was then utilized for asset transactions on the platform.

The R3 CONSORTIUM was established in 2014, with founding members JPMorgan Chase, Barclays, and another nine world-renowned banks. In 2016, R3 started developing the Corda platform, a type of "enterprise blockchain." Nodes in Corda require permission to join and transactions are validated through a "trusted notary" mechanism, making it a rather centralized system that relies on trust in third parties for transaction verification. Corda is not a strictly defined blockchain but rather a distributed ledger with similar characteristics, specifically designed for the financial industry.

CADcoin shares similar principles with Fedcoin in terms of value anchoring and conversion mechanisms. However, they differ in their target markets, with Fedcoin focusing on retail transactions and CADcoin targeting wholesale markets. Correspondingly, Fedcoin represents a new currency form that can establish novel monetary policies, while CADcoin serves as a form of deposit certificates and operates more as a settlement method powered by technological advancements.

Rod Garratt noted that, in terms of payment efficiency alone, CADcoin may be considered a step backward compared to existing electronic payment systems. However, the experiment with CADcoin validates the concept of simultaneous clearing and settlement, leading to increased efficiency within the business model.[15]

An additional distinction between CADcoin and Fedcoin is that Fedcoin aims to digitize cash while preserving cash-like anonymity. CADcoin primarily functions as a settlement tool for institutions, with anonymity and privacy not being its primary objectives. Nevertheless, to address the confidentiality requirements of participating institutions regarding transaction data, rules for data read/write or zero-knowledge proof technology can be implemented to achieve the desired level of privacy.

CADcoin

- Issuer/Participants: Bank of Canada, Canadian Payments Association, six commercial banks, and the R3 consortium
- Technology: Blockchain (for transaction) and centralized database (for issuance)
- Model: A combination of account-based system and blockchain (centralized issuance but decentralized transaction)
- Objective: Support the reserve system with blockchain technology
- Type of currency: Wholesale
- Project Status: Experimental
- Digital Currency: wholesale CBDC (technically categorized as a strict digital currency, but not universally accessible)

5. Ubin: An Experiment with Wholesale CBDC

Following CADcoin, the Monetary Authority of Singapore (the Singaporean central bank) initiated a project called Ubin, a collaboration involving technology firms like R3 and multiple banks such as HSBC, JPMorgan Chase, and DBS. In this project, three blockchain platforms— Corda, Fabric, and Quorum—were utilized to compare their transaction efficiency, privacy, high availability, and finality.[16]

Fabric, a blockchain developed by IBM, began its development in 2014. In 2015, Linux established the Hyperledger Blockchain Foundation, and IBM donated Fabric to Hyperledger. Fabric is a typical "permissioned" and "consortium" blockchain designed for enterprises and business alliances. It is currency-less and does not rely on Proof-of-Work (PoW) or Proof-of-Stake (PoS) consensus algorithms. Instead, it employs a transaction flow of "transaction proposal - endorsement - transaction submission - ordering - validation - broadcasting," which essentially relies on a centralized node for ordering service. In essence, Fabric is a modular and easy-to-implement blockchain.

Quorum is a blockchain project developed by JPMorgan Chase (later merged with ConsenSys in 2020). It is based on Ethereum technology but implements significant modifications to meet the needs of financial industry consortiums. Quorum is a permissioned and

[15] For CADcoin, please refer to Garratt, Rod. "CAD-coin versus Fedcoin." *R3 Report* 15 (2016).

[16] For Project Ubin, please refer to https://www.mas.gov.sg/schemes-and-initiatives/Project-Ubin.

consortium blockchain where only authorized nodes can participate. Its consensus mechanism is not based on PoW or PoS but utilizes the Raft consensus algorithm, which improves consensus speed but can only be used for a limited number of known nodes. A notable innovation in Quorum is the design of "private transactions," where each node maintains private transaction data alongside the publicly shared ledger among all nodes.

Banks participating in the Ubin project opened regulatory accounts on MEPS + and recorded their deposits as "Continuous Depository Receipts," which are reusable deposit certificates. The balances in these accounts were synchronized with the distributed ledger. Daytime interbank transaction settlements relied on the distributed ledger, enabling real-time settlements of "Continuous Depository Receipts."

Ubin is a wholesale CBDC designed for wholesale operations. With Ubin, the objective of the Monetary Authority of Singapore was to enhance settlement efficiency utilizing a distributed ledger system.

UBIN

- Issuer/Participants: Monetary Authority of Singapore and R3 consortium
- Technology: Blockchain (for transactions) and centralized database (for issuance)
- Model: Combination of an account-based system and blockchain (centralized issuance, decentralized transaction)
- Objective: Support the reserve system using blockchain technology
- Currency Type: Wholesale
- Project Status: Experimental
- Digital Currency: Wholesale CBDC (technically categorized as a strict digital currency, but not universally accessible)

6. Stellar: A Comprehensive Experiment of CBDC for Wholesale and Retail

The Bank of Japan (the Japanese central bank), in collaboration with the European Central Bank, embarked on a project called Stellar in 2016 to explore the application of distributed ledger technology in financial infrastructure. The Stellar project comprised three phases.[17]

The first phase aimed to verify the improvements and enhancements of liquidity in payment systems using distributed ledger technology. The second phase focused on studying the application of distributed ledger technology in securities trading, specifically examining the possibility of achieving Delivery vs. Payment (DvP) through blockchain. The third phase involved researching the use of distributed ledger technology for cross-border payment transactions.

The Stellar project utilized two blockchain platforms, Fabric and Corda, to test their performance and other differences. DvP, or Delivery vs. Payment, is a transaction method where securities and funds are settled simultaneously on the settlement date and are interdependent settlement conditions. In traditional systems, interfaces between the securities systems and fund settlement systems are required, resulting in an asynchronous process.

---

[17] For more information on the Stellar Project, please refer to The European Central Bank and the Bank of Japan. "Synchronised Cross-Border Payments," June 2019. https://www.ecb.europa.eu/paym/intro/publications/pdf/ecb.miptopical190604.en.pdf.

With the emergence of digital currencies and tokenized securities through smart contracts, true DvP can be achieved, where funds transfer and securities transfer occur simultaneously within a single blockchain transaction.

The first and second phases of the Stellar project pertain to wholesale central bank digital currency operations, while the third phase focuses on retail payment operations. By the issuance of digital currency, the Bank of Japan aims to leverage the settlement efficiency of distributed ledger and blockchain technologies to innovate the architecture of settlement systems.

STELLAR

- Host/Participants: Bank of Japan, European Central Bank
- Technology: Blockchain, Centralized Database
- Model: Combination of Account Balance and Blockchain; Centralized Issuance, Decentralized Settlement
- Purpose: Innovate the architecture of settlement systems
- Currency Type: Wholesale in Phases 1 and 2, Retail in Phase 3
- Project Status: Experimental
- Digital Currency: Technically classified as a strict digital currency

7. e-Krona: Digital Cash for Small Payments

In 2017, Sveriges Riksbank (the central bank of Sweden) initiated the development program for e-Krona, an electronic currency. The technical collaborator for this project is Accenture PLC. Their objective is to issue a central bank digital currency to replace cash and use it specifically in small-scale personal payment scenarios. The Swedish central bank has no plans to issue a central bank digital currency in the near future. The purpose of e-Krona is to conduct research on distributed ledger technology from a technological perspective.[18]

E- KRONA

- Issuer: Sveriges Riksbank
- Technology: Blockchain, Centralized Database
- Model: Combination of Account Balance and Blockchain; Centralized Issuance, Decentralized Settlement
- Purpose: Utilize blockchain technology for small payments
- Currency Type: Retail
- Project Status: Experimental
- Digital Currency: Technically, it is classified strictly as a digital currency

---

[18] For more information on e-Krona, please refer to https://www.riksbank.se/en-gb/payments-cash/e-krona/

7.4 Digital Yuan: The Grandest-Scale Experiment of Retail CBDCs

7.4.1 The Journey of China's CBDC

In 2014, the People's Bank of China (PBOC), as the Chinese central bank, initiated the research on virtual currencies such as Bitcoin. In 2016, they held a digital currency seminar and established the Digital Currency Institute (DCI) in the same year. This institute subsequently took the lead in conducting the social pilot on the digital renminbi (RMB). This was followed by the lauch and operationalization of a blockchain-based trade finance supply chain platform in 2018. By the end of 2019, the pilot testing of digital RMB began in four cities.

Currently, the digital RMB stands as the world's pioneering central bank digital currency to be utilized on a large scale. While it draws inspiration from blockchain technology, its primary approach and model closely resemble that of Fedcoin. Nevertheless, there exist numerous disparities in terms of the technical specifics and specific models.

China has been at the forefront of central bank digital currency research and development. It was the first major country to pilot a CBDC for public users. According to the White Paper of the People's Bank of China on the Development of China's Digital Renminbi, released in July 2021, as of November 2020, this bank had conducted pilot tests of the digital RMB in ten cities, including Shenzhen, Suzhou, Xiong'an, and Chengdu, covering different regions such as the Pearl River Delta, Yangtze River Delta, Beijing-Tianjin-Hebei, central China, western China, northeastern China, and northwestern China. By the end of June 2021, this venture had yielded 1.32 million digital RMB worth of pilot scenarios over 20.87 million individual digital wallets, and over 3.51 million corporate digital wallets opened.

The main milestones of digital RMB:

- 2014: The People's Bank of China initiates researching virtual currency technologies like Bitcoin.
- 2016: A digital currency seminar is held.
- 2016: The Digital Currency Institute is established.
- 2018: A blockchain-based trade finance supply chain platform is launched.
- End of 2019: The digital RMB starts pilot testing in four cities.
- 2021: By June, there were 1.32 million digital RMB pilot scenarios, over 20.87 million individual digital wallets, and over 3.51 million corporate digital wallets opened.

7.4.2 The Operation Mode and Advancements of Digital RMB

1. Centralized Management and Two-tier Operation Mode

The digital RMB adopts centralized management and two-tier operation mode, with the People's Bank of China (PBOC) at the center of the digital RMB operation system. The PBOC is responsible for issuing the digital RMB to commercial banks[19] and managing the entire lifecycle of the digital RMB, including issuance, cancellation, interconnectivity between institutions, and wallet ecosystem management. At the same time, commercial banks are responsible for providing exchange and circulation services of the digital RMB to the public.

Digital RMB adopts a "two-tier operation model," where the PBOC does not directly interact with customers. They still need to open a "digital wallet" through commercial banks to use the digital RMB and conduct transactions.

Digital RMB is stored and transacted through dedicated digital wallets. The transaction records of digital RMB are stored in the central database of the respective commercial banks, and relevant transaction information is also uploaded to the PBOC's central database.

The first direct central bank digital currency in Ecuador was not successful; however, China's two-tier distribution model may have considered important lessons from its history. From the current perspective, providing customer services directly by the central bank also goes beyond the scope of its responsibilities. Under the two-tier operation mode, commercial banks provide digital RMB services to customers, which allows for the exploration of technological diversity by commercial banks without altering the current financial structure (Table 7.4).

- Production phase: The PBOC generates the digital RMB as the issuance fund and stores it in the issuance repository.
- Issuance phase: Based on the application demand from commercial banks, the PBOC transfers the digital RMB from the issuance repository to the banks' repositories.
- Circulation phase: Users apply for the exchange of digital RMB from the bank's repository to their digital wallets. When users engage in transfer transactions using digital RMB, it essentially involves the transfer of value between two digital wallets, enabling value transfer.
- Diversified Digital RMB Wallets.

In digital RMB, a software wallet "provides services through mobile payment apps, Software Development Kit (SDK), and Application Programming Interface (API)." Typically, users can download the digital RMB wallet app onto their mobile phones, such as iPhone, and use it without any hardware association. In contrast, a hardware wallet "uses security chips and other technologies to enable the functions

[19] In China, the entities authorized to operate the digital RMB, currently being commercial banks, are referred to as designated operating institutions and cooperating institutions. Designated operating institutions have direct access to the digital RMB ledger maintained by the People's Bank of China (PBOC), while cooperating institutions can only access the PBOC through designated operating institutions or other approved institutions, primarily clearing and settlement organizations.

Table 7.4 Various wallets or transactions envisaged for digital RMB

Digital RMB		Progress	Features
Software wallet	Category I, II, III (real name)	Large-scale pilot	Different levels of customer due diligence correspond to different functionality and permissions
	Category IV (controllably anonymous)		Opened through a bank and linked to a mobile phone number: controlled anonymity
Hardware wallet	Real Name	Small-scale pilot	Wallet embedded in specific device
	Anonymous		
Transaction	Dual offline transactions	Conceptual design	Value transfer can be achieved offline by both parties

of e-CNY. It is supported by IC card, mobile phones, wearable objects, and the Internet of Things devices."[20] In the conceptual design, digital RMB wallets could be embedded in hardware devices, eliminating the need for software downloads.

In addition, The Digital Currency Institute of the People's Bank of China has envisioned a dual offline transaction mode, which allows direct value transfer between parties without relying on the Internet. Specifically, in offline transactions, the currency unit has already been transferred, but the transaction information has not been communicated to the People's Bank of China and the commercial bank. During the offline period, digital RMB is disassociated from electronic system tracking and monitoring, resembling anonymous cash transactions.

RISK FACTORS IN DUAL OFFLINE TRANSACTIONS FROM AN ANTI- MONEY LAUNDERING PERSPECTIVE

From an anti-money laundering perspective, dual offline transactions present two specific risk factors that should be taken into account.

Firstly, there is a factor of increased risk associated with dual offline transactions. While these transactions still involve electronic transfers, which are more convenient and faster than cash transactions, they inherently carry a higher level of risk compared to cash transactions.

Secondly, there is a risk reduction factor to consider. Once the dual offline transactions are brought online, all transaction records are uploaded to centralized servers, thereby enhancing traceability in comparison to cash transactions. As a result, the duration of the offline period, the frequency of transactions, and the transaction amounts during offline periods become crucial factors in determining the risk level of dual offline transactions.

In the current pilot phase, only software wallets are widely promoted and used; hardware wallets and dual offline transactions are still in the conceptual and experimental stages.

Inspired by ***the classification management approach*** of bank accounts in today's China, digital software wallets have implemented a similar framework. In this

[20] Please refer to Working Group on E-CNY Research and Development of the People's Bank of China. "Progress of Research & Development of Digital RMB in China," July 2021. http://www.pbc.gov.cn/en/3688110/3688172/4157443/4293696/2021072014364791207.pdf.

approach, wallets are categorized into four distinct classifications based on the level of customer identification strength. Each wallet category is assigned specific limits for single transactions, daily transaction volumes and balance thresholds, ensuring a tailored and secure transaction experience.

The People's Bank of China classifies software wallets into two groups: real-name and anonymous. Real-name wallets have anti-money laundering requirements similar to existing bank accounts, implementing a classification management approach that further divides real-name digital wallets into three categories. Different requirements apply for opening wallets based on their permission levels, with varying corresponding functionality and permissions. Higher-level Category 1 and Category 2 wallets introduce an additional method of digital identity verification, linking them to the customer's own bank account.

Regarding the allowance for certain conditions of anonymous wallets, unlike existing accounts, anonymous wallets allow customers to open anonymous wallets (Category 4 wallets) under specific conditions. However, this anonymity is not absolute but rather controlled, so we can call Category wallet as controllable anonymous wallet. Users need to open an anonymous wallet using their mobile phone number, which, in theory, can be traced back to the user's true identity by law enforcement agencies based on China's real-name registration system for mobile phone numbers. Due to weaker due diligence requirements for Category 4 wallet customers, the functionality and permissions of these wallets are the lowest (Table 7.5).

Table 7.5 Classification and requirements of software wallets

	Category I	Category II	Category III	Category IV
Application method	Face-to-face at the counter only	Electronic channels allowed	Electronic channels allowed	Electronic channels allowed
Identity verification requirements	Face recognition; ID number and name; mobile number; linking to and verifying through bank account	Face recognition; ID number and name; mobile number; linking to and verifying through bank account	Face recognition; ID number and name; mobile number	Mobile number
Quantity limit	One per person per institution	One per person per institution	One per person per institution	One mobile phone number per institution
Linking to bank account	Required	Required	Not Required	Not Required

Source Compiled from the digital wallet service agreements of designated operating institutions, including the Industrial and Commercial Bank of China, Agricultural Bank of China, Bank of China, China Construction Bank, and Bank of Communications (as of November 2, 2021)

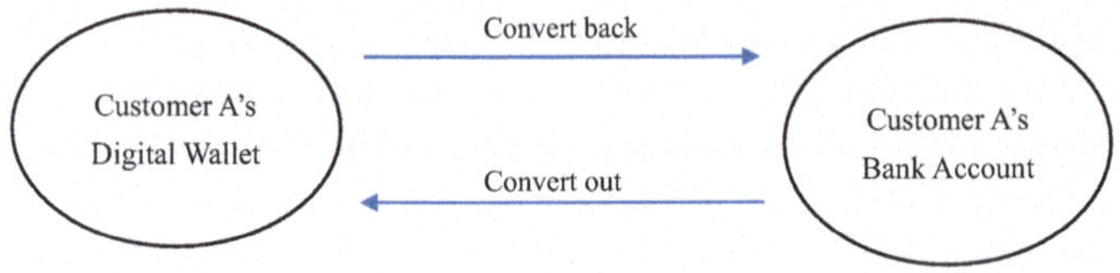

Fig. 7.5 Withdrawals and deposits between digital wallet and bank account

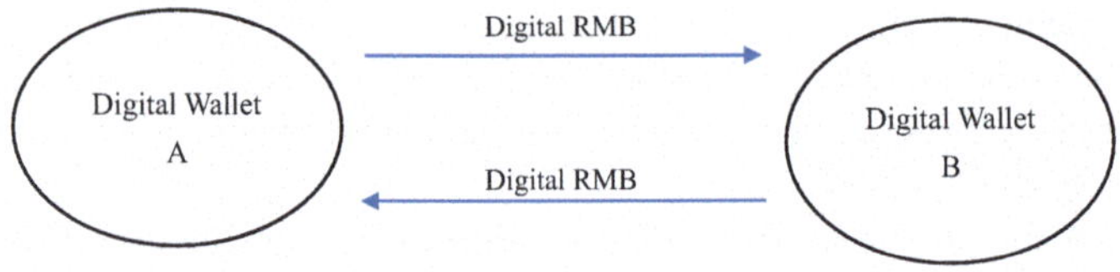

Fig. 7.6 Fund transfers between digital wallets

3. Digital RMB Transaction Modes

Digital RMB, using digital wallets as the carrier, enables functions such as withdrawals, deposits, fund transfers, and payments. All these transaction modes have corresponding counterparts in the existing financial system.

The withdrawal and deposit transactions in digital wallets are similar to fund transfers between third-party payment accounts and linked bank accounts (Fig. 7.5).

From a user experience perspective, transfer transactions between digital wallets are similar to bank account transfer transactions (Fig. 7.6), with the only difference being that the value transfer between digital wallets is recorded by both the central bank and the commercial banks simultaneously.[21]

7.4.3 What Does the Digital RMB Change?

First, digital currency has increased the amount of information available to the central bank. In terms of accounting, digital currency is recorded by both commercial banks and the central bank. This means that digital currency no longer requires a separate clearing and settlement process (as discussed in Sect. 2.4.2), as payments can be settled directly through the central bank. This not only significantly improves payment efficiency but also allows the central bank to capture a complete and detailed record of all transactions (Table 7.6).

[21] In the dual offline mode, the transfer transaction is initially recorded for accounting purposes, and payment confirmation is only issued after payment verification has been completed when connected to the network at a later stage. This transaction model is unique to digital RMB but only in the conceptual stage.

Table 7.6 Main characteristics of digital RMB compared with the traditional model

	Traditional Model	Digital RMB	Explanation
Issuer	The People's Bank of China	The People's Bank of China	
Service providers	Financial Institutions (mainly commercial banks)	Financial Institutions (mainly commercial banks)	
Transaction medium	Bank Accounts	Digital Wallets	
Transaction method	Account-to-account Account-to-cash	Account-to-wallet Wallet-to-wallet Wallet-to-cash	Transactions between digital wallets enable instant settlement, improving payment efficiency
Accounting method	User's accounts recorded by financial institution	Synchronized recording by financial institutions and the central bank	Technically, the central bank has the potential to monitor micro-level fund flows for digital RMB
Programmability	Not possible	Possible	Technically, digital currency has the potential for programming

Under the traditional two-tier system, fund flows between users are recorded by individual commercial banks, which information cannot be directly accessed by the central bank. While the central bank can understand the macroeconomic flow of money through aggregated data reported by financial institutions, it is not able to track the flow of each individual fund.

However, through central bank digital currency, the central bank can monitor the flow of every single fund. This provides the central bank with the potential to enhance the effectiveness of monetary policy and improve its ability for in-depth supervision, offering unlimited possibilities in terms of technology.

Currently, although the central bank does not possess specific customer identity information (which is held by commercial banks), it still requires sophisticated institutional arrangements and technical means to effectively protect customer privacy. For example, limitations on the use of customer data (such as only allowing macro data analysis) can be specified in the law, and a separation of user identity information can be implemented between the central bank and commercial banks.

Second, digital RMB has programmability. Programmability has the potential to have a significant impact on business models and payment methods. The most prominent application of programmability is in automatic payment transactions. Many existing cryptocurrencies have been utilized for online gambling through automatic payment transactions. To this end, the designers of digital RMB, recognizing the dual nature of programmability, have taken a cautious approach and explicitly state that digital RMB incorporates programmability through loading smart contracts that do not affect the currency's functionality, promoting innovation in business models while ensuring security and compliance.

7.4.4 The Unique Design of Digital RMB: Ensuring a Two-Tier Financial System

Regardless of the means of implementation, the issuance of Central Bank Digital Currency (CBDC) will have significant impacts on the central bank, the overall monetary system, the economy, and users. Therefore, central banks around the world are exercising extreme caution. After years of research, deliberation and experimentation, China's central bank has started implementing digital currency. It can be observed that the policy formulation takes into careful consideration the potential risks involved and attempts to prevent and mitigate them either through technological means or policy mechanisms.

1. **The Potential Impacts of Digital RMB**

As pointed out in Sect. 2.4.3 of this book, the current financial system operates on a two-tier structure known as "Central Bank-Commercial Bank" framework. Commercial banks directly serve customers who deposit cash into banks, and the banks expand the money supply through lending. However, CBDC has the potential to change this existing "Central Bank-Commercial Bank" axis.

If the Central Bank Directly Provides Services to Users

CBDC can technically allow users to bypass commercial banks and make payments directly through the central bank. If individuals are permitted to access the central bank's balance sheet or if the public is allowed to open accounts with the central bank for transactions using legal tender, this would bring a fundamental change to the existing two-tier structure. The following potential issues may arise:

SELF- POSITIONING OF THE CENTRAL BANK. Being a government entity, the central bank lacks market experience and technological capabilities. In terms of providing payment and financial services to users, it does not have a competitive advantage compared to private enterprises. Moreover, as a non-profit institution, the central bank lacks motivation for innovation and there is a risk of creating monopolies, which could stifle payment innovations by private institutions. In the design of digital RMB, efforts have been made to mitigate these risks and provide more space for commercial banks and institutions to leverage their advantages.

CENTRALIZATION IS RISKED BY STEMMING FROM STRENGTHENING THE ROLE OF THE CENTRAL BANK. Under the digital RMB model, with data and computations being centralized in the central bank, there is a systemic risk. If the central bank's information becomes compromised, it could lead to disastrous privacy breaches.

If Deposits Converted into CBDC

Even though it is prohibited for users to directly access the central bank's balance sheet, to prevent the disruption of the mechanism of credit creation through lending, the central bank must ensure the M0 attributes of digital RMB. CBDC represents a new form of currency backed by the central bank's credit. It is a liability of the central bank, which represents national credit and is risk-free. From an absolute safety perspective, the public is naturally inclined to hold CBDC. From a technological perspective, each CBDC unit is unique and traceable, so it can neither be mixed with commercial banks' assets nor lent externally (at least in theory for now).

Under the premise of constant total quantity, the increase in central bank digital currency implies a decrease in bank deposits. Assuming the complete disappearance of commercial deposits, banks would become "narrow banks" and lose their ability to create money. With the entire population holding central bank digital currency, the current "fractional reserve system" would transform into a "100% reserve system." The central bank would have direct control over the money supply, in contrast to the current method of control through interest rates and money supply.

WHAT IS A NARROW BANK?

A narrow bank, also known as a 100% reserve bank, is a type of commercial bank where all deposits must be fully supported by central bank reserves. Narrow banks no longer issue loans and do not have the function to expand credit; they simply serve as channels for central bank currency injection.

After the introduction of CBDC, if a central bank intends to maintain the existing money creation model, it must establish a mechanism to ensure that commercial bank deposits do not undergo a massive conversion into CBDC. Otherwise, the ability of commercial banks to create money would vanish, rendering them narrow banks.

To prevent such drastic changes, the demand for CBDC among the public can be controlled through interest rate settings. If CBDC is interest-free, or if its interest rate is lower than that of bank deposits or even negative, people would not feel inclined to convert all their bank deposits into CBDC.

2. Understanding Risk Mitigation in the Design of Digital RMB

Based on publicly available information, the design and pilot process of China's digital currency, the digital RMB, has fully taken into account the potential impact. Two key designs have been implemented to minimize this risk:

- The Two-layer Issuance System: Preventing Depositors from Abandoning Banks

Digital RMB adopts a "two-layer issuance system," where the People's Bank of China (PBOC) does not directly interface with customers. Instead, customers use the digital RMB through a "digital wallet" provided by commercial banks.

Given the two-layer issuance system, commercial banks continue to provide digital RMB services, which enables the exploration of diverse technological solutions by commercial banks and avoids a monopolistic control of payments by the central bank.

- The Positioning of Digital Yuan's M0: A Price Mechanism to Prevent Deposit Flight to CBDC

Another issue related to traditional narrow banking is whether digital RMB will accrue interest. The Whitepaper of Digital RMB published in 2021) emphasizes that digital RMB is positioned as M0, therefore, it is not interest-bearing. We consider this as an implicit pricing mechanism to prevent depositors from converting their funds into CBDC.

Traditionally, individual deposits in financial institutions reflect the credit of these institutions, and deposit certificates serve as their repayment commitment. Since there is a risk of financial institutions being unable to fulfill their repayment obligations, the interest paid to depositors contains a compensation for this risk. However, digital RMB is recorded directly by the central bank and is equivalent to cash, representing the highest level of security: even if the financial institution operating the digital RMB goes bankrupt, the digital currency can be specifically linked to each individual's digital wallet, establishing a one-to-one relationship between the digital currency and its owner.

In this sense, compared to traditional deposits, digital RMB is a risk-free asset. If it also accrued interest, rational individuals would be inclined to choose a safer form of currency when faced with similar returns. In other words, if digital RMB also provided interest, depositors would likely consider moving their funds to the risk-free digital RMB.

3. **Summary**

China's central bank digital currency, at least for the time being, is merely a change in payment methods and has not altered the structure of the existing financial system. However, it is essential to closely monitor the potential issues that may arise, such as the reduction in bank deposits due to the increasing use of the digital currency. To maintain a balance, it will be necessary to control the proportion of digital currency and bank deposits through price mechanisms or other measures.

7.5 Wholesale CBDC Cross-Border Experiment: A Multilateral Central Bank Digital Currency Bridge

7.5.1 Challenges in Cross-Border Payment Within Distributed Central Bank Systems

Within a domestic currency system, wholesale central bank digital currency primarily improves settlement efficiency. Even if we assume that a country's domestic currency settlement system is entirely decentralized, this would only represent a marginal improvement in terms of efficiency. However, changes in the settlement system within the international monetary system would bring about structural transformations. It

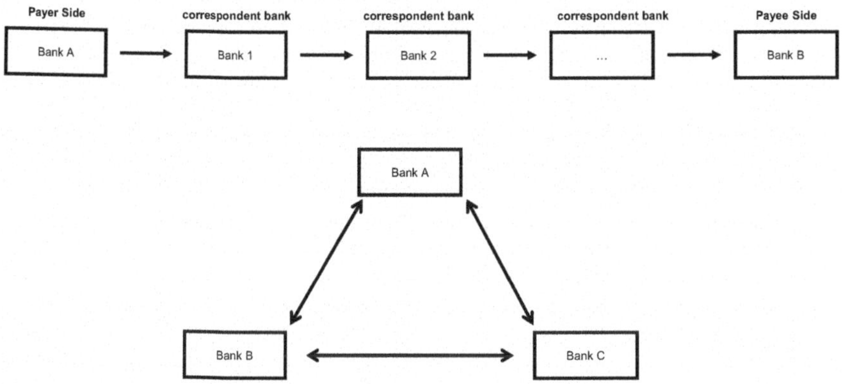

Fig. 7.7 Illustration of a corresponding bank settlement model

can be said that the decentralized technological approach aligns well with the current international central system landscape, and it may even present an optimal solution to enhance the current international settlements. Many digital currency innovations may be developed for the sake of innovation itself, but addressing cross-border payments through distributed principles is driven by a strong practical need.

Firstly, central banks are distributed entities, and there is no central bank of central banks. For example, the fiat currencies of Euro, US Dollar, Japanese Yen, and Chinese Yuan are issued by their respective central banks. While within Europe, sovereign nations have relinquished their coinage powers to a supranational central bank—the European Central Bank, in the broader international context, it appears unlikely that a "world central bank" will emerge anytime soon.

Secondly, in a distributed central bank environment, cross-border clearing is undertaken by international organizations, primarily SWIFT, and settlement is facilitated through correspondent banking, which is slow and costly. The correspondent banking model entails complex workflows and expensive procedures, resulting in high costs and extremely slow transaction speeds (see Fig. 7.7). In terms of cost, cross-border payments based on correspondent banking account for approximately 0.5% of the transaction value, and the average payment transaction speed is 2–3 days.[22]

THE CASE OF TRANS- BORDER PAYMENTS

Existing electronic payment systems are centralized, with nations being equal entities and each having an independent monetary and payment system. However, cross-border payments are costly and slow. If you have sent a telegraphic transfer in US dollars to relatives or friends abroad, you may have experienced this.

If one wants to remit money from Beijing to BNP Paribas (BNP) in Paris, France, they would first need to choose a Chinese bank, such as China Construction Bank (CCB). Both BNP and CCB need to open a correspondent account with a commercial bank in the United States, which could be, respectively, at CITI Bank (CITI) and Bank of America (BOA). In this

[22] Sun, Huarong. "Research on the Development Status, Challenges and Countermeasures of Cross-Border Payment Business of Banking Institutions." *Financial Theory & Practice*, no. 12 (2020). (孙华荣:《银行跨境支付业务发展及监管策略研究》, 载《金融理论与实践》2020年第12期).

scenario, BNP and CCB are respondent banks, while CITI and BOA are correspondent banks. Once the remitter has completed the remittance process at CCB, the settlement between the two banks would be conducted through the Society for Worldwide Interbank Financial Telecommunication (SWIFT) system. It would be made between the correspondent accounts that BNP and CCB has opened in the United States, which in our case, would be respectively at CITI and BOA. In other words, for USD cross-border payments, the final transfer of funds would be achieved between the correspondent accounts established in the United States.

In the transaction process between CITI and BOA, the ultimate settlement is conducted through the Federal Reserve of the US, with CITI and BOA serving as agents for BNP and CCB to access the Federal Reserve for settlement purposes.

A similar process would be followed for cross-border remittances in other currencies.

7.5.2 Multilateral Central Bank Digital Currency Bridge: A Promising Experiment

Ripple has utilized blockchain technology to provide a peer-to-peer network among commercial banks, attempting to create a clearing system to substitute SWIFT. This reduces the cost of international remittances performed through SWIFT to some extent; however, the settlement still relies on corresponding banks.

The authors of this book believe that the true game-changer in future cross-border payments lies in the Multilateral-Central Bank Digital Currency Bridge (mBridge). The mBridge enables direct cross-border payments between commercial banks while ensuring the monetary sovereignty of each country's central bank. Among the existing potential models, through its clever design, mBridge strikes the best balance between leveraging blockchain to enhance cross-border payment efficiency and maintaining central bank control over digital currencies.

A Range Of Cross- Border Payment Models Based On CBDC

Central banks around the world are unlikely to give up their currency sovereignty. Even if they issue their own central bank digital currencies (CBDCs) and allow them to freely circulate on public blockchains, central banks cannot accept relinquishing control. The Bank for International Settlements (BIS) has grouped various cross-border payment models based on CBDC into three categories:

The first is the "compatible model," where each country builds and operates its own CBDC system, and then establishes payment settlement between these independent CBDC systems through a set of agreed specifications and unified systems, similar to the current SWIFT system.

The second is the "interlinked model," where countries consider interoperability when building their own CBDC systems, following agreed-upon clearing and settlement mechanisms and adhering to prescribed interface specifications.

The third is the "single multilateral model," where multiple central banks collaboratively develop rules and build a single digital currency cross-border payment and settlement platform. Commercial banks, as settlement participants, join the platform through their respective central bank nodes.

The mBridge project belongs to the third category. Through its clever design, it seems to strike an optimal balance between enhancing cross-border payment efficiency using blockchain technology and maintaining central bank control over digital currencies. Its core ideas are as follows:

1. Commercial banks that join the Currency Bridge blockchain settlement platform can freely use their respective digital currencies for settlement, which is performed on a peer-to-peer basis.
2. Commercial banks that join the Currency Bridge must be authorized by their domestic central banks.
3. Central bank nodes participate in the consensus mechanism as accounting nodes, while commercial bank nodes have operational capabilities but do not participate in data consensus.
4. Payment data is only shared among the counterparties and the respective central banks.

The mBridge project was inspired by blockchain and distributed ledger technology. The development platform for this project is based on a specialized distributed ledger technology designed specifically for the cross-border payments of central bank digital currencies (CBDCs). This ledger is called the "mBridge Ledger" (shown in Fig. 7.8).

On the mBridge Ledger, after reaching consensus between central banks, they can connect their respective CBDCs and execute direct settlement and clearing on the currency bridge. For central banks without a CBDC system, they can still connect their Real-Time Gross Settlement (RTGS) systems directly. In this case, the central bank can issue its own CBDC specifically for cross-border payments on the currency bridge. Settlement and clearing for commercial banks can then be directly carried out by their respective central banks, eliminating the need for SWIFT and intermediary banks.

On the mBridge Ledger, commercial banks from different monetary jurisdictions can achieve direct payments. In the blockchain structure, central bank nodes are connected to each other in a complete graph, with each node serving as a validator node responsible for bookkeeping and generating blocks. Commercial bank nodes, on the other hand, are ordinary nodes that connect to their respective central bank nodes, synchronize data, and perform various functional operations but do not participate in the consensus algorithm (shown in Fig. 7.9).

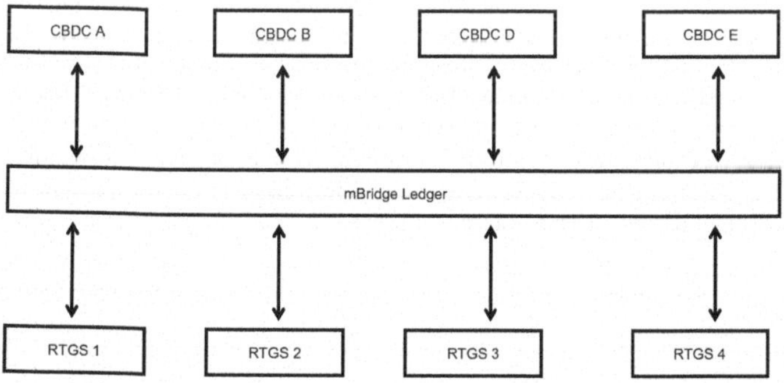

Fig. 7.8 The mBridge Ledger

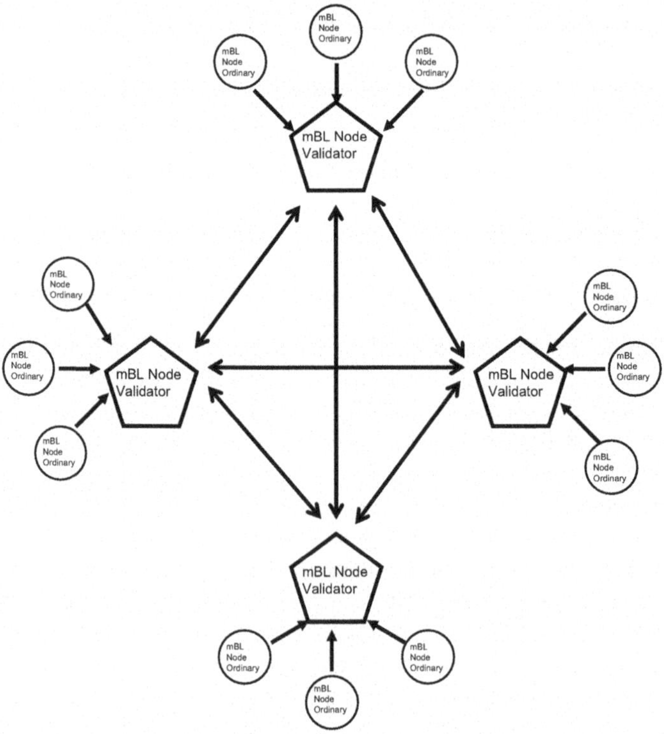

Fig. 7.9 Execution of the consensus algorithm

Commercial banks achieve point-to-point direct settlement by connecting to the currency bridge through their respective central banks (shown in Fig. 7.10).

THE THREE PHASES OF MBRIDGE

The Inthanon-LionRock project, a collaboration between Thailand and Hong Kong, was the precursor to the mBridge project. In the first and second phases of the project, the blockchain network was called the "corridor network," which enabled the interoperability of digital currencies from different jurisdictions. The Corda R3 blockchain was used in the first phase, which is a decentralized database inspired by blockchain technology and designed specifically for permissioned networks, unlike Bitcoin and Ethereum blockchains.[23] In the second phase, the project adopted the Hyperledger Besu blockchain, which is based on Ethereum client technology but is compatible both with permissioned chain consensus algorithms like PoA and IBFT, and public chain consensus algorithms like PoW and PoS, combining the advantages of public and private chains.[24]

The technology choices in the first and second phases reflect the project's understanding of the requirements for cross-border digital currency payments in terms of blockchain ledgers,

[23] BIS Innovation Hub. "Project mBridge—Connecting Economies through CBDC," October 2022. https://www.bis.org/publ/othp59.pdf.

[24] BIS Innovation Hub. "Project mBridge—Connecting Economies through CBDC," October 2022. https://www.bis.org/publ/othp59.pdf.

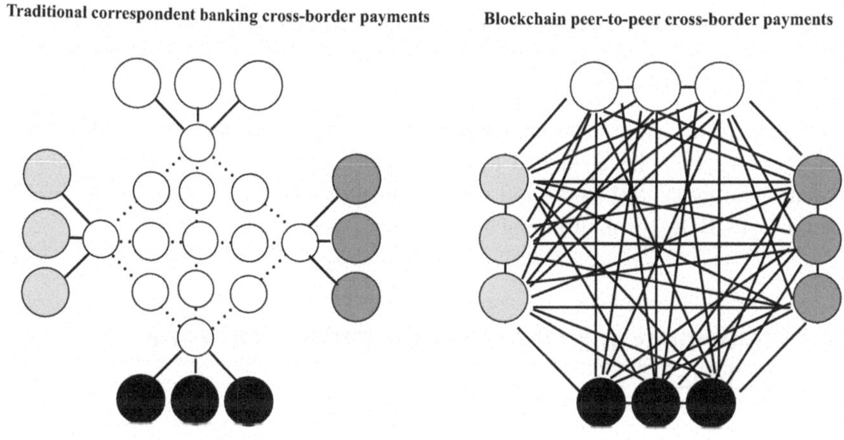

Fig. 7.10 Cross-border peer-to-peer payments by commercial banks

consensus algorithms, and privacy protection. These requirements differ significantly from the commonly used technologies in the industry for public and permissioned chains.

In the third phase, the Digital Currency Institute of the People's Bank of China (PBOC) joined the project in 2021, with the institute's chairperson leading the technical committee. The project was subsequently renamed as the "Multilateral Central Bank Digital Currency Bridge" (mBridge) and focused on studying the feasibility of utilizing CBDC for multilateral cross-border payments.

In terms of the operation process, there is an important difference between the "corridor network" and the mBridge. In the corridor network model, the issuance and destruction of digital currencies take place outside the corridor network blockchain system, and then they are mapped through interfaces into the corridor network as Depository Receipts (DR), which are traded within the corridor network. Contrarily, in mBridge, the issuance and destruction process occurs on the mBridge itself and the blockchain is involved only in adjusting reserve account balances (and digital currency balances if already existing).[25]

Looking back to the transition from the corridor network to mBridge, the involvement of the Digital Currency Institute of the People's Bank of China and the appointment as the chair of the technical committee were key factors. This marked an enhancement in the team's technological capabilities, resulting in the development and breakthroughs of the Currency Bridge project, which now aligns more closely with the specific requirements of the digital currency scene with their self-developed technologies and system designs.

For the development of blockchain for mBridge, the Digital Currency Institute of the People's Bank of China collaborated with Tsinghua University, led by internationally renowned cryptologist Wang Xiaoyun. The consensus algorithm used among central bank nodes differs from blockchains like Bitcoin; it adopts a permissioned chain approach, reaching consensus among a limited number of certified nodes. The consensus algorithm, called "Dashing," was developed by the Digital Currency Institute of China and Tsinghua University. It is a byzantine fault tolerant (BTF) algorithm that can tolerate (n-1)/3 faulty nodes, which may be unresponsive or even send wrong messages within the consensus process. "Dashing" is similar to the Hotstuff consensus algorithm, which uses digital signatures to guarantee message integrity and a lead node to collect consensus messages, significantly improving

[25] Hong Kong Monetary Authority and Bank of Thailand, Inthanon-LionRock, 2019.

efficiency compared to traditional BFT algorithms. "Dashing" employs weak certificates and a uniquely designed asynchronous BFT framework called "Star," further enhancing efficiency compared to Hotstuff.[26]

Overall, the mBridge project has evolved through different phases since its conception, incorporating the enhanced technological capabilities and collaborations of the participating central banks and research institutions, thus aiming to explore the potential of CBDC for multilateral cross-border payments.

7.6 Motivations and Objectives for CBDC: The Case of China

"Motive" refers to the inner drive of individuals, that is, why people take action, while "purpose" means what the actors expect to gain from their actions. This section examines the subjective "motivations and objectives" of central bank digital currency. However, the question of whether the objective can be achieved is a judgment based on objective reality.

In Chap. 3, we analyzed the inspirations brought by blockchain technology to central banks, that is, which technologies central banks are willing and able to use. Here, we aim to analyze whether central banks must adopt digital currency to achieve certain motivations and objectives. In other words, is it inevitable to take the path of digital currency to achieve these objectives?

Globally, China has taken the lead in the development of CBDC. As the first major economy, it has initiated large-scale trials of CBDC targeting public users. Therefore, we can take China and digital renminbi (or Digital Yuan) as the example to analyze the motivation and objective of CBDC. Digital Yuan has always been a hot topic in media reports, with numerous experts providing various interpretations of it. To explore which unique contributions can be brought about by digitalizing currency, we have summarized these interpretations into ten aspects and analyzed each of these so-called motivations and objectives.

For instance, some media outlets claim that digital currency can promote the internationalization of renminbi. However, we believe that currency internationalization is essentially an economic and political issue instead of a technological one. Another example is the belief that digitalizing legal tender can improve financial inclusion. Nonetheless, we reckon that China's existing electronic payment systems are already highly developed and widespread, and the incremental impact of digital legal tender would be extremely limited. On the contrary, digital currency offers traceability and programmability, providing new regulatory tools for monetary policy and a comprehensive oversight that the existing electronic payment systems cannot offer.

---

[26] Duan, Sisi, Haibin Zhang, Xiao Sui, Baohan Huang, Changchun Mu, Gang Di, and Xiaoyun Wang. "Byzantine Fault Tolerance with Weak Certificates." *IACR Cryptol. ePrint Arch.*, 2022, 625.

Table 7.7 Motivations and objectives from the payment and settlement aspects

Motivations and objectives	Technological necessity	Does CBDC bring unique contributions?	Comments
Cash substitute	No need for blockchain or distributed ledger technology	No	The goal of replacing paper cash seems more like finding a positioning for digital legal tender rather than a genuine motivation and objective
New settlement structure	Blockchain, distributed ledger, cryptocurrency chains	Yes	Despite the lower efficiency of blockchain transactions, central banks value blockchain technology for breaking the previous multi-tier settlement model and improving settlement efficiency under the "peer-to-peer payment" model
Convenient transactions and low cost	No need for blockchain or distributed ledger technology	To a limited extent	Payments and transactions are already convenient and low-cost with the current centralized technology. CBDC offers limited convenience and cost reduction compared to physical currency

7.6.1 Payment and Settlement

1. CBDC as a Cash Substitute

With the prevalence of online banking and third-party payment systems, the proportion of cash (banknotes and coins) has greatly decreased in China.[27] Considering the decline of banknotes and the gradual arrival of a cashless society, the disappearance of banknotes seems to be a trend, and whether to replace them or not has become irrelevant (Table 7.7).

Cash is the base currency of the central bank, hence the phasing out of cash signifies a decrease in the importance of this monetary asset. The Digital Yuan, positioned as an electronic form of M0, aims to replace cash while achieving controlled anonymity in terms of privacy. It retains the advantages of paper money while overcoming weaknesses such as money laundering. Therefore, the goal is not to eliminate existing cash but to upgrade paper money to enhance the status and proportion of the "new cash," which logically aligns with the purpose of substituting cash.

In summary, the goal of replacing banknotes seems more like finding a positioning for the digital currency, rather than a true motivation or purpose.

[27] Since 2003, the proportion of M2 fell by 5%. Please refer to Yao, Qian. "An Analysis of the Economic Performance of the Digital Fiat Currency." *Studies of International Finance*, no. 1 (2019). (姚前:《法定数字货币的经济效应分析》, 载《国际金融研究》2019 年第 1 期。).

2. New Settlement Structure

Central banks of various countries are unlikely to renounce control over their power to issue currency. They also place significant importance on the role of currency in regulating the economy and will be disinclined to abandon such a crucial tool. However, they are not concerned about the control of payment and settlement services because these services, which target users, are best provided by competitive commercial institutions. This is also the reason why central banks support online banking and third-party payment systems in the development of digital currency.

As Gang Di, one of the core developers of Digital Yuan, has acknowledged, the current design of CBDCs in major countries utilizes a centralized issuance mechanism with direct real-time settlement on distributed ledgers, greatly improving settlement efficiency.[28] This is also the purpose and motivating factor for central banks, such as Canada, the United Kingdom, and Singapore, to experiment with digital currencies.

Different Forms Of Currencies Have Different Settlement Methods. In the case of cash payment, it is completely peer-to-peer and decentralized. For example, if Sophia sends 100 yuan to Alex, Alex can verify the authenticity of the 100 yuan banknote and accept it, completing the payment. Meanwhile, the central bank, as the issuer of the 100 yuan banknote, does not have any information about this transaction.

With the emergence of electronic payments, Sophia can use online banking or mobile banking applications to pay Alex 100 yuan. In essence, Sophia uses bank deposits to pay Alex, and the payment process is recorded digitally in the books of commercial banks to facilitate value transfer.

For interbank transactions, banks still need to arrange settlement through central banks after clearing. Therefore, although online banking payment is completed instantaneously on the user side, the actual clearing and settlement process still takes a long time (refer to Sect. 2.4 for more details).

CBDCs, drawing on blockchain technology, can achieve value transfer either through recording on a blockchain ledger or through the transfer of value tokens, similar to the transfer of banknotes during cash payments. Thus, there is no need for additional clearing and settlement, resulting in improved efficiency in payment settlement. This provides the inspiration brought by blockchain technology to central banks and the technical feature that many central banks value, as payment settlement efficiency is improved through payment settlement.

Although the Digital Yuan aims to utilize a new settlement architecture, eliminating clearing and settlement stages and improving payment efficiency, it does not currently prioritize using a distributed ledger for peer-to-peer settlement between commercial banks in its technical design but continues to rely on the centralized account databases of central banks and commercial banks as the settlement system.[29]

[28] Di, Gang. "Analysis of Digital Currency." *China Finance* 17 (2018): 52–54. (狄刚:《数字货币辨析》, 载《金融科技》2018 年第 17 期。).

[29] Yao, Qian. "Prototype Concept of China's Legal Digital Currency." *China Finance*, no. 17 (2016): 13–15. (姚前:《中国法定数字货币原型构想》, 载《中国金融》2016 年 第 17 期。).

Table 7.8 Motivations and objectives from the payment and settlement aspects

Motivations and objectives	Technological necessity	Does CBDC bring unique contributions?	Comments
More effective monetary policy tools	Cryptocurrency chain for traceability Smart contracts for programmability	Yes	These are among the most valuable aspects brought about by central bank digital currency (CBDC) technology. They can only be achieved through blockchain, distributed ledger, and smart contract technologies, which traditional methods cannot accomplish
Penetrative oversight			Blockchain, distributed ledger, and other digital currency technologies offer powerful regulatory capabilities, enabling penetrative oversight through the comprehensive monitoring of capital flows

However, the technological characteristics of the Digital Yuan, as a retail CBDC, still impact the settlement system by upgrading it to a level where the central bank's credit control system and commercial banks' account systems work together. This settlement mode, similar to the circulation of banknotes, although not achieving complete peer-to-peer settlement, is different from the current hierarchical clearing and settlement model that relies on electronic reserves, and improves settlement efficiency.

7.6.2 Monetary Policy and New Tools for Financial Regulation: Precision Targeting and Penetrative Oversight

JP Koning's concept for CBDC has recognized that CBDC will serve as a new monetary tool. Electronic forms of currency can potentially become instruments for implementing negative interest rates, which is a challenging prospect within the existing financial system (as excessive negative rates by banks could lead to cash withdrawals by depositors). The People's Bank of China has conducted in-depth research on the impact of Digital Yuan on monetary policy and found that this influence could be great and enhance the effectiveness of such policy (Table 7.8).[30]

[30] Yao, Qian. "Optimization of Current Monetary System by Central Bank Digital Currency and Its Issuance Design." *Studies of International Finance*, no. 4 (2018). (姚前:《法定数字货币对现行货币体制的优化及其发行设计》, 载《国际金融研究》2018 年第 4 期。).

The ability of legal digital currency to impact monetary policy stems from its three characteristics of being an electronic form, having traceable ledger structure, and programmability.

MONITORING THE FLOW OF CENTRAL BANK DIGITAL CURRENCY THROUGH BLOCKCHAIN

Under the current technological conditions, the management of fiat currency by central banks involves regulating the **overall** quantity and price at a **macro** level. This is because both cash and bank deposits are difficult to trace and are homogenous in nature. Banknotes of the same denomination are indistinguishable without close examination, and balances in bank accounts are challenging to differentiate and track. **As a result, central banks lack control over the distribution and flow of currency, and regulatory measures can only rely on post-event investigations to impose penalties as a deterrent.**

Additionally, the existing monetary policy often falls short of expectations. For example, many media outlets have pointed out that loans to the real estate sector should be redirected towards supporting the manufacturing industry, while funds should be channeled towards high-efficiency and environmentally friendly industries instead of low-efficiency and outdated production capacity.

However, CBDC offers the potential to enhance the precision of monetary policy. Leveraging blockchain or similar technologies, CBDC can be controlled through smart contracts to ensure that funds are specifically allocated to targeted entities, such as small and micro enterprises, or to areas that require support, such as ecological conservation, agriculture, and water resources.

From a technological perspective, digitalized legal currency provides potential tools for tracing and controlling capital flow. It can assist the central bank in monitoring currency and implementing more effective monetary policies by enabling the precise analysis of currency stock, flow, and velocity using comprehensive currency data held by banks.

Furthermore, once Digital Yuan achieves programmability, algorithmic precision targeting will become possible, fundamentally enhancing the central bank's ability to control the flow of currency and ensuring the effective execution of monetary policies.

Similarly, financial regulatory authorities can leverage capital flow to enhance their capacity for penetrative oversight, including monitoring illegal financial activities and tracing criminal funds.

7.6.3 Financial Innovation and Financial Inclusion

Bitcoin, as a cryptocurrency, has a unique design in terms of its technological architecture and privacy model, allowing users to make payments and receive funds without the need for an account and only based on a public–private key address. Due to not requiring an account, virtual currencies like Bitcoin do bring about financial inclusion, enabling people in areas without bank branches to engage in electronic payments and potentially reduce costs. Current electronic payment methods, such as

Alipay and WeChat Pay, can achieve similar convenience as Bitcoin without considering regulatory requirements such as real-name verification for account opening. In small-value transactions, China's digital currency, the digital renminbi, does not require real-name verification either, thus achieving the same level of inclusiveness as Bitcoin (Table 7.9).

However, the promotion of financial inclusion through new payment methods needs to be considered from an incremental perspective. In recent years, with the development of electronic payments and the widespread adoption of third-party payment providers, China has already achieved a high level of financial inclusion. The group of people who can use digital renminbi typically already have access to existing electronic payment services (such as Alipay and WeChat Pay) through their smartphones. Furthermore, China has eliminated fees for interbank electronic remittances, making domestic electronic payments essentially cost-free.

Therefore, in a context where electronic payments are highly developed, widely adopted, and have low cost in China, the incremental financial inclusion brought about by digital renminbi is limited.

Table 7.9 Motivations and objectives from the perspectives of financial innovation and inclusion

Motivations and objectives	Technological necessity	Does CBDC bring unique contributions?	Comments
Financial innovation	Smart contracts	Yes	This is one of the most valuable aspects brought about by the technology related to CBDCs and can only be achieved through blockchain, distributed ledger, and smart contract technologies. However, due to risk factors, the interface for smart contracts seems not be opened in the short term for digital yuan
Financial inclusion	No need for blockchain or distributed ledger technology	No	The technology brought about by blockchain fundamentally does not contribute to financial inclusion. It only creates an illusion of financial inclusion due to regulatory advantages. If current online banking and mobile payment methods would be exempted from regulatory requirements, they could also achieve similar convenience

7.6.4 Internationalization of RMB

Most CBDCs have not set internationalization as a primary objective. This is likely because these experiments have taken place in countries that already have freely convertible international currencies. For instance, the US dollar has already achieved internationalization within the current payment system. Similarly, CBDC experiments in Canada, the UK, and Singapore do not prioritize internationalization. Although Japan's experiment does involve cross-border settlements with Thailand, its focus is primarily on improving the settlement system rather than actively pursuing currency internationalization.

During the design and pilot phase of the digital renminbi, there has been significant attention from various sectors of society regarding whether it can foster the internationalization of Chinese currency. Some media speculations have even suggested that facilitating cross-border payments and building a new clearing and settlement system are important objectives of digital renminbi.

Digital renminbi seems not to embody the path toward RMB internationalization, as currency internationalization is not a technological problem. Technology is neither a sufficient nor a necessary condition. From a historical perspective, the internationalization of the British pound and the US dollar has had no relation to payment technology. Some third-world countries have also experimented with official digital currencies, such as Ecuador's Dinero Electrónico, but this did not change their currency status.

The research and development group of digital renminbi of the People's Bank of China expressed a clear statement in the white paper of digital RMB on the development progress of internationalization:

> Cross-border payments involve many complex issues such as currency sovereignty, foreign exchange management policies, exchange settlement arrangements, and regulatory compliance requirements. It is a challenging field that the international community is committed to addressing together. Currency internationalization is a natural market choice and is essentially determined by economic fundamentals, as well as factors such as the depth, efficiency and openness of the currency and financial markets.

The author of this book agrees with the aforementioned viewpoints. While it is acknowledged that solutions like mBridge may contribute to reducing reliance on the US dollar in cross-border transactions, such reduction is considered limited. It is important to recognize that technological factors are just one aspect of currency internationalization and not always the primary driver.

7.6.5 Competing Against Virtual Currencies

Bitcoin and its numerous cryptocurrencies are not suitable as retail currencies, as the limitations imposed by their underlying technology hinder their adoption as a widespread payment method. However, in 2019, Diem's proposal did stimulate central banks worldwide to somewhat accelerate research on blockchain technology. As discussed in Chap. 5, Sect. 5.9, with Facebook having 2.7 billion users, if Diem were to become the universal currency within the Facebook community, Facebook would possess a control surpassing that of any sovereignty (Table 7.10).

The motivation to combat private currencies does not seem sensible, as private currencies can simply be prohibited through regulatory measures. CBDCs are primarily aimed at leveraging blockchain and distributed ledger technology to enhance the efficiency of the legal currency system.

However, pursuing technological advancement for the sake of technology itself provides a valid and logical motive for studying and competing against cryptocurrencies. Particularly when a careful analysis reveals the evident neutral characteristics within blockchain and distributed ledger technology, central banks are even more enticed.

Therefore, to keep pace with the ever-changing financial landscape, it is reasonable for central banks to prioritize learning and understanding cryptocurrencies. By gaining knowledge and expertise in the technologies of cryptocurrencies, central banks can equip themselves with the necessary technical advantage to sustain the widespread acceptance and utilization of legal currencies.

Table 7.10 Motivations and objectives of competing against virtual currencies

Motivations and objectives	Technological necessity	Does CBDC bring unique contributions?	Comment
Competing against virtual currencies	Blockchain, distributed ledger smart contracts	No	The underlying technical flaws of virtual currencies hinder their adoption as a mainstream payment method. Governments can also enact legislation to prohibit virtual currencies. Central banks primarily focus on learning blockchain technology and improving the efficiency of the fiat currency payment system

Part III
When it Comes to Regulation

Chapter 8
Virtual Currency in the Context of Financial Regulation

Which virtual currencies trigger financial oversight? What attributes do virtual currencies have under the financial regulatory framework? What are the implications of decentralization in financial regulation?

This chapter highlights that the convertibility attribute of virtual currencies triggers financial regulations. For convertible virtual currencies, they may have the attributes of money, value transfer and investment under the financial regulatory framework. In this chapter, we also illustrate that the decentralized degree of virtual currencies determines who bears the regulatory responsibilities and what those entail, which subsequently poses new requirements for regulatory technology.

The existing financial regulatory system has at least three players: monetary authority (central bank), market regulator (securities regulation and investor protection), and anti-money laundering regulator. Non-convertible (closed) virtual currencies, such as Q coins, are merely electronic goods with limited use within specific online spaces. On the other hand, convertible (open) virtual currencies can serve as payment and investment tools, thereby carrying significance for financial regulation purposes. Consequently, these virtual currencies possess three main attributes in the context of financial regulation: from a monetary perspective, they can act as substitutes for legal tender payment instruments; from an investment perspective, they can be treated as securities; and from an anti-money laundering perspective, they can be perceived as means of value transfer.

To assess whether various phenomena related to virtual currencies, including the recent rise of non-fungible tokens (NFTs), possess financial regulatory significance and how these should adhere to existing financial regulations, we need to follow two steps (see Fig. 8.1).

Firstly, we must determine whether they possess convertibility: if they are convertible, they will have financial attributes; otherwise, they are merely limited-purpose goods typically referred to as "utility tokens."

Y. Wu and W. Zhu, *The Fundamentals of Digital Currency*,
https://doi.org/10.1007/978-981-97-8261-1_8

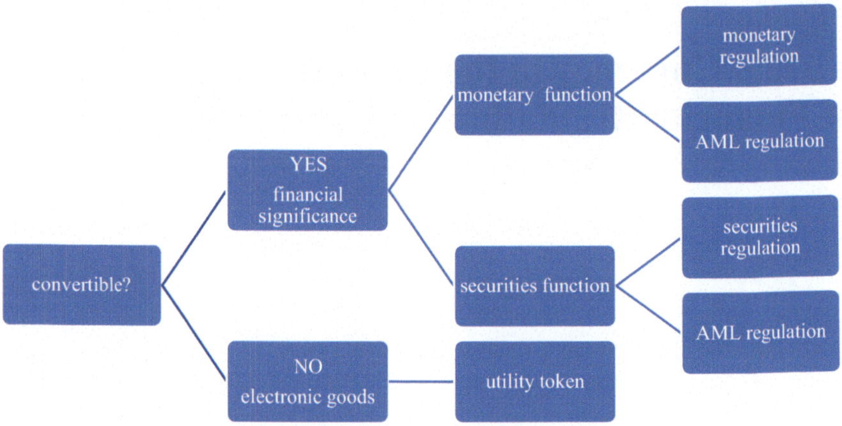

Fig. 8.1 Assessing the financial attributes of virtual currency

Secondly, we need to assess whether they exhibit monetary functions or securities attributes. If so, they should respectively comply with monetary regulation (payment regulation, prudential regulation, etc.) and securities regulation.

8.1 Convertibility: Determinant of the Financial Attributes of Virtual Currencies

Only when virtual currencies have unrestricted conversion will they have the potential to become financial products, making financial regulation necessary. As stated in Sect. 3.4 of this book, if a virtual currency is not convertible, it is more like electronic goods that serve limited purposes due to the unidirectional nature of their transactions.[1] If a virtual currency can be freely transferred between different entities, it possesses convertibility.

8.1.1 Convertibility as a Prerequisite: Consensus Among Monetary Authorities and Anti-Money Laundering Regulators

Monetary authorities have long recognized that virtual currencies may have multiple technological paths and must go beyond technology itself to explore their financial essence. In fact, based on the financial essence of virtual currencies, in 2012,

[1] See European Central Bank. "Virtual Currency Schemes," October 2012. https://www.ecb.europa.eu/pub/pdf/other/virtualcurrencyschemes201210en.pdf, p. 5.

the European Central Bank (monetary authority of the Eurozone) classified them into "convertible" and "non-convertible" categories. The former can be transferred between different users, enabling exchange with legal tender and other virtual currencies, while the latter is designed for specific communities and entail single-purpose tokens. From a regulatory perspective, the fundamental difference lies in whether the virtual currency can be transferred between different users. In the official documents of international organizations and regulatory authorities reviewed in this book, this document was the earliest to mention the regulatory significance of convertibility.

The above standard quickly gained acceptance in anti-money laundering regulation and has become a consensus among anti-money laundering authorities. The U.S. Department of the Treasury was the first to articulate this position in its first regulatory guidance on virtual currencies in 2013, stating that virtual currencies subject to anti-money laundering regulation were limited to "convertible virtual currencies."[2] In 2014, the Financial Action Task Force (FATF), an international standard-setting organization for anti-money laundering, accepted and acknowledged this stance in "*Virtual Currencies: Key Definitions and Potential Anti-Money Laundering and Counter-Terrorist Financing Risks.*"[3] In 2019, the FATF adopted international anti-money laundering standards for virtual currencies and published corresponding guidance entitled "*Guidance for a Risk-Based Approach to Virtual Assets and Virtual Asset Service Providers,*" officially confirming this standpoint and elevating it to a global mandatory rule.[4]

Monetary authorities and anti-money laundering authorities are highly aligned in the scope of regulated virtual currencies. While monetary authorities recognize that only convertible virtual currencies can perform monetary functions (as a means of payment, medium of exchange, and store of value), for anti-money laundering authorities, the activities they regulate are not limited to the transfer of legal tender but encompass various forms of "value transfer." As such, both consider convertibility as a prerequisite for determining whether virtual currencies should be subject to regulation.

Virtual currencies are able to act as a medium of exchange, thus can substitute legal tender in value transfers. As a result, there is a close connection between the execution of monetary functions and the role of virtual currencies as a means of value transfer.

---

[2] See United States Department of the Treasury Financial Crimes Enforcement Network. "Application of FinCEN's Regulations to Persons Administering, Exchanging, or Using Virtual Currencies," March 2013. https://www.fincen.gov/resources/statutes-regulations/guidance/application-fincens-regulations-persons-administering.

[3] See Financial Action Task Force. "Virtual Currencies, Key Definitions and Potential AML/CFT Risks," June 2014. http://www.fatf-gafi.org/media/fatf/documents/reports/Virtual-currency-key-and-potential-aml-cft-risks.pdf, p. 26.

[4] Financial Action Task Force. "Guidance for a Risk-Based Approach to Virtual Assets and Virtual Asset Service Providers," June 2019. https://www.fatf-gafi.org/media/fatf/documents/recommendations/RBA-VA-VASPs.pdf, par. 14.

8.1.2 Convertibility: A Prerequisite for Securities

Convertibility is a standard proposed from the perspective of monetary authorities and anti-money laundering authorities, while securities regulatory authorities do not often directly use convertibility as a classification standard. The US Securities and Exchange Commission (SEC), for instance, does not adopt a classification standard like "convertibility," but instead uses the classification of "utility tokens" and "securities tokens." However, upon careful examination of SEC's regulatory classification standards, it becomes evident that they align with the concept of convertibility. Here, we make an attempt to explore the consistency between the two regulatory methods.

According to the SEC classification, "utility tokens" are limited to specific uses in certain domains, representing proof of purchase for usage rights, distinct from regulated "security tokens." In 2019, the SEC's formal regulatory decision further clarified the characteristic of non-convertibility for utility tokens.[5] That is, if a token cannot be exchanged with the outside world, it will then fail to meet the definition of a security under securities law and fall outside the scope of securities regulation. In other words, from the SEC's perspective, a purely closed virtual currency is only considered a "utility token," while an open or convertible virtual currency may potentially qualify as a "securities token" subject to securities regulation.

> While securities are often associated with company interests, such as stocks and bonds, this assumption does not hold true in all cases. It is relatively straightforward that virtual currencies can perform the functions of currency and serve as a means of value transfer. However, intuitively, virtual currencies differ significantly from traditional securities such as stocks and bonds. The U.S. Securities and Exchange Commission (SEC) has stated in its regulatory policy that traditional securities are indeed based on corporate interests, but this is not the essence of securities. The SEC still adheres to the "Howey test," which consists of four criteria to determine whether a specific investment qualifies as a security.[6]

Therefore, from the standpoint of the SEC, convertibility is a prerequisite triggering regulation. When a virtual currency allows for transferability beyond its closed space of single-directional use, enabling exchanges between different entities, it will then prompt the SEC to determine whether it qualifies as a security by applying the four criteria of "Howey test." Similarly, the so-called "hybrid" tokens, which have both closed-space usage and the ability to be transferred between different entities, will also trigger regulators to determine whether they are classified as securities.[7]

---

[5] The Division of Corporation Finance, U.S. Securities and Exchange Commission. "SEC No-Action Letter (TurnKey Jet, Inc.)," April 3, 2019. https://www.sec.gov/divisions/corpfin/cf-noaction/2019/turnkey-jet-040219-2a1.htm.

[6] See Clayton, Jay. "Statement on Cryptocurrencies and Initial Coin Offerings," December 11, 2017. https://www.sec.gov/news/public-statement/statement-clayton-2017-12-11#_ftnref5.

[7] SEC Chairman Jay Clayton's statement differentiates between 'utility tokens' and 'securities tokens,' noting that tokens having both attributes are classified as 'securities tokens' and are subject to securities regulation. See Clayton, Jay. "Statement on Cryptocurrencies and Initial Coin Offerings," December 11, 2017. https://www.sec.gov/news/public-statement/statement-clayton-2017-12-11#_ftnref5.

Convertibility is a prerequisite for a token to be considered a "security," but whether it meets the sufficient conditions for classification as a security still depends on fulfillment of the four criteria of the Howey test, especially the third and the fourth.

How to apply the Howey test to determine whether a virtual currency qualifies as a security? The Securities Act of 1933 of the United States does not provide a general definition of securities but uses a combination of specific types of securities, such as stocks, bonds, debentures, notes, and transferable shares, along with flexible descriptions to define the scope of securities. This includes evidences of indebtedness, investment contracts, certificates of interests in profit-sharing agreements, and other similar instruments under the category of securities, allowing for legal flexibility (15 U.S.C. § 77b(a)(1) (2017)).

In the landmark case of *SEC v. WJ Howey Co.* (1946), the U.S. Supreme Court established a general test to determine whether an investment qualifies as a security. In particular, the so-called Howey test consists of four elements: 1) an investment of money, 2) in a common enterprise, 3) with an expectation of profits, and 4) derived primarily from the efforts of others. While the first two elements are generally satisfied in practice, the key challenge lies in determining the presence of the last two elements.[8]

In 2017, the United States Securities and Exchange Commission (SEC) provided a comprehensive explanation of its regulatory stance on the nature of virtual currencies, particularly in their investigation of Dao tokens.[9] The SEC stated that Dao tokens fully satisfy the four elements of the "Howey test." Due to the typical significance of Dao tokens, their analysis holds value for understanding other virtual currency issuance practices. These elements include: (1) investment of money (using fiat currency or virtual currency, which is also considered money); (2) being in a common enterprise (not discussed in detail); (3) having an expectation of profits (expecting the appreciation of the value of Dao tokens); and (4) derived primarily from the efforts of others (from the efforts of management and founders).

As virtual currencies often claim to operate within a spontaneous order in the absence of a real governing body, the key point in this case is the fourth element. The SEC carefully analyzed the governance structure of the Dao and pointed out that voting rights on the platform are decentralized, and Dao token holders do not possess meaningful control. The true control remains in the hands of a few individuals such as the founders. In this way, the profits of Dao token holders are derived from the efforts of these few individuals who truly control the DAO.

---

[8] For further details, please refer to U.S. Securities and Exchange Commission. "Framework for 'Investment Contract' Analysis of Digital Assets," April 3, 2019. https://www.sec.gov/corpfin/framework-investment-contract-analysis-digital-assets.

[9] U.S. Securities and Exchange Commission. "Report of Investigation Pursuant to Section 21(a) of the Securities Exchange Act of 1934: Dao (Release No. 81207)," July 25, 2017. https://www.sec.gov/files/litigation/investreport/34-81207.pdf.

8.2 The Triple Attributes of Convertible Virtual Currencies: Mapping of the Regulatory System

The existing financial regulation has two major goals: prudential regulation and conduct regulation.[10] Prudential regulation comprises macroprudential regulation and microprudential regulation. The former aims to maintain stability of the financial system and is generally overseen by the central bank acting as the monetary authority, while the latter focuses on the soundness of individual financial institutions and is overseen by the central bank or separate prudential regulatory agencies. Conduct regulation is aimed at creating and maintaining fairness and transparency in financial markets for the protection of financial consumers, such as the mandatory disclosure of information in securities markets and safeguarding consumers' rights to fair trading.[11] In the existing fiat currency system, the central bank is responsible for currency issuance, and due to credit expansion through financial intermediaries (typically commercial banks), prudential regulation issues arise.

Anti-money laundering regulation is not traditionally considered as means of financial regulation. It was established in the 1970s by the United States to combat the increasing drug-related crimes by imposing anti-money laundering obligations on banks, with the aim of preventing and detecting criminal activities utilizing the financial system.[12]

The United States has a typical multi-tiered regulatory system, and its regulation of virtual currencies involves at least three levels: virtual currency remittance businesses licensed by each state, anti-money laundering regulation implemented by the U.S. Treasury for virtual currencies, and regulation of virtual currency issuance and transactions from a securities regulation perspective by SEC.[13]

Inspired by the multiple regulatory dimension of virtual currencies in the United States, we can map the financial regulatory system onto virtual currencies and argue that convertible virtual currencies have three attributes: from a monetary perspective, they can perform the functions of a medium of exchange, a store of value, and a unit of account; from an investment perspective, they are securities investments (or at

[10] Taylor, Michael. *Twin Peaks: A Regulatory Structure for the New Century*. London: Center for the Study of Financial Innovation, Dec. 1995.

[11] The Group of Thirty. "The Structure of Financial Supervision Approaches and Challenges in a Global Marketplace," 2008.

[12] In different countries, the anti-money laundering regulation of financial institutions may be implemented by various departments, including: central banks (such as in China), treasury departments (such as in the United States), police departments (such as in Australia), financial conduct regulatory authorities (such as in the United Kingdom), and dedicated specialized departments (such as in Russia).

[13] In the United States, the Securities and Exchange Commission (SEC) and the Commodity Futures Trading Commission (CFTC) have overlapping authorities regarding securities in certain situations where they intersect with commodities. As for virtual currencies, both regulatory bodies assert their regulatory authorities and implement regulations, but for the sake of simplicity, in this chapter, we focus our discussion solely on the SEC as the securities regulator.

least a type of investment that should be regulated); from an anti-money laundering perspective, they serve as a means of value transfer (see Table 8.1).

In 2021, Non-Fungible Tokens (NFTs) emerged as a way of storing and recording data on the blockchain. In the age of the Internet, information can be replicated at zero financial cost, such as copying a webpage or an image. In this "unrestricted" digital playing field, blockchain enables the creation of a unique digital file for an artwork, assigning it a distinct code similar to Bitcoin, which makes it unique and facilitate transactions. As these tokens store records of unique and non-replaceable artworks (such as paintings and music), they are referred to as Non-Fungible Tokens.

Non-Fungible Tokens have emerged as a form of electronic art collections. Whether NFTs constitute virtual currencies in terms of financial regulation and whether they trigger financial regulatory actions can be determined using the decision-making process outlined at the beginning of this chapter. Due to their inherent openness on the blockchain, Non-Fungible Tokens can be transferred between different entities, making them resemble convertible virtual currencies.

In addition, it is necessary to assess the characteristics of Non-Fungible Tokens to identify if they constitute currency, securities, or means of value transfer. For instance, if a specific Non-Fungible Token has already gained widespread acceptance as a means of payment, regulatory considerations from the perspective of payments and anti-money laundering may be warranted. If a Non-Fungible Token can be divided and traded between unspecified parties

Table 8.1 The regulatory issues of virtual currencies

Attribute	Regulatory content	Regulators	Examples of regulators	Regulatory issues
Money	Payment, clearing and settlement; legal tender	Central bank	People's Bank of China Bank of England	Impact on the fiat currency system not yet significant
	Financial soundness	Prudential regulator	People's Bank of China (Macro), CBIRC (China, Micro) Bank of England	Only conceptual discussions on prudential issues are in progress
Securities	Investor protection, market order	Conduct regulator	CSRC (China), FCA (UK), SEC (US)	Suitability for retail investors is controversial; The main challenges include fraud and price manipulation
Means of value transfer	Anti-money laundering	AML regulator	People's Bank of China U.S. Treasury FCA (UK)	Urgent need for regulation due to severe money laundering and criminal activities

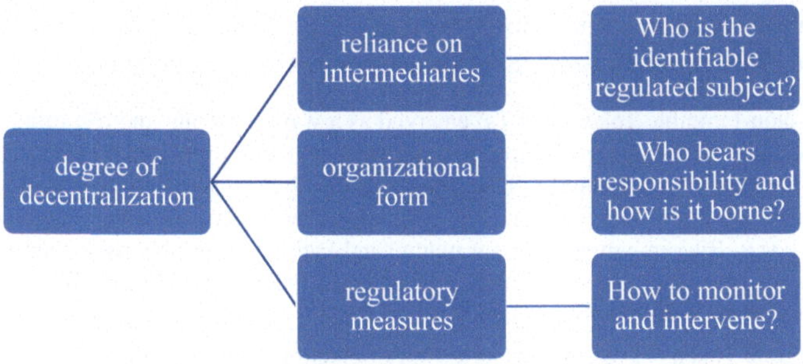

Fig. 8.2 The impacts of decentralization on financial regulation

with the purpose of gaining profits, regulatory measures from the securities perspective may need to be implemented.

8.3 The Implications of Decentralization for Financial Regulation

As much as the technological arrangements of virtual currencies differ, so does their degree of decentralization. From a regulatory perspective, we should closely consider the specific degree of decentralization and analyze which technological features change the key concerns of regulation. This helps us assess the specific impact of the characteristics of decentralized technology on financial regulation (see Fig. 8.2).

8.3.1 Who Bears the Regulatory Responsibilities?

The first impact of decentralization on financial regulation is the matter of who should be accountable for financial regulation. The degree of decentralization determines the reliance on financial intermediaries, and changes in this reliance lead to alterations in the "identifiability of regulated subjects" (see Table 8.2).

The more centralized a digital currency, the easier it is to identify the concerned obligated entity and the more effectively the regulated subjects can be determined to fulfill comprehensive obligations. Conversely, the opposite statement also holds true. For specific financial regulation, the focus of implementing regulatory policies is on the regulated subject or the obligated entity. In the current monetary system, financial intermediaries like banks act as hubs for financial activities, and regulatory rules are designed around these financial intermediaries, who are the main focus of financial regulation.

The challenge brought by decentralization is that related activities can, to some extent, bypass financial intermediaries, making it difficult for regulators to find the

Table 8.2 The degree of decentralization and identifiable regulated subjects

Degree of decentralization	Characteristics	Typical example	Reliance on intermediaries	Identifiable regulated subjects
Completely decentralized	Algorithm-based issuance, peer-to-peer payments	Bitcoin	No Reliance	Virtual currency exchange and transfer service provider
Issuance centralized Others decentralized	Issuer guarantees redemption; custodian safeguards assets; peer-to-peer payments	USDT	Limited Reliance	Virtual currency exchange and transfer service provider; issuer; custodian
Payment decentralized Others centralized	Central bank responsible for issuance, clearing & settlement; digital wallet provided by financial institutions	Digital RMB	Strong Reliance	Digital wallet provider; participator authorized by central bank
Completely centralized	Issuer guarantees redemption; custodian safeguards assets; issuer-controlled centralized servers handle payments, clearing & settlement	WebMoney	Complete Reliance	Virtual currency exchange and transfer service provider; issuer; custodian

focal point for achieving their regulatory objectives. Taking Bitcoin as an example, for large-scale matching transactions to take place, it is necessary to rely on cryptocurrency exchanges. To this end, the international anti-money laundering standards set by the Financial Action Task Force (FATF) cover the regulation of various service intermediaries and participants involved in exchange, transfer, issuance, custody, sales, and more. These entities are required to adhere to anti-money laundering measures equivalent to those imposed on financial institutions.

However, because on-chain governance activities (such as modifying code rules, conducting "forks," etc.) are decentralized, all current regulatory rules can only apply to on-chain transaction activities involving service intermediaries. To give an example, the financial regulator has the authority to establish rules governing exchange platforms, allowing them to impose restrictions on transfers between specific blockchain addresses. As exemplified in Sect. 4.5, Coinbase adhered to the sanction requirements of the US government and refused transactions involving addresses suspected to be associated with Russia. When it comes to the voting mechanisms within the Bitcoin blockchain, however, the regulator currently lacks the capability to enforce any rules.

"Fork" Is A Term Borrowed From Software Engineering That Describes The Branching Of Software Versions. As a common example, when a software version is upgraded, the upgraded version and the initial version become two separate branches. This situation is referred to as a software fork.

In the cryptocurrency community, this concept is used to describe a situation where, due to disagreements, a group of participator modifies the code of a cryptocurrency, which will deviate from the main version, and releases a new version, creating a new cryptocurrency distinct from the initial one. BCH (Bitcoin Cash) and BSC (Binance Smart Chain) are such forks of Bitcoin.

These forks often occur due to differing philosophical beliefs about the financial order of cryptocurrencies and different technological pursuits. When a fork emerges, the initial cryptocurrency splits into separate and distinct cryptocurrencies, much like the plot of a martial arts novel in which a dispute emerges within a sect, resulting in some disciples separating and forming their own sect, thereby establishing a new faction.

8.3.2 What Do Those Responsibilities Entail?

The second impact of decentralization on financial regulation is who should be accountable for financial regulation. Decentralization has led to new organizational structures, which in turn impact the way responsibilities are assumed. Let us take the example of The DAO, the most controversial new organizational form.

Bitcoin strives to establish a decentralized order and has created a community governance model based on the idea of "code is law." The DAO (decentralized autonomous organization), a distributed software application, was launched on the Ethereum blockchain in 2016, further experimenting with the concept of decentralized autonomous organization. It operates as a decentralized platform governed by predetermined rules, without any central authority, where all token holders on the platform have direct voting rights.

The Experiment of The DAO With Decentralized Autonomous Organizations Began In April 2016 With A Massive Crowdfunding Campaign In The Ethereum Community. It aimed to establish a decentralized autonomous organization called "The DAO." It was envisioned as a risk investment fund that operates without any physical organization or centralized management. In practice, The DAO is a distributed software application comprising smart contracts written in code and deployed on the Ethereum blockchain. The platform runs according to predetermined rules and is not controlled by any individual or centralized entity. It is often referred to as a "virtual organization" or a "decentralized autonomous organization."

The code modification of The DAO can only be achieved through the majority consensus of DAO tokens.[14] Enabled by the elements of "virtual currency" and "smart contracts," the concept of an unmanaged "virtual organization" became possible through the DAO, as envisioned by David in B-Money.

The DAO was developed and operated by Slock.it, a German company founded by Christoph Jentzsch and Simon Jentzsch, the former being an early core developer in the Ethereum community.

[14] Jentzsch, Christoph. "Decentralized Autonomous Organization to Automate Governance." White paper, November 2016. https://download.slock.it/public/DAO/WhitePaper.pdf.

The DAO involves two main roles: investors and entrepreneurs. Investors exchange ether for DAO tokens through the Ethereum network, effectively obtaining digital equity, while entrepreneurs submit proposals and deploy smart contracts to apply for investment from The DAO. The first entrepreneur to submit a funding proposal to The DAO was Slock.it.

THE DAO'S CROWDFUNDING CAMPAIGN BEGAN IN MAY 2016, with investors sending ether to The DAO's smart contract address in exchange for virtual shares. After four weeks of fundraising, The DAO raised around 12 million ether.[15]

On July 25, 2017, the U.S. Securities and Exchange Commission (SEC) issued a report asserting that DAO tokens were securities; it stated that virtual currencies similar to DAO tokens, issued on the blockchain, should be subject to securities laws and regulations. Although The DAO claimed to be a "crowdfunding contract," it did not meet the exemption criteria provided by crowdfunding regulations.[16]

The SEC declaring The DAO's issuance of securities as illegal sparked discussions about the issue of responsibility in such decentralized autonomous organizations. As previously mentioned, the internal governance of blockchain poses fundamental challenges in the future. Decentralized autonomous organizations lack any tangible organizational structure, making existing legal entities (such as corporations, general partnerships, and limited partnerships) unsuitable. From a legal perspective, The DAO lacks the necessary statutory requirements, even without considering the requirement for legal registration. Additionally, it is short of the appropriate management framework and allocation of internal and external responsibilities that would classify it as a corporation or limited partnership. While a general partnership could be determined based on the fact of joint actions, the creators of The DAO hold significant control, while ordinary token holders do not possess meaningful control.[17] Therefore, the liability assumed by all participants seems unfair.

In 2017, The DAO was deemed illegal by the U.S. SEC for issuing securities, leading to discussions on the issue of accountability for such decentralized autonomous organizations. As pointed out by Yun Wu and Wei Zhu, the internal governance of blockchain poses fundamental challenges for the future.[18] These decentralized autonomous organizations lack any tangible organizational structure, making the application of existing market entities (mainly including corporations, general partnerships, and limited partnerships) clearly inadequate. Under the current

---

[15] U.S. Securities and Exchange Commission. "Report of Investigation Pursuant to Section 21(a) of the Securities Exchange Act of 1934: The DAO," 25 July 2017. https://www.sec.gov/files/litigation/investreport/34-81207.pdf.

[16] U.S. Securities and Exchange Commission. "Report of Investigation Pursuant to Section 21(a) of the Securities Exchange Act of 1934: The DAO," 25 July 2017. https://www.sec.gov/files/litigation/investreport/34-81207.pdf.

[17] U.S. Securities and Exchange Commission. "Report of Investigation Pursuant to Section 21(a) of the Securities Exchange Act of 1934: The DAO," 25 July 2017. https://www.sec.gov/files/litigation/investreport/34-81207.pdf.

[18] Wu, Yun, and Wei Zhu. "Anti-Money Laundering Regulation over Virtual Currencies: A Starting Point to Depart from Autonomous Order." *Law and Economy*, no. 2 (2021): 79–97.

legal framework, corporations and limited partnerships require registration, which the The DAO platform obviously lacks. Even without considering the requirement for legal registration, from a normative perspective, the The DAO platform is missing an organizational management framework and a consensus on internal and external responsibilities, making it difficult to constitute a corporation or limited partnership. Certainly, a general partnership can be determined based on factual common action and the The DAO platform can be regarded as a general partnership within the existing legal framework. However, as the SEC pointed out, the initiators of the The DAO platform have actual control, whereas ordinary holders of DAO tokens are not sufficient to form meaningful control.[19] It is clearly unfair for all participants to bear unlimited joint and several liability.

Some Chinese papers suggest treating The DAO as a limited partnership, designating those with control over the platform (participating addresses) as general partners and ordinary participants (participating addresses) without control as limited partners.[20] Certain U.S. studies propose that none of the existing organizational models are suitable for The DAO and recommend classifying it as a new type of "hybrid entity," combining elements of limited liability companies, corporations, and partnerships.[21]

8.3.3 What New Demands Does Regulatory Technology Face?

The third impact of decentralization on financial regulation is that decentralization requests new regulatory technologies. The varying degrees of decentralization have presented new requirements for the monitoring techniques and intervention methods employed by regulators.

For Bitcoin, activities on the blockchain are anonymous and the tracing capabilities are limited, only allowing tracking of transaction addresses. This can be understood as masked individuals conducting transactions with cash, where the transaction process can only be established through the serial numbers on the banknotes. As mentioned earlier, existing anti-money laundering regulations require virtual currency service providers to fulfill similar anti-money laundering obligations as banks by constructing a traceable transaction system associated with real identities. However, for peer-to-peer transactions not relying on virtual currency service providers, i.e., pure on-chain transactions, traceability is limited to the extent of

[19] U.S. Securities and Exchange Commission. "Report of Investigation Pursuant to Section 21(a) of the Securities Exchange Act of 1934: The DAO," 25 July 2017. https://www.sec.gov/files/litigation/investreport/34-81207.pdf.

[20] See Guo, Shaofei. "A Study on the Legal Nature of 'Decentralized Autonomous Organizations.'" *Social Science Journal* 3 (2020): 96–104. ''See also Wang, Qingsong. "Defining the Nature of Internal Relationships and Attribution in Blockchain Systems." *Law Journal* 5 (2019): 130–142.

[21] Nielsen, Timothy. "Cryptocorporations: A proposal for legitimizing decentralized autonomous organizations." *Utah L. Rev*, 2019, 1105–1129, p. 1105.

"masked person cash transactions" (transactions from one address to another on a public chain). Therefore, in order for regulators to monitor blockchain transactions, they must employ more extensive information and utilize various data and scenario matching techniques for effective monitoring.

Existing regulations intervene by targeting identifiable regulated entities and forcing them to achieve regulatory objectives, such as compelling them to improve internal control and governance structures, up to the point of revoking licenses or business permits. All of this is based on the clear identification of the regulated entities and the responsibility bearers. For regulating decentralized blockchain activities and organizations, this poses significant challenges and may require empowering the state as a "super code controller" to achieve effective intervention.

Chapter 9
Formation of a Global Anti-Money Laundering Regulatory Network

Why does virtual currency regulation begin with anti-money laundering? How do AML authorities regulate virtual currencies to address anonymity? How will AML regulation push the blockchain toward transparency?

This chapter explains that AML efforts are essential for regulation due to the anonymity of digital transactions. Authorities require service providers to identify customers and report suspicious activities. Here, we emphasize that AML regulation is not just a compliance requirement but a transformative force that is reshaping the future of virtual currencies, prompting the blockchain to move toward transparency. Undoubtedly, this will mitigate the risks associated with illegal activities.

9.1 Why Does Virtual Currency Regulation Begin with Anti-Money Laundering? Regulators' Logic

The severe price manipulation, speculation, rampant laundering, and misuse of virtual currencies for criminal activities underscore the necessity for their regulation. IImportantly, in regulatory practice, a nation's intervention in virtual currencies is multidimensional (as we have discussed in Chaps. 6 and 8), each presenting distinct levels of urgency and necessity.

Given that the impact of virtual currencies on the traditional currency system has yet to fully manifest, and discussions around associated prudential concerns are still ongoing, monetary authorities find themselves mostly in an observational position regarding virtual currencies. Concurrently, major nations like the United States, grappling with concerns about investor suitability, have refrained from permitting any public issuance of virtual currencies. The global community has yet to establish a broad consensus on how to responsibly issue virtual currencies to the general public, with few positive instances of registration or approval. Instead, due to issues

Y. Wu and W. Zhu, *The Fundamentals of Digital Currency*,
https://doi.org/10.1007/978-981-97-8261-1_9

such as price manipulation and fraud that continue to dominate the investment landscape, leading nations frequently approach virtual currency regulation through mechanisms like administrative penalties and judicial investigations. Simultaneously, the escalating concern of money laundering through virtual currencies has prompted anti-money laundering authorities worldwide to collectively acknowledge the compelling necessity and urgency of regulating these digital assets.

At the current stage, the urgency and necessity associated with the three forms of regulation concerning the monetary attributes, securities attributes, and value transfer means attributes of virtual currencies differ significantly. However, a common ground for urgent action lies in addressing the dual imperatives of combatting virtual currency price manipulation and fraud, as well as effectively countering money laundering through virtual currencies, yielding a focal point in anti-money laundering regulation.

1. Virtual Currencies Have Not Posed a Significant Threat to the Traditional Currency System: The Tolerant Stance of Monetary Authorities

Due to their inherent flaws in serving as a store of value and a medium of exchange, since the inception of Bitcoin on January 9, 2009, virtual currencies have not created noteworthy impacts or influences on existing currency systems. As these currencies are far from reaching a stage where they can compete with fiat currencies, most countries, except for a few with absolute prohibitions, have adopted a tolerant attitude towards them while upholding fiat currency as the sole legal tender.

Meanwhile, the emergence of new digital currencies, including privately issued virtual currencies and central bank-issued "central bank digital currencies," has led to conceptual discussions about the continued relevance of traditional financial intermediaries (such as banks) and the amplification of monetary credit. Prudent regulation is not an immediate concern at this stage since these issues remain in the conceptual discussion phase.[1]

In summary, the issues of currency sovereignty and related financial stability are currently not prominent, with no immediate necessity or urgency for regulation.

2. Virtual Currencies Seem Not Suitable for Ordinary Investors: The Postponement of Public Issuance

The core objective of securities regulatory authorities is to protect public investors, and the boundary between regulation and non-regulation lies in meeting the needs of investor protection. Only products suitable for the risk tolerance of the general public can be publicly solicited and issued, warranting regulatory oversight; otherwise, exemptions may apply. The fundamental question perplexing regulators worldwide is to what extent virtual currencies are suitable for ordinary investors. Regulatory authorities lack a clear and affirmative answer, as there is significant divergence and controversy among professional investors regarding the intrinsic value of virtual currencies. Taking the United States as an example, no virtual currency or financial

[1] See BIS, Central Bank Digital Currencies 6 (CPMI Papers No. 174, March 2018), available at: https://www.bis.org/cpmi/publ/d174.pdf.

products of virtual currency targeting the general public have been registered or approved.[2]

The lack of underlying assets supporting virtual currencies raises significant doubts about their intrinsic value, with substantial disagreements among professional investors on whether they possess any such value.[3] Renowned investor Warren Buffett has referred to Bitcoin as a "gambling device" and "rat poison."[4] While Buffett's understanding may not necessarily reflect the truth, it highlights the substantial dispute over the intrinsic value of Bitcoin within the global elite investor community.

Doubts regarding intrinsic value represent a fundamental issue for virtual currencies, and a credible judgment may only emerge after an extended record of market dynamics. Consequently, there is also a lack of broad consensus within the international community on how to issue virtual currencies to ordinary investors, with few positive instances of registration or approval. Instead, due to prevalent issues such as price manipulation and fraud in the investment domain, major countries primarily regulate virtual currencies through administrative penalties, judicial investigations, and similar measures.

3. Anti-Money Laundering Regulation as a Priority

As previously mentioned, the high inherent risks of anonymity and transnationality associated with virtual currencies make them prone to money laundering and illicit

---

[2] In 2017, the Chicago Mercantile Exchange (CME) listed bitcoin futures, but the participants in futures trading were not public investors but qualified investors or professional investors.

[3] The discussion here on the intrinsic value of virtual currencies is limited to non-stablecoins like Bitcoin, which lack asset backing and exhibit significant volatility. Due to the lack of value anchoring in Bitcoin, stablecoins, also known as asset-linked stablecoins, have emerged, backed by fiat currencies or physical assets. USDT, with the US dollar being its reserve asset, is the most typical and widely used stablecoin. Additionally, Facebook's proposed Libra, also known as the Diem project, initially planned to use a basket of currencies as its reserve assets. There are also stablecoins backed by commodities, such as DGX (Digix Gold Tokens), with gold as the reserve asset. However, these stablecoins require custody of the supporting assets and face notable investor protection issues. Some studies have raised doubts about whether issuers of these stablecoins possess sufficient assets, as exemplified by the reservations regarding the reserve assets backing USDT in the earlier mentioned paper by Griffin et al. (2019). Furthermore, some asset-linked stablecoins are backed by other virtual currencies, and the effectiveness of maintaining stablecoin value depends on the value stability of the supporting asset.

In a broader sense, algorithm-based stablecoins are also classified as stablecoins. These stablecoins maintain their value by adjusting the total token supply through algorithms. In other words, when the value of the stablecoin decreases, a portion of the tokens is burned to maintain price stability, and vice versa. However, algorithm-based stablecoins have not proven to be effective in practice in maintaining their value, as illustrated by the case of NuBits. The definition and scope of algorithm-based stablecoins, however, remain subject to debate and will not be further elaborated here. Please refer to FSB, *Regulation, Supervision and Oversight of "Global Stablecoin" Arrangements: Final Report and High-Level Recommendations*, 9–10 (2020). Also see Dirk Bullmann, Jonas Klemm, and Andrea Pinna, *In Search for Stability in Crypto-assets: are Stablecoins the Solution?*, ECB Occasional Paper No. 230, 23 (2019).

[4] Yun Li, Warren Buffett Says Bitcoin is a "Gambling Device" with "a lot of Frauds Connected with It," CNBC, May 4 2019, at Market, available at: https://www.cnbc.com/2019/05/04/warren-buffett-says-bitcoin-is-a-gambling-device-with-a-lot-of-frauds-connected-with-it.html.

activities. According to existing data, the use of virtual currencies to support money laundering and criminal activities is substantial both in relative and absolute terms. In an article published in October 2018, the then-president of the FATF urged jurisdictions to pay attention to the severity of virtual currencies being exploited for criminal activities, stating that "Virtual assets and financial crime now go hand in hand."[5] Due to the escalating issue of money laundering through virtual currencies, anti-money laundering authorities worldwide have collectively recognized that the necessity and urgency of regulating virtual currencies is of realistic concern.

Additionally, from the perspectives of investor protection and maintaining market order, anti-money laundering regulation can create a framework conducive to curbing severe fraud and manipulation in the virtual currency market, reducing barriers of entry for ordinary investors. The anonymity associated with virtual currencies makes it challenging to trace lost assets, and fraud and price manipulation are also difficult to detect. In its official opinion rejecting the application for a Bitcoin financial product by the Winklevoss twins in 2018, the U.S. SEC noted that the Bitcoin (underlying asset) market is not "inherently resistant to fraud and manipulation" and lacks sufficient preventive measures to curb fraud and manipulation.[6] Therefore, financial products based on Bitcoin as the underlying asset are deemed unsuitable for ordinary investor participation. We think that the establishment of anti-money laundering regulation will significantly contribute to establishing a traceable system for transactions, fundamentally enhancing the capacity to identify and discover illegal activities, thereby restraining illegal activities through virtual currencies and purifying the market and transactions from them.

Consequently, the dual objectives of combating virtual currency price manipulation and fraud and addressing money laundering through virtual currencies converge in the realm of anti-money laundering regulation.

---

[5] Marshall Billingslea, Virtual Assets and Financial Crime Now Go Hand in Hand, Financial Times, Oct. 28, 2018, at Opinion.

[6] In countries with a securities issuance approval system, regulatory authorities are expected to make substantive judgments on behalf of investors. However, even in countries that operate under a securities registration system, such as the United States, regulatory authorities do not completely forgo a substantive review of securities. The SEC has repeatedly rejected applications for financial products publicly issued based on Bitcoin as an underlying asset. In 2018, in rejecting the Winklevoss application for a Bitcoin financial product, the SEC noted that Under United States securities laws, the question of whether there is intrinsic value is for investors to determine, yet the SEC has the authority to review whether the underlying asset market (Bitcoin) is inherently resistant to fraud and manipulation, or whether there are adequate preventative measures in place to suppress fraud and manipulation. See Securities Exchange Act Release No. 83723 (July 26, 2018), 83 FR 37,579 (Aug. 1, 2018).

9.2 Regulatory Attempts Initiated by the International Community: Anti-Money Laundering as the Starting Point

The relationship between virtual currencies and fiat currencies, as well as the impact of virtual currencies on the financial system, have been subjects of an open discussion. Yet there is no definitive consensus on whether virtual currencies are suitable for ordinary investors. However, concerns about speculation, fraud and severe money laundering issues have compelled authorities worldwide to respond with substantive measures.

Since 2013, the Financial Action Task Force (FATF) has undertaken research on the money laundering risks associated with virtual currencies. In June 2014, the FATF released a report titled "Virtual Currencies: Key Definitions and Potential AML/CTF Risks," providing a comprehensive overview of relevant definitions and involving a study on the money laundering risks associated with virtual currencies while incorporating criminal cases. In June 2015, the FATF issued the "Guidance for a Risk-based Approach to Virtual Currencies," exploring how FATF standards are applicable to virtual currencies.

After extensive research and deliberations, regulatory authorities from diverse jurisdictions within the FATF framework achieved a consensus on anti-money laundering regulations for virtual currencies. The pivotal moment occurred during the FATF plenary meeting held in Florida, USA in June 2019, where the anti-money laundering standard was officially adopted, accompanied by its comprehensive guidance titled "Guidance for a Risk-Based Approach to Virtual Assets and Virtual Asset Service Providers." This marked the first set of regulatory standards, among all international organizations, specifically formulated and approved for virtual currencies. Basically, it established international consensus on anti-money laundering regulation for virtual currencies.

This milestone represented a significant leap forward in addressing the challenges posed by virtual currencies, providing a standardized framework for countries to assess and implement anti-money laundering measures in the context of virtual assets and service providers. The international community, through the FATF, has demonstrated its commitment to tackle the unique risks associated with virtual currencies, marking a crucial step in the evolving landscape of global financial regulations.

THE UNCROWNED KING: FATF. The Financial Action Task Force (FATF), launched by the G7 summit in 1989, started as an intergovernmental organization to tackle the hazards of money laundering and to promote and coordinate international anti-money laundering actions. Over time, it has evolved into a body setting international standards for combating money laundering. Currently, the FATF comprises 39 full members (including two regional organizations), with more than 200 countries and jurisdictions worldwide participating in the FATF or FATF-style regional bodies. The FATF Secretariat is housed at the headquarters of the Organisation for Economic Co-operation and Development (OECD) in Paris.[7] Its standards comprise "the 40 Recommendations," where each recommendation and its interpretative note

[7] Please refer to the official FATF website at https://www.fatf-gafi.org/about/.

are endowed with equal binding force.[8] To assess the implementation of these recommendations across nations, the FATF has developed a comprehensive and rigorous "Assessment Methodology," encompassing forty compliance indicators (aligned with the 40 Recommendations) and eleven effectiveness indicators (derived from the 40 Recommendations, each indicator is called "Immediate Outcome"), with each indicator containing several criteria.[9]

The distinctive feature of the 40 Recommendations lies in framing a series of requirements around anti-money laundering, covering five aspects, namely, criminal justice, anti-money laundering supervision, international cooperation, the enforcement of United Nations targeted financial sanctions, and more. This framework spans various domains, ranging from judiciary to law enforcement, regulation, and to diplomacy.

The binding nature of the 40 Recommendations affects over 200 economies globally. Unlike most international organizations, the FATF has devised a comprehensive evaluation methodology, urging member states to adhere to the standards through mutual assessments. Members falling short of compliance face financial countermeasures and sanctions, akin to financial sanctions. With core FATF member nations holding sway over major freely convertible currencies and international payment settlement systems, the collective implementation of financial sanctions by these nations has the potential to isolate any economy from the global financial system. This formidable set of evaluation mechanisms, infused with tangible consequences, positions the anti-money laundering standards set by the FATF as internationally recognized and enforceable.

Taking the example of United Nations targeted sanctions resolutions, unlike the United Nations Security Council that lacks detailed technical mechanisms to enforce resolutions, the FATF, acting as a technical organization, has established a comprehensive set of standards. These mandate that domestic laws in each country must provide a legal basis for implementing targeted financial sanctions resolutions (Recommendation 6, Recommendation 7, where "targeted" implies sanction lists for individuals and entities). Moreover, they require effective execution (Immediate Outcome 10 & Immediate Outcome 11). Through mutual assessments among members, the FATF identifies legal and enforcement deficiencies in various countries and proposes remedial suggestions. Thus, through technical standards, the FATF propels the global implementation of United Nations targeted sanctions resolutions.

In legal terms, the Financial Action Task Force is a temporary international working group without international legal personality. Its secretariat relies on the Organization for Economic Cooperation and Development to enjoy some privileges associated with international organizations, such as diplomatic immunity. However, owing to its prowess in financial sanctions, few other technical standards from international organizations carry such robust binding force. Thus, the FATF is often hailed as the "uncrowned king" of international regulation in financial circles, earning the moniker of "little United Nations."

In June 2019, through the addition of "interpretative note" to Recommendation 15 (New Technologies), the FATF specified the regulatory requirements for virtual currencies. The standards employ a cascading impact approach, explicitly enumerating which existing recommendations are applicable to virtual currencies and how

[8] The full title of the "40 Recommendations" is "International Standards on Combating Money Laundering and the Financing of Terrorism & Proliferation (amended June 2019)," commonly referred to in the industry as the "FATF Recommendations 2012" or "40 Recommendations".

[9] The full title of the "Assessment Methodology" is "Methodology for Assessing Technical Compliance with the FATF Recommendations and the Effectiveness of AML/CFT Systems (amended October 2019)," which is generally referred to within the industry as "Methodology 2013" or "Assessment Methodology".

they should be applied. In October 2019, the FATF modified the "assessment methodology" based on the revised "40 Recommendations." As per the decision of the FATF plenary, a preliminary review of the implementation by countries and regions was conducted in June 2020. Based on this initial review, targeted comprehensive assessments were subsequently organized.

The newly adopted anti-money laundering standards for virtual currencies by the FATF encompass industry entry, anti-money laundering regulatory requirements, and international cooperation, among others. These standards have a direct and revolutionary impact on the operational models and industry development of virtual currencies.

9.3 International Anti-Money Laundering Standards for Virtual Currencies

1. Respecting National Positions on Virtual Currency Legitimacy: Prohibition or Regulation?

To dispel potential misconceptions about the legitimacy of "virtual currencies," the FATF has rebranded them as "virtual assets" and issued a statement explicitly stating its non-endorsement of their legal status.[10] In line with the FATF's regulatory approach towards casinos, if a country successfully prohibits virtual currencies, formal regulatory measures may be unnecessary. Conversely, for nations permitting virtual currencies, the establishment of regulatory frameworks becomes imperative to meet FATF standards. Countries adopting prohibition measures, such as China, must implement effective actions, including legal sanctions, to align with FATF standards. For countries embracing virtual currencies, robust and effective regulatory measures are a necessity.[11]

2. Applying Established Standards for Financial Activities and Institutions to Govern Virtual Currency Activities and Service Providers

The pre-existing framework for preventing money laundering focuses on making sure that certain entities, like financial institutions and "designated non-financial businesses or professions" (DNFBP), meet their obligations regarding preventing money laundering. The main goal of authorities overseeing these rules is to ensure that these entities fully comply with their anti-money laundering responsibilities.

Adding to the existing two categories of entities with obligations, the FATF introduced a third category of Virtual Asset Service Providers (VASPs), which are responsible for carrying out the anti-money laundering obligations. Oversight and regulation are in place to monitor these service providers to make sure they meet the goals set

[10] FATF Statement, Regulation of Virtual Assets (*Paris, France, Oct. 19, 2018*).

[11] FATF, Guidance for a Risk-Based Approach to Virtual Assets and Virtual Asset Service Providers, paras. 32, 67 (June 2019).

Table 9.1 Comparison between virtual asset service providers (VASPs) and banks

	Banks (typical anti-money laundering obligated entities)	Virtual asset service providers (VASPs)
Nature of activity	Value transfer	Value transfer
Activities	Custody and control of fiat currency	Custody and control of virtual currencies
Anti-money laundering obligations	Core trio of anti-money laundering obligations and more	Core trio of anti-money laundering obligations and more

by anti-money laundering regulations. From the perspective of technical neutrality, the simple logic applied by the FATF is that the standards used for financial institutions and activities should also apply to VASPs and activities involving virtual assets (Table 9.1).[12]

VASPs bear the same anti-money laundering obligations as banks, encompassing 12 standards from "Recommendation 10" to "Recommendation 21." The core trio of obligations entails conducting customer due diligence,[13] maintaining customer and transaction records, and reporting suspicious transactions to the designated national financial intelligence unit.

3. The Scope of Regulation Encompasses All "Virtual Asset Activities"

FATF regulatory rules define entities based on the essence of their "activities," considering "Virtual Asset Service Providers" as entities or individuals conducting business by offering services for "virtual asset activities." For clarity, the FATF enumerates key "virtual asset activities" in its *Guidance for a Risk-Based Approach to Virtual Assets and Virtual Asset Service Providers* of 2019, including:

(1) Exchange between fiat currency and virtual currency;
(2) Exchange between different types of virtual currencies;
(3) Transfer of virtual currencies;
(4) Custody and management of virtual currencies;
(5) Participation in the issuance and sale of virtual currencies or the provision of services to them.

[12] During the discussion, the original proposal was to categorize virtual asset activities directly as financial activities, and to include virtual asset service providers within the scope of "financial institutions." This would mean that existing rules would automatically apply. The representatives agreed with this regulatory approach, but some argued that such arrangement was too generic on a technical level and failed to address the unique issues and concerns associated with virtual currencies. Consequently, the final solution was to add an "interpretative note" to "Recommendation 15," which specifically lists which existing rules apply and which should be applied with heightened requirements.

[13] According to "Recommendation 10," customer due diligence (CDD) requirements are more comprehensive than what we typically refer to as "customer real-name systems": it involves not only verifying the accuracy of customer identities but also identifying the ultimate controlling natural persons or ultimate beneficial owners behind legal entity customers, as well as understanding the purpose and nature of the customer's business.

Table 9.2 Comparison of scope of typical anti-money laundering obligations

Aspect	Traditional currency system	Virtual currency system	Explanation
Self-custody and use	User personally holds cash (in a safe)	User personally holds private keys (non-custodial wallet)	Institutions providing means for cash storage (e.g., safe manufacturers) are not obligated entities for anti-money laundering; nor are institutions offering technical services related to the personal custody and use of virtual currencies
Third-party custody and use	User holds funds through a bank (bank account)	User holds funds through a service provider (custodial wallet)	Banks act as value transfer agents and are obligated entities for anti-money laundering; likewise, VASPs fall under the category of obligated entities for anti-money laundering

Prior to the above guidance, some countries only regulated the anti-money laundering aspects of the direct exchange between virtual and fiat currencies. However, FATF standards extend the regulatory oversight to encompass all virtual currency transfer activities, especially those involving transfers between different virtual currencies (Table 9.2).

Understanding "virtual asset activities" is crucial to comprehend the concept of "custodial wallet," which the FATF uses as an illustrative example in setting its rules. When enumerating the scope of the aforementioned "virtual asset activities," the FATF seems to assume that, within these activities, service providers gain control over virtual currencies through "custodial wallets." Similar to a bank account, a "custodial wallet" entails that users can store their private keys of their virtual currencies while granting control to the service provider, and they can instruct the service provider to transfer virtual currencies held in this wallet.

Should users opt not to utilize third-party custody for virtual currencies, they are using a "non-custodial wallet." This can be likened to a personal safe for storing cash, representing a storage method under the owner's individual control. Providing "non-custodial wallet" services is akin to offering secure storage solutions, involving technical services that fall outside the scope of anti-money laundering regulation (Table 9.3).

When referring to a virtual currency trading platform or exchange in this book, we essentially mean a typical "Virtual Asset Service Provider" (VASP). Customers usually store their virtual currencies in the platform's "custodial wallet," and the platform facilitates matched transactions based on user instructions.[14]

4. Establishing Industry Entry Thresholds to Prevent Regulatory Evasion

[14] In addition, there are also physical electronic terminals, such as Bitcoin ATMs, and the activities of purchasing and transferring virtual currencies through these physical terminals are subject to FATF rules on virtual currency regulation. For some virtual currency platforms, if they only publish price information and do not engage in any trading activities, they do not fall under regulated

Table 9.3 Comparison of virtual currency custodial wallets with bank and securities accounts

	Bank account	Securities account	Virtual currency custodial wallet
Custody object	Fiat currency	Securities	Virtual currency
Custody control method	Bank manages and controls funds in the account	Securities broker manages and controls securities	Wallet provider manages and controls assets in the custodial wallet
Transaction method	Based on user instructions	Based on user instructions	Based on user instructions
Government authority exercise	Regulators can monitor fund flow through bank accounts; the government can legally instruct the freezing of assets in bank account	Regulators can monitor securities asset flow through securities accounts; the government can legally instruct the freezing of assets in securities account	Regulators can monitor fund flow through custodial wallets; the government can legally instruct the freezing of assets in custodial wallet

The FATF imposes threshold requirements for entry to the industry. Each jurisdiction must adopt a registration or approval system, and VASPs must obtain registration or licensing before offering virtual asset services. Specifically, the provider's place of establishment, operation, and the customer's location may all require the service provider to apply for registration or licensing. When the service provider is a legal entity, its place of establishment is mandatory for registration or licensing application, while for a natural person, it is the business location that requires registration or licensing. This minimal set of mandatory rules ensures that VASPs are registered, licensed and regulated in at least one jurisdiction. It is designed to prevent offshore services, where an entity registers in one jurisdiction but provides services in another, avoiding regulatory oversight. The objective is to guard against the establishment of "regulatory havens" or "regulatory gaps," ensuring a global network of collaborative regulation.

5. Strengthening International Cooperation to Prevent Regulatory Arbitrage

International cooperation is a crucial aspect of existing FATF standards. "Recommendations 37" to "Recommendations 40" outline judicial assistance, cross-border asset freezing and confiscation, extradition, and other forms of international cooperation. To comprehensively enhance international collaboration in the virtual currency domain, the FATF extends these requirements to all regulatory areas beyond anti-money laundering. In the new standard, it is highlighted that countries may have different regulatory bodies for virtual currencies with varying perspectives on the nature and nomenclature of virtual currencies. However, these differences should

activities. For the scope of regulation, see FATF, *Guidance for a Risk-Based Approach to Virtual Assets and Virtual Asset Service Providers*, paras. 33–54 (June 2019).

not impede international cooperation in regulatory information exchange, aiming to prevent regulatory arbitrage.[15]

6. The Stricter Application of Regulatory Standards

The FATF acknowledges the inherently higher risks associated with virtual assets. As such, it mandates stricter application of certain standards based on a risk-based approach, which relates to two primary areas:

First, governmental agencies enforce anti-money laundering regulations for virtual assets, and these regulatory responsibilities cannot be delegated to industry self-regulatory bodies. Under the FATF framework, obligated entities encompass financial institutions and DNFBPs, each subject to varying levels of importance and risk. The FATF standards dictate that government institutions must oversee regulatory compliance for financial institutions, while non-financial institutions may be subject to regulation by self-regulatory organizations. Given the unique risk profile of virtual asset services, the FATF mandates that only government institutions can regulate them.

Secondly, considering the transnational nature of virtual currencies and their higher inherent risk of money laundering, any value transfer of virtual assets is uniformly presumed to be cross-border transactions and subjected to more stringent anti-money laundering requirements than existing cross-border transactions. According to FATF standards, financial institutions must conduct customer due diligence for occasional transactions, whether domestic or cross-border, when the amount reaches 15,000 USD or EUR (whichever is lower). For cross-border transactions, financial institutions must verify the accuracy of customer identities when the transaction amount reaches 1000 USD or EUR (whichever is lower)—an aspect of customer due diligence. However, the new standards stipulate that for occasional transactions involving virtual currencies, customer due diligence must be performed once the transaction reaches 1000 USD or EUR (whichever is lower).

9.4 The Transformative Impact of International Anti-Money Laundering Standards on the Industry Ecosystem: Regulators' Expectations

The international anti-money laundering (AML) standards of the FATF are catalyzing a transformative shift in the operational frameworks and ecosystems of the financial industry. These reforms, shaped by regulatory foresight and clear expectations, aim to streamline compliance and enhance security across the board. Here is a synthesized breakdown of their revolutionary effects:

[15] As stated in paragraph 8, sentence 2 of the FATF's "Interpretative Note to Recommendation 15": "In particular, supervisors of VASPs should exchange information promptly and constructively with their foreign counterparts, regardless of the supervisors' nature or status and differences in the nomenclature or status of VASPs.".

1. Scope of Impact

The new international AML standards have altered the financial ecosystem and operational modes of the entire industry. Transactions between individuals using "non-custodial wallets" (completely peer-to-peer transactions without any external services) remain outside the purview of regulation. However, any transactions facilitated by a third party, such as those stored and transferred through a trading platform, fall within the regulatory framework. This significantly mitigates risks and aligns with the basic regulatory logic and technological characteristics of the industry. From a risk control perspective, non-custodial wallets demand high technical expertise from users. Without adequate knowledge, not only correct transactions are difficult to execute but also there is a high risk of losing virtual currencies, limiting their use to a few users. In terms of regulatory logic, the focus is on commercial activities instead of private individual actions. Technologically, peer-to-peer transactions without external services are hard to detect, akin to cash transactions by the general public, and regulating these would not conform to the cost–benefit principle of regulation.

2. Entry Thresholds and Preventing Offshore Havens

FATF rules have set basic entry thresholds, preventing an unregulated "free-for-all" in the industry. To avoid regulatory arbitrage across jurisdictions, the FATF also demands that industry access controls are implemented at the establishment level, coupled with strengthened international cooperation requirements.

3. End of Anonymity and Embedded AML Monitoring

As per FATF rules, service providers, just like banks, must register all customers with real identities, scrutinize the background and purpose of transactions, and report suspicious transaction information to the government. Consequently, AML monitoring is comprehensively integrated into virtual currency transaction services. The ability of the state to "track funds" extends from the existing financial system into the virtual realm, allowing for a deeper tracking of virtual world transactions.

4. Promotion of Investor Protection through AML Rule Implementation

Regulatory concerns about investor suitability for virtual currencies largely stem from the lack of traceability. The establishment of AML infrastructure will largely address traceability issues, providing a solid foundation to combat market manipulation and investment fraud. We believe that under effective AML regulation, securities authorities in various countries may change their stance on the suitability of virtual currencies for investors, potentially allowing them to become investable financial products for the public under certain conditions.

9.5 For Whom Does the Bell Toll? a Global Anti-Money Laundering Network Taking Shape

In June 2019, the Financial Action Task Force (FATF) passed international anti-money laundering (AML) standards for virtual currencies. The two superpowers, China and the United States, passed the relevant compliance assessment for virtual currency anti-money laundering (the assessment of "Recommendation 15") in 2020 and 2021, respectively. These two nations represent divergent paths in virtual currency policy: China prohibits virtual currency transactions, while the United States allows them. China has proven to the FATF its effective prohibition of virtual currencies, while the United States has demonstrated the establishment of an AML regulatory framework for virtual currencies that meets the standards.

According to FATF statistics, since 2020, an increasing number of countries and regions have established virtual currency AML frameworks. As of June 2023, among 151 countries and regions surveyed by the FATF, 90 explicitly allowed virtual currency transactions, 16 prohibited them, and 45 remained undecided. Of the 90 that allowed virtual currencies, 77 had established the corresponding AML legal systems, 11 were in the process of legislating, and only two had taken no action. Among the 16 that prohibited virtual currency transactions, 9 had already taken regulatory or law enforcement measures (we can assume that at least these 9 had corresponding prohibitive laws). According to these statistics, at least 86 of the 151 surveyed countries and regions had established AML legal regimes, covering major global economies such as China, the US, Europe, and Japan, accounting for 57%.[16] There is reason to believe that this percentage will significantly increase under the strong deterrence mechanisms of the FATF, especially with the fifth round of mutual evaluations launched in 2023.

AML requirements dictate that virtual currency transactions must implement real-name systems, carrying the same AML obligations as banks. Virtual currencies traded through exchanges no longer possess the advantage of anonymity (if this was ever an advantage compared to traditional financial institutions). But more importantly, once trading is real-named, blockchain addresses transacting with exchange wallets are also tagged. Most blockchains are public (at least Bitcoin and Ethereum are such), so once an address is linked with a specific identity, the blockchain becomes transparent.

As the number of transactions between exchange wallets and blockchain addresses increases, the transaction network and the blockchain become more transparent. For example, if the identity of certain address owners is known, other addresses transacting with them can then be marked. Even if the real identities of some address owners cannot be confirmed, relationships can be inferred based on transaction patterns with known identities. We believe that under this "network effect," blockchains are tending toward transparency. Chapter 2 of this book introduced how US virtual currency exchanges monitored blockchain addresses associated with

---

[16] FATF (2023), *Targeted Update on Implementation of the FATF Standards on Virtual Assets/VASPs*, FATF, Paris, France, https://www.fatf-gafi.org/content/fatf-gafi/en/publications/Fatfrecommendations/targeted-update-virtual-assets-vasps-2023.

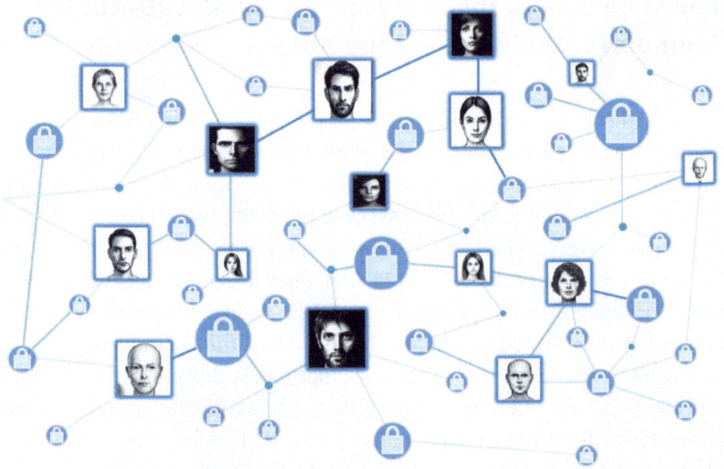

Fig. 9.1 Network effects drive the increasing transparency of blockchain

Russia in real time to comply with US sanctions, and froze assets transferred to exchanges. It can be conjectured that compared to traditional cash, from a privacy standpoint, the disadvantages of blockchain are becoming increasingly apparent (Fig. 9.1).

Once the anti-money laundering regulatory network is formed, virtual currency exchanges will be entirely domesticated, much like the banks we see today. Regulators can then fully impose legal requirements on virtual currency exchanges, even if the exchanges operate outside their jurisdiction. For instance, a country with foreign exchange controls may instruct foreign virtual currency exchanges to refuse wallet services to its citizens to prevent asset transfers via virtual currencies. While such notices are often non-binding, most private institutions cannot oppose state power, as we often see at present. Global regulators could also treat virtual currency exchanges as financial institutions, akin to the requirements of tax information exchange agreements (like CRS), demanding the reporting of citizens' financial information to their home country's tax departments.

Table 9.4 Activities related to public companies and virtual currency communities

	Public companies	Virtual currency communities	Current regulatory practices for virtual currencies
Internal governance (on-chain governance)	Amendments to bylaws	Code rule modifications	Untested in practice
	Stock issuance	Increase in total virtual currency	Untested in practice
	Corporate spin-offs	"Forks"	Untested in practice
External activities (on-chain transactions)	Stock issuance	ICOs	Only negative practices
	Trading rules (preventing price manipulation)	Trading rules (preventing price manipulation)	Only negative practices
	As a means of value transfer	As a means of value transfer	Comprehensive regulatory rules

9.6 Where Will Regulation Further Extend?

9.6.1 "External Activities" Versus "Internal Governance": The Limits of Anti-Money Laundering Rules

We can liken a self-operating virtual currency community to a "public company," where "on-chain governance" refers to the community's internal governance mechanism. This includes the rules for code modifications, those for increasing the total amount of virtual currency, and "forking" (where a subset of miners vote with their feet, creating a new chain based on the original one). These internal voting activities are largely similar to a company's internal governance system, and "on-chain transactions" are analogous to the issuance and circulation of a public company's stock outside the company itself (Table 9.4).

Chinese existing anti-money laundering regulatory rules only touch upon external activities, specifically when they serve as a means of value transfer. Since major regulatory authorities have not approved or registered any virtual currency as a publicly issued financial product, there is a complete gap in the internal governance practice of virtual currencies; existing practices are limited to penalties and actions against market manipulation and the unauthorized issuance of virtual currencies.

Bitcoin has created a community governance model where "code is law." Filippi and Loveluck took Bitcoin governance as an example, dividing blockchain governance into two levels: "governance by infrastructure" and "governance over infrastructure" that interact with each other, ultimately manifesting in "governance over infrastructure," i.e., code modifications.[17] Modifications to code rules are akin to

[17] Primavera De Filippi & Benjamin Loveluck, *The Invisible Politics of Bitcoin: Governance Crisis of a Decentralized Infrastructure*, 5(4) Internet Pol'y Rev. (2016), available at: https://policyreview.info/articles/analysis/invisible-politics-bitcoin-governance-crisis-decentralised-infrastructure.

amendments to a public company's bylaws, representing the pinnacle of power and rights within corporate governance, the foundation for all other powers and rights.

Regarding internal governance, existing securities regulatory rules can only be applied to blockchain governance if the virtual currency is approved or registered by regulatory authorities. From a regulatory view, the challenge is how to apply the existing concepts of public company regulation to blockchain governance to achieve the goal of protecting ordinary investors. Meanwhile, from an industry perspective, the extent to which a decentralized governance order can achieve sound governance remains to be seen under the current legal framework.

9.6.2 "Internal Governance": The Fundamental Challenge for the Future

For regulators, on-chain internal governance represents a novel issue, which involves at least the following three fundamental challenges:

Firstly, from a normative perspective, "what constitutes good governance?" Securities regulators have set up a basic framework and method for public company governance, establishing a universally recognized standard for good governance. However, the extent to which these standards apply to autonomous communities is subject to debate, and so as the amount of exploration into different governance models that regulation will allow. Blockchain autonomous communities have existed for a much shorter time than corporations, with comparatively few experiences and cases to draw robust conclusions from, making it an iterative process of exploration.

Secondly, from the perspective of accountability, autonomous communities intrinsically lack a tangible entity or organizational structure. How can real-world regulators identify regulatory subjects and duty-bearers? Participants in public chains can be anonymous (note that the aforementioned anti-money laundering rules do not require blockchain participants to be real-named, but only to register their real names with service providers when transacting externally), and such communities lack a tangible organizational structure. So, who fulfills the obligations set by regulation? How are duty-bearers identified? The "Dao" platform attempted to achieve the ideal of a "decentralized autonomous organization," although this venture was halted when its issuance of "Dao tokens" was deemed by the U.S. SEC as an unregistered security offering. However, the "Dao" platform brought forth the fundamental questions of defining the legal nature and responsibility of new types of organizations within blockchain autonomous communities.[18]

[18] If we build on existing laws, such organizations should be considered as "general partnerships." The main reason is that the establishment of a legal person or a limited partnership in most countries is predicated on registration, and since "DAO" is not registered, it cannot constitute a legal person or a limited partnership under the law; a "general partnership" does not require registration and can arise based on a common contractual action, hence "DAO" can be considered as a "general partnership," which means that all participants may bear joint and multifaceted liability. According to Laila Metjahic, at least under the legal framework of the United States, classifying the organization

Lastly, from the perspective of legal enforcement, blockchain communities are governed by code. But then, how can regulators compel autonomous communities to modify the code? Should the law endow regulators with the power of a "super code controller?" And, if a "super code controller" changes the code, will community participants choose to vote with their feet?

as a partnership does not affect the characterization of its ICO activities as a securities offering. See Laila Metjahic, *Deconstructing the DAO: The Need for Legal Recognition and the Application of Securities Laws to Decentralized Organizations*, 39 Cardozo L. Rev. 1533, 1533–1568 (2017).

Chinese scholars generally assert that ordinary participants should not bear unlimited joint liability, and therefore, it is more appropriate to classify it as a "limited partnership." For a more in-depth discussion of related issues, see Wang, Qingsong. "The Nature and Attribution of Internal Relations in Blockchain Systems." *Law Science* 5 (2019): 130–142. (汪青松:《区块链系统内部关系的性质界定与归责路径》, 载《法学》2019 年第5期 第130–142页。).

Part IV
The Future of Digital Currency

Chapter 10
An Emerging Republic of Supremacy: Super-Regulator and New Pontiff of the Digital Age

How will the advent of a super-regulator of blockchain redefine global sovereignty? Could this super-regulator assume the role of a "new Pontiff" in the modern digital era?

In this chapter, we trace the evolution of global hegemony from the British Empire's territorial control to the United States' intangible control via the dollar system. This chapter anticipates how blockchain technology could create a super-regulator, the Republic of Supremacy, whose jurisdiction could reach individuals directly, just as the Pope transcended all kingdoms, directly ruling over all subjects of kings in the High Middle Ages. History might turn back to the time before the Peace of Westphalia, and this "new Pontiff" could alter the equilibrium of power, law and finance, posing a substantial challenge to the foundational principles of nation-states and their sovereignty.

From the Renaissance and the Age of Discovery, the British Empire and the United States of America stood as the only two nation-states to genuinely wield global power. The British Empire brandished tangible control through vast territories, exerting global influence through physical dominance. In contrast, the United States pioneered a new form of global dominance: intangible control via the pervasive influence of the dollar payment system.

The stark contrast between these two powers is underscored by their methods of exerting influence. While the British Empire operated within the framework of the 1648 Peace of Westphalia, which established the principles of modern international law and the sovereignty of states over their territories, it was the United States that challenged this system. The British Empire, a "model student" of the Westphalian system, extended its state power globally through colonial ports and trade routes, controlling merchant ships and commercial activities. Conversely, the United States disrupted and subverted this system, leveraging its financial system to compel foreign banks to adhere to its laws by threatening to cut off their access to the dollar—a strategy that effectively bypassed traditional sovereign boundaries.

Y. Wu and W. Zhu, *The Fundamentals of Digital Currency*,
https://doi.org/10.1007/978-981-97-8261-1_10

This practice provoked a reevaluation of traditional international law and introduced new paradigms in international relations.

In the blockchain era, the government capable of controlling the most universally used blockchain will extend its power to every corner of the globe, becoming an unparalleled super-regulator that can operate beyond the established notions of national sovereignty. The possible advent of such super-regulator suggests that the long-standing principles of state sovereignty and international law may become obsolete, potentially leading to the unraveling of the Westphalian international system. This phenomenon might lead to the global distribution of power being significantly reshaped; we could experience a return to a pre-Westphalian era, with the emergence of a "new Pontiff" who would exert dominance over the traditional concept of nation-states.

10.1 The First Phase of Global Power: Territorial-Based Physical Control of the British Empire

During my undergraduate studies of law in China, I enrolled in a course called Maritime Law, which introduced concepts like maritime liens and in rem actions. For legal learners in civil law countries like China, these concepts often appeared somewhat out of place, as they did not align easily with basic civil law principles, presenting a certain incongruity. It was only through further study that we fully understood that the foundational systems and concepts of modern maritime law were established by British judges. Today, international treaties have incorporated and disseminated these British-established systems and concepts, serving as templates for domestic law in nations across the globe. Consequently, maritime laws worldwide predominantly derive from the British legal system. To aid student comprehension, our teachers traced these laws back to their origins and often referred to centuries-old cases from the London courts. Initially, it was puzzling why maritime disputes from other nations were adjudicated in British courts. We learned that this jurisdictional reach stemmed from the British Empire's control of the world's crucial ports where the Empire's judgments could be enforced. Unless a vessel operated solely within the territorial waters of its own country, once it docked in a port under British control, it became subject to law enforcement by British courts.

In the era of the British Empire, engaging in international trade inevitably meant dealing with ports under British control, which in turn meant being subject to the jurisdiction of the Empire. Thus, through its physical control over the maritime trade channels, the British Empire possessed global jurisdiction.

10.2 The Second Phase of Global Power: Dollar-Based Non-Physical Control of the United States

The U.S. dollar serves as the primary currency for international trade settlements, with all interbank dollar transactions ultimately settling through the United States. The vast majority of the world's foreign exchange reserves are in dollars, and one's "dollar wealth" can be ultimately represented as a number within the Federal Reserve's accounting system. Thus, by controlling the dollar, the United States extends its national power into international trade, with the ability to seize and freeze anyone's dollar-denominated bank assets. This abstract form of power transcends the traditional boundaries of nations and sovereignty. The term "long-arm jurisdiction," often heard in legal contexts, exemplifies this type of power that crosses international borders.

The end of World War II saw the establishment of the Bretton Woods system, which pegged various national currencies to the US dollar, thereby solidifying its role as the foundation for other currencies. Although the dollar's supremacy has since been challenged, with the euro, pound sterling, Japanese yen and others gaining significant shares of international trade, its foundational status has been unchanged. According to statistics from the Society for Worldwide Interbank Financial Telecommunication (SWIFT), a platform for transnational banking transaction information, approximately 40–50% of international trade settlements are conducted in dollars, and the International Monetary Fund (IMF) indicates that the dollar has consistently accounted for 50–60% of official global reserve currencies in recent years.[1]

With the advancement of technology, the role of cash in international transactions has diminished, with payments being facilitated primarily by banks through instruments such as letters of credit, bills of exchange, and wire transfers. Interbank settlements no longer involve physical cash movement but are finalized through central banks. In other words, in the digital age, an individual's bank assets are digits on a bank's ledger, and the collected deposits of a bank are merely numbers on the central bank's ledger; thus, the physical form of currency has lost its decisive role.

In recent years, the United States has exploited its pivotal role in dollar clearing and settlement, extending its jurisdictional reach to banks in other countries. For instance, if the U.S. government wanted to access customer and transaction information from BNP Paribas in France, traditional international law would require it to go through the French government (via judicial assistance, for example). For example, a century ago, BNP Paribas could have ignored a direct request from the U.S. government without consequence. Today, however, the U.S. wields the "dollar" as an ultimate instrument, able to demand relevant information directly from BNP Paribas's New York branch. If the branch refuses, the U.S. government can cut off its dollar transactions, effectively incapacitating its international business and relegating it to a domestic French bank. Faced with this monetary policy cudgel, banks dare not defy.

---

[1] Johnson, Carter, and Alexandre Tanzi. "Dollar Usage in Global Payments in July Rises to Record, Swift Says." Bloomberg, August 24, 2023. https://www.bloomberg.com/news/articles/2023-08-24/dollar-usage-in-global-payments-in-july-rises-to-record-swift-says.

In addition, the U.S. can take further assertive measures, such as ordering BNP Paribas to seize the assets of a French customer within France and to redirect them to accounts specified by the U.S. authorities. Non-compliance could lead the U.S. government to enforce the assets held by BNP Paribas in its correspondent banking accounts within the United States. The only way for BNP Paribas to object to the U.S. government's demands would be to close its correspondent banking accounts in the United States, but this would also mean that BNP Paribas could no longer conduct transactions in U.S. dollars.

Without deploying military force or making physical threats, the U.S. can effortlessly obtain personal bank information from other countries or freeze and confiscate bank assets on foreign soil, an unprecedented feat in human history. Despite protests from other nations, this gateway of financial control has not been shut.

What is more, in the blockchain era, this kind of power will be set to widen even further; the nation that gains control of the blockchain will become the global super-regulator.

10.3 The Republic of Supremacy: A Future Super-Regulator

In Part II, we delved into the structure of blockchain-based economy, emphasizing two key elements poised to revolutionize the paradigm: smart contracts and virtual currencies. Now, let us embark on a thought experiment. Imagine a nation known as the "Republic of Supremacy," a dominion surpassing the combined might of all historical empires.

Thought Experiment: There exists a super-regulator, that is, the "Republic of Supremacy," in the year 203X. A virtual currency, V-Coin, accounts for 50% of global trade settlements, 70% of the world's foreign exchange reserves are held in V-Coin, and 50% of the world's population conducts daily transactions in it. V-Coin is supported by 100 nodes, all located within the territory of the Republic of Supremacy, and the 100 ultimate individuals with voting rights over these nodes are also based within its borders. The Republic of Supremacy would compel these nodes to encode the following rules:

(1) The Government of the Republic of Supremacy serves as the super-node, exercising authority to command the execution or cessation of smart contracts based on its court decisions.
(2) The Government of the Republic of Supremacy retains the prerogative to seize, freeze or confiscate V-Coin in accordance with its court rulings.

The U.S. dollar payment system maintains control solely over financial institutions, limiting the extraterritorial reach of the United States to these entities and indirectly governing individuals through them. Conversely, blockchain technology establishes a direct connection with individuals. Thus, a government mastering the blockchain can extend its national authority extraterritorially to every individual, marking the true dissolution of the concept of sovereignty.

10.4 Top Secret: How the Republic of Supremacy Crafted V-Coin

With the proliferation and development of blockchain technology, machine power has created a digital order that pertains to many areas, such as global finance and commerce, and has exerted a profound impact on international power structures. The Republic of Supremacy has a deep understanding of machine power and digital order, and is a world leader in blockchain technology. It has issued its digital currency, V-Coin, with the aim to establish it as a new globalized digital currency, thus achieving international hegemony greater than the maritime jurisdiction of the historic British Empire or the dollar payment authority of the United States. The Republic of Supremacy has meticulously designed V-Coin with the highest secrecy:

Firstly, the payment and settlement processes of V-Coin must be decentralized, facilitating "payment concurrent with settlement." The circulation of V-Coin is free worldwide, and its protocol is open and transparent. Any application can integrate with the V-Coin value protocol. Only in this way can states, institutions and individuals worldwide use V-Coin with confidence. Even those hostile to the Republic of Supremacy would not oppose V-Coin because it functions as a digital token of value and its payment and settlement processes are as free as physical cash.

Secondly, there may be two *potential issuance strategies* for V-Coin. In the first scenario, if the Republic of Supremacy is confident enough, it could adopt a centralized issuance model, unilaterally determining the supply of V-Coin while ensuring the stability of its value. Alternatively, the Republic of Supremacy could establish certain rules or even invite various nations and large organizations to join an issuance committee, adjusting the supply according to agreed-upon rules, resembling a rule based issuance approach. However, overall, it is unlikely that V-Coin would be issued like Bitcoin, such as with a fixed algorithm and a set amount.

Thirdly, the *consensus protocol* for V-Coin, which is the blockchain consensus mechanism, cannot be in the form of a public blockchain. While being self-assured, the Republic of Supremacy would not want to take such a risk. Whether there are 100 nodes or 1000, control must inevitably remain with the Republic of Supremacy. In extreme cases, all nodes could be within the Republic, but that would be too blatant and unsightly. A more common approach would be to form an alliance with many friendly nations, allocate a small portion of nodes to these countries and operate the nodes collectively, thus maintaining both substance and appearance.

Fourthly, as V-Coin payment and settlement are decentralized and the nodes are distributed across many countries, *power has effectively been transferred to machines*. Although the V-Coin is issued by the Republic of Supremacy, machines have taken over its governance, and the digital order of V-Coin has been established.

Nations, organizations, and individuals around the world, whether friendly or hostile to the Republic of Supremacy, tend to trust the automated power and digital order of the V-Coin to the extent that it can be widely accepted as a direct form of currency.

Crucially, the Republic of Supremacy must *retain the authority to modify* the V-Coin value protocol or amend the blockchain's source code. Certainly, the Republic would not frivolously alter the code, as it could affect the credibility of V-Coin. It would rather form a development committee through the alliance, ceding some power to allied states and organizations in order to maintain an open-discussion atmosphere within the alliance. Ultimately, regardless of these detours, the final decision-making power would be kept within the Republic of Supremacy. When necessary, it should be able to persuade all node nations to amend the code together, thereby altering the digital order. What is most important is the hegemony of machine power, while controlling this kind of power is the art of politics.

10.5 From V-Coin to V-Contracts: The Advent of a New Global Legal Order

The impact of V-Coin, meticulously crafted by the Republic of Supremacy, extends far beyond that of the U.S. dollar, whose influence is confined to global banks and financial institutions, reaching private individuals. V-Coin, as a digital currency, extends its influence to global organizations and natural persons worldwide who download the corresponding app wallet. This means that both global companies and individuals operate within the digital order based on V-Coin. If all trade and retail transactions are conducted using V-Coin, then any disputes arising in these processes will inevitably fall under the jurisdiction of V-Coin's master, the Republic of Supremacy, and be adjudicated by its judicial system. Thus, monetary transactions transcend being mere financial transactions; they directly affect judicial authority over commerce. Consequently, organizations and individuals worldwide using V-Coin find themselves subject to the governance of a transnational authority.

While the payment and settlement processes of V-Coin are decentralized and possibly privacy-protecting, its code can still incorporate regulatory policies that allow for the freezing of addresses that violate the regulatory requirements. The global proliferation of V-Coin inevitably leads to the centralization of global finance on the V-Coin platform, perhaps directly on the V-Coin blockchain or another blockchain initiated by the Republic of Supremacy. Digital finance, written in code and deployed on the blockchain, is based on the V-Coin value protocol. These machine-based finance codes may not be written by the Republic of Supremacy but are certainly bound by standards set by committees under its control, conforming to those standards. Moreover, these machine finance products must also comply with laws and regulations established by the Republic of Supremacy.

Digital currency acts as the foundation, but the Republic of Supremacy's ambitions go beyond that. Within the digital order, business contracts necessitate a foundational digital currency for value agreements and a reliable machine authority for enforcement. Hence, the Republic of Supremacy offers the blockchain infrastructure for deploying digital contracts, now known as V-Contracts. These smart contracts, extending beyond the international trade scope of the former British Empire, are integral for domestic trade, real estate transactions, and supply chain executions, converging global commerce into a third dimension beyond time and space.

The nature of this smart contract platform can be summarized as follows:

1. The goal of V-Contracts is not to entirely replace each country's commercial or property law but to establish machine authority and a digital commercial order. Nevertheless, the V-Contract order will inevitably supplant parts of the legal content of other countries, albeit indirectly. To attract more users, the designer will enable V-Contracts to be compatible with and supportive of the business-related laws of as many countries worldwide as possible.
2. V-Contracts will require a super-foundational law to bind all users, tentatively named the Constitution of V-Contracts. This should be as inclusive as possible to accommodate the laws of other nations. It would primarily cover the basic ethos and procedures of V-Contract governance, crucial codes for users, and some basic commercial rules that can reach a consensus, such as the protection of property rights, the prohibition of fraud and forgery, among other fundamental principles.
3. V-Contract agreements will cater to various industries with intricate ties to the real world. For instance, health insurance contracts must rely on health data, while real estate contracts depend on geographic location information, construction data, community governance, and property appraisal information. The collection of this data could be resolved through technical means, like IoT device collection, or by relying on people or organizations for collection. Operating on the principle of machine authority, the V-Contract ecosystem will incorporate numerous IoT protocols and standards, and will engage many trusted third parties to provide services on the platform.
4. For the protocol code maintenance of V-Contracts, similar to V-Coin, the Republic of Supremacy will consider and balance various factors, organize committees, build alliances with many participating nodes, and distribute some power to other participants, thereby forming a fundamentally trustworthy machine authority. Nevertheless, control over this machine authority will still be retained by the Republic of Supremacy.

With the rapid development of digital technology, people are constructing an ever-expanding virtual world. This is achieved by using digital means to describe the real world and seamlessly integrating it into the virtual world, being an unstoppable trend. In the digital world, human capabilities are greatly enhanced. As the digital world grows and becomes enriched with more content, resources and capabilities, machine power brings digital order, and those who control this order will emerge as formidable international hegemons. This level of power, leveraging the authority of machines, will permeate into people's everyday work and life.

10.6 Republic of Supremacy: The New Pontiff Arrives

In medieval Europe, the subjects of each kingdom were first and foremost the congregants of the Pope, who wielded direct jurisdiction over them through marriages, taxes, judicial matters, and more. For over a thousand years, the Pope remained a sovereign entity above all kingdoms. This era persisted until 1648, when European nations finally chose to sit down and negotiate after the Thirty Years' War, jointly establishing order and forming the Westphalian system. It consisted of a series of treaties that defined how states would handle their affairs through consultation, establishing a new world order. Thus began the retreat of divine authority and the establishment of state sovereignty, separating the internal affairs of states from their foreign relations, and setting guidelines for international interaction through international law.

The development of blockchain technology could turn history full circle, as the Republic of Supremacy, which controls the blockchain, could become the "Papal State" of the new tech world, establishing and maintaining a new international order.

First, the Supreme Court of the Republic of Supremacy would become the highest global court, superseding those of all other nations. Because the courts of the Republic of Supremacy can command smart contracts and enforce V-Coin assets, global trade disputes, and even individual disputes, would likely opt for jurisdiction in the courts of the Republic of Supremacy, ascribing it global judicial reach. Similar to maritime disputes that once voluntarily sought the jurisdiction of the British Empire, people tend to choose courts whose rulings can be enforced, not wanting their decisions to be just an empty check. With the enforcement power in the hands of the courts of the Republic of Supremacy, courts of other nations would effectively become subordinate, with the courts of the Republic of Supremacy acting as the de facto supreme courts of other nations.

Second, the laws of the Republic of Supremacy would turn into supranational law that the whole world obeys. In medieval Europe, every subject was a member of the Pope's congregation at the same time, and the Pope held the unique ultimate punishment: excommunication, equivalent to depriving a person of their soul. In the blockchain era, the Republic of Supremacy could directly punish foreign citizens residing in their own countries, such as confiscating or freezing their V-Coin assets and restricting their transactions with V-Coin. They could use this as leverage to demand that citizens of other countries comply with the orders and laws of the Government of the Republic of Supremacy. The long-arm jurisdiction frequently used by the United States is based on bank control and therefore can and only can be used on targeted individuals and cases. Each instance of exercising this authority is met with countermeasures or opposition from other powers, so it must be done cautiously. However, the jurisdiction of the Republic of Supremacy could reach individuals directly, issuing universal laws and orders, and requiring individuals from other countries to obey, just as the subjects of medieval kingdoms complied with the Pope's laws and orders.

Third, the regime of the Republic of Supremacy would become a world authority above other powers. In today's global economy, if trade sanctions are conventional weapons, then financial sanctions are nuclear weapons, with unparalleled power. In the blockchain era, the Republic of Supremacy could impose financial sanctions on hostile nations and their government leaders, similar to what the United States does today, including freezing their V-Coin assets and requiring everyone to stop doing business with them. The only difference is that the Republic of Supremacy could directly control all global transaction information and all virtual assets, unilaterally launching "nuclear strikes" against other powers at any time. Possessing this kind of "superweapon" beyond the reach of other nations, the Republic of Supremacy would become a world authority above other powers.

In the era of blockchain economy, whichever regime controls the blockchain will possess a level of power beyond sovereign borders. The traditional Westphalian international system, which defines sovereignty by borders, will dissolve and be restructured, and a new Pontiff with far-reaching authority will emerge once again.

Chapter 11
From Cryptocurrency to Blockchain: Machine Power and Digital Order

Can machines exercise authority? To what extent are machines capable of acting autonomously and making decisions? Do "machine power" and "digital order" imply that machines can dominate over humans, or could they suggest that machines are enforcers of a human-designed order? Why is digital currency considered as the most ideal 'beachhead' for deploying blockchain technology to realize machine power establishing a digital order?

In Chapter 11, we explore how the digitization of currency challenges traditional financial systems and introduce a new paradigm of machine-driven social order. We address the conceptual shift from human-dependent financial systems to machine-operated blockchain networks, considering the implications for societal rules and governance in the digital era. This chapter is an insightful examination of the transformative impact of blockchain technology on currency and societal structures.

11.1 A Product of the Natural Progress of Technology

The technological development of cryptocurrency inevitably led to the emergence of blockchain technology, a foreseeable fact arising from the pursuit of digitizing currency, requiring a complete elimination of reliance on physical entities. While not all digital currencies are necessarily based on blockchain, the exploration of digital currency technology naturally yielded the emergence of blockchain technology.

As tautological as it may appear, since the construction of blockchain order must begin with currency, digital currency inevitably serves as the foundation of blockchain. This is due to the unique nature of currency-based human order. Currency represents the most abstract form of social order, as it can exist independently of any physical goods and can function as a tool to measure credit. Once a consensus is reached regarding the value of a particular item, it can be adopted as a form of currency.

Y. Wu and W. Zhu, *The Fundamentals of Digital Currency*,
https://doi.org/10.1007/978-981-97-8261-1_11

From a different perspective, the advent of blockchain technology is an inexorable outcome resulting from the constant technological progress and advancement in human society. Specifically, on the one hand, the evolution of social order inherently leads to the establishment of a digital order supported by machine power; on the other hand, the implementation of blockchain is crucial for the utilization of machine power.

The technological development of digital currency has followed a long journey, with blockchain representing the latest milestone. In the 1990s, eCash first utilized asymmetric encryption technology to combat counterfeit digital currencies. Subsequently, technologies such as HashCash and reusable proofs of work (RPoW) leveraged hash algorithms to quantify the computational costs associated with digital currencies. The inclusion of timestamping technology provided digital files with a time attribute. The theoretical concepts of B-Money and BitGold explored the ideas of digital currencies and smart contracts within the realm of the online world. Bitcoin, however, revolutionized the playing field by seamlessly integrating asymmetric encryption, peer-to-peer networks, hash costs, timestamps, and consensus algorithms into a cohesive and technically flawless digital currency. As a significant technological feat, the proof-of-work consensus algorithm played a groundbreaking role, enabling value to be exchanged within an open network without the need for centralized institutional trust. Collectively, this technology constitutes what we now refer to as blockchain.

As illustrated in Fig. 11.1, the development of digital currency is a progressive journey towards enhancing the digitization level within the sphere of currency, which naturally leads to the emergence of blockchain technology. The figure comprises four distinct diagrams, each illustrating a currency mode from both the physical and digital worlds. They provide a comprehensive view of the degree of digitization in terms of payment, clearing & settlement (hereinafter referred to as settlement), and issuance within various currency models.

In cash mode, physical paper notes and coins constitute payment in the real world, with no settlement process involved. The issuance of currency relies on the central bank, which prints and mints the money. In this mode, the digital world is not needed.

Moving to electronic payment mode, no physical cash is used for payment in the real world. However, realizing payment still requires the involvement of commercial banks (along with the user's cards, computers or mobile phones) in the real world to facilitate the operation of a balance sheet in the digital world. The settlement process in the real world is dependent on both the commercial banks and the central bank, and is also operated by these two kinds of banks but through a balance sheet in the digital world. Issuance relies on the central bank in the real world and is operated by the central bank through a balance sheet in the digital world. The balance sheet in electronic payment mode is SIMPLE digitization, representing only the balance of currency (it is simple because the balance is merely the accounting record of the TOTAL AMOUNT of the real-world currency. In other words, the currency in the electronic payment mode has no digital entity.) Unlike cash mode, electronic payment mode has a simple balance sheet in the digital world but relies on more physical entities in the real world.

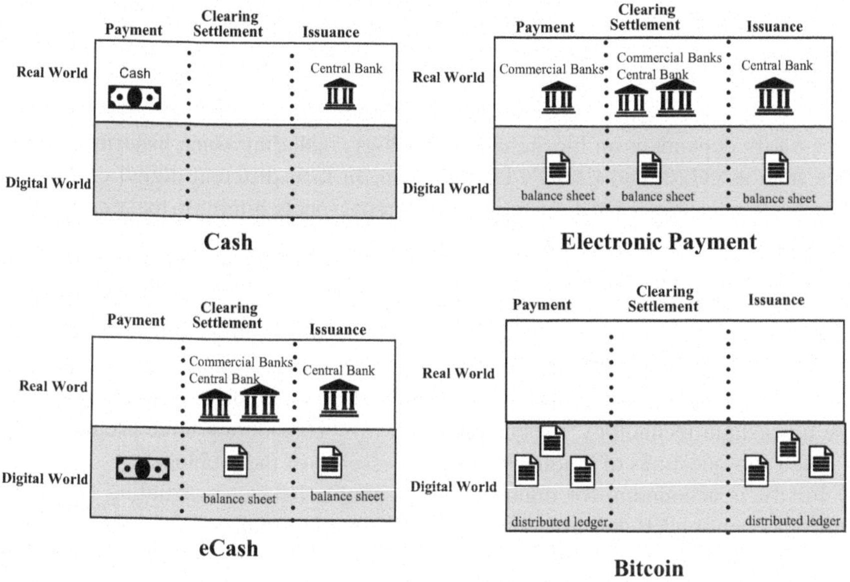

Fig. 11.1 Digitalization degrees of four different modes of currencies

In the eCash mode, physical cash is not required in the payment process, and there is no reliance on commercial banks. Instead, this mode uses encrypted strings that represent currency in the digital world (please note that, as an important milestone, money has a digital entity in the digital world, for each specific encrypted string represents EACH specific currency). Otherwise, the settlement and issuing processes are similar to the electronic payment mode. It can be observed that eCash relies on fewer physical entities in the real world and has a higher digitization level in the digital world because of encrypted strings that represent currency itself.

The technological development path of digital currency follows gradually diminishing reliance on physical entities in the real world and increasing digital entities in the digital world. Therefore, the ultimate goal of technology is to eliminate all real-world dependencies and enhance digital entities in the digital world, which is brought about by blockchain technology, such as Bitcoin.

In the Bitcoin mode, physical cash and reliance on commercial banks are not required in the payment process. Instead, currency is represented in a distributed ledger in the digital world. In this way, there is no need for a settlement process, and the issuing process depends on this distributed ledger instead of the central bank. Compared to eCash, electronic payment and cash modes, Bitcoin has a higher level of digitization. Based on our current understanding, Bitcoin represents the pinnacle of digitization.

Upon closer examination, the payment and issuing processes of Bitcoin still of course rely on numerous mining machines in the real world. However, these mining machines are decentralized among many miners with no singular entity performing exclusive tasks; hence, in logical terms, Bitcoin does not rely on any SINGLE specific entity in the real world. This zero dependency in the real world is equal to logical zero dependency.

Must digital currencies use blockchain technology? Digital currencies are not necessarily dependent on blockchain technology, including some historical examples such as eCash and China's Digital Yuan. In fact, different digital currencies achieve varying degrees of digitization in different aspects, aiming to make currencies computable and programmable.

Nonetheless, the highest level of pursuit in digitization requires the use of blockchain technology. This means that the issuance, payment and settlement processes are all entrusted to machines and algorithms, eliminating the need for human and organizational reliance.

To comprehensively answer the question of whether digital currencies must use blockchain technology, we can approach it by considering three progressively focused sub-questions to gradually grasp the essence of the problem.

Firstly, is accounting for digital currency simple balance accounting or digital entity accounting? Balance accounting only records a balance for each account, reflecting the way the current financial system operates. Digital entity accounting involves creating different levels of digital entities for digital currencies, similar to gold or cash. It builds data structures for various functionalities, such as "digital crypto strings," "digital yuan," "transactions," "blocks," etc. Accounting for these digital entities is similar to managing the inventory of gold or cash. Using these digital entities, rich functionalities like traceability and programmability can be achieved. If only simple balance accounting is employed, it is usually classified as electronic currency and not considered as true digital currency. (Remember what we have just mentioned about "SIMPLE." Balance accounting only records the TOTAL AMOUNT, while the accounting of digital entity records each specific currency.) For instance, Alipay, WeChat Pay or PayPal can be considered electronic payments and do not qualify as "digital."

Secondly, when it comes to digital currency, is there a pursuit of rich functionalities beyond simple accounting? In other words, can digital currency be programmed? Well, under the current technology system of balance accounting, achieving programmability is not possible; it can only be realized when a digital entity model is implemented. While programming work can be performed within the current centralized database technology, it is primarily focused on manipulating "balances" rather than the currency itself. Thus, it can be classified as programmable payment, but not as programmable currency.

Thirdly, is accounting for digital currency executed in a single ledger or multiple ledgers? For reference, a single ledger refers to having only one ledger controlled by a single party (institution or individual), and other users have to trust this party, which constitutes the current monetary order. Multiple ledgers refer to a distributed ledger where all involved parties, including users, participate in accounting and maintain the ledger jointly. Then, one might ask which one is better, a single ledger or multiple ledgers? Since single ledger has been the mainstream for a long time, people are accustomed to it and have no issues with it. However, a single ledger is similar to a computer not being connected to the Internet, while multiple ledgers can be likened to interconnected computers. Trend wise, multiple ledgers are the inevitable future development, for which blockchain is referred to as the value protocol of the Internet. Before the emergence of blockchain, digital value was restricted to individual machines, but with blockchain, digital value can be interconnected. Blockchain typically employs the digital entity accounting model, so this third level generally needs to be based on the first level. For digital currencies to use the multiple ledger model, so far only blockchain is the available option. Not any model that does not use blockchain can be considered a true multiple ledger. Bitcoin achieved all three levels at once, and when designing digital currency, the desired level can be chosen based on the requirements.

Leading up the advent of blockchain, people recognized the lack of a value protocol on the Internet and the lack of scarcity in the digital world. Following Nick Szabo's analogy, how can we simulate gold in a computer? How can a digital string bear as much value as gold? To solve this challenge, when it comes to current technology, blockchain is the only avenue to explore. There is no alternative. If Satoshi Nakamoto had not invented blockchain, it would have been someone else.

Iin the history of digital currencies, Nick Szabo's "Bit Gold" and Wei Dai's "B-Money" represent early pursuits of blockchain. As early as 1998, these two individuals described the fundamental characteristics of blockchain in their respective communications. They did not implement the code, however, and it can be observed that their exploration of open and distributed systems was not extensive. The objective of Bit Gold was to develop a protocol that creates tamper-proof units of value on a network, independent of third parties. B-Money aimed to construct a virtual world on the Internet that does not rely on governments, enabling legal bindings for identity, currency and contracts. After Satoshi Nakamoto published the whitepaper of Bitcoin, he communicated with Wei Dai that he had designed something similar to B-Money.

Was the emergence of blockchain technology inevitable? As shown in Fig. 11.2, humanity's pursuit of improving computability has never stopped. Stemming from our awareness of our own weaknesses, we expect to delegate more and more execution functions to machines. In the pursuit of precise social order, we prefer to rely on machine calculations to maintain societal rules. The core technological means for empowering machines is clearly blockchain. Therefore, from a trend perspective, the emergence of blockchain is inevitable.

But hang on, would blockchain have emerged without the relevant research on digital currency? Nowadays, blockchain technology can be applied in various fields, but its initial implementation undoubtedly positions it into the realm of digital currency. Currency represents the most abstract and fundamental value in society, becoming the natural choice to be impacted by value protocols on the Internet. Hence, the emergence of blockchain is an 'organic' result of, and certainly connected to, digital currency.

The relationship between currency and digitization has been eloquently discussed in previous works. As proposed in The Evolution of Money, "The central concept of money—the irreducible nut of the matter—is therefore that it is a means to attach exact, timeless, Pythagorean numbers to the fuzzy and transient concept of real-world value. The point of doing this is to

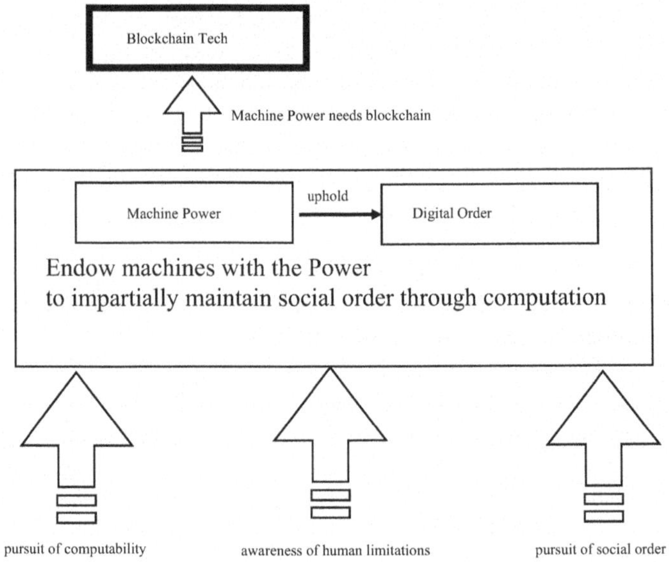

Fig. 11.2 The inevitable emergence of blockchain

> facilitate certain transactions (e.g. tax payment, exchange, settling of scores, rewards, motivating people) by shifting them to a mathematical space, with its addition, subtraction, and compound interest." In addition, Marshall McLuhan stated that: "Money as a social medium or extension of an inner wish and motive creates social and spiritual values, a communication medium that conveys value."
>
> According to a number of monetary theorists and economists, the essence of currency is to digitally describe the value of the real world. Before the advent of computer digitization technology, people had to rely on the characteristics of gold or silver, and paper vouchers for counting. Thus, the transition of currency towards digitization is a return to its core essence. The emergence of blockchain technology initially revolved around digital currencies but turned out to hold profound significance far beyond them; it has brought about a transformative shift in power and order, which even its inventors did not foresee. This shift has been gathering momentum and has finally rooted quietly with the birth of digital currencies and blockchain.

With the development of information, networking and digitization, programming code has become increasingly vital for the foundation of societal production and daily life. Code, developed by humans and representing their intentions, is executed by machines with high efficiency and precision. However, the execution of code prompts several questions.

First, how can code represent the will of many individuals or parties? The lifecycle of a program consists of two stages: development and execution. During development, code must reflect the will of many individuals or parties and can only be produced through negotiation and confirmation by a collective. However, during execution, code cannot represent the will of multiple parties since a machine can only be controlled by one party.

Second, how can code be trustworthy and reliable? The early Internet gave rise to the notion of "code is law." However, treating website code as law is naive if we expect laws to be transparent, stable and fair. Website code represents the will of the website owner, who has the freedom to write and modify it as they wish, while users can only comply with code rules so long as they do not participate in the formulation of "code law." Hence, code law on the Internet is neither trustworthy nor reliable.

Third, code significantly improves productivity, effectively executing calculations, driving machine production, and processing information. But can code maintain social order? Can it constrain and guide human behavior like morals and laws, providing people with predictable expectations for their actions?

The study of digital currencies has brought about the birth of blockchain technology, which addresses the above three questions. Blockchain inconspicuously introduces a wave that shifts power to machines, allowing digital technology to maintain and shape social order. Technological development may appear accidental, sporadic and unpredictable, as if conceived by genius. However, on a larger scale, technology evolves spontaneously, driven by the needs of human civilization and silently progressing alongside humanity. If, in the history of technological revolution, waves chase each other, dazzling the eyes, the machine power and digital order brought by blockchain rise like vast waves, accompanied by faint thunder, gradually emerging on the horizon towards the new digital realm.

11.2 New Tools to Maintain Social Order

The Bitcoin system does not require maintenance by a centralized institution but relies on numerous mining machines to preserve trust in the system. Is it possible to destroy this system? Well, there could be two methods. The first one is widely known as a "51% attack." When one party controls more than 51% of the total network computing power, they can engage in "double spending" and potentially change previous transaction history (although it is more difficult to change older transaction history). Based on the total network computing power in October 2021 (162 EH) and the approximate computing power of a single computer (68 TH/s, which is equal to 68 trillion hash calculations per second), it would require 1.22 million mining machines to reach 51% computing power. According to market prices at that time, the total value of these machines would amount to 15 billion yuan. In addition, a substantial amount of electricity costs would be incurred to operate these machines for a double spending attack. However, the major problem is that the attacker would only gain the value of a few transactions in a single block, which would be outweighed by the associated costs. It would be more profitable to support the Bitcoin network with the resources. While it is theoretically possible to continue increasing computing power to maliciously destroy Bitcoin, the attacker would ultimately be left with nothing in exchange for their great efforts.

The other method of destroying Bitcoin has been less often discussed: corrupting the developer community through bribery. Trust in the Bitcoin system is based on the vast number of mining machines running Bitcoin node software, with the developers of these software programs having the authority to modify and update the code. The Bitcoin developer community consists of several hundred volunteer programmers, of which five core developers have the ability to submit code changes. Technically, it is possible to convince these core developers to modify the Bitcoin code with malicious intent to completely destroy the Bitcoin network. However, the mining operators would not agree to run such code as it would be detrimental to their profits. Besides, if the core developers were to engage in actions that harm Bitcoin, they would lose their charisma and reputation within the developer community. Even if the power to destroy Bitcoin was significant enough to convince all developers and mining operators, users would hold the final line of defense: if they were to discover that the developers and mining operators were attempting to destroy Bitcoin to cause the value of their coins to plummet, they would do everything possible to stop it. In this way, the order of Bitcoin is established and maintained on the alliance of millions of machines, and this power derives from the consensus of the vast community of developers, miners and users of Bitcoin.

The fundamental goal of Bitcoin's creator(s) was to eliminate the need for third-party trust, as well as the necessity of central banks, commercial banks, and other financial institutions. Through a peer-to-peer network, Bitcoin enables the issuance and settlement of currency. To achieve this goal, Satoshi Nakamoto designed the UTXO ledger structure, blockchain, and proof-of-work mechanism. In the absence of third-party trust, who fills this trust gap? How can users have confidence in that the received bitcoins are genuine, transactions are not counterfeited, and completed transactions will not be reversed?

Strictly speaking, the filling of this trust gap is achieved through a systematic structure. The first layer of the system is supported by mathematics, algorithms and programs: machines replace third-party institutions, running programs and algorithms to provide trust. The second layer of the system is comprised of developers, mining operators, users, and other individuals that form the Bitcoin community. Through organization and market behavior, these participants uphold the fairness and rationale of mathematics, algorithms and software, as the masters of the first-layer machines. Although they hold the ultimate power, they delegate the direct authority of implementation to the machines. If they want to exert power over them, they need to modify the code and algorithms, and this means that they must engage in negotiations within the community and take collective action after reaching a consensus. To draw an analogy with a political system, the community formed by developers, mining operators and users acts as the legislative body and does not directly govern. They only establish laws but delegate the power to enforce these laws to the government and the judicial system.

As shown in Fig. 11.3, the blockchain program runs on machines (mining machines), maintaining the currency ledger. The consistency of these programs, algorithms and data is ensured by the consensus algorithm. These machines collectively form an organic system that must act consistently and cannot deceive, lie or act maliciously. If a machine is inconsistent, it will be removed from the system.

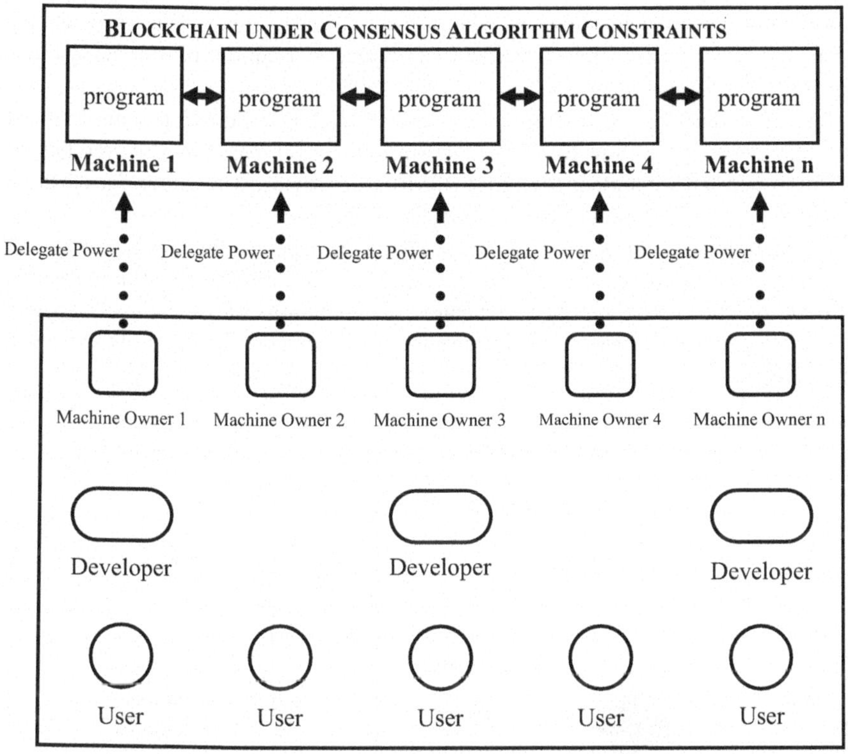

Fig. 11.3 The architecture of machine power in blockchain

Each machine has an owner, but they do not have the right to arbitrarily change the algorithms and data on the machine. If changes are made without authorization, the machine will be excluded from the blockchain system. As such, it is the consensus algorithm that forces machine owners to delegate power to the machines. This delegation of power is a logical means of authorization; physically, the machine still belongs to the owner, who can manipulate it at will. However, to remain in the blockchain, the owner must give up the ability to arbitrarily modify the machine's code.

Developers may appear to have greater power, but the developer community has an open-source mechanism. The decisions of core developers are supervised by the community, and the entire process is transparent and open. More importantly, for modifications made by developers to the program to be accepted, they must obtain recognition from the miner owners. If the majority of miner owners are unwilling to install the code written by developers, the latter will lose their power. Therefore, the relationship between developers and miner owners is based on negotiation. Ultimately, power lies with the users. If users are dissatisfied, they will leave the community, resulting in a loss of value for the virtual currency. Therefore, developers and miner owners must consider and respect the opinions of user groups (see Fig. 11.4).

The key aspect of constructing this system (including the development of virtual currency programs) is how to delegate power to the machines. Blockchain relies on machine power to maintain the order of virtual currency. This order, based upon machine power as a tool, is a new creation of digital order.

Social order encompasses a wide range of aspects, from the fundamental values of life, liberty and property to smaller details such as refraining from spitting in public and avoiding offensive language. To achieve and maintain order at all levels, society has developed various solutions through its evolution, such as the tools of ethics, laws, and more.

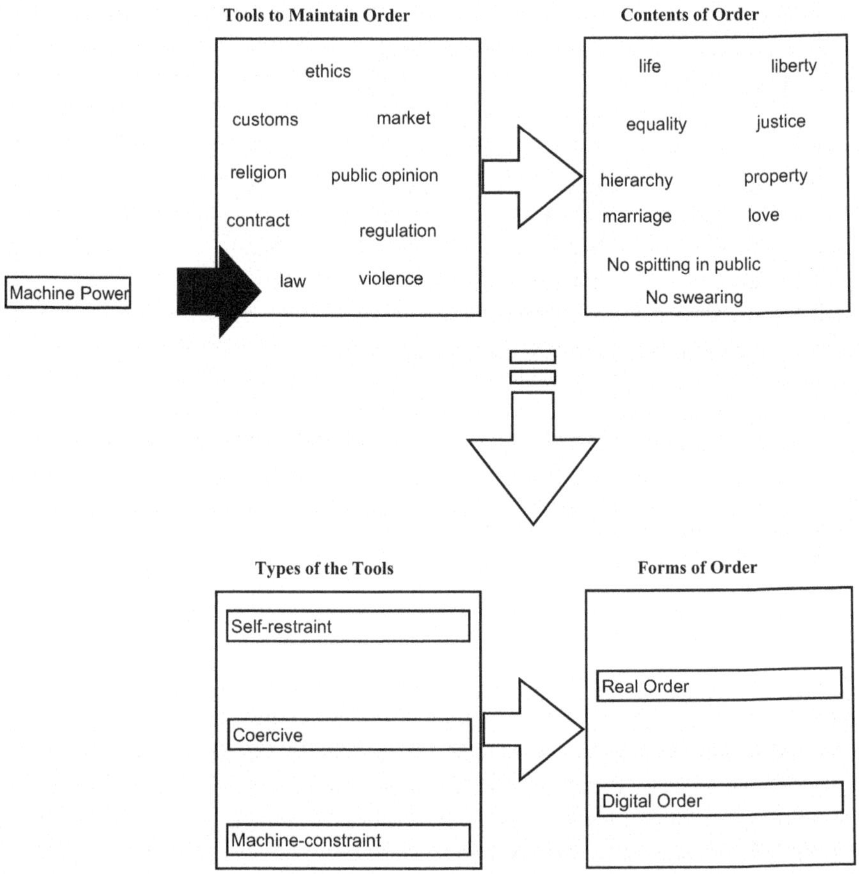

Fig. 11.4 Machine power as a new tool to introduce digital order

The inclusion of machine power as a tool for maintaining social order is a natural outcome of the development of digital technology and social order. With the introduction of machine power, digital order emerges. As a result, our understanding and classification of order also transform. Types of order tools include self-restraint, such as ethics, beliefs, customs, and markets; and coercion, such as laws, command, and violence. (Here, we discuss only "machine power," not "machine rights." This book focuses on the concept of machine-derived power and does not delve into robotic ethics or any futuristic topics such as machine rights or welfare.)

The concept of "machine power" in this book refers to the responsibility given to machines, allowing them to act autonomously and make decisions within their scope of given responsibility. This connotation is not as much of a sci-fi as it may seem. It simply refers to which tasks can be assigned to machines for automatic execution and which affairs machines can handle. If we broaden the concept of machines from computers to all types of machinery, then "machine power" has long been applied in control theory and automation systems. An automated control system adjusts its actions based on parameters from the surrounding environment. This means that in the motion of a mechanically automated control system, humans have given the machines the power to operate under specific conditions. The constraints imposed by humans on machines are purely general principles, namely, the automatic control algorithm. For example, when a missile tracks a target, its direction, posture, and speed during flight are determined by the missile's computational component. In a steel rolling mill, when rolling steel plates, the thickness of the plates remains constant, but the various parameters of the rolling mill are calculated by the control system. With the development of mechanization, automation and computer networks, humans have delegated many capabilities to machines. However, using machine power to maintain social order is a new issue, and it all begins with blockchain.

The designers of Bitcoin have a clear vision of challenging the current monetary system and financial order. The issuance process of Bitcoin is not dependent on the banking system and credit but on the computing power competition among numerous miners. The payment and settlement processes also transcend centralized structures and achieve trusted execution in a peer-to-peer network. After the emergence of smart contracts, decentralized finance such as unmanned open finance also appeared, and these models challenge the current or traditional financial and monetary order. The operation of traditional currency and financial orders revolves around human action, relying on laws, regulations, institutions, conventions, markets, and violent punishments to constrain human behavior and achieve a healthy order. The underlying force that supports and maintains the operation of the new Bitcoin order is entirely different from that fueling traditional order:

IT IS THE POWER OF MACHINES!

11.3 Envisaging the Rise of Machine Power and the Future of Digital Order

Can machines possess authority? To what extent can they act autonomously and make decisions? "Machine power," as discussed in this book, refers to the autonomy and decision-making authority delegated to machines within their operational scope. It considers which tasks can be automated and managed by machines. At present, blockchain is the only technology that can truly empower machines. Running blockchain nodes, machines can operate independently beyond the owner's control.

Behind the myriad of terms like digital currency, blockchain, DAO, and Web3 lies the essence of entrusting power to machines and code, a phenomenon referred to as "machine power." Indeed, digital currency has led to the advent of blockchain technology. However, in essence, digital currency is merely the most ideal beachhead for the deployment of blockchain. Money is a ledger of value that must be trustworthy, and blockchain embodies this trust, enabling machines to manage the monetary order.

Historically, monetary order was maintained by laws and violence as the support of laws; now, it is sustained by blockchain-operated machines, with order encoded in software. This "digital order" also means societal order dependent on technological tools for successful action and cooperation. Our book argues that "digital order" represents a shift where machines take over the maintenance of social order from humans, which previously necessitated mainly manual or computational tasks.

It is clear that "machine power" and "digital order" are not about machines dominating humans, as we have seen in science fiction. Instead, machines are enforcers of human-designed order; an order that is the foundation of society, which was shaped over millennia by instincts, customs, laws, and markets. Blockchain code now replaces these, serving as a new instrument for social order.

This scale of transformation is more profound than the financial changes brought by digital currency. By delegating power to machines, "digital order" can be enforced with absolute precision. In this new order, the anticipated counterpart to human actions is not another person but a computer program. This evolution of order represents a leap into a new intellectual era, where we acknowledge our shortcomings and use machines to transcend them. "Machine power" and "digital order" signify a small step for humanity but a leap into a new social evolutionary phase.

——This marks the end of human childhood.[1]

[1] Homage to Arthur C. Clarke's seminal science fiction novel *Childhood's End*, acknowledging his insights into human evolution and societal transformation".

References in English

Adam Hayes, "Cryptocurrency Value Formation: An Empirical Study Leading to a Cost of Production Model for Valuing Bitcoin." *Telematics and Informatics* 34, 7 (2017): 1308–1321. https://papers.ssrn.com/sol3/papers.cfm?abstract_id=2648366.

Allman, Eric. "An introduction to the source code control system." *University of California at Berkeley, Working paper* (1980).

Andreas, M. Antonopoulos. "Mastering Bitcoin: Unlocking Digital Cryptocurrencies." *O'Reilly Media*, 2016, 63.

Bank for International Settlements. "Implications for Central Banks of the Development of Electronic Money," October 1996. https://www.bis.org/publ/bisp01.pdf.

Bech, Morten L., and Rodney Garratt. "Central Bank Cryptocurrencies." BIS Quarterly Review, September 2017. https://ssrn.com/ abstract=3041906.

Beermann, Johannes. "Cash and Cryptocurrencies from the Perspective of Central Banks." *Financial Market Research*, no. 12 (2019): 109–112.

Billingslea, Marshall. "Virtual Assets and Financial Crime Now Go Hand in Hand." Financial Times, October 29, 2018. https://www.ft.com/content/8e26bba2-d91f-11e8-aa22-36538487e3d0.

BIS, Central Bank Digital Currencies 6 (CPMI Papers No. 174, March 2018), available at : https://www.bis.org/cpmi/publ/d174.pdf.

BIS Innovation Hub. "Project mBridge - Connecting Economies through CBDC," October 2022. https://www.bis.org/publ/othp59.pdf.

Bjerg, Ole. "Designing New Money - The Policy Trilemma of Central Bank Digital Currency." *Copenhagen Business School Working Paper*, 2017.

Broadbent, Ben. "Central Banks and Digital Currencies." *Speech by Deputy Governor for Monetary Policy, Bank of England to the London School of Economics*, 2 March 2016.

Bullmann, Dirk, Jonas Klemm, and Andrea Pinna. "In Search for Stability in Crypto-Assets: Are Stablecoins the Solution?" *ECB Occasional Paper* 23, no. 230 (2019).

Bünz, Benedikt, Jonathan Bootle, Dan Boneh, Andrew Poelstra, Pieter Wuille, and Greg Maxwell. "Bulletproofs: Short Proofs for Confidential Transactions and More." *2018 IEEE Symposium on Security and Privacy (SP)*, 2018, 315–334.

Carney, Mark. "The future of money." *Scottish Economics Conference. Edinburgh: Edinburgh University*. 2018.

CFTC. "CFTC Orders Tether and Bitfinex to Pay Fines Totaling $42.5 Million," October 15, 2021. https://www.cftc.gov/PressRoom/PressReleases/8450-21.

Chair Gary Gensler. "Statement on the Approval of Spot Bitcoin Exchange-Traded Products," January 10, 2024. https://www.sec.gov/news/statement/gensler-statement-spot-bitcoin-011023.

Chaum, David, Amos Fiat, and Moni Naor. "Untraceable electronic cash." *Advances in Cryptology—CRYPTO'88: Proceedings 8*. Springer New York, 1990, 319–327

Y. Wu and W. Zhu, *The Fundamentals of Digital Currency*,
https://doi.org/10.1007/978-981-97-8261-1

Chaum, David. "Blind Signatures for Untraceable Payments." *Springer EBooks*, 1983, 199–203. https://doi.org/10.1007/978-1-4757-0602-4_18.

Chaum, David, Amos Fiat, and Moni Naor. "Untraceable Electronic Cash." *Lecture Notes in Computer Science*, 1990, 319–327. https://doi.org/10.1007/0-387-34799-2_25.

Ciphertrace. "Q2 2019 Cryptocurrency Anti-Money Laundering Report - CipherTrace," February 10, 2020. https://ciphertrace.com/q2-2019-cryptocurrency-anti-money-laundering-report/.

Clayton, Jay. "Statement on Cryptocurrencies and Initial Coin Offerings," December 11, 2017. https://www.sec.gov/news/public-statement/statement-clayton-2017-12-11#_ftnref5.

Coleman, Lester. "UCLA Finance Professor Nominates Satoshi Nakamoto For Nobel Prize." CCN.Com, 4 March 2021. https://www.ccn.com/ucla-finance-professor-nominates-satoshi-nakamoto-nobel-prize/.

Committee on Payments and Market Infrastructures and the Markets Committee, Bank for International Settlements. "Central Bank Digital Currencies," March 2018. https://www.bis.org/cpmi/publ/d174.pdf, p.6.

Danezis, George, and Sarah Meiklejohn. "Centrally Banked Cryptocurrencies," February 2016. https://doi.org/10.14722/ndss.2016.23187.

Del Castillo, Michael. "New York Attorney General Warns That Kraken Cryptocurrency Exchange Could Be Violating Regulations." Forbes, September 18, 2018. https://www.forbes.com/sites/michaeldelcastillo/2018/09/18/new-york-attorney-general-warns-kraken-cryptocurrency-exchange-could-be-breaking-the-law/#6ff8ef67380f. Accessed on March 5, 2021.

Dewey, Caitlin. "Everything We Know About Ross Ulbricht, the Outdoorsy Libertarian Behind Silk Road." Washington Post, October 3, 2013. https://www.washingtonpost.com/news/the-switch/wp/2013/10/03/everything-we-know-about-ross-ulbricht-the-outdoorsy-libertarian-behind-silk-road/. Accessed on November 25, 2021.

Di, Gang. "Analysis of Digital Currency." *China Finance* 17 (2018): 52–54.

Dirk Bullmann, Jonas Klemm, and Andrea Pinna, *In Search for Stability in Crypto-assets: are Stablecoins the Solution?*, ECB Occasional Paper No. 230, 23 (2019).

Duan, Sisi, Haibin Zhang, Xiao Sui, Baohan Huang, Changchun Mu, Gang Di, and Xiaoyun Wang. "Byzantine Fault Tolerance with Weak Certificates." *IACR Cryptol. ePrint Arch.*, 2022, 625.

Engert, Walter, and Ben Siu-Cheong Fung. "Central Bank Digital Currency: Motivations and Implications." *Bank of Canada Staff Discussion Paper*, no. 2017–16, 2017.

European Banking Authority. "EBA Opinion on 'Virtual Currencies,'" July 2014. https://eba.europa.eu/file/44764/download?token=DeE-57CM, p.12.

European Central Bank. "Virtual Currency Schemes," October 2012. https://www.ecb.europa.eu/pub/pdf/other/virtualcurrencyschemes201210en.pdf.

Fan, Yifei. "Analysis of Policy Significance Regarding the Positioning of Digital Currency M0." *Financial Times*, no.001(15 Sept. 2020).

Fan, Yifei. "China's Central Bank Digital Currency Should Adopt a Double-Layer Issuance System." *Financial View*, no. 3 (2018)

Fan, Yifei. "Several Considerations on Central Bank Digital Currency." *First Financial Daily*, 26 Jan 2018, A05; Di, Gang. "Analysis of Digital Currency." *China Finance* 17 (2018): 52–54.

Fan, Yifei. "The Theoretical Foundation and Architectural Choice of China's Legal Digital Currency." *China Finance*, no. 17 (2016): 10–12

Fantacci, Luca. "Cryptocurrencies and the Denationalization of Money." *International Journal of Political Economy* 48.2 (2019): 105–112.

FATF (2023), *Targeted Update on Implementation of the FATF Standards on Virtual Assets/VASPs*, FATF, Paris, France, https://www.fatf-gafi.org/content/fatf-gafi/en/publications/Fatfrecommendations/targeted-update-virtual-assets-vasps-2023.

FATF Statement, Regulation of Virtual Assets (*Paris, France, Oct. 19, 2018*).

FATF, Guidance for a Risk-Based Approach to Virtual Assets and Virtual Asset Service Providers, paras. 32, 67 (June 2019).

Feng, Yingzi, and Wei Jin. "Prominent Figures Hurriedly Dissociate Themselves as Space Chain Plunged 90%." *Huaxia Times*, 9 April 2018, 13.

Financial Action Task Force. "Guidance for a Risk-Based Approach to Virtual Assets and Virtual Asset Service Providers," June 2019. https://www.fatf-gafi.org/media/fatf/documents/recommendations/RBA-VA-VASPs.pdf.

Financial Action Task Force. "Virtual Currencies, Key Definitions and Potential AML/CFT Risks", June 2014. http://www.fatf-gafi.org/media/fatf/documents/reports/Virtual-currency-key-and-potential-aml-cft-risks.pdf.

Finklea, Kristin. "Dark Web," *Congressional Research Service*, R44101 (2017), 3, https://fas.org/sgp/crs/misc/R44101.pdf. Accessed November 15, 2021,

Fitzgerald, F. Scott. "The Crack-Up." *The Crack-up*. New York: New Directions, 1993, 69.

Foley, Sean, Jonathan R. Karlsen, and Talis J. Putnins. "Sex, Drugs, and Bitcoin: How Much Illegal Activity Is Financed Through Cryptocurrencies?" *Review of Financial Studies*, 32.5 (2019): 1798–1853.

Friedman, Milton, and Anna J. Schwartz. *Monetary Trends in the United States and United Kingdom: Their Relation to Income, Prices, and Interest Rates, 1867–1975*. University of Chicago Press, 1982.

FSB, *Regulation, Supervision and Oversight of "Global Stablecoin" Arrangements: Final Report and High-Level Recommendations*, 9–10 (2020).

FSB Financial Stability Board. "Regulation, Supervision and Oversight of 'Global Stablecoin' Arrangements: Final Report and High-Level Recommendations," 2020, 9–10.

Fu, Zhu. "Analyzing the Impact of Virtual Currency on the Current Monetary System from the Perspective of Q Coin." *Financial Economics* 4 (2008).

Furukawa, Yuki. "Former Mt. Gox CEO Mark Karpelès Gets Suspended Jail Term." Bloomberg, March 15, 2019. https://www.bloomberg.com/news/articles/2019-03-15/former-bitcoin-baron-mark-karpeles-gets-suspended-jail-term. Accessed on March 5, 2021.

Gandal, Neil, et al. "Price manipulation in the Bitcoin ecosystem." *Journal of Monetary Economics* 95 (2018): 86–96.

Gennaro, Rosario. "Quadratic Span Programs and Succinct NIZKs without PCPs." *Advances in Cryptology–EUROCRYPT 2013: 32nd Annual International Conference on the Theory and Applications of Cryptographic Techniques, Athens, Greece, May 26–30, 2013*, Springer Berlin Heidelberg, 2013, Proceedings 32.

Gertchev, Nikolay. "The Money-Ness of Bitcoins." Mises Daily, April 4, 2013. https://mises.org/mises-daily/money-ness-bitcoins.

Gollnick, Clare, and Emily Wilson. "Separating Fact from Fiction: The Truth about the Dark Web." *Terbium Labs*, 2016, https://dsimg.ubm-us.net/envelope/385643/510233/The%20Truth%20About%20The%20Dark%20Web.pdf. Accessed on November 25, 2021.

Graeber, David. *Debt: The first 5000 years*. Penguin UK, 2012, 21–23.

Greco, Thomas. *Money: Understanding and creating alternatives to legal tender*. Chelsea Green Publishing, 2001, p.22.

Griffin, John M. and Amin Shams. "Is Bitcoin Really Un-Tethered?" *The Journal of Finance*, 75.4 (2020): 1913–1964.

Guo, Shaofei. "A Study on the Legal Nature of 'Decentralized Autonomous Organizations.'" *Social Science Journal* 3 (2020): 96–104,

Gurley, John G., and Edward S. Shaw. *Money in a Theory of Finance*. Brookings Institution Press, 1960.

Hankins, Aaron. "Bitcoin Begins the Week with a Stumble; SEC Announces Adviser for Digital Assets." MarketWatch, June 4, 2018. https://www.marketwatch.com/story/bitcoin-begins-the-week-on-a-sour-note-2018-06-04. Accessed on March 5, 2021.

Hayek, F.A. *Denationalization of Money: The Argument Refined*. 3rd ed. London: The Institute of Economic Affairs, 1991, 51–53.

Hertzog, Eyal, Guy Benartzi, and Galia Benartzi. *Bancor Protocol: Continuous Liquidity for Cryptographic Tokens through Their Smart Contracts*, 2017.

Hopwood, Daira, Sean Bowe, Taylor Hornby, et al., "Zcash protocol specification." GitHub: San Francisco, CA, USA, 4, 220(2016): 32.

Innes, A. Mitchell. "The Credit Theory of Money." *The Banking Law Journal* 31 (1914): 151–168, p.155. http://www.newmoneyhub.com/www/money/mitchell-innes/the-credit-theory-of-money.html.
Innes, A. Mitchell. "What Is Money?" *The Banking Law Journal*, 1913, 377–408, p.392. http://www.newmoneyhub.com/www/money/mitchell-innes/what-is-money.html.
Jentzsch, Christoph. "Decentralized Autonomous Organization to Automate Governance." White paper, November 2016. https://download.slock.it/public/DAO/WhitePaper.pdf.
Jin, Panshi, et al. "SOA-Based New Generation Banking System Architecture for Banking Group." *Computer Systems and Applications* 25, no. 12 (2016): 42–52.
Johnson, Carter, and Alexandre Tanzi. "Dollar Usage in Global Payments in July Rises to Record, Swift Says." Bloomberg, August 24, 2023. https://www.bloomberg.com/news/articles/2023-08-24/dollar-usage-in-global-payments-in-july-rises-to-record-swift-says.
Keatinge, Tom, and David Carlisle. "Virtual Currencies and Terrorist Financing: Assessing the Risks and Evaluating Responses," 2018. https://www.europarl.europa.eu/RegData/etudes/STUD/2018/604970/IPOL_STU(2018)604970_EN.pdf, p.18.
Koning, J. P. "Fedcoin," October 19, 2014. http://jpkoning.blogspot.com/2014/10/fedcoin.html.
Kumar, Aditi, and Eric Rosenbach. "The Truth about the Dark Web." *Finance & Development* 56, no. 3 (2019): 22.
Laila Metjahic, *Deconstructing the DAO: The Need for Legal Recognition and the Application of Securities Laws to Decentralized Organizations*, 39 Cardozo L. Rev. 1533, 1533–1568 (2017).
Legge, James. "The analects," in *Sacred Books of the East*, vol. 1, Chinese Text Project, https://ctext.org/analects/ens. Accessed on 6 September 2023.
Li, Chong. "The Development of Virtual Currency and the Reconstruction of Monetary Theory and Policy." *The World Economy* 8 (2003)
Li, Yun. "Warren Buffett Says Bitcoin Is a 'Gambling Device' with 'a Lot of Frauds Connected with It.'" CNBC, May 4, 2019. https://www.cnbc.com/2019/05/04/warren-buffett-says-bitcoin-is-a-gambling-device-with-a-lot-of-frauds-connected-with-it.html.
Locascio, Vincent R. *The Monetary Elite Vs. Gold's Honest Discipline*. Weltanschauung Financial Pr, 2005, 106–107.
Mankiw, N. Gregory. *Principles of Economics*. 8th ed. Cengage Learning, 2018, p.605.
Marshall Billingslea, Virtual Assets and Financial Crime Now Go Hand in Hand, Financial Times, Oct. 28, 2018, at Opinion.
Marx, Karl. *A Contribution to the Critique of Political Economy*. Chicago: Charles H. Kerr& Company, 1904, p.212.
McLeay, Michael, Amar Radia, and Ryland Thomas. "Money Creation in the Modern Economy." *Bank of England Quarterly Bulletin* Q1 (2014): 14–27.
Mullan, P. Carl. *History of Digital Currency in the United States*. New York: Palgrave Macmillan, 2016'.
Nakamoto, Satoshi. "Bitcoin: A Peer-to-Peer Electronic Cash System." *Decentralized Business Review*, 2008. https://bitcoin.org/bitcoin.pdf.
Nielsen, Timothy. "Cryptocorporations: A proposal for legitimizing decentralized autonomous organizations." *Utah L. Rev*, 2019, 1105–1129, p.1105.
Ouyang, Yu, and Michael A. Morgan. "The Contemporary Presidency: How Presidents Utilize Their Emergency Powers." *Presidential Studies Quarterly*, 2019, 718–732.
Pang, Jinju, et al. *Political Economy*. 5th ed. Higher Education Press, 2014, 50–52.
People's Bank of China. "2020 Overall Operation of the Payment System Report," March 24, 2021. https://www.gov.cn/xinwen/2021-03/24/content_5595427.htm.
Polasik, Michal, Anna Iwona Piotrowska, Tomasz Piotr Wisniewski, and Radosław Kotkowski. "Price Fluctuations and the Use of Bitcoin: An Empirical Inquiry." *International Journal of Electronic Commerce* 20, no. 1 (2015): 9–49. https://www.researchgate.net/publication/280570108_Price_Fluctuations_and_the_Use_of_Bitcoin_An_Empirical_Inquiry.

Primavera De Filippi & Benjamin Loveluck, *The Invisible Politics of Bitcoin: Governance Crisis of a Decentralized Infrastructure*, 5(4) Internet Pol'y Rev. (2016), available at : https://policyreview.info/articles/analysis/invisible-politics-bitcoin-governance-crisis-decentralised-infrastructure.

Reed, Chris. "Online and Offline Equivalence: Aspiration and Achievement." *International Journal of Law and Information Technology* 18, no. 3 (2010): 248–273.

Robinson, Matt, and Tom Schoenberg. "Bitcoin-Rigging Criminal Probe Focused on Tie to Tether." Bloomberg, November 20, 2018. https://www.bloomberg.com/news/articles/2018-11-20/bitcoin-rigging-criminal-probe-is-said-to-focus-on-tie-to-tether.

Rooney, Kate. "As Bitcoin Nosedives, Regulators Said to Be Investigating Whether It Was Propped Up Illegally." CNBC, November 20, 2018. https://www.cnbc.com/2018/11/20/regulators-investigate-whether-bitcoin-price-was-propped-up-illegally.html. Accessed on March 5, 2021.

Shuai, Qinghong. "Q Coin, U Coin, POPO Coin, and Electronic Currency." *E-Commerce* 1 (2007)

"Special Committee on the Termination of the National Emergency" of the 93rd Congress. "The Report of the Special Committee on the Termination of the National Emergency (Senate Report 93–549)." November 19, 1973, 2. https://ia902207.us.archive.org/24/items/senate-report-93-549/senate-report-93-549.pdf.

Stalinsky, Steven. "The Cryptocurrency-Terrorism Connection Is Too Big to Ignore." Washington Post, December 17, 2018. https://www.washingtonpost.com/opinions/the-cryptocurrency-terrorism-connection-is-too-big-to-ignore/2018/12/17/69ed6ab4-fe4b-11e8-83c0-b06139e540e5_story.html. Accessed on November 25, 2021.

State-Of-The-Dapps. "Sotd-Www/Pages/About.Vue at Master · State-of-the-Dapps/Sotd-Www." GitHub, n.d. https://github.com/state-of-the-dapps/sotd-www/blob/master/pages/About.vue. Accessed on 17 September, 2023. The original statement is "And remember... smart contracts are neither smart, nor contracts!"

Sun, Huarong. "Research on the Development Status, Challenges and Countermeasures of Cross-Border Payment Business of Banking Institutions." *Financial Theory & Practice*, 2020.

Szabo, Nick. "Secure Property Titles with Owner Authority," 1998. http://szabo.best.vwh.net/securetitle.html. Also available at: https://www.fon.hum.uva.nl/rob/Courses/InformationInSpeech/CDROM/Literature/LOTwinterschool2006/szabo.best.vwh.net/securetitle.html.

Szabo, Nick. "Smart contracts: building blocks for digital markets." *EXTROPY: The Journal of Transhumanist Thought, (16)* 18.2 (1996): 28.

Taylor, Michael. *Twin Peaks: A Regulatory Structure for the New Century*. London: Center for the Study of Financial Innovation, Dec. 1995.

The European Central Bank and the Bank of Japan. "Synchronised Cross-Border Payments," June 2019. https://www.ecb.europa.eu/paym/intro/publications/pdf/ecb.miptopical190604.en.pdf.

The Committee on Payments and Market Infrastructures, Bank for International Settlements. "Digital Currencies," November 2018. https://www.bis.org/cpmi/publ/d137.pdf. p.6.

The Division of Corporation Finance, U.S. Securities and Exchange Commission. "SEC No-Action Letter (TurnKey Jet, Inc.)," April 3, 2019. https://www.sec.gov/divisions/corpfin/cf-noaction/2019/turnkey-jet-040219-2a1.htm.

Tobin, James. "The Case for Preserving Regulatory Distinctions." *Restructuring the Financial System: A Symposium Sponsored by the Federal Reserve Bank of Kansas City*, 1987, 167–183.

United States Department of the Treasury Financial Crimes Enforcement Network. "Application of FinCEN's Regulations to Persons Administering, Exchanging, or Using Virtual Currencies," March 2013. https://www.fincen.gov/resources/statutes-regulations/guidance/application-fincens-regulations-persons-administering.

U.S. Congress. "An Act to Provide for Increased Participation by the United States in the International Development Association and to Permit United States Citizens to Purchase, Hold, Sell, or Otherwise Deal with Gold in the United States or Abroad." Pub. L. No. 93–373, 88 Stat. 445. 1974.

U.S. Securities and Exchange Commission. "Framework for 'Investment Contract' Analysis of Digital Assets," April 3, 2019. https://www.sec.gov/corpfin/framework-investment-contract-analysis-digital-assets.

U.S. Securities and Exchange Commission. "Report of Investigation Pursuant to Section 21(a) of the Securities Exchange Act of 1934: The DAO," 25 July 2017. https://www.sec.gov/files/litigation/investreport/34-81207.pdf.

U.S. Securities and Exchange Commission. "Report of Investigation Pursuant to Section 21(a) of the Securities Exchange Act of 1934: Dao (Release No. 81207)," July 25, 2017. https://www.sec.gov/files/litigation/investreport/34-81207.pdf.

Van Alstyne, Marshall. "Why Bitcoin Has Value." *Communications of the ACM* 57, 5 (2014): 30–32. https://www.researchgate.net/publication/273609426_Why_Bitcoin_Has_Value.

Vigna, Paul. "Which Digital Currency Will Be the Next Bitcoin?" The Wall Street Journal, December 19, 2017. https://www.wsj.com/articles/which-digital-currency-will-be-the-next-bitcoin-1513679400.

Wang, Qingsong. "Defining the Nature of Internal Relationships and Attribution in Blockchain Systems." *Law Journal* 5 (2019): 130–142.

Wang, Qingsong. "The Nature and Attribution of Internal Relations in Blockchain Systems." *Law Science* 5 (2019): 130–142.

Wang, Wei. "Modernized Payment System: China's Payment and Clearing Expressway." *Financial Electronization*, no. 10 (2019): 63–64.

Wang, Yang, and Ye Pan. "Beware of Blockchain Becoming a 'Golden Signboard' for Scams." *Economic Reference News*, 11 November 2019, 5.

Webmoney. "WebMoney Transfer Code," https://www.wmtransfer.com/eng/legal/codex.shtml, paragraph 1.3.1. Accessed on 27 May 2021.

Werner, Richard A. "Can banks individually create money out of nothing? — The theories and the empirical evidence." *International Review of Financial Analysis*, no. 36 (2014): 1–19.

White, Lawrence H. "The World's First Central Bank Electronic Money Has Come–and Gone: Ecuador, 2014–2018," n.d. https://www.alt-m.org/2018/03/29/the-worlds-first-central-bank-electronic-money-has-come-and-gone-ecuador-2014-2018/.

World Wide Web Foundation. "Three Challenges for the Web, According to Its Inventor." World Wide Web Foundation, 12 March 2017. https://webfoundation.org/2017/03/web-turns-28-letter/.

Working Group on E-CNY Research and Development of the People's Bank of China. "Progress of Research & Development of Digital RMB in China," July 2021. http://www.pbc.gov.cn/en/3688110/3688172/4157443/4293696/2021072014364791207.pdf.

Wray, L. *A Primer on Macroeconomics for Sovereign Monetary Systems*. UK: Palgrave Macmillan, 2012.

Wu, Yun, and Wei Zhu. "Anti-Money Laundering Regulation over Virtual Currencies: A Starting Point to Depart from Autonomous Order." *Law and Economy*, no. 2 (2021): 79–97.

Wu, Yun, and Wei Zhu. "Virtual Currencies: A Failed Social Experiment of Private Currencies?" *Financial Regulatory Research*, no. 6 (2020). https://www.researchgate.net/publication/373111648_Virtual_Currencies_a_Failed_Social_Experiment_of_Private_Currencies. Accessed on 24 Aug 2023.

Xu, Zhong, et al. "Exploration of Central Bank Digital Currency Theory." *China Finance*, no. 17 (2016): 33–34

Yang, Wenjie. "Development of China's Modernized Payment System." *China Finance*, no. 14 (2017): 18–20.

Yang, Yueqi. "Coinbase Blocks 25,000 Crypto Wallets Linked to Russian Users." Bloomberg News, March 7, 2022. https://www.bnnbloomberg. ca/coinbase-blocks-25–000-crypto-wallets-linked-to-russian-users-1.1733821?ms.

Yao, Qian. "An Analysis of the Economic Performance of the Digital Fiat Currency." *Studies of International Finance*, no. 1 (2019).

Yao, Qian. "Optimization of Current Monetary System by Central Bank Digital Currency and Its Issuance Design." *Studies of International Finance*, no. 4 (2018).

Yao, Qian. "Prototype Concept of China's Legal Digital Currency." *China Finance*, no. 17 (2016): 13–15.

Yao, Qian. "Some Thoughts on Central Bank – Issued Digital Currency." *Journal of Financial Research*, no. 7 (2017): 78–85

Zarate, Juan. *Treasury's War: The Unleashing of a New Era of Financial Warfare*. Hachette UK, 2013.

Zhou, Lei, and Jie Chen. "Study of Use of Blockchain Technology in National Digital Currency." *Journal of Hangzhou Insititute of Financial Studies*, no. 6 (2018): 27–31.

References in Chinese

Pang, Jinju, et al. *Political Economy*. 5th ed. Higher Education Press, 2014, 50–52 (逄锦聚等,《政治经济学(第五版)》, 高等教育出版社, 2014年, 第50–52页。)

Wu, Yun, and Wei Zhu. "Virtual Currencies: A Failed Social Experiment of Private Currencies?" *Financial Regulatory Research*, no. 6 (2020). https://www.researchgate.net/publication/373111648_Virtual_Currencies_a_Failed_Social_Experiment_of_Private_Currencies. Accessed 24 Aug 2023. (吴云和朱玮, 虚拟货币: 一场失败的私人货币社会实验,《金融监管研究》, 2020年第6期, 第6–20页。)

Li, Chong. "The Development of Virtual Currency and the Reconstruction of Monetary Theory and Policy." *The World Economy* 8 (2003).(李翀, 虚拟货币的发展与货币理论和政策的重构,《世界经济》, 2003年第8期。)

Shuai, Qinghong. "Q Coin, U Coin, POPO Coin, and Electronic Currency." *E-Commerce* 1 (2007).(帅青红, Q 币、U 币、POPO 币与电子货币,《电子商务》, 2007年第1期。)

Fu, Zhu. "Analyzing the Impact of Virtual Currency on the Current Monetary System from the Perspective of Q Coin." *Financial Economics* 4 (2008). (付竹, 以 Q 币为视角探析虚拟币对现行货币体系的影响,《金融经济》, 2008年第4期。)

Yang, Wenjie. "Development of China's Modernized Payment System." *China Finance*, no. 14 (2017): 18–20.(杨文杰, 中国现代化支付系统发展,《中国金融》, 2017年第14期, 第18–20页。)

Wang, Wei. "Modernized Payment System: China's Payment and Clearing Expressway." *Financial Electronization*, no. 10 (2019): 63–64.(王伟, 现代化支付系统——中国支付清算高速路,《金融电子化》, 2019年第10期, 第63–64页。)

Beermann, Johannes. "Cash and Cryptocurrencies from the Perspective of Central Banks." *Financial Market Research*, no. 12 (2019): 109–112.(约翰内斯·比尔曼, 中央银行视角下的现金与数字货币,《金融市场研究》, 2019年第12期, 第109–112页。)

Yao, Qian. "Prototype Concept of China's Legal Digital Currency." *China Finance*, no. 17 (2016): 13–15. (姚前, 中国法定数字货币原型构想,《中国金融》, 2016年第17期, 第13–15页。)

Fan, Yifei. "China's Central Bank Digital Currency Should Adopt a Double-Layer Issuance System." *Financial View*, no. 3 (2018).(范一飞, 中国央行数字货币应采用双层投放体系,《金融博览》, 2018年第3期。)

China's Digital Currency Research Institute. "A method and system for generating digital currency." *Chinese Invention Patent: CN110751467A*. Public Release Date: 4 Feb 2020. (中国人民银行数字货币研究所, 一种数字货币的生成方法及系统, 中国发明专利号 CN110751467A, 公开日期: 2020年2月4日。)

China's Digital Currency Research Institute. "A method and system for recalling digital currency quotas." *Chinese Invention Patent: CN110619567A*. Public Release Date: 27 Dec 2019. (中国人民银行数字货币研究所, 一种数字货币的额度回收方法及系统, 中国发明专利号 CN110619567A, 公开日期: 2019年12月27日。)

China's Digital Currency Research Institute. "A method and system for circulation of digital currency." *Chinese Invention Patent: CN110659889A*. Public Release Date: 7 Jan 2020. (中国人民银行数字货币研究所, 一种数字货币的流通方法及系统, 中国发明专利号 CN110659889A, 公开日期: 2020年1月7日。)

Yao, Qian. "Some Thoughts on Central Bank – Issued Digital Currency." *Journal of Financial Research*, no. 7 (2017): 78–85.(姚前, 关于央行法定数字货币的若干思考,《金融研究》, 2017年第7期, 第78–85页。)

Xu, Zhong, et al. "Exploration of Central Bank Digital Currency Theory." *China Finance*, no. 17 (2016): 33–34.(徐忠、汤莹玮、林雪, 央行数字货币理论探讨,《中国金融》, 2016年第17期, 第33–34页。)

Fan, Yifei. "The Theoretical Foundation and Architectural Choice of China's Legal Digital Currency." *China Finance*, no. 17 (2016): 10–12.(范一飞, 中国法定数字货币的理论依据和架构选择,《中国金融》, 2016年第17期, 第10–12页。)

Fan, Yifei. "Several Considerations on Central Bank Digital Currency." *First Financial Daily*, 26 Jan 2018, A05.(范一飞, 关于央行数字货币的几点考虑,《第一财经日报》, 2018年1月26日, 第A05版。)

Di, Gang. "Analysis of Digital Currency." *China Finance* 17 (2018): 52–54.(狄刚, 数字货币辨析,《中国金融》, 2018年第17期, 第52–54页。)

Wu, Yun, and Wei Zhu. *Digital Currencies: The Rise of Machine Power and the Future of Digital Order*. Zhejiang University Press, 2022. (吴云和朱玮,《数字货币: 机器权力的兴起与数字秩序的未来》, 浙江大学出版社, 2022年。)

Zhu, Wei, Yun Wu, and Bo Yang. *A Short History of Blockchain*. China Financial Press, 2020.(朱玮、吴云和杨波,《区块链简史》, 中国金融出版社, 2020年。)

Wu, Yun, Hongjiao Xue, and Wei Zhu. "Money Laundering Through Virtual Currencies: Inherent Risk, Typological Analysis and Regulatory Responses." *Financial Regulatory Research*, no. 10 (2021): 1–19. (吴云、薛宏蛟和朱玮, 虚拟货币洗钱问题研究: 固有风险、类型分析与监管应对,《金融监管研究》, 2021年第10期, 第1–19页。)

Wu, Yun, and Wei Zhu. "Digital Currencies and Virtual Currencies Subjected to Regulation: A Trans-disciplinary Perspective from Law, Finance and Technology." *Journal of Shanghai University of Political Science and Law*, no. 6 (2021): 66–89.(吴云和朱玮, 数字货币和金融监管意义上的虚拟货币: 法律、金融与技术的跨学科考察,《上海政法学院学报(法治论丛)》, 2021年第6期, 第66–89页。)

Wu, Yun, and Wei Zhu. "Anti-Money Laundering Regulation over Virtual Currencies: A Starting Point to Depart from Autonomous Order." *Law and Economy*, no. 2 (2021): 79–97.(吴云和朱玮, 虚拟货币的国际监管: 以反洗钱为起点走出自发秩序,《财经法学》, 2021年第2期, 第79–97页。)

Guo, Shaofei. "A Study on the Legal Nature of 'Decentralized Autonomous Organizations.'" *Social Science Journal* 3 (2020): 96–104. (郭少飞, "去中心化自治组织"的法律性质探析,《社会科学》, 2020年第3期, 第96–104页。)

Wang, Qingsong. "The Nature and Attribution of Internal Relations in Blockchain Systems." *Law Science* 5 (2019): 130–142.(汪青松, 区块链系统内部关系的性质界定与归责路径,《法学》, 2019年第5期, 第130–142页。)

Fan, Yifei. "Analysis of Policy Significance Regarding the Positioning of Digital Currency M0." Financial Times, no.001(15 Sept. 2020). (范一飞, 关于数字人民币M0定位的政策含义分析,《金融时报》, 2020年9月15日, 第001版)

Jin, Panshi, et al. "SOA-Based New Generation Banking System Architecture for Banking Group." Computer Systems and Applications 25, no. 12 (2016): 42–52. (金磐石、朱玉红、胡宪忠、李骁, 基于SOA的银行集团"新一代"系统架构,《计算机系统应用》, 2016年第25卷第12期, 第42–52页。)

Feng, Yingzi, and Wei Jin. "Prominent Figures Hurriedly Dissociate Themselves as Space Chain Plunged 90%." *Huaxia Times*, 9 April 2018, 13. (冯樱子和金微, 太空链破发90% 大佬纷纷撇清关系,《华夏时报》, 2018年4月9日, 第13版。)

Wang, Yang, and Ye Pan. "Beware of Blockchain Becoming a 'Golden Signboard' for Scams." Economic Reference News, 11 November 2019, 5. (王阳和潘晔, 警惕区块链成行骗"金字招牌",《经济参考报》, 2019年11月21日, 第5版。)

Zhou, Lei, and Jie Chen. "Study of Use of Blockchain Technology in National Digital Currency." Journal of Hangzhou Insititute of Financial Studies, no. 6 (2018): 27–31.(周雷、陈捷,《国家数字货币应用区块链技术初探》,《杭州金融研修学院学报》, 2018年第6期, 第27–31页。)

Sun, Huarong. "Research on the Development Status, Challenges and Countermeasures of Cross-Border Payment Business of Banking Institutions." *Financial Theory & Practice*, no.12 (2020).(孙华荣, 银行跨境支付业务发展及监管策略研究,《金融理论与实践》, 2020年第12 期。)

Yao, Qian. "An Analysis of the Economic Performance of the Digital Fiat Currency." Studies of International Finance, no. 1 (2019). (姚前,《法定数字货币的经济效应分析》,《国际金融研究》, 2019 年第 1 期。)

Yao, Qian. "Optimization of Current Monetary System by Central Bank Digital Currency and Its Issuance Design." *Studies of International Finance*, no. 4 (2018). (姚前,《法定数字货币对现行货币体制的优化及其发行设计》,《国际金融研究》, 2018 年第 4 期。)

The People's Bank of China,. "2020 Overall Operation of the Payment System Report," March 24, 2021. https://www.gov.cn/xinwen/2021-03/24/content_5595427.htm.(中国人民银行:《2020年支付体系运行总体情况报告》)

Chinese Laws and Regulations

法律文件

The Provisional Measures for the Administration of Online Games (Order No. 49 of the Chinese Ministry of Culture in 2010) (《网络游戏管理暂行办法》(文化部令 2010 年第 49 号))

The Announcement on Preventing the Financing Risks of Token Offerings(The People's Bank of China, along with six other competent authorities, 2017) (2017 年, 中国人民银行等七部委颁布了《关于防范代币发行融资风险的公告》)

SPRINGER NATURE

GPSR Compliance

The European Union's (EU) General Product Safety Regulation (GPSR) is a set of rules that requires consumer products to be safe and our obligations to ensure this.

If you have any concerns about our products, you can contact us on ProductSafety@springernature.com

In case Publisher is established outside the EU, the EU authorized representative is:

Springer Nature Customer Service Center GmbH
Europaplatz 3
69115 Heidelberg, Germany

The manufacturer's authorised representative in the EU is Springer Nature Customer Service Centre GmbH, Europaplatz 3, 69115 Heidelberg, Germany. If you have any concerns regarding our products, please contact ProductSafety@springernature.com

Printed and bound by CPI Group (UK) Ltd, Croydon, CR0 4YY

01/10/2026

02225858-0006